EMPIRE AND HISTORY WRITING IN BRITAIN *c.*1750–2012

MANCHESTER
1824

Manchester University Press

❧ HISTORICAL APPROACHES ❧

Series editor

Geoffrey Cubitt

The Historical Approaches series aims to make a distinctive contribution to current debate about the nature of the historical discipline, its theory and practice, and its evolving relationships to other cultural and intellectual fields. The intention of the series is to bridge the gap that sometimes exists between learned monographs on the one hand and beginners' manuals on the other, by offering works that have the clarity of argument and liveliness of style to appeal to a general and student readership, while also prompting thought and debate among practising historians and thinkers about the discipline. Titles in the series will cover a wide variety of fields, and explore them from a range of different angles, but will have in common the aspiration of raising awareness of the issues that are posed by historical studies in today's world, and of the significance of debates about history for a broader understanding of contemporary culture.

Also available:
Geoffrey Cubitt *History and memory*
Matthew Kempshall *Rhetoric and the writing of history, 400–1500*

EMPIRE AND HISTORY WRITING IN BRITAIN c.1750–2012

Joanna de Groot

Manchester University Press
Manchester And New York
distributed in the United States exclusively by Palgrave Macmillan

Published by Manchester University Press
Oxford Road, Manchester M13 9NR, UK
and Room 400, 175 Fifth Avenue, New York, NY 10010, USA
www.manchesteruniversitypress.co.uk

Distributed in the United States exclusively by
Palgrave Macmillan175 Fifth Avenue, New York,
NY 10010, USA

Distributed in Canada exclusively by
UBC Press, University of British Columbia, 2029 West Mall,
Vancouver, BC, Canada V6T 1Z2

British Library Cataloguing-in-Publication Data
A catalogue record for this book is available from the British Library

Library of Congress Cataloging-in-Publication Data applied for

ISBN 978 0 7190 9045 5 hardback

ISBN 978 0 7190 9046 2 paperback

First published 2013

Typeset by JCS Publishing Services Ltd, www.jcs-publishing.co.uk
Printed in Great Britain by Bell & Bain Ltd, Glasgow

CONTENTS

ACKNOWLEDGEMENTS

The production of texts, knowledge and understanding in the humanities is largely an individual, even lonely, process, but it is never undertaken wholly alone. It is a pleasure as well as a proper scholarly and professional convention for me to acknowledge the support, interest and help from which I have benefited while working on this book

To my long-standing colleagues and good friends Jane Rendall and Peter Biller I owe considerable gratitude for sharing intellectual insights, and for reading and commenting on drafts of the text. Other colleagues in the History Department at York whose ideas and suggestions have been valuable to me include Sabine Clark, Simon Ditchfield, Mark Jenner, Chris Renwick and Allen Warren. More generally I really appreciate the friendly and lively presence of all my colleagues in the department, which has helped me to keep going over the years. At a time when academic life is constrained by intensifying work pressures and by managerialism they maintain a level of professional commitment and collegial solidarity which is exemplary and reassuring.

Among a wider circle of friends and colleagues I would like to thank Bain Attwood, Catherine Hall, Richard Holt, Ann Kaloski Naylor, Zoe Laidlaw and Keith McClelland. They have stimulated and supported me in many ways over the years, as well as providing important specific inputs to my thinking about the book, and I feel privileged to have shared debates and conversations with them.

Coming closer to the actual process of completing the book, I warmly thank Geoff Cubitt and Emma Brennan for their editorial contributions, and for the combination of encouragement and judicious pressure which has got me through the final stages of the work.

Outside the academic setting of my work a number of people have made important contributions to my efforts. My research has been enhanced by the hospitality, good companionship and gorgeous food provided by 'outlaw' Dick Muskett on my many visits to London. Betsy knows very well what she has contributed by way of challenge and support, and I am delighted to acknowledge that publicly. My sister Lucy has an unerring talent for focusing on what really matters, and for combining crisp realism with humour and generous concern, even when her own life has its serious pressures. Her ongoing support and stimulus have been essential to me and I love her for that as well as many other things.

PREFACE

The history of historical practice is both fascinating and challenging. It can take people 'into the engine room' or 'behind the scenes' and show aspects of that practice which enhance and enrich the study and understanding of the past. It can also challenge and even alienate people by producing complex and uncertain insights or using over-elaborate language and argument. It can slide into list-like accounts of authors, texts or 'schools' of historical writing rather than identifying themes or issues which might clarify those accounts. Alternatively, it can become very abstract and detached from the actualities and inconsistencies involved in researching, thinking, and writing about the past.

It will be for readers to judge whether this text has avoided such pitfalls, but its purpose is to follow a particular thread of investigation and interpretation through the story of history writing in 'Britain' since the mid eighteenth century. That thread, or theme, is the impact of involvement in empire on historical practice over that period. The first chapter sets out the contextual and conceptual underpinnings for the investigation in some detail, but here it will be useful to flag up some key aspects of the text. It contributes to recent historiography by arguing for the constitutive role of empire in the culture and mentalities as well as in politics and material life in those 'Atlantic Isles' known variously as 'the United(?!) Kingdom', 'the British(?!) Isles' and 'Great Britain'. Rather than detaching empire from the history of 'Britain' as a separate topic, which in some contexts can be useful, this text is attentive to imperial elements in the story of 'British' history writing. It offers a different perspective on existing narratives of history writing in Britain in its varied scholarly and popular forms by raising questions of imperial influence within those narratives. By positioning imperial themes

within an account of 'British' history writing, the text thereby offers
a postcolonial take on the story of historical practice. It may even
add something to political and cultural histories of the United
Kingdom and its empire by reframing understandings of the role of
history writing and historical texts within those histories.

It might well be thought that such large agendas are over
ambitious and impractical for a single text, but there is potential
value in putting forward one overarching narrative, even if
inevitably partial and selective, as a basis for discussion and analysis.
In order to create such a narrative I have adopted a number
of guiding strategies. I have sought to combine discussion of
innovative historical practice and of elite or canonical texts in any
period with a consideration of texts which maintained established
practice addressed more diverse constituencies and borrowed or
adapted from the dominant canon. This approach is based on an
understanding of the story of history writing as revealing layers
of thought and conventions built up over time which continue to
shape historians' practices, and inheritances from the past which
play a role in the present. Many texts combine older and newer
ideas and assumptions, whether or not this is acknowledged. Recent
works relevant to this book illustrate this point. John Darwin's
magisterial account of the 'British world system' sets British imperial
involvements in a grand geopolitical narrative, using conventions of
imperial history shaped by the influence of previous generations of
historians who had sought to link material and political analyses.[1]
He also identifies recent work on a 'British world' and on the
cultural politics and political cultures of empire in the UK. While
critical of 'cultural' approaches to the history of empire (critiqued
by reference to a rather untypical example of the genre), at various
points his discussion acknowledges its relevance to his own grand
narrative. Although he does not engage with recent work on the
mutually constitutive relations of colonies and metropole, his use
of earlier views of the importance of local circumstances and 'men
on the spot' and interest in public opinion at times converges with
that work.[2] As a sophisticated grand narrative it sidesteps other
approaches without excluding them. Its conventional scholarly
sensitivity to complexity, as well as its overarching agenda of
presenting empire as an ever-shifting 'project' rather than a stable
entity, bring it closer to recent concerns with the provisionality and
uncertainty in historical narrative than may have been intended.

In her study of two 'architects of imperial Britain', the father
and son Zachary and Thomas Macaulay, Catherine Hall moves
between the lives and writings of her two protagonists and the
shaping of politics and imperial activities in 'Britain' between the
1780s and the 1850s.[3] Their activities and ideas were shaped by
imperial connections to the West Indies, West Africa and India. In
turn, their work as political activists, authors and colonial officials
shaped action and thinking in those domains, whether the legacy
of abolitionist politics, the articulation of reform programmes in
India, or elaborations of ideas of race, civilisation and empire in
their writings. Careful readings of private letters and journals as
well as historical texts and political writing by both Macaulays allow
the development of an account which simultaneously explores the
personal formation of two 'imperial men' and of political culture/
cultural politics of Britain and empire. These established historical
skills support an innovative approach using concepts and methods
in recent postcolonial and gender history and insights from
social and psychological analysis. Acknowledging the influence of
established conventions of intellectual history and biography, it
draws on feminist and cross-cultural thought to connect personal
and political, domestic and imperial strands in the life stories of
the Macaulays, and the worlds which they inhabited.[4]

These two works on empire are sharply contrasted, and in
some senses opposed to one another, but both illustrate how
there are no simple lineages or paths of development in historical
practice. Shared legacies, professional conventions and new
methods, interpretations or controversies operate in specific ways
at particular moments in time and for particular practitioners. It
is for this reason that this text combines a chronological with a
thematic structure. It surveys the role of empire in history writing
across different periods but insists strongly that continuities are
as significant as changes over time. It also identifies three themes
relevant to the analysis throughout the time dealt with in the book.
More will be said in the first chapter about the historical contexts
underpinning these three themes, but it is worth indicating here
the connections identified as worth investigation. Firstly, I suggest
that, since British imperial activities and interests often involved
issues of war, politics and governance, it is worth exploring their
impact, if any, on historical writing about the state, its institutions
and its dealings with subjects or citizens. Secondly, since imperial

encounters brought 'British' people into contact with other societies, I consider how 'imperial' influences did, or did not, shape historians' treatments of social life, and their notions of civilisation and progress, or their opposites. Thirdly, since imperial contacts involved articulating cultural and political as well as material differences, I examine the entwining of imperial involvements, history writing and notions of 'race' and 'nation'. Thus the overall inquiry undertaken in the text can be consistent in its treatment of the question of empire and history writing, and ground itself in a reasoned approach to the possible links between them, while using the chronological structure to do justice to specificity, continuity and change. A scene-setting opening section to each chronological chapter will provide the context for the thematic discussion by setting out the routes by which empire entered into British lives, including those of historians, in each given period.

The challenge is to attend to the multiple and divergent versions of the past which can be found in the historical writings produced in any of the periods covered by the book, while investigating the themes which have been identified. The use of different kinds of writing in each period is intended to address that challenge. While inevitably selective, the range of works examined can give the reader some sense of both patterns and divergences in historical practice in each of the four time periods under discussion. It may seem that there is not enough discussion of works dealing explicitly with histories of empire, which deserve a narrative of their own but are clearly relevant to the concerns of this text. While such works might seem the most obvious material needed for a study of empire and history writing, it is one of the main contentions of the book that this question needs to be taken up by looking at many kinds of such writing. The limits and effects of imperial involvement on historical practice need to be examined across a spectrum of historical practice, and can be indirect or incidental as well as direct and explicit. The outlines of material, political and cultural circumstances at the start of each chronological chapter will provide a basis for discussion of both kinds of influence, or lack thereof.

Such a discussion requires careful attention to the external influences on particular texts and their producers without slipping into deterministic readings of such influences. Nonetheless, a study of history writing which draws attention to the cultural resources available to their writers in any given period, and to the political and material underpinnings of those resources, can enrich our appreciation of such writing. As will be seen, imperial connections, activities and imaginings were a part, albeit only one part, of the cultural universe within which British history writing was produced. It is the role of that part of culture which is the subject of the book.

Notes

1 J. Darwin, *The empire project: the rise and fall of the British world system, 1830–1970*, Cambridge, 2009. He explicitly acknowledges the influence of work by John Gallagher ('the shrewdest historian of modern British imperialism'), Richard Robinson, Peter Cain and Anthony Hopkins, whose key works appeared between the 1950s and the 1990s, and he asserts the importance of traditional military and diplomatic approaches (pp. xi, xii–xiii).

2 Darwin, *Empire project*, pp. 14–15 (critique), pp. 5, 41–9, 92–106,146–8, 212–16, 439–42, 445–7 are instances where other elements are woven into the predominantly politico-strategic narrative.

3 C. Hall, *Macaulay and son: architects of imperial Britain*, New Haven, CT, 2012.

4 Hall, *Macaulay and son*, pp. xv–xix, 67–8, 127–37, 140–9, 309–19.

🌿 1 🌿

EMPIRE AND HISTORY WRITING:
SETTING THE SCENE

> There are two ways to lose oneself: by a walled segregation in the particular, or by a dilution in the 'universal'. (Aimé Césaire)[1]

The quotation above opens up some of the main issues discussed in this book. At a moment when the French faced demands for decolonisation in Algeria and Indo-China, the Martiniquais intellectual and politician Aimé Césaire announced his resignation from the French Communist Party in a public 'letter' to Thorez, its leader. Césaire is best known for his development of the idea of 'negritude' to explore the social and cultural distinctiveness of Caribbean people of African origin, and of colonial subjects in Africa. An activist as well as an intellectual, he had recently campaigned for the recognition of the French-ruled Caribbean island of Martinique as a *département* of France. His 1955 *Discourse on colonialism* criticised the brutalising effects of colonial power on both colonial rulers and colonial subjects, arguing for radical change to emancipate those subjects from colonial control and to liberate European societies from class oppression.[2] Thorez was preoccupied with steering his party through the minefields of Stalinism, of class, anti-colonial politics and French nationalism. Communists of that period were challenged by perceptions of their participation in anti-German resistance in France between 1940 and 1945 as both patriotic and self-interested, and by the pursuit of leftist class concerns alongside anti-colonialism and Cold War politics. What political and historical perspectives might link commitments to, or criticisms of, class, nation and empire? Did patriotic narratives of the French past support the reform of 'Greater' (that is, imperial) France, or encourage decolonisation? Could colonial subjects share universal ideals of progress, emancipation and, as Césaire put it, 'respect for peoples and cultures' with the metropolitan French, or were 'difference' and particularity to be the basis of liberation? Césaire's statement identifies the problems and limitations of each extreme and links historical 'national' to colonial concerns.

Similar dilemmas faced people in the United Kingdom and its empire at the same period. West Indians of African origin who had fought in the British armed services during the Second World War faced new difficulties and discrimination in the 'mother country' when they entered the UK in the 1950s as migrants seeking to work and settle. Labour governments struggled to reconcile conflicting views on the merits of empire, commonwealth and decolonisation with the protection of 'British' interests and the pressures of the Cold War and anti-colonial movements. After 1951 their Conservative successors faced challenges in Egypt, Malaya, Kenya, Iran and Korea, as well as rising material expectations and difficulties in the UK. When members of the British public challenged the brutal official mistreatment of Mau Mau rebels in Kenya, they attacked its 'un-English' character and its betrayal of a history of support for justice and Christian values most recently associated with the repudiation of Nazi war crimes.[3] History, patriotism and morality were mobilised to oppose colonial misconduct from across the right–left political spectrum, just as campaigners for colonial independence or against apartheid in South Africa drew on narratives of a 'British' past and values to underpin their case. Interpretations of history were brought to bear on the politics of empire and the writing of 'national' history needed to address the significance of empire.

Césaire critiqued two approaches to politics and social thought which were popular in the 1950s and continue to be so. Anti-colonial nationalism produced political demands by people claiming a cultural uniqueness which they associated with a specific 'national' identity, paralleled in some of the 'black' politics emerging in South Africa and the USA. Appeals to particular shared histories, cultures and customs had been a staple of political movements from American resistance to British rule in the 1760s to Zionist, African and Arab nationalisms, or racialist and anti-immigrant politics in the mid twentieth century. As with politics based on workplace or religious affiliation, emphasis on specific experiences

– past or present – constructed particularism, sustaining political loyalty and activism in opposition to those seen as having different and conflicting interests. A leading Iranian nationalist politician, Hussein Makki, wrote patriotic history in the 1940s, just as the Kenyan leader Jomo Kenyatta drew on anthropological work he had done at the London School of Economics before the Second World War to project his anti colonial politics. However, the 1950s was also a period of drives towards universalising projects for progress, whether in development economics or the United Nations with its associated agencies and declarations. Commitment to material development, human rights and social or political modernisation assumed that they were universally applicable and desirable goals. It shaped the politics of postcolonial states, international agencies and professional, largely western, 'experts'. Confidence that knowledge and reason should be the basis for improving lives in any society, and that 'prosperity', 'justice' or 'progress' were, or should be, the same everywhere, reached back to eighteenth-century European thought on progress and human needs.

Of course, many reformers, policymakers, commentators and activists combined elements from both these approaches, arguing for the adaptation of universal principles to specific local conditions, or for parallels and similarities within 'national' or social diversity. Those who opposed imperialism or universalist policies in the name of 'national' or cultural particularity often drew on ideas from non-indigenous sources. Conversely, development planners used comparative methods and recognised the need to know and deal with specific 'customary', 'tribal' or religious institutions. This will be explored further in Chapter 5 of this book. Nonetheless it was not surprising that Césaire identified particularism and universalism as distinct and persuasive ideologies that were shaping political and intellectual endeavour in his time. The certainties of Cold War strategists, of development specialists and of both the opponents and defenders of European imperialism did indeed use these ideologies, which had wide appeal in politics, the media and scholarship. Just as the 1950s saw the emergence of influential arguments for the distinctive experience, needs and interests of what was becoming known as the 'third world', and the celebration of its histories and cultures, so there were learned and popular advocates of the view that this was a moment when progress and liberty could be made available to all. Interestingly, both views appealed to history. If examples of the particularist outlook might be the anti-colonial west African politicians and writers Kwame Nkrumah and Leopold Senghor, the American academic and government official Walt Rustow could exemplify the universalist viewpoint. Rustow was a senior foreign policy adviser, a noted hawkish backer of US intervention in Vietnam, a professor at Columbia, MIT, Oxford and Cambridge, and the author of academic studies of the history of Soviet society and of economic development. While Senghor and Nkrumah sought to connect the distinctive past of African societies to modern demands for recognition and equality, Rostow universalised his scholarly formulations of the 'stages of economic growth' in support of free market economics and US hegemony. Current political concerns entwined with thinking and writing about the past of states, peoples and empires.

This book explores two important and related elements in the particular history of British history writing. Firstly, it looks at how debates on the significance of empire and colonialism in stories of the past of Britain and other places have developed over the last 250 years. The view that imperial relationships and activities have influenced colonial rulers or those wielding material, political or cultural power, and those subordinated to such power, has a long and contested history. Debates over slavery, colonial rights and colonial expansion in eighteenth- and nineteenth-century political movements – like arguments about empire in both pro- and anti-American politics today, or TV programmes on empire and slavery – illustrate continuing public, political and intellectual concerns. Political and popular interest intersects with academic controversy about interpretations of 'imperial' dimensions in modern European, and also Roman, Chinese, American and Middle Eastern history. Successful films and exhibitions on the Roman Empire, the Ottoman Turks or the 'First emperor of China', show the powerful attraction of 'imperial' subject matter.[4] So do academic debates on the 'barbarian invasions' of the Roman empire in the fourth and fifth centuries CE, or on the fate of indigenous American peoples following the arrival of Europeans, as well as comparative studies of different empires.[5] This book follows such persistent and changing concerns with colonial and imperial elements in the European past from the eighteenth century to the present and examines their role in the writing of history.

The other 'imperial' influence which has shaped British history writing has done so by influencing the terms, approaches and assumptions applied to the study of the past more generally. Much of the vocabulary and organising ideas regularly used by historians since the eighteenth century, whether or not they wrote on 'imperial' matters, has meanings and associations stemming from British involvement in global and imperial activities and relationships. Terms like 'progress', 'nation' or 'civilisation', which have been common currency in historical thought and texts since that time, acquired a distinctive character through European contacts with a wider world, augmenting and sometimes redirecting other meanings. Ideas of 'advanced' (as against 'backward') or of 'civilised' (as against 'barbarous' or 'decadent') cultures, governments or societies have been shaped by contacts between Europeans, inhabitants of America and Africans since the era of New World conquest and slavery. This supplemented the effects of contact between Europeans and inhabitants of Asia, which had expanded from medieval involvements in the Middle East into a web of trade, conquest, exploration and missionary activity. Classical and medieval thought on human unity and diversity, and on virtue and prosperity – like the initial impact of European contacts with the Americas and Asia – were continuing influences. However, the growing eighteenth-century European involvement in the wider world had key effects on European thought. It produced a wealth of information, ideas and images which became resources for new thinking about human society and about political and historical change, which fed into historical writing. From the 1750s the emergence of varied ideas about what constituted a 'nation' or 'race' underpinned nation making, empire building, economic change and social reform in that period, and also the writing of global, national and comparative histories. This book tracks the embedding of the terminology of 'nation', 'people', 'progress' and 'civilisation' in the work of British historians and in debates about these terms, through to the present era of decolonisation and postcolonial global politics.

These two features of the history of history writing have interacted to position imperial and colonial elements centrally within historical texts and practices. Recently, a number of historians have emphasised that European imperial and colonial roles over the last three centuries have shaped social, political and cultural development within Europe rather than being external or additional to it.[6] They have shown how histories of overseas empire are histories of the formation of modern states and societies *in* Europe as much as they are histories of European involvement and impact in the rest of the world. The activities and outlook of governments, entrepreneurs, intellectuals, migrants and clergy within Europe were increasingly affected by growing contact and concern with this wider world. Commercial, shipping and investment practices in early modern Spain, Portugal, Britain, France and the Netherlands adapted to meet new opportunities and difficulties overseas, thereby affecting material life in those countries. Political and religious institutions and policies which had been developed to meet the needs of governance and religious conversion in European overseas settlements and trading posts influenced political and religious experience in what came to be called the metropole. From the shaping of the Counter-Reformation papacy to the English shipping and insurance industries, political and economic lives were transformed by extra-European involvements. Furthermore, European ways of depicting and understanding themselves came to draw on information, speculation and information about various peoples and ways of life outside Europe.[7]

The discussion here presents arguments for this view and for alternatives. It will suggest that just as politicians, commentators, and voters have been concerned with imperial expansion, colonisation and competition for global power, so too historians' awareness of those issues has influenced their accounts of the past. Historians are exposed to the current interests and concerns of their society, and their awareness of *contemporary* debates about chattel slavery, about European and anti-colonial nationalism, and about political or social reform, or international power struggles has affected their work. Anthony Grafton has shown how the aims and methods of historians in the sixteenth century were shaped by the political and religious controversies of their time. As will be seen, eighteenth-century historians like Catharine Macaulay, Edward Gibbon and William Robertson considered the history of the Roman empire in the context of contemporary debates over imperial power and colonial settlement in India and north America.[8] Images of violence and destruction associated with the French Revolution hovered around nineteenth-century portrayals of protest and unrest in the UK. At the same period, legacies of Protestant belief similarly informed historical discussions of religious issues in sixteenth- and seventeenth-century England.

Global conflicts in the 'Napoleonic' era, the 1857 conflict in India, the growth of settler dominions and of organised opposition to colonial rule have all affected historical work on empire, as do decolonisation and global politics today. Equally importantly, they added new meanings to the terminology used more widely by historians in narratives and analyses of national and social pasts.

This book will explore imperial strands in historical practice, which includes researching the past, formulating questions about the past and organising ideas and material arising from research, as well as writing on the past or commenting on the historical work of others. It will consider two important areas of that practice. It will describe and analyse the role of stories and interpretations of empire in British accounts and analyses of the past produced since the mid-eighteenth century. It will show various ways in which the subject of empire and colonies became embedded in historical narratives and how that has been critiqued and contested. By examining views and debates on empire offered in historical writing for different audiences (scholars, children, popular readerships), it will illustrate the contested place of empire in constructions and perceptions of the past, with their varied changes and continuities. The aim is to trace the ways in which stories and ideas about colonies and imperial power were included or identified within narratives of 'national' history, or indeed separated or excluded from them, enhancing understanding of the historic place of empire in British culture. Whether as a space for exotic and pleasurable imaginings in fiction or advertising, a practical concern for business and government or an inspiring political or moral theme for educators and politicians, the imperial past has been an ongoing resource within that culture.

Secondly, the book will consider the influence of encounters with the wider world on the language, ideas and assumptions in British historians' conceptual and methodological 'toolkits', providing a fuller view of how and why they do what they do. In order to get the most from historical texts it is important to be aware of the implications and associations of terms and approaches used in those texts. When some past activity is called 'progressive', or a society or policy is said to be 'civilised', or some people are termed a 'nation', it is worth asking what meanings are being given to these concepts, and to pay attention to the history behind ideas of 'progress', 'nation' or 'civilisation'. Scholarly work in cultural history, the history of ideas and the history of medicine and religion has shown how concepts have complex histories. What came to be termed 'science' in the nineteenth century was previously known as 'natural philosophy', just as 'science' had referred to a very different set of intellectual or academic activities in medieval times.[9] Notions of 'empire', 'family', 'nation', 'industry', 'revolution' and 'insanity' (to name just a few examples) have changed over time, and thus gained, lost and kept uses or meanings. Such changes influence both the choice of terms by those who write texts, and the way in which readers understand them. This book looks at terms which have been flavoured by the increasingly global horizons of British experience, and of British perceptions of the past since the eighteenth century, bringing 'colonial' associations into history writing about topics which may not be themselves 'colonial'. Basing itself on this understanding of the 'made-ness' of language and meaning, it will extend readers' grasp of historians' practices and of their effects.

As a basis for the historical study in the main part of the book it will be useful to say more about the two issues which will be studied so that readers can be clear what is under discussion. This provides a framework for the chronological analysis in the next three sections, and for the assessment of recent and future developments in the final section of the book.

'Empire' and 'nation' in historical narrative

At least since Luís de Camões' 1572 epic poem *The Lusiads* affirmed Portuguese identity by celebrating Portuguese overseas exploration and conquest, the placing of imperial expansion within 'national' narratives has featured in European imagining and writing of the past. Europeans now linked stories of their own societies to stories of empire by celebrating the bringing of Christianity to the 'heathen' or successful overseas rivalry with European competitors and by comparing contemporary imperial achievements with empires of the ancient past. European 'colonial' consciousness had a longer history, associated with the *reconquista* in Spain, 'German' conquest/settlement in middle and north-eastern Europe, or Anglo-Norman incursions into Ireland and Wales, as well as 'crusades' in the eastern Mediterranean. This expansionism combined the aspirations of western European military elites with those of the reorganised western church, and of merchant networks in both the Mediterranean and northern Europe. As historians like Robert Bartlett have argued, it contributed significantly to the formation of 'European' and Latin Christian identities influenced by experiences of conquest, conversion and settlement. Significantly, what became understood as elements in a core identity were often formed on the moving frontiers of war and settlement in central Europe, Ireland, Greece or the Iberian peninsula. Shared frameworks of power and culture were established by laws and charters, the work of religious orders and papal influence, and wielded by conquering aristocracies whose 'Frankish' energy, boldness and brutality were seen as sources of their success. This common identity worked alongside awareness of the diversity among the European elites who claimed it, while stimulating views of social and cultural difference flavoured by ethno-racial thinking which allowed them to distinguish themselves from Irish, Slavic, Jewish, Greek or 'Saracen' others.[10]

A new feature of the early modern period was the appearance of European concepts of a 'nation' associated with state and dynastic power, with constructions of shared history and culture, and in some cases with the assertion of a global presence. These associations took diverse forms. The emergence of the Dutch 'United Provinces' in the seventeenth century was linked to Protestantism, the Orange dynasty and resistance to Hapsburg power, but also to the success of a 'United East India Company', and rivalry for land and profit in America, the Indies and the Caribbean. These themes were woven into both their political and colonial practices and narratives of their past.[11] English counterparts crafted their own 'national' consciousness out of experiences of seventeenth-century political and religious conflict, and of overseas settlement and assertion against European competitors, expressed in historical accounts of that period. Narratives of an 'English' past, in which Protestantism, 'liberty' and property rights were established through a political compact between state, church and property owners, were linked to celebrations of international commercial and colonial success, and of English control of all the 'British' Isles.[12] The remaking of Roman Catholicism as a global faith linked the re-forming of religious organisation and practice to commercial and colonial links stretching from Mexico to Japan. These developments parallel those shaping Louis XIV's France with ambitions in India, the Americas and the Middle East, as well as in Europe, and to imperial and ethnic thought in Safavid Iran, Habsburg/Bourbon Spain, Qing China, or the Ottoman lands.[13] Any monolithic or totalising view of interaction between ethnic, imperial or 'national' thought and practice would be misleading, but nonetheless it should be recognised as a developing feature in the sixteenth to eighteenth centuries.

The theme of relations and tensions between understandings and meanings of 'nation' and of 'empire' in Britain will be followed from the eighteenth century to the debates of the present time. By the late seventeenth century stories and memories of the past supported particular views of the relationships between ruling dynasties, shared language, religion or customs, and state structures of taxation, law and military organisation in which 'nation' and 'empire' entwined. The Spanish *reconquista* and American conquests, like Dutch French, and English overseas commercial and colonial expansion, fed visions of 'national' specificity that linked trans-national ideals (prosperity, Christianity, liberty, civilisation) to that expansion. Dealing with the 'savage' Irish or Native Americans, arguing that global trade and settlement served 'national' interests, brokering arrangements between governments, trading companies, elites and colonists embedded these connections in varied forms. The growth of cities with 'colonial' roles (Seville, Nantes, Bristol, Amsterdam, Marseilles, London) linked urban life and work, whether of bankers or dock workers, to global activities. The creation of legal and administrative systems to manage government interests in overseas trade or settlement brought such activities into the 'national' as well as regional political sphere. Trading companies and crown and proprietary colonies linked the state to European ventures in America, Asia and the Caribbean. The production of travel writings, visual images and scholarly or religious texts spread images, information and ideas about a wider world into varied cultural settings. Reports of the lives of 'native' peoples, sermons about freeing Christians captured by North African pirates, and figures of be-feathered indigenous Americans or turbaned Turks in pageants or advertising began to disseminate in Europe. The influence of such material in the British context will be a central theme in this book.

Rather than treating notions of 'empire' and nation' as isolated from one another, this text examines their conflicts and interactions over time. When the nineteenth-century scholar Ernest Renan asked the question, 'What is a nation?' he explicitly distinguished 'nations' from empires like those of the Romans and the Ottoman Turks, and both present-day scholars and earlier writers and politicians – not to mention anti-imperial nationalists – have opposed the claims of empire and nation.[14] In order to follow developments in the period discussed in this book, it will be useful to draw attention to the uses and meanings which have been acquired by the terms 'nation' and 'empire' in a European setting. Derived from Latin terms for rule and command (both civilian and military), 'empire' came to signify territories under the rule of a particular regime. It embraced the definition of Henry VIII's 'realm of England' as an 'empire' in the 1533 Act in Restraint of Appeals, Roman ideas of world empire and views of the medieval Holy Roman Empire. An *imperium* might include communities with diverse social structures, customs, languages or beliefs, and involve subsidiary, if not subordinate, governing groups and leaders with varied relationships to the imperial regime. Notions of empire have also been associated with the conquest and state control of far-off peoples, and with territorial expansion and settlement. The term *colonia*, initially used to describe settlements of Greek migrants or demobbed Roman soldiers away from their places of origin, became linked to accounts of expansion and empire in varied ways. Europeans encountering the states and dominions of Chinese, Inca or Mughal rulers applied the term 'empire' to those polities, implying some sort of comparability, despite their difference from European experience. Images and stories of the Roman empire shaped western European history writing as well as political thought and institutions. They were associated variously with effective and civilising power, with questions of tyranny, decline and corruption, and with glamour, luxury and violence.

These resources were complemented by a similarly complex repertoire of uses and meanings for the idea of 'nation'. Early use to name people thought to have common descent and/or geographical origin developed into a term which identified a 'nation' by possession of shared language, customs, social institutions, laws or beliefs linked to kinship or place of origin.[15] Such an identity might be claimed by a group of people for themselves and/or attributed to them by others, using stories of their ancestry, heroes, victories, sufferings and adventures. History, myth and memory contributed to the making and transmission of views of shared identity and might inform actions based on those views (demands for rights, persecution, resistance to external intervention, discriminatory treatment). Stories of Jews as a people with shared descent ('children of Abraham'), place of origin and experience (Old Testament narratives of triumph migration, suffering and liberation) can be compared with ancient Greek accounts of their origins, migrations and conflicts in the eastern Mediterranean. Tales of ancient Indo-Europeans, or at least of their elites, in India appear in popular legend and Sanskrit poetry (the *Mahabharata*), just as oral narratives of ancestors and clan lineages have been used to construct shared pasts in African communities. Scholars have debated the distinctions between these 'ethnies' and more recent 'national' versions of history and identity. They have compared the practice of linking history, culture and politics in Jewish and anti-Jewish politics, in Roman distinctions between 'Roman' and 'Greek' and in 'modern' nationalisms.[16] Such links supported practical and moral arguments for different forms of government, whether in changing Venetian views of the Ottoman regime in relation to its European counterparts, or in English common lawyers' interest in 'Anglo-Saxon' traditions of government. They could also support beliefs and theories about the origins and basis of human cultural and social difference shaped by Christian theology and classical ideas of climate, civilisation and ethnicity.[17] This book will consider the role of such connections in British history writing.

Categories of both 'empire' and 'nation' have relied to a significant extent on distinctions and interactions between 'us' and 'them', 'self' and 'other'. 'Imperial' ideals and practices dealt with relationships between rulers and ruled and the incorporation or control of plural societies within an 'imperial' structure. Such relationships and institutions might be seen as 'civilising' missions (in Roman or nineteenth-century European empires) or as expressions of dynastic power and virtue (as with Habsburg, Chinese or Ottoman rule) or the duty of a 'superior' group towards 'inferior' others. Significantly, the empire which aroused pride and controversy in eighteenth-century Britain was described in 'national'/territorial ('British') and not in dynastic ('Hanoverian') terms. Ideas of the 'nation' invoked the solidarity and inclusion said to define particular groups through shared culture, descent, physical location or supposed inherent qualities. Those very definitions necessarily exclude or separate out 'others' who are said not to share the characteristics claimed for a particular 'nation'. Such thinking has supported claims to national 'rights' or destiny and/or policies designed to distinguish and discriminate between 'real' members of the 'nation' and immigrants, minorities or 'outsiders', however defined. Irish people in England, 'Slavs' in Germany, Jews and Roma people in many European countries and indigenous or migrant groups in the USA, like 'colonial' or former colonial subjects in imperial metropoles, have faced policies and prejudices founded on just such distinctions.

Since historians have regularly used concepts of 'nation' and 'empire' in their work since the eighteenth century, it is important to consider the assumptions and omissions associated with these terms in particular historical contexts. One crucial but often unnoticed expression of selection/exclusion in history writing is the frequent use of the term 'we' to address readers in a vast number of history texts. While drawing those readers into a relationship with the text, author or subject matter, this usage also asserts or imagines common bonds, which of course ignores or denies the diversity of those readers. What is imposed or concealed when 'national' histories assume that all readers are part of that nation or part of it in the same way? What are the effects of histories of single-sex institutions (armies, convents, parliaments before the twentieth century) which ignore homosociality, or of histories of some particular religion which address readers as though they were all attached to that faith? Who is the 'we' being addressed by experienced scholars writing for young, popular and non-specialist readers? These questions of exclusion or oversimplification could be discussed extensively in relation to almost every text to be discussed in this book. However, by raising them at the start of this text, readers are at least alerted to a powerful rhetorical device whose familiarity may make it invisible, but whose frequent presence is especially relevant for discussions of 'empire' and 'nation'.

Like Renan, some historians treat 'empire' and 'nation' as distinct and even competing political categories, but it should equally be recognised that the emergence of some 'nations' has had significant 'imperial' features. The development of government structures in the Netherlands was shaped by networks of global and colonial trade and settlement, as can be seen from the interest of the newly established rulers of the United Provinces in commercial patents and a successful United East India Company. The emergence of 'Britain' since the late thirteenth century involved assertions of English dominance in Wales, Scotland and Ireland, as well as expansion and competition in continental Europe, the Atlantic and Asia. While new issues and forms of imperial activity and thought developed from the eighteenth century, the relationships of empire and nation examined in this book were rooted in an extended history rather than suddenly emerging in recent times. This was reflected in versions of 'national' history which traced and celebrated the story of the 'nation' through stories of imperial achievement, or conversely expressed anxieties that the 'national interest' might be threatened by 'imperial' commitments. In this respect, historical writing paralleled political debates on the same questions. Imperial expansion or reform might be seen as an expression and test of national virtues or a manifestation of national destiny, as well as a marker of success and power. Equally, it could be criticised as unworthy of national virtues, and even dangerous to them, as well as to material and political interests. It will be seen that such anxieties and ambitions played their role in depictions of the nation as well as in political decisions and controversies. From eighteenth- and nineteenth-century debates about slavery and imperial wars to twentieth-century disagreements over decolonisation and apartheid, the British – like other Europeans – concerned themselves with the 'national' significance of imperial issues. Disagreements among politicians, commentators and historians over whether empire was peripheral or central to the interests and meanings of the nation themselves constructed and maintained connections between the two.

The concept of mutually constitutive relationships between 'nation' and 'empire' forms part of the framework for discussions of empire and history in this book. Eighteenth-century controversies over what kind of state management of overseas endeavours, if any, would enhance the prosperity of state and economy were conducted in terms of the benefit to the 'nation' and of 'national' moral standing. So too were nineteenth-century debates over the dangers and obligations of imperial rule, which often went beyond the practical concerns of politics and government. As will be seen, the rhetoric of responsibility, prosperity or virtuous profitability ('doing well by doing good') were developed and criticised in religious and secular discussion; questions of the abolition of slavery, of investment in colonies and emigration and of imperial 'duty' towards indigenous peoples were discussed as issues with 'national' significance. It will be seen that notions of an imperial civilising mission, whether Christianising, protective or reforming, entwined imperial activities with ideas of national identity, national character and national destiny. The ability to bring the rule of law, 'enlightened' religious and moral standards, 'rational' social and economic practices or even preparation for self government to 'less fortunate' peoples entered the self-image of various European, including British, publics. It makes sense to examine how such publics 'knew' who they were through 'knowing' their difference from, and relationship to, colonial others. Ideas about bringing distinctively 'French' forms of order and rationality to Algeria, or a uniquely 'British' commitment to liberty, reform and property to India or South Africa played formative roles in imaginings and understandings of a French or British nation. Just as 'colonial' products (tobacco, sugar, coffee, tea; later cotton, jute, rubber or petroleum) were domesticated within European mass consumption, and just as colonial investment helped in 'metropolitan' economic development, so information and ideas about colonial activity shaped European 'national' identities. Empire might thus be embedded in collective 'national' memories and used or debated in schools, churches and the media as well as elections or parliaments.

This story can be explored through the study of areas of life ranging from parliamentary debate and household expenditure to religious, academic and leisure activities, and – in the case of this book – the activity of history making. The book traces the effects of ideas of empire on studies of the past, looking at the extent to which 'empire' formed the subject matter of such studies, and at the 'empire origins' of ideas, questions and terms used by historians. It treats 'history' as a term covering the whole range of activities involved in producing and presenting accounts of the past, and 'historians' as a term to describe those who undertake them. Activity begins with the choice of topics to study and the selection of material for investigation of the chosen topic. The planning and design of research and decisions to include or exclude particular issues or types of material are as much part of the making of 'history' as any written or other outputs of research. So too is the planning and organisation of the interpretation and description of material. Interpreting and describing the past involves selection, emphasis and decisions about views on the topic being discussed, which all affect what is included/excluded or prioritised/ marginalised within the text. It also involves important choices about language and style (argumentative, detached, dramatic, descriptive, humorous) which are integral to any text, rather than optional extras. Historians also make choices about how to present their work – choices influenced not only by their own aspirations (do they want their own TV series, or to be published in the most prestigious journal in their field?) but also by programme makers', academics' or publishers' views of what might be saleable or relevant. Such choices in turn affect decisions about the language, argument and information used to depict the past.

Historians' depictions of the past have taken forms ranging from TV programmes (with academic consultants or presenters) and learned monographs, to texts for non-academic readers, exhibition catalogues and school textbooks. These depictions overlap with and influence the wider sphere of cultural presentations of the past. Current views of the British anti-slavery campaigns can draw on radio discussion among academics and broadcasters, the politician William Hague's commercial biography of William Wilberforce, museum displays on the ending of the slave trade, school lessons or academic texts. A scholarly work on Elizabeth I's minister Walsingham is read in daily instalments on radio, where leading academics are gathered to discuss the history of sport, party politics or religion. Examination of earlier depictions of the past also reveals a diversity of forms and the influence which those forms have had on one another. Themes and terms cross between popular and scholarly accounts, between secular and religious texts, between written and visual depiction or between texts aimed at children and those intended for adults. A theatrical farce like Gil Vicente's *Auto da India* could dramatise conflicts over Portuguese interests in Asia and north Africa among sixteenth-century Portuguese court factions and Lisbon elites. Men like the German Hans Staden, the French Huguenot de Léry, and the Jesuit Acosta advocating Christian beliefs among American peoples related their endeavours in terms of dangerous adventure and ethnographic debate on human cultures as well as religious mission.[18] Historical stories often appear in political speeches and pamphlets, especially when authors have moved between political, literary and intellectual activities. These can refer to familiar episodes like the Battle of Britain, or be like Enoch Powell's obscure but subsequently memorable allusion to 'rivers of blood' in his notorious 1968 speech on immigration. To consider the role of information, ideas and experiences derived from involvement in empire in the development of historical practice opens up a complex cultural and intellectual field.

This brief account of the range of activities involved in history making and historical practice is the basis for an exploration of the entry of imperial elements into that practice. It enables discussion of empire as a subject for British historians and also allows questions to be asked about the 'imperial' flavour of concepts or stories used in other contexts. Responses to contact and conflict in 'imperial' settings has contributed to ideas and frameworks used by writers on past societies in Britain and elsewhere. These can be seen in Han Chinese dealings with peoples in inner Asia, or in Greek and Roman experiences of settlement and conquest from the Atlantic to the Black Sea. Similar stimuli came from medieval western European involvements with central and eastern European peoples, and with Muslim societies in the eastern and southern Mediterranean. From the fifteenth century they were supplemented by European responses to exploration, conquest, commerce and colonial settlement beyond Europe. These formed a cultural repertoire increasingly used by Europeans as their activities in a wider world expanded from the eighteenth century onward, and could be used in a growing body of investigation and interpretation of the past. As cross-cultural and comparative approaches became both esteemed and popular, the ideas of social structure and historical change which were created entered historians' terminology, and cultural resources derived from global imperial contacts shaped their ideas. This process is discussed more fully in Chapter 2.

Most important among the toolkit of terms which historians brought into regular use have been the notions of civilisation, progress and ethnic or national identity around which much historical writing has been organised. It is useful to remember that these concepts have been developed not as isolated categories, but through comparison and differentiation among different communities, polities and cultures and the use of 'othering'. When Greeks and Romans created ideas of politics and civilisation rooted in their own urban life and governance (the Greek *polis*, the Roman *civitas*), they did so by contrasting their own 'civilised' achievements with the 'barbarian' practices of peoples beyond their boundaries. Certain benchmarks of legal and political institutions, of urban settlement, religious practice and literate elite culture were used by writers as defining marks of their own cultures and as general criteria for 'civilisation'. When they wished to warn readers of dangers or weaknesses which might undermine empire or civilisation, they might, like Tacitus or Herodotus, praise some 'barbarian' practices while criticising others. They experimented with explanations of human difference, using both hierarchical and non-hierarchical models of diversity, and considering both climatic and social origins for that diversity. Such views drew on imperial and colonising experiences, whether or not they were applied directly to accounts of those experiences.[19]

Another strand of comparative analysis emerged within the cultural framework of Christianity, creating definitions of the states and communities of 'Christendom' against 'Muslim' equivalents in the Mediterranean area, or of Jewish groups, and 'heathens' in northern or eastern Europe. Western European views of their distinctive political and cultural interests and identities were formed by reference to these cultural and political 'others'. The expansion of European states and settlements, and related developments in knowledge and thought, established norms and understandings of 'religion', 'civilisation' and 'good' government for use in historical writing.[20] Paradoxically, these ideas built on exchanges of ideas and information across the Muslim–Christian divide, as Arab thought and versions of classical texts reached western European scholars. By the fifteenth century Europeans had developed a range of distinctions and hierarchies of desirable and/or virtuous social, political or cultural practice which influenced ideals and aspirations, if not practical politics.

The practice of associating particular characteristics with particular groups of people, using ethnographic information, theories of inherent or acquired human difference and stories of conquest, conversion and colonisation established patterns of thinking directly relevant to this book. The legacies of classical thought and empire making and the formation and expansion of medieval Christian states and communities fed into intellectual and political views of identity, difference and plurality. Combinations of state policy, cultural perception and social relationships shaped situations as diverse as the multicultural communities of twelfth-century Sicily, the treatment of Jews in medieval Europe or tension between 'German' and 'Italian' interests in the Holy Roman Empire. When Europeans began to depict the newly met peoples of the Americas they combined classical and biblical motifs with information brought back to Europe and existing conventions of fable and myth to portray Caribbean, Mexica or north American peoples. They posed warriors with Aztec shields and ornaments like classical heroes, or nude American women like figures of Eve and Venus, and assimilated accounts of 'New World' people within existing European accounts of 'wild men', 'Asiatic' tribes, and ancient Picts.[21] Legend, humanistic classical learning and Christian thought were used to make sense of newly encountered peoples and present them as partly attractive and interesting, and partly frightening or 'barbarous'. They could be shown simultaneously as beings surviving from before the biblical Fall or Noah's flood, as living in a classical 'golden age and as practitioners of strange, perhaps 'savage', customs from tattooing to cannibalism.

In addition, these contacts stimulated new ideas and images of human difference as some artists and writers sought to depict the 'otherness' of distant peoples and their own distant ancestors. By the late sixteenth century Jesuit writers with a global mission to convert sketched out ideas of staged human development from 'barbarism' to 'civilisation', English artists portrayed Inuit people, and German books depicted costumes from non-European societies alongside those of different ranks and occupations in western Europe.[22] These depictions combined information from European accounts of conquest and colonisation with 'signature' images identifying 'Americans' by putting them in feather headdresses and skirts (a misreading of imported American feather garments first made in 1505). Depictions of 'Tartars' might offer an exotic fantasy of the savage warrior seen in a 1577 German 'costume book', or more ethnologically informed presentation as in a similar work of 1610.[23] They linked curiosity and fantasy about distant peoples with European religious and political concerns of the time. The presentation of different characteristics of various human groups thus combined the familiar and the unfamiliar by repeated use of stereotypes, or by recasting 'exotic' people and their practices in forms recognisable to European audiences.

By the 1520s exotic Aztec 'others' from America appeared alongside European peasants and criminals in image collections for Charles V, identified ethnically but also incorporated into his court entourage, as their homeland was incorporated within his empire.[24] Images from the wider world became points of reference in European politics, as when a Dutch commentator on the killing of the de Witt brothers used the image of Brazilian cannibalism to convey its brutality, or opponents wrote of the 'Turkish' despotism of Oliver Cromwell. Likewise, 'exotic' figures could be assimilated to European convention. A 1549 picture of the Ottoman ruler Suleiman II showed him in a dramatically exotic/stereotypical 'Turkish' turban, while presenting him in the monarch-on-horseback style familiar in portraits of his contemporaries Charles V and Francis I.[25]

The beginnings of the Atlantic trade in enslaved Africans added new features to a long history of European assumptions about the practice of enslavement, and added understanding of human differences and/or 'inherent' suitability for enslavement. Colonial, national and racial thinking entwined in the ideas and images of preachers, politicians and intellectuals and their audiences, as they did in discussions about the new commercial and colonial ventures pursued by Europeans in the Americas, Africa and Asia. The Turkish and Iranian carpets appearing in sixteenth- and seventeenth-century European paintings 're-presented' these 'eastern' products as signs of affluence 'at home' in Europe, as well as of European contact with the societies where they were produced. For the English in north America or Ireland in the sixteenth and seventeenth centuries, contacts with trading partners, colonial subjects, rivals or allies generated intellectual, moral and political debates as well as practical concerns. They combined comparative discussion of different customs or governments, judgemental ranking of 'civilised'/'barbarous', or 'godly'/'heathen' practices and the pleasurable accumulation of 'curious' information and objects from distant places. The growing body of material depicting and defining European 'peoples' in relation to a whole range of 'others' could also be used to shape ideas of 'national' destiny, character and expansion. These might be associated with Christian missionary aims, with Protestant and Catholic rivalry and with commitment to increasing 'national' prosperity and grandeur. Indeed, it can be argued that the new perceptions of being a 'nation' coming into use in the sixteenth and seventeenth centuries were linked to experiences of overseas expansion and competition, and to ideas of nations as sharing and promoting particular versions of 'civilisation'. As western 'Christendom' divided along religious lines during the sixteenth century, rulers' support for rival versions of Christianity created powerful connections between state, faith and identity which were projected into overseas settlement, conquest and commerce, with lasting effects.

These developments can be seen in public art and architecture, in the political ideas of rulers and intellectuals, and in history writing. The use of a 'black legend' of Spanish mistreatment of Caribbean and American peoples, like the depiction of 'American' figures in ceremonies designed for Habsburg emperors, embedded new colonial contacts and images in the politics of Catholic–Protestant conflict and dynastic expansion. Puritan and Anglican texts and sermons, drawing parallels between the persecution of heretics by the Inquisition and Spanish cruelty to indigenous Americans, contributed to self-images of Englishness bound up with Protestantism and with ideas of a colonial mission. Early histories of English settlement in north America helped to shape *English* identities by celebrating their ability to manage American 'natives' through Christian love and offers of the benefits of civilisation rather than fear. Spanish conquest and settlement in central and southern America during the sixteenth and seventeenth centuries likewise contributed to dynastic and religious self-fashioning as monarchy and religious orders made use of the colonial spaces which they had opened up. The new Dutch Republic's commercial empire in the East and West Indies sustained confidence in providential purpose as well as material and political power.

Entwined with the religious and political conflicts which shaped the relations of European states and peoples over the sixteenth and seventeenth centuries were new contacts with a wider world, which contributed to European ideas of nation and civilisation. Just as contact with peoples in the Americas stimulated thinking on these ideas, as Europeans assimilated newcomers to existing world views and considered their 'differentness', so contact with Ottoman and Asian societies also became a source for European self-fashioning. These contacts established new European commercial relationships and privileges, while also reinforcing Christian stereotypes of

Muslim beliefs and practices. Europeans were dealing with powerful, complex and effective states and societies, and with the challenge of making sense of a growing range of encounters. The romance, speculation and prejudice with which Europeans viewed Ottomans, Indians or Japanese were fused with religious, commercial, political and military concerns in their depictions of 'the Turk' or 'the Hindu'. Significantly, such ideas and images were used as much to further religious and political debate within European societies as to depict or analyse 'eastern' people. Shifting Venetian views of the 'despotism' of Ottoman rulers combined practical attempts to deal with 'the east' with romance and fantasy, refiguring both in the context of diplomatic and commercial concerns. Protestant English use of Islam as a counterweight to images of Catholic states of the Counter-Reformation, and also as a symbol of fanaticism, tyranny and decadence, was a similar feature of early modern culture.[26] The 'us' of Venetian or English historians, commentators and policymakers was entwined as well as contrasted with the 'them' in the east.

By the later seventeenth century significant links had been established between western European understandings of overseas expansion, of civilisation and of developing views on 'national identity'. Practices of 'othering' used 'information' about newly encountered peoples to create not only attractive or horrifying imaginings of exotic foreigners, but also new understandings of national identity by contrasting the latter with the former. The distinctive shared qualities of a 'nation' could be established through comparison and contrast between its own virtues, successes and qualities and the deficiencies, faults and limitations of others, both European and non-European. In an English setting this might juxtapose Protestant and constitutional government to Roman Catholic absolutist rule, or eastern despotism and superstition. It might contrast the orderly industrious productivity of property-owning English traders and colonists with the practices of indigenous Americans or 'lazy' Africans and 'orientals'. It might focus on 'savage', 'heathen' and 'barbarous' customs (polygamy, cannibalism, tattooing, idol worship) in other societies in order to affirm the moral and social worth of the 'national' culture and values. Such comparisons consolidated beliefs and explanations of the virtues of English national character by setting up these oppositions, just as French responses to Ottomans, north American 'Indians', or enslaved Africans shaped their ideas of their 'national' identity. While images and ideas of other peoples could be, and often were, used by Europeans in many other ways, their 'othering' role in the history of nationalistic thought and politics became a significant feature of western culture.

When eighteenth-century thinkers designed their particular accounts of the rise and progress of civilisation in general, or of specific governments and societies, they did so within this well-established framework. As shown in the next chapter, there were distinctive new elements in these accounts, but the continued role of the established themes and images was also important. This study offers a view of how longer-established and newer ideas coexist, rather than one replacing the other in some linear process. Just as each human being combines their genetic or family inheritance in a new form without losing that inheritance, so views of nation, empire and civilisation were refigured without existing elements disappearing. Rather than seeing such changes as some uncomplicated move forward over time, it is more useful to take a 'genealogical' approach, acknowledging the variety, and sometimes inconsistency, of the ideas influencing historians at any given time. The persistence of established views, the creative capacity to pursue diverse and incompatible lines of thought and the echoes or effects of concepts and images from one period in another all contribute to particular narratives of the past. In material terms it should be remembered that some historical writing had a very long shelf life. To take one instance: as Macaulay's *History of England* swept to long-lasting success in the mid-nineteenth century, David Hume's work of eighty years earlier was still being reprinted, and others will be noted in due course. The discussion here will recognise the rich accumulation of understandings and depictions of 'nation', 'civilisation' and 'empire' which have informed history writing in the UK.

'Empire' and related themes

While recognising the complexity of this body of ideas, it will be useful to organise the discussion of empire and history writing by addressing themes which appeared regularly in writing on empire and have influenced history writing more generally. These have created associations between the concept of 'empire' and other terms regularly used by historians. The arguments in this book focus on three sets of connections found in history writing produced since the later eighteenth century. One set links notions of empire to those of state, government and citizenship; a second set links them to ideas of progress and civilisation; a third links them to concepts of race and nation. Each link is introduced here as a prelude to the specific consideration of how they operated in different periods.

Empire, state and citizenship

'Empire' is, of course, a term most obviously used to refer to forms of state power and governmental structures. It is applied to states as diverse as that of the Romans in the second century CE, the Tang Chinese in the eighth, the Mongols in the thirteenth, the Ottomans or Spanish in the sixteenth, the British in the nineteenth and the Soviets in the twentieth century. It draws attention to how rulers and ruling elites involved in conquest or settlement adapted, maintained or reinvented their exercise of power in order to control and exploit the peoples and territories they subjugated or colonised. Key features of the Roman, Ottoman, Spanish or British 'state' (laws, armies, administration, policy making) were remade in response to imperial expansion. This changed their functions and meanings for people in the 'metropole' (Italy, Istanbul, Spain, the UK) as well as imperial subjects elsewhere. The making of the Roman empire between the rule of Augustus (27 BCE–14 CE) and that of Hadrian (117–38 CE) involved remodelling existing institutions (the senate and the proconsular system of government) while continuing to work with local allies and elites, and to maintain military control and the flow of revenue. Divine emperors, client rulers and the circulation of imperial officials, resources and soldiers were part of life at the core of the empire and in its frontier zones.[27] The reshaping of Ottoman power in the fifteenth and sixteenth centuries linked frontier warrior and nomad forms of authority and exploitation to new ways of extracting revenue and manpower for the regime, adapting state relationships with clients, allies and vassals. New forms of dynastic, administrative and military power shaped life in the imperial centres of Istanbul and Edirne, as well as in regional centres (Aleppo, Cairo, Belgrade) or on the Balkan and Azerbaijani frontiers.[28]

The Spanish conquest of lands in central and southern America likewise stimulated creative adaptation of systems of land allocation, labour organisation and state oversight. These were rooted in the *reconquista* of the Iberian peninsula, in indigenous Inca or Mexica practices, and in new methods and opportunities created in the colonial setting. The partnership of crown and church, their negotiation with local interests and circumstances, and the web of uneven authority shaping plantation slavery, and religion as well as governance affected subjects of Spanish rule in the peninsula as well as the 'colonies'.[29] The development of state and empire in 'Britain' similarly affected the English, and the Scots, Irish and Welsh whom the English variously tried to control, incorporate or ally with, as well as settlers or trading companies active overseas. Early uses of the term 'empire' relate to Tudor assertions of royal autonomy, the union of the Scottish and English crowns under James I and Anglo-Scottish aspirations to settle parts of the island of Ireland.[30] They drew on understandings of Roman notions of *imperium* disseminated by lawyers, rulers and scholars during the Middle Ages, and on the theory and practices of 'composite monarchy' developed by European rulers to manage diverse domains acquired by inheritance, agreement or conquest. 'Latecomers' to European colonial expansion, seventeenth-century English entrepreneurs and governments experimented with various forms of venture in trade and settlement, which, if insecure and limited, supported real if fluctuating relationships between state, colonisation, trade and empire. In the later part of the century legislation to regulate trade and colonial settlement, and new naval and military policies developed in the context of the Stuart restoration and the 1688 revolution indicate important shifts linking changes in the conduct of war and state finance to global commercial and colonial interests. The reorganisation of the East India Company, the passing of the Navigation Acts and the setting-up of the Board of Trade, the National Debt and the Bank of England established a mesh of connections between government, finance, entrepreneurship and global expansion.[31]

In all these situations involvement in imperial and global ventures altered the role and significance of state structures for all who lived within them. The term 'empire' carried new meanings in which imperial and global perspectives became entwined in 'domestic' politics. This involved rearrangements of landholding, taxation and legal authority, and conflicts between different vested interests, and also debate about the character of state power and legitimacy. Such conflicts and debates indicate not only the provisional and unstable character of connections between ideas of 'state' and those of empire, but also how early modern European fears and aspirations for their states were acquiring imperial and colonial associations. Spanish controversies over the 'nature', status and rights of indigenous Americans – like later discussions of slavery, colonial political representation and state interests in commerce, religious conversion or settlement – involved rulers, intellectuals, assemblies and propagandists. Important issues emerged from their thinking. What were the challenges and opportunities for rulers seeking to consolidate central and colonial power? What forms of authority, autonomy and accountability were desirable within the state and its dependencies? What were the roles and rights of different kinds of subjects? Such questions linked concerns about political systems and practices within Spain, the Netherlands, France or Britain, to issues of colonial and commercial power and management. Of course, notions of 'empire' and 'state' were not connected in these ways for all Europeans, but the developments which brought them together in 'Britain' were not unique. From the seventeenth century, when writers created narratives of crown, law, power and constitution they did so in terms which had a global flavour.

References to classical, Christian and local concepts or precedents are significant as evidence that early thinking in Britain on overseas empire entwined with other traditions, but also indicate how close that thinking was to mainstream interests in law, government and power. The embedding of John Locke's discussion of the legitimacy of English settlement in north America in a general treatise on government is a noted example of how overseas commercial expansion and settlement were understood as part of the framework of 'domestic' politics and government. It drew on polemical and scholarly uses of legend, rhetoric and learned argument which for a century had debated the roles of trade, liberty and religion in a 'Britain' or 'England' seen as including trade and colonial ventures or at least aspirations in the Caribbean, Ireland, India and North America. Early modern perceptions of the 'English' or 'British' state were flavoured with experiences of governmental attempts to impose English authority in Ireland, to negotiate relationships with colonial entrepreneurs and assemblies, and to manage international trade. By the early eighteenth century practical experience combined with idealistic and ideological ambition in views of an imperial state supporting liberty and commerce.[32]

The sermons, pamphlets and treatises in which English and Scottish writers reflected on experiences of colonial endeavour and rivalry with European competitors, and their political, moral and legal implications, also commented on relations between colonisers and those they encountered. As they developed arguments for annexing territory, controlling its existing occupants and challenging rival claims to authority, the question of the rights or status of 'natives', or of chartered companies, colonial settlers and enslaved people, entered discourses of liberty, justice and subjecthood. Although, as will be seen, much of this discussion concerned the material and cultural characteristics of 'natives', it also dealt with political questions of the validity of treaties made with them, or of their rights to property. State regulation of English trading and settlement initiatives, and legal frameworks of overseas indenture and transportation, as well as global military and diplomatic activities connected governing institutions to imperial endeavours.[33] English attempts to establish English law in early modern Ireland, war and diplomacy with native Americans, 'aboriginal' Australians or Maoris, like legal and political demands from colonial subjects, consolidated connections between state action and empire. While policies towards enslaved people, natives and indentured servants enabled the propertied and powerful to control and exploit them, they were nonetheless embodied in codes and ordinances which placed their power within the domain of law and political debate.[34] One task of this book will be to track how texts dealing with British political and constitutional history have conveyed or ignored its 'imperial' aspects.

Empire and 'civilisation'

A second thematic connection between empire and historical practice involves approaches to the study of past societies and cultures. As imperial ideas entered mainstream thought on law and government, they came to influence European notions of civilisation. From the fifteenth century, increasingly diverse and prolonged contacts between Europeans and peoples in Asia, Africa and the Americas promoted comparative and analytical discussion of the economic, political, religious and cultural practices of different societies. As already noted, commentators drew on classical and humanist concepts of 'civilised' and 'barbarous', on reports and legends of distant peoples, on experiences of the 'crusades' and on scholarly texts, as well as information from the new contacts. As they sought to convey the 'difference' of unfamiliar societies while assimilating them within existing frameworks of knowledge, authors deployed notions of savagery and civilisation, culture and barbarism, Christian and infidel, extending and modifying them as they did so. Common topics for comment were how societies met material needs (agriculture and manufacture, or lack of them), how they reproduced themselves (sexual and marriage practices) and how they regulated themselves (the presence or absence of law, religion, family structures and government).[35]

Growing numbers of descriptions and commentaries on various peoples and societies moved from anecdote and compilation to evaluate and make sense of the material being presented for their readers. Their use of biblical history and theory, of the environmental and cultural ideas of classical authors and accounts of earlier European encounters with Mongols, Middle Eastern peoples or Africans was modified by new contacts. Over time, European speculations and theories combining these existing ideas with new thinking began to judge and evaluate other societies, which also reshaped how terms like 'civilised' or 'godly' were used within European thought. European perceptions of themselves as 'civilised' or 'Christian', and others as less so, involved contrast and comparison using a single ethnocentric standard, distinguishing between more and less civilised ways of living. Such distinctions established judgements and hierarchies among various cultures and societies, but, equally importantly, they shaped how Europeans described, defined or debated their own. In earlier periods crusading ideas and experiences contributed to the growth of notions of a Christian Europe or European Christendom defined against the 'Saracens' or 'heathens' beyond its terrain, or Jews and heretics within it.[36] From the fifteenth century such notions were further developed with reference to Africans, Asians or Native Americans.

These developments stimulated debates about the origins of, and connections between, different human groups, and how they might fit into biblical narratives of the peopling of the world after Noah, or classical accounts of migration and the emergence of 'civilised' life.[37] As Europeans considered similarities and differences between human societies, they consolidated ideas of their own social, political cultural and religious identities and achievements. Their views of their own societies and cultures drew on their ideas and imaginings of others, whether favourable or unfavourable, opinionated or nuanced. Views of craft production in the Mughal empire, religious practices in the kingdom of Kongo or the dress and sex lives of Algonquins and Ottomans flavoured European perspectives on their own forms of religion, government, production or marriage. Contrasting tyranny with good government, religion with idolatry or superstition, productive labour and social order with idleness and savagery, Europeans used comparisons and assumptions drawn from contact with other societies to make sense of themselves.

This process fed discussion about how human groups developed and disseminated their social, political and cultural practices. Western Europeans created stories of the development of civilisation from barbarism, and human capacity to learn political and economic skills or 'true' religion. Over the seventeenth and eighteenth centuries they experimented with various ways to describe and explain not only variation between societies in different parts of the world (climate or environment) but also change and development (historical or evolutionary influences). As already noted, theories of evolution or stages of human development can be found in some sixteenth-century writings and were to become an important means to make sense of human history similarity and differences. When native inhabitants of the east coast of north America were compared to the ancient Pictish inhabitants of Scotland, connections were made between the American present and the Scottish past which compared and contrasted forms of 'savagery'. These could suggest that Algonquins, like Scots, might 'advance' from a less to a more 'civilised' state, or that they were locked into a savage condition outside processes of change – a view with interesting implications for their place in historical narrative. If peoples in Asia could not be portrayed as 'without history' in the same way as indigenous Americans, comparisons like those of Fynes Moryson between people in the Ottoman empire and the Irish also created a common terrain of 'exotic' discussion. The 'barbarity' and 'savagery' attributed to the indigenous Irish population from the twelfth-century English conquest gained new resonance during the Elizabethan 'reconquest', with which Moryson was associated, as he was with Elizabethan ventures in the Middle East.[38]

'Civilised' modern Europeans were placed at the head of a hierarchy of more or less civilised societies, established by use of an enlarged repertoire of knowledge and ideas. Importantly for the discussion in this book, that position was historicised as the outcome of a development by which Europeans had 'progressed' beyond others, whether in arts and sciences, governmental institutions or Christian virtue. By the eighteenth century European understandings of what it meant to be 'civilised', and accounts of the emergence of civilised societies, were underpinned by global comparisons. The legacy of classical and Christian thought on these issues was being modified by new European involvements with a wider world. Like the relationship between ideas of state and government and ideas on empire, references to civilisation and to progress, or their opposites – barbarism, savagery and decadence – carried global associations with them. In the British case this was reinforced by a Protestantised culture in which virtue and progress were associated with that faith. It played a role in British views of Irish 'savages', of Ottoman 'tyranny' and of native American 'superstition', as it did in their comparisons and contrasts with Roman Catholicism and Islam. When historians created accounts and interpretations of the past they could draw on this legacy, whether or not they dealt directly with the subject of empire or colonies.

Empire and race

Western European debates on similarities and differences between themselves and other societies and peoples fostered a third set of relationships embedding imperial associations in the language and concepts used by historians. The process of comparing, distinguishing and accounting for similarity or difference raised questions about what might be inherent unchanging human characteristics, as against those affected by education, religion or social intervention. Early discussions of this topic focused on whether newly encountered peoples in Africa or the Americas could become Christians, or were capable of settled life of the kind Europeans considered 'civilised'. They also assessed the achievements of what they saw as more sophisticated governments, crafts or cultures. The 'temporalisation' of these discussions by use of notions of change over time, whether degeneration, advance or cyclical movement, was paralleled by interest in what might be the 'innate' qualities of specific groups of humans as opposed to humans in general. There is a long history of 'proto-racial' thinking in classical and medieval texts which considered the role of climate or physiological difference in determining the characteristics of particular groups (Jews, 'northern' as opposed to 'southern' peoples). Greek and Roman thinking on human difference considered inherited or inherent qualities and descent to be important features as well as climate, environment and culture; similar concerns appeared in Judaic thought.[39]

From the late fifteenth century this tradition was modified by the reports and speculations arising from a wider range of European contact with diverse societies. If native Americans were 'degenerate' survivors of the post-Noah dispersal of humanity, or of 'antique' (that is, classical) peoples,[40] how could observers explain their 'failure' to create forms of government, society or productive activity which Europeans regarded as 'civilised'? As European settlers and entrepreneurs increasingly depended on the labour of enslaved Africans to make a success of commercial agriculture in the Caribbean and mainland America, was enslavement to be justified in terms of the inherent characteristics of those being enslaved? As the numbers of non-European converts to Christianity grew, what arguments might be made for or against their capacity for ordination or responsibility in the church? More generally, debates about the diversity or unity of humanity now drew on resources from this enlarged range of contacts, feeding into existing views about the distinctive or innate characteristics of peoples within Europe as well as beyond.

It is in this context that ideas both of 'race' and of 'nation' were developed into the forms which have been so influential since the eighteenth century. It is worth noting that terms like 'people', 'race' and 'nation' were used quite interchangeably and inconsistently in political texts, travel writing and scholarly work. Ideas and assumptions about the identity and interests of 'the English', or 'the French' were entwined with ideas about human difference emerging from global trade, empire and exploration, blurring the distinctions between these categories. It was less a matter of assertions about the unity of humanity, or the 'essential' and distinctive characteristics of particular human groups, than of a field of thought and representation in which these elements jostled alongside each other. As will be seen, ideas and images from science, history, medicine, philosophy and literature all fed into thinking about what features made up a 'people', about whether such features were inherent or acquired, and about hierarchies and differences between various 'peoples'.

Studies of 'nationalist' thought and politics and the role of imagined and learned ideas about 'nations' have tended to focus on accounts of European thought and its influence outside Europe, and less often on racial influences in European politics.[41] However, it is important to consider how developing views about 'national' identity cross-fertilised with understandings of 'race' which drew on global contacts. European writers often used both European and non-European examples in descriptions of the 'manners and customs' of different peoples, in scholarly thought on different types of society or government, and in celebrations of 'folk' cultures as manifestations of 'authentic' ethnic identity. Their writings often slipped from comparative judgements into arguments about the inherent, fixed and inherited characteristics of specific human groups. Discussions of physical attributes, of family, political or legal forms, and of custom, language and religion were used to define and fix the identity of 'peoples', 'nations' or 'races' across the world. Europeans also argued over whether the diversity of cultural, physical and social forms among humans indicated variation within a single species or the existence of separate species, and over whether or how to construct a hierarchy of human groups. It is within that contested domain that writers in the UK created 'national' histories using categories and stories with imperial associations. Whether relating 'British' involvement in Ireland, or comparing 'English'/'British' national character, government and culture with colonial and European others, notions of a 'people' or 'nation' (a 'we' or 'us'?), which became key terms in history writing, were flavoured by such associations.

These comments are no more than an introduction to the three sets of connections between experiences and understandings of empire and historical practice. As this book tracks the history of history writing in Britain from the mid-eighteenth to the twenty-first century, showing how accumulated layers of ideas, information and images provided resources for historians, each set of connections will be examined within a chronological period. This allows clearer discussion of the extent and limits of 'imperial' elements in history writing, shaped both by the legacy of concepts developed over time, and by the links between the concepts described here. In British history writing the subject matter of empire also became a topic in itself. 'National' narratives of material life have dealt with global entrepreneurial networks from the East India and Levant Companies and the slave trade in the eighteenth century to British Petroleum and the City of London in the twentieth. War, conquest and settlement, from seventeenth-century ventures in Ireland, Virginia and Massachusetts, to twentieth-century involvement in Zimbabwe, Iraq and Palestine, have also entered 'national' stories of the UK. Histories of English/British society and culture could also have an imperial flavour, through accounts of how migration, missionary work or the spread of cricket and Shakespeare, projecting that culture into a wider world, while influencing 'national' identity 'at home'. The extent to which such stories figured in histories of England or Britain and their treatment in such histories can also be related to anxieties and disagreements about empire at different periods, as understood and depicted by historians of the time.

Equally, it is important to consider how historians' vocabulary was affected by the languages of description and analysis emerging from 'imperial' experiences and available for discussion of government, society, ethnicity and civilisation outside specifically colonial settings. The development of terms deployed to interpret law and policy making, material and moral progress or 'national' identity which had developed in that way raises questions about the role of such terms in the texts in which they appeared. If ideas of the rule of law or social progress in the UK used actual or implied comparison with practices elsewhere, how has that shaped beliefs in a civilising mission supporting the global exercise of British power, whether in Australia in the 1830s or Afghanistan in the 2000s? How is our understanding of history writing affected by a critical study of its universalising, relativist or ethnocentric discussions of liberty, prosperity or justice in past societies? Who is included in the 'we', 'our', and 'us' so regularly used in historical writing? What have been the variations and continuities in the imperial associations within notions of 'state', 'nation', 'progress' and 'civilisation' used in that writing?

The argument here is not that 'imperial' influences have dominated British history writing since the mid-eighteenth century, but rather that there are threads of such influence which are worth attention. Like other explorations of the constitutive role of empire within UK history over the last three centuries, this book suggests that, as with other areas of culture and life, the domain of history writing has been receptive of, and has contributed to, British imperial experience. An account and analysis of the imperial strand in the history of history writing can illuminate the traces of 'empire' in the 'metropolitan' UK, as well as exploring a significant aspect of that history. By using both chronological and thematic approaches, it will be possible to situate both these topics in the distinctive circumstances of particular periods, and to depict the layers and varieties of meaning built into concepts over time. It offers a way to appreciate the fluctuating, contested but identifiable presence of 'empire' in British history writing.

Notes

1 A. Césaire, *Lettre à Maurice Thorez*, Paris, 1956, p. 15.
2 A. Césaire, *Discourse on colonialism*, trans. J. Pinkham, New York, 1972.
3 See D. Branch, *Defeating Mau Mau, creating Kenya*, Cambridge, 2009; C. Elkins, *Britain's gulag: the brutal end of empire in Kenya*, London, 2005; S. Alam, *Rethinking Mau Mau in colonial Kenya*, Basingstoke, 2007.
4 Examples from the last decade are blockbuster exhibitions at the Royal Academy on the Chinese, Aztecs and Turks and highly successful British Museum exhibitions on empires in Iran and China, as well as on the Roman emperor Hadrian, and films like *Gladiator* (2000), *Alexander* (2004) *Kingdom of Heaven* (2005) on the Crusades, and TV series on the Roman empire (2005, 2007) and the first Chinese emperor (2006).
5 See G. Halsall, *Barbarian migrations and the Roman west*, Cambridge, 2007; C. Wickham, *The inheritance of Rome*, London, 2010; K. Kupperman, *Indians and English*, Ithaca, NY, 2000; N. Salisbury, *Manitou and Providence*, Oxford, 1982; U. Bitterli, *Cultures in conflict*, Stanford, 1989; D. Cook, *Born to die: disease and the New World conquest*, Cambridge, 1998; J. Krippner-Martinez, *Rereading the conquest*, Philadelphia, 2001; M. Restall, *Seven myths of the Spanish conquest*, Oxford, 2003.
6 Key work on this theme by Antoinette Burton, written between 1994 and 2011 is collected in her *Empire in question*, Durham, NC, 2011, especially chs 1–3, 12, 14, 15; other important contributions are C. Hall, *Civilising subjects*, Cambridge, 2002, and her section in C. Hall *et al.* [eds.], *Defining the Victorian nation*, Cambridge, 2000; and 'The rule of difference: gender, class, and empire in the making of the 1832 Reform Bill', in I. Blom [ed.], *Gendered nations*, Oxford, 2000; S. Gikandi, *Maps of Englishness*, New York, 1996; M. Sinha, *Colonial masculinity*, Manchester, 1995; M. Sinha, 'Teaching imperialism as a social formation', *Radical History Review*, 67:1 (1997), pp. 175–86; C. Hall and S. Rose [eds.], *At home with the empire*, Cambridge, 2006.
7 See, for example, the work of A. Pagden, notably, A. Pagden, *The fall of natural man: the American Indian and the origins of comparative ethnology*, Cambridge, 1986; A. Pagden, *Spanish imperialism and the political*

imagination, New Haven, CT, 1990, 1998; and A. Pagden, *Lords of all the world*, New Haven, CT, 1995; Bitterli, *Cultures in conflict*; S. Schwartz [ed.], *Implicit understandings*, Cambridge, 1994; F. Nussbaum, *Torrid zones*, Baltimore, MD, 1995; F. Nussbaum [ed.], *The global eighteenth century*, Baltimore, MD, 2003; R. Rocher, *The complexion of race*, Philadelphia, 2000; S. West [ed.], *The Victorians and race*, Aldershot, 1996; K. Wilson [ed.], *A new imperial history*, Cambridge, 2004; Hall and Rose, *At home with the empire*.

8 A. Gratton, *The footnote: a curious history*, Cambridge, MA, 1997; K. O'Brien, *Narratives of enlightenment: cosmopolitan history from Voltaire to Gibbon*, Cambridge, 1997, chs 5, 6, and K. O'Brien, 'Empires, history and emigration', in C. Hall and K. McLelland [eds.], *Race nation and empire*, Manchester, 2010; J.G. Pocock [ed.] *Varieties of British political thought*, Cambridge, 1993, chs 8, 9.

9 See B. Barnes and S. Shapin [eds.], *Natural order: historical studies of scientific culture*, London, 1979; S. Shapin, *Never pure: historical studies of science*, Baltimore, MD, 2010.

10 R. Bartlett, *The making of Europe: conquest, colonization and cultural change, 950–1350*, London, 1994 makes this an organising theme and specific aspects are developed on pp. 18–23, 101–5, 187–96, 197–242, 252–5, 269–314; D.Abulafia [ed.], *New Cambridge medieval history, vol. 5*, Cambridge, 1999 has sections on the Mediterranean and on the northern and eastern European frontiers (chs 17–25); see also D. Abulafia and N. Berend [eds.], *Medieval frontiers: concepts and practices*, Aldershot, 2002; D. Palmer and N. Standen [eds.], *Frontiers in question: Eurasian borderlands, 700–1700*, Basingstoke, 1999, chs by Moreno, Stephenson, Power, Ellis, Rowell, Williams; R. Bartlett and A. Mackay [eds.], *Medieval frontier societies*, Oxford, 1989; J. Ray, *The Sephardic frontier*, Ithaca, NY, 2006; J. Muldoon, *Identity on the medieval frontier*, Tampa, 2003; A. Murray [ed.], *The clash of cultures on the medieval Baltic frontier*, Aldershot, 2009; J. Muldoon *et al.* [eds.], *The expansion of Latin Europe, 1000–1500*, Aldershot, 2008–9, vols 1, 3; J. France, *The crusades and the expansion of Catholic Christendom*, London, 2005; J. Phillips, *The medieval expansion of Europe*, Oxford, 1998.

11 See T. Brady [ed.], *The political economy of merchant empires*, Cambridge, 1991; M. Hart, *The making of a bourgeois state*, Manchester, 1993; J. Israel, *The Dutch republic*, Oxford, 1995; J. Tracy [ed.], *The rise of merchant empires*, Cambridge, 1990; S. Chaudhury and M. Morineau [eds.], *Merchants, companies and trade*, Cambridge, 1999; J. de Vries, *The first modern economy*, Cambridge, 1997, chs 4, 9, 10, 13; P. Emmer and F. Gaastra [eds.], *The organisation of interoceanic trade in European expansion*, Aldershot, 1996; L. Blusse, 'The run to the coast: comparative notes on early Dutch and English expansion and state formation in India', *Itinerario*, 12 (1988), pp. 195–214.

12 See, for example, D. Armitage, *The ideological origins of empire*, Cambridge, 2000; N. Canny, 'Fashioning "British" worlds in the seventeenth century', in N. Canny *et al.* [eds.], *Empire, society, and labour*, Mansfield, PA, 1997; J. Greene, 'Empire and identity from the Glorious Revolution to the American Revolution', in P. Marshall [ed.], *Oxford history of the British empire, vol. 2: the eighteenth century*, Oxford, 1998; D. Armitage and M. Braddick [eds.], *The British Atlantic world, 1500–1800*, Basingstoke, 2002, chs 6, 10.

13 A. Wright, *The Counter-Reformation: Catholic Europe and the wider world*, Aldershot, 2005; S. Peabody, *'There are no slaves in France': the political culture of race and slavery in the ancien regime*, Oxford, 1996; W. Cohen, *The French encounter with Africa*, Bloomington, IN, 1980; I. McCabe, *Orientalism in early modern France*, Oxford, 2008; J. Ames, *Colbert, mercantilism and the French quest for Asia*, Chicago, 1996; D. Goffman and C. Stroop, 'Empire as composite: the Ottoman polity and the typology of dominion', in B. Rajan and E. Sauer [eds.], *Imperialisms: historical an literary investigations*, Basingstoke, 2004.

14 E. Renan, 'What is a nation?' (1882), translated in H. Bhabha, *Nation and narration*, London, 1990, pp. 8–22.

15 A. Smith, 'Were there nations in antiquity?' and S. Reynolds, 'The idea of the nation as a political community', in L. Scales and O. Zimmer [eds.], *Power and the nation in European history*, Cambridge, 2005; E. Dursteler, 'Ideas of nation in the pre-national era', *Brigham Young University International Forum Series*, 1999.

16 A. Smith, *The ethnic origins of nations*, Oxford, 1998, part 2; A. Smith, *Myths and memories of the nation*, Oxford, 1999, part 1; A. Hastings, *The construction of nationhood*, Cambridge, 1997; J. Armstrong, *Nations before nationalism*, Chapel Hill, NC, 1982.

17 L. Valensi, *The birth of the despot: Venice and the Sublime Porte*, Ithaca, NY, 2009; R.J. Smith, *The gothic bequest, medieval institutions in British thought*, Cambridge, 1987; C. Kidd, *The forging of races*, Cambridge, 2006; I. Hannaford, *Race: the history of an idea in the west*, Baltimore, MD, 1996; P. Springborg, *Western republicanism and the oriental prince*, Oxford, 1991, part 2.

18 S. Raman, '"The ship comes well laden": court politics, colonialism and cuckoldry in Gil Vicente's *Auto da India*', in Rajan and Sauer, *Imperialisms*; J. de Léry, *History of a voyage to the land of Brazil* (trans. and ed. J. Whately), Berkeley, CA, 1990; H. Staden, *True history* (trans. M. Harbsmeier), Durham, NC, 2008; J. de Acosta, *Natural and moral history of the Indies* (ed. J. Mangan), Durham, NC, 2002.

19 J. Rives, 'Introduction' to his edition of Tacitus, *Germania*, Oxford, 1999, pp. 1–75; B. Isaac, *The invention of racism in classical antiquity*, Princeton, 2004; M. Eliav-Feldon *et al.* [eds.], *The origins of racism in the west*, Cambridge, 2009, chs 1–4; E. Gruen, *Rethinking the other,*

Princeton, 2010; C. Glacken, *Traces on the Rhodian shore: nature and culture in western thought from ancient times to the end of the eighteenth century*, Berkeley, 1973, chs 2, 6; J. Muldoon [ed.], *Travellers, intellectuals and the world beyond medieval Europe*, Aldershot, 2010.

20 Eliav-Feldon *et al.*, *Origins of racism*, chs 5–11; Bartlett, *The making of Europe*; T. Husband, *The wild man: medieval myth and symbolism*, New York, 1980; R. Bernheimer, *Wild men in the Middle Ages*, London, 1970; J. Friedman, *The monstrous races in medieval art and thought*, Syracuse, NY, 1999; J. Rubies [ed.], *Medieval ethnographies*, Aldershot, 2009; C. Ingrao [ed.], *The Germans and the east*, West Lafayette, IN, 2008, chs 1–4.

21 H. Honour, *The new golden land*, New York, 1975, chs 1–5 and images on pp. 14, 62, 65, 68, 72, 78, 85, 98, 102–3,119; M. van Groesen, *Representation of the overseas world in the de Bry collection of voyages*, Leiden, 2008; O. Dickason, *The myth of the savage and the beginnings of French colonialism in the Americas*, Edmonton, 1997; P. Mason, *Infelicities: representations of the exotic*, Baltimore, MD, 1998; M. Greer *et al.* [eds.], *Re-reading the 'black legend': the discourse of race and religious difference in the Renaissance empires*, Chicago, 2007; M. Quilligan [ed.], 'Theodore de Bry's voyages to the new and old worlds', special issue of *Journal of Medieval and Early Modern history*, 41:1 (2011), pp. 1–66.

22 De Acosta, *Natural and moral history*; E. Brancaforte, *Visions of Persia*, Cambridge, MA, 2003, pp. 52, 55, 122.

23 P. Mason, *Infelicities: representations of the exotic*, Baltimore, MD, 1998, pp. 16–41; Brancoforte, *Visions*, pp. 51–7.

24 A. Satterfield, 'The assimilation of the marvellous other: reading Christoph Weiditz's "Trachtenbuch" (1529) as an ethnographic document', MA thesis, University of South Florida, 2007.

25 Mason, *Infelicities*, p. 63; Hans Eworth *c*.1520–74 (Flemish portraitist of Tudor monarchs and nobles) *Suleiman II*, http://commons. wikimedia.org/wiki/FileHans_Eworth (accessed 18 August 2012); N. Matar, 'Renaissance England and the turban', in D. Banks [ed.], *Images of the other: Europe and the Islamic world before 1700*, Cairo, 1996.

26 Valensi, *Birth of the despot*; M. Dimmock and A. Hadfield [eds.], *The religions of the book: Christian perceptions, 1400–1660*, Basingstoke, 2008, chs 2, 3, 5, 8; M. Soykut, *Italian perceptions of the Ottomans*, Oxford, 2011; D. Goffman, *Britons in the Ottoman empire, 1642–60*, Seattle, WA, 1998; D. Goffman, *The Ottoman empire and early modern Europe*, Cambridge, 2002; E. Dursteler, *Venetians in Constantinople*, Baltimore, MD, 2008; N. Matar, *Turks, Moors and Englishmen in the age of discovery*, New York, 1999; N. Matar, *Britain and Barbary*, Tampa, FL, 2005; N. Bisaha, *Creating east and west: Renaissance humanists and the Ottoman Turks*, Philadelphia, 2006.

27 J. Lendon, *Empire of honour*, Oxford, 1997; C. Ando, *Imperial ideology and provincial loyalty in the Roman empire*, Chicago, 2000; C. Ando,

Law language and empire in the Roman tradition, Philadelphia, 2011; G. Woolf, *Becoming Roman*, Cambridge, 1998; G. Woolf, 'Becoming Roman, staying Greek',*Cambridge Classical Journal*, new series, vol.40 (1994), pp. 116–43; P. Brunt, *Roman imperial themes*, Oxford, 1990.

28 B. Tezcan, *The second Ottoman empire*, Cambridge, 2010; C. Imber, *The Ottoman Empire, 1350–1650: the structure of power*, Basingstoke, 2002; R. Abou el Haj, *Formation of the modern state: the Ottoman empire 16th to 18th centuries*, Syracuse, NY, 2005; H. Karateke [ed.], *Legitimizing the order: the Ottoman rhetoric of state power*, Leiden, 2005; C. Kafadar, *Between two worlds: the construction of the Ottoman state*, Berkeley, CA, 1995; J. Hathaway [ed.], *Mutiny and rebellion in the Ottoman Empire*, Madison, WI, 2002; J. Hathaway, *The politics of households in Ottoman Egypt*, Cambridge, 1997; L. Darling, *Revenue raising and legitimacy*, Leiden, 1996; S. Faroqhi, *The Ottoman empire and the world around it*, London, 2004; E. Eldem *et.al.* [eds.], *The Ottoman city between east and west*, Cambridge, 1999; K. Barkey, *Bandits and bureaucrats: the Ottoman route to state centralization*, Ithaca, NY, 1994.

29 A. Knight, *Mexico: the colonial era*, Cambridge, 2002; A. Caneque, *The king's living image: the culture and politics of viceregal power in colonial Mexico*, London, 2004; T. Herzog, *Defining nations: immigrants and citizens in early modern Spain and Spanish America*, New Haven, CT, 2003; C. MacClachlan, *Spain's empire in the New World*, Berkeley, CA, 1988; A. Pagden, *Spanish imperialism and the political imagination*, New Haven, CT, 1990; S. Stein and B. Stein, *Silver, trade, and war: Spain and America in the making of early modern Europe*, Baltimore, MD, 2000; H. Thomas, *Rivers of gold: the rise of the Spanish empire*, London, Weidenfeld and Nicholson, 2003; H. Kamen, *Spain's road to empire*, London, 2003.

30 Armitage, *Ideological origins*.

31 N. Canny [ed.], *Oxford history of the British empire, vol. 1: origins of empire*, Oxford, 1998; Armitage and Braddick, *British Atlantic world*; J. Tracy [ed.], *The rise of merchant empires*, Cambridge, 1993; P. Lawson, *The East India Company: a history*, London, 1993; K. Chaudhuri, *The English East India Company, 1600–40*, London, 1965; K. Chaudhuri, *The trading world of Asia and the English East India Company*, Cambridge, 1978; I. Watson, *Foundation for empire: English private trade in India, 1659–1760*, Delhi, 1980; K. Andrews, *Trade, plunder and settlement*, Cambridge, 1984; R. Brenner, *Merchants and revolutionaries*, Princeton, 1993; N. Zahedieh, *The capital and the colonies*, Cambridge, 2010.

32 B. Arneil, *Locke and America*, Oxford, 1996; J. Tully, *An approach to political philosophy: Locke in contexts*, Cambridge, 1993; R. Meek, *Social science and the ignoble savage*, Cambridge, 1976, ch. 2.

33 E. Mancke, 'Empire and state', in Armitage and Braddick, *British Atlantic world*, and 'Negotiating an empire: Britain and its overseas

peripheries, 1550–1780', in C. Daniels [ed.], *Negotiated empire: centres and peripheries in the Americas*, London, 2007.

34 J. Greene [ed.], *Exclusionary empire: English liberty overseas, 1600–1900*, Cambridge, 2010.

35 M. Hodgen, *Early anthropology*, Philadelphia, 1964; Meek, *Social science*; K. Kupperman, *America in European consciousness, 1493–1750*, Chapel Hill, NC, 1995; Honour, *New golden land*; Matar, *Turks, Moors and Englishmen*; A. Cirakman, *From 'the terror of the world' to 'the sick man of Europe': European images of the Ottoman empire and society*, Oxford, 2002; I. Kamps and J. Singh [eds.], *Travel knowledge*, Basingstoke, 2001; S. Anderson, *An English consul in Turkey*, Oxford, 1989.

36 B. Kedar, *Franks, Muslims and oriental Christians in the medieval Levant*, Aldershot, 2006.

37 See M. Hodgen, *Early anthropology*, Philadelphia, 1971; P. Hulme, *Wild majesty: encounters with Caribs from Colombus to the present day*, Oxford, 1992.

38 T. Harriot, *A brief and true account of the new found land of Virginia*, London 1590, has similarly posed images of east coast indigenous Americans and of 'Picts' and their neighbours; Fynes Moryson, *An history of Ireland from 1599–1603*, London, 1735 edn, pp. 373–7; *Itinerary*, London, 1617, part 1, book 3, ch. 4 comments on the lack of industriousness of interest in hunting among Turks in words similar to those used of the Irish; part 3, book 4, ch. 2, (p. 180) compares the headscarves of Irish women to those of Turks.

39 D. Goldenberg, *The curse of Ham*, Princeton, 2003; B. Isaac, *The invention of racism in classical antiquity*, Princeton, 2004; Eliav-Feldon *et al.* [eds.], *Origins of racism*; E. Gruen [ed.], *Cultural identity in the ancient world*, Berkeley, CA, 2011.

40 J. Lafitau, *Moeurs des sauvages ameriquains comparées aux moeurs des premiers temps*, Paris, 1724, uses many classical comparisons, notably vol. 1, chs 3, 5, 6, while also pioneering ethnographic commentary; see also Mason, *Infelicities*, chs 1, 4, 5; Dickason, *Myth of the savage*, chs 2–4.

41 Classic discussions are B. Anderson, *Imagined communities*, London, 1983; E. Gellner, *Nationalism*, Oxford, 1983; E. Hobsbawm, *Nations and nationalism*, Cambridge, 1990; more recent studies which deal with ethnicity and empire to some extent include T. Baycroft, *Nationalism in Europe*, Cambridge, 1998.

2

EMPIRE AND HISTORY WRITING
C.1750–1830

Now the great map of mankind is unroll'd at once; and there is no state or gradation of barbarism and no mode of refinement which we have not at the same instant under our view. The very different civility of Europe and of China; the barbarism of Persia and Abyssinia; the erratic manners of Tartary and of Arabia; the savage state of North America and New Zealand. (Edmund Burke to William Robertson, on reading his *History of America*, 10 June 1777)[1]

In 1773, Hester Chapone, a writer associated with the 'bluestocking' network of women intellectuals, set out a programme for the study of history by young women. She noted that British history was a global subject, both because of British connections with other 'nations', and because 'you may pass to every quarter of the earth and still find yourself in the British dominion'.[2] Her comparisons of various societies and her celebration of the extent, wealth and power of the British empire capture a moment of imperial growth (in India) and of controversy (in America), of awareness of the advantages and challenges of 'luxury' and prosperity, and of modern 'philosophical' history. As well as recommending classical authors, she directed readers to modern writers like Hume, Robertson, Pufendorf and Voltaire, advising them to set their study of British history in its European and global context. Twenty years later, the Scottish scholar William Robertson, author of acclaimed histories of Scotland, America and the Emperor Charles V, reflected on the growth of European global power since the sixteenth century:

Thus the commercial genius of Europe, which has given it a visible ascendant over the three other divisions of the earth, by discerning their respective wants and resources and by rendering them reciprocally subservient to one another, has established an union among them, from which it has derived an immense increase of opulence, of power, and of enjoyments.[3]

Setting out a history of contact since 'ancient times' beside comments on contemporary Indian customs, politics, religions and economic activity, he linked European dominance in global trade to social, political and cultural development in Europe. He did so when British expansion in India, settlement in Australia, Canada and west Africa, and trade with China, were reshaping their great power status, just as growing international exports, and debates on free trade, slavery and population were politicising trade and production. These widely read authors used a framework of new interests in historicising and comparing societies and morals, new models of ancient, medieval and modern history and a sense of Britain's global power and centrality. Their consciousness of British predominance was set in a 'cosmopolitan' analysis of European progress and of the thinking of European intellectuals, and it enacted important views of gender, nation, power and empire.[4] Their texts were to be reissued regularly for over half a century, as part of a repertoire of history writing which reached considerable readerships.

For Britons in the later eighteenth and early nineteenth century, perceptions and understandings of the past had their distinctive historical context. Just as British governments and entrepreneurs were increasingly affected by circumstances beyond Europe as well as those within the 'British' Isles and in Europe, so accounts of the past and depictions of the 'nation' drew on a similarly extended and complex range of connections. After setting out the changing conditions within which discussion of empire and writing on the past were taking place, this chapter discusses how these fed into the subject matter and the practice of history writing, using the sets of connections presented in the previous chapter. While it is easy to emphasise the scale and impact of change in both the circumstances and the character of history writing, it is equally important to recognise the limits and complexity of their effects and the diversity of responses to particular historical circumstances.

In the 1750s the state and society encompassing the Irish, English, Welsh and Scottish inhabitants of the 'British' Isles could be seen as commercially and internationally successful, with significant overseas colonial and trading bases and flourishing exports of local products and re-exported overseas goods. In variable and complex ways these activities were stimulating urban growth and consumption, rural manufacturing networks and agricultural and manufacturing innovation. They were also linked to political and social conditions in which propertied and entrepreneurial interests were able to flourish within and beyond the 'British' Isles. Current analyses of social and material transformation in these islands emphasise its unevenness and variability, and consider it as a process which extended across the whole eighteenth and early nineteenth centuries, rather than as a sudden development at the end of that period.[5] Surges in cotton textile and iron production, and in non-European commerce, from the 1770s were important but rather specific aspects of a much longer and more complex set of changes that included the commercialisation of agriculture and the expansion of retailing and transport to supply domestic as well as overseas markets. These changes were manifest in the growth of towns and new occupations, in the political and religious debates and innovations which accompanied change, and in the use of both old and new ideas to express and make sense of such change, and to support or resist it. Between the 1750s and the 1830s many key elements of life in Britain and Ireland altered significantly, whether patterns of residence, work and consumption, new kinds of political movements or new cultural and intellectual influences ranging from political economy to evangelical Protestantism.

Among these changes three areas can be identified as particularly relevant for the practice of history writing. Firstly we need to consider the extension of British connections with a wider world, and the growing interdependence of 'British' and others within that world as material factors in 'British' experience. Secondly we will look at political change, whether internal to the 'British' Isles, as with the Acts of Union of 1707 and 1801 and growing debates on constitutional reform, or external, as with the imperial and continental conflicts of European powers and the effects of the French and American Revolutions. Thirdly we will examine the repertoire of cultural resources and intellectual tools on which writers of history in this period could draw, exploring both persistent and innovative elements in that repertoire. These varied features came together to constitute the matrix within which historical writing was produced.

One obvious change in the world in which British history writing took place was its expanding space, and increasingly interdependent position within that space. By the 1750s seventeenth-century initiatives in trans-Atlantic settlement and plantation agriculture, and in organised Asian trade, were transforming the lives and experiences of a wide range of people in the 'British' Isles. Relatively small groups of traders, settlers, investors and wealthy consumers had been key protagonists in the development of North American colonies, East India Company commerce and West Indian plantations in the seventeenth century; this situation changed significantly during the eighteenth century. Population increase and economic growth in the British colonies in North America generated a series of farming, trading and plantation communities whose productivity and increasing prosperity made them significant producers, entrepreneurs and consumers. By the 1820s the independent United States was expanding territorially and demographically, and elaborating its agrarian, commercial and manufacturing production.[6] By the 1740s the East India Company had established increasingly strong competitive commercial bases and networks of local support in the Indian subcontinent, dominating the export of Asian products to Europe. From the 1780s British political influence and territorial conquest in India grew rapidly, so that by the 1820s Britain was a major military and ruling power in the subcontinent.[7] The plantation economies of the West Indies, and of European colonies from Maryland to Brazil, generated not only important new commercial agricultural products, but also the profitable and essential trade in enslaved Africans who provided the bulk of the plantation labour force.[8] In the southern hemisphere the establishment of British interests in South Africa, Australia and New Zealand in the early nineteenth century opened up new possibilities for trade, settlement and colonial power. Movements of people (sailors, soldiers, migrants, traders), of investment, of products (raw materials, manufactures, foodstuffs) and of services (banking, shipping, colonial administration, insurance) westward across the Atlantic, southward to Africa and the Pacific and eastward to Asia, and back to Europe, linked many Britons to this larger world.[9] While not on the scale of later developments, these changes had already begun to have an impact on the UK, and beyond.[10]

These patterns of expansion had consequences. From the 1760s British interests in India stimulated the expansion of trade and political relations with China, Iran, south-east Asia and the Gulf. Changing conditions and European rivalries in the Ottoman empire likewise encouraged new patterns of British commercial and political involvement in the eastern Mediterranean. In addition to the spread of European trade and settlement, European exploration further extended European global connections and awareness. As well as the well-publicised Pacific voyages of Anson, Bougainville and Cook, the period between the 1740s and the 1830s saw Britons travelling to Tibet, Central Asia and the north-west Canadian coast, and exploring the Australian and North American interiors.[11] This fed a growing literate interest in travel writing and altered the understanding of the physical world, its varied human communities and the place of 'Britain' within it, while fostering various commercial, scientific and political aims. New forms of travel narrative, texts with various blends of information, imagination and political argument, and presentations of 'exotic' material about distant peoples on stage or in the visual arts contributed to the presence of this material in settings from metropolitan theatre to the chapbooks sold in rural communities.[12] Alongside written and visual depictions of distant places, maps, material objects and botanical and zoological collections brought physical evidence from distant places into British libraries, gardens and learned or public institutions.[13]

These developing links between Britain and a wider world involved interdependence as well as extension, as global colonial and commercial influences played an increasingly important constitutive role in the lives and activities of diverse groups of Britons. While historians continue to debate the extent and precise impact of colonial and global influences on British economic development between the mid-eighteenth and early nineteenth centuries, the presence of these influences was a visible and material reality. The reshaping of financial practices and institutions and the expansion of shipping and related industries – such as the investment of colonial and overseas commercial profits in land and agriculture and their contribution to urban growth in Britain – can all be connected to changing British involvement in the wider world.[14] Various British manufactures came to make use of imported raw materials, tried to emulate exotic 'eastern' equivalents or were aimed at colonial consumers and, in the case of the shipping industries, at the actual practices of overseas trade. Many Britons became regular consumers of plantation and Asian products as it became normal to drink Chinese tea, imported by the East India Company, sweetened with sugar produced on West Indian plantations, to smoke tobacco and to use cotton for clothes, furnishing fabrics and handkerchiefs.[15] Quite apart from all those directly involved in global and colonial activities, many everyday patterns of work, dress or food and drink in Britain were thus shaped by connections to enslaved Africans, West Indian and American plantation owners, Indian or Chinese traders and peasants and North American farmers. The experience of 'being British' was thereby remade, as existing work or consumption habits came to coexist or cross-fertilise with new elements. From the emulation of 'eastern' styles by British textile industries (the 'Paisley shawl') to the remaking of daily diets and social gatherings around tea drinking or smoking, 'British' life came to encompass 'global' features and to depend on global and colonial relationships.

If the meanings of being 'British' were changing as such relationships became materially and socially embedded in everyday experience, they were also affected by political developments. Political divisions between Tories, Whigs, Jacobites, 'independents' and government supporters – like religious divisions between Anglicans, Roman Catholics and Nonconformists – had their origins in the seventeenth century, and still fuelled mid-eighteenth-century ideas and conflicts. Different understandings of the 'revolution' of 1688–89 and the political and constitutional relationships between monarchy, parliament, propertied elites and the Anglican church which emerged in the late seventeenth and early eighteenth century were inflected by the growth of British commercial, diplomatic and colonial involvements as a major power. Frequent references to the links between commerce, 'liberty' and global prestige and influence, like political controversies over British overseas commitments, whether to the Hanoverian interests of the monarchy or to armed conflict with European rivals for global advantage, embedded imperial and global elements in both elite and popular politics. Factional manoeuvres by ambitious politicians and broader expressions of political feeling, rooted in established and influential party or religious loyalties, linked new versions of patriotism and empire to inherited and, importantly, historically framed, views of English/British liberties, religious toleration or monarchical and parliamentary power.[16]

Particularly significant for the writing of 'national' histories were the changing relationships between the dominant English and the

Welsh, Scottish and Irish residents of the 'British' Isles. The 1707 Act of Union with Scotland and unresolved issues there, which fed into 'Jacobite' challenges to Hanoverian rule in 1715 and 1745, were paralleled by material developments which affirmed distinctive aspects of Scottish society while linking it to other parts of Britain. As with people of Welsh background, complex issues of mutual and divergent interests, ranging from religious affiliation to economic development, were reshaping politics and ideas in this period.[17] In Ireland the legacy of seventeenth-century conflicts and settlements, and the impact of the American colonists' challenge to British rule, stimulated political self-assertion among Anglo-Irish and Irish communities, culminating in the 1798 rising and the ensuing 1801 Act of Union which established the 'United Kingdom'. These political developments were underpinned by a web of cultural and economic exchanges and conflicts involving land, access to public life and communal relations.[18] Older practices of English stereotyping of Welsh, Scots or Irish, and claims for autonomy in Ireland and Scotland, were supplemented by new interest in Scots, Welsh and Irish pasts and cultural identities, and by contests around political rights and the character of the union, which persisted over the next two centuries. Inherited accounts and myths were developed by new poetic, archaeological and ethnographic approaches to the cultures and histories of peoples in the 'British' Isles.[19] Political issues were also entwined with a range of socio-economic exchanges which shaped interdependent, if unequal, relations between the various parts of the kingdom through the movements of people and goods, and by the active involvement of Scots and Irish soldiers, settlers, entrepreneurs and missionaries in 'British' imperial activities. One of the issues now facing historians was the depiction (or dismissal) of the differences, interactions and distinctive characteristics of the 'four nations' of the United Kingdom and the story of emergent English dominance within that kingdom. As will be seen, their understandings of state, nation and empire were shaped by views of that story.

The 'four nations' structure of the UK posed questions about power and inclusion which became increasingly debated themes in English and British politics from the 1760s through to the 'reform decade' of the 1830s. Periods of British involvement in global warfare from the 1750s to the 1780s and again from the 1790s to 1815 highlighted imperial and trans-national aspects of 'national' politics.

The American colonists' challenge to royal and parliamentary sovereignty and their winning of independence – like the debates over parliamentary representation and corruption, and over imperial policies on slave trading and Indian affairs – brought such issues into the foreground. Arguments about the rights of colonial assemblies or non-Anglicans, or about the conduct and accountability of East India Company officials and parliamentary placemen, were added to older concerns over relations between crown, church of England, government ministers and parliament.[20] An emergent language of 'rights' drew on established dissident discourses of 'country' politics and liberty going back to the seventeenth century, and on newer concepts of 'natural' law, rights and liberty. These were reinforced by the political activism of the American and French Revolutions, which underpinned notions of 'the people' and their politics with powerful conflicts and protests, and with lasting ideological and cultural innovations. British and Irish responses to that politics ranged from populist and radical claims for political rights to sophisticated defensive arguments against violent and disruptive change and the abstract ideals which legitimised it. Substantial legislative and administrative changes enacted between the 1790s and the 1830s, including new arrangements for imperial governance and new welfare and electoral structures, embedded assumptions about the capacity for sensible improvement within patriotic self-images of the 'English' or 'British' people or nation. Celebrations of a distinctively 'English' or British story of constitutional progress rooted in the gradual development of honoured traditions or in the assertion of 'the rights of freeborn Englishmen' became powerfully significant for contemporary politics, linking current conflicts and new aspirations to narratives of the past.

More generally the changes experienced by the generations of historians writing between the 1750s and the 1830s can be seen as influences on their depictions of the past. New patterns of employment, land rights and investment expanded the role of money wages and purchased goods, and hence of market forces and fluctuations, albeit unevenly, across the social spectrum. The commercialisation of many areas of life, from agricultural production to household adornment, stimulated both enthusiasm for the prosperity and 'refinement' available to growing sections of the population, and anxiety over the actual or potential corrupting effects of luxury and consumerism. Connections between female impropriety and a taste for Chinese porcelain, the gender and class issues posed by the spread of tea drinking, and economists' debates on the role of consumption, all featured in public discussion from the 1770s to the 1830s.[21] This gave an edge to narratives of the past, which moved uneasily between emphasis on material and on 'moral' progress, and discussion of imperial and colonial developments raised such issues very vividly. Discussion of the excesses and immorality of slave traders and returning Indian 'nabobs', or of the dangers of the commodities which came from the plantations or Asia, and the tensions between patriotism and criticism surrounding colonial wars and conquests, posed questions about 'national' destiny, character and virtue. Stories of the rise of a 'polite and commercial' (that is, civilised and trade-oriented) nation might be patriotic celebrations of British achievement or more anxious discussions about the risks to the 'nation' of market and material success.

One important strand in discussion of those questions was an increasingly explicit concern with gender, in which the specifically 'feminine' or 'feminising' character of consumption was a regular theme. This was part of a wider set of gender developments which took a number of forms. There was increasing public interest in the gendered specifics of various political, moral or social roles, norms and expectations whereby progress, citizenship, consumption, domestic life and education were described and debated in relation to femininity and masculinity; various groups of women entered into those activities exploring, confirming and critiquing gender norms though writing, debate and educational, religious or philanthropic activity, which itself stimulated further contest over their activities. More specifically, this period saw the emergence of women writers of a range of historical texts ranging from grand narrative to books for children; assumptions and images of patriotism, virtue and civilised conduct were shaped by reference to 'manly' or 'womanly' qualities and to codes of gender and sexual conduct, as well as to comparisons of the 'customs and manners' of societies around the globe. Writers and commentators were also aware of the emergence of female readerships for historical texts. While a writer like Hume might commend his sceptical political analysis of seventeenth-century political conflict to a male friend, he envisaged that friend's wife being moved by his emotive depiction of the execution of Charles I.[22] As will be seen, ideas of social change and social order made central use of gender rights, roles and relations as key criteria for judging types of society and their state of development. A work like Robert Henry's 1771 *History of Great Britain* claimed that the respectful treatment of women by the Celts and Britons at the time of the Roman conquest was a mark of virtue, prefiguring medieval chivalry, even if those peoples were 'in the lowest stages of civilisation'.[23] Such approaches interacted with religious, medical and literary images of gender differences and norms in which domesticity, physiology and moral prescriptions often combined. Anxieties over women's intellectual agency and patriotic constructions of femininity were located in comparative accounts of the distinctive history of marriage and gender relations which emphasised a distinctive European story of manners and morals, and/or recent progress.[24]

Patterns of movement and migration also affected views of 'English' or 'British' identity which were being transformed by the global and colonial lives and activities of administrators, settlers, enslaved people, traders, plantation managers, convicts, sailors, missionaries and members of the armed services. This created networks and webs within which settlers connected to families 'back home', administrators or members of the armed forces or merchant navy moved across oceans and territories, and entrepreneurs and financiers managed transnational interests. In doing so they carried with them and reshaped 'English' or 'British' ideas and practices in Britain as well as overseas. Such connections are exemplified by a Baptist East India Company official in Sumatra combining administrative duties, business and the moral regulation of his community there, or an English housekeeper incorporating 'Indian' recipes into her cooking, or the former slave Equiano negotiating difference, respectability and Englishness in London (and Belfast) anti-slavery circles.[25] This added further dimensions to the cultural and political impact of movement within the United Kingdom, which shaped views about the distinctive identities of 'country bumpkins' and urban sophisticates, or of those defined according to their Welsh, Yorkshire, Irish, Devon or Scottish origins. Were these diversities more significant, for good or ill, than some shared 'Englishness' or 'Britishness'? Were the expanding urban environments of eighteenth- and early nineteenth-century Britain and Ireland, and the colonial and commercial activities which flourished there, testimony to the achievements and inherent qualities of the 'British' or a threat to those qualities?

What were the advantages and problems of Irish migration to Britain, or of encouraging colonial migration with its associated impact on the governance and rights of 'native' peoples? Were the highly visible effects of technological change and market forces (railways, bankruptcies, protest movements) evidence of ongoing progress, or of dangerous, damaging, unpredictable or unsustainable influences? Did the social mobility and the material change and instability of an increasingly market-centred society provide evidence of the moral worth and 'character' of English (or British) society and institutions, or a challenge to their continued survival? Writers on the 'national' past, like commentators on the contemporary scene, embedded such concerns in their texts.

Alongside social and political developments, we should consider the cultural resources and intellectual tools available to historians between the mid-eighteenth and the early nineteenth century. Established traditions of placing historical narratives within frameworks of Christian and classical reference, linking accounts of the past to the operations of Providence, to biblical narratives, and to ancient Greek or Roman comparisons, continued to be influential. Innovative accounts and analyses of society and politics associated with the 'new' historical practices of the Scottish enlightenment, discussed below, were also deeply engaged with earlier religious and political approaches. As Colin Kidd robustly argues, 'respect for the authority of the Bible, one's confession and the established institutions of church and state' was a significant component in eighteenth-century ideas of history and identity.[26] So too were the partisan commitments and debates which flavoured historical writing with affirmations and critiques of various Whig, Tory, 'republican' and 'patriot' politics, forming a dominant pattern in eighteenth-century history writing Even sophisticated historical texts like those of David Hume or Catharine Macaulay were placed by some commentators on a 'Whig'/'Tory' party spectrum of narratives of seventeenth-century politics, as well as being seen as modern sceptical or philosophic accounts.

To them were now added other images and ways of thinking, enquiring and explaining. Some might be stimulated by the experience of social change and political controversy, producing new depictions of disorder or disruption, or of progress and liberty. Others drew on newer theories of human development and 'human nature', most particularly those concerned with the diversity or unity among human beings, the processes of social change and connections between material, political and cultural aspects of human societies. These theories included Montesquieu's consideration of relationships between social and political power, attempts, notably by Scottish thinkers, to create materialist accounts of the 'stages' of human development, and scholarly explanations of the common characteristics and/or significant differences among human beings. As will be seen, these discussions emphasised broad shifts and trends and collective endeavour or experience, rather than individual events or persons, or divine providence, although history writing organised around these latter themes continued to flourish. Indeed, Hume and Robertson, when writing on the Scottish and English past, combined interest in conveying character and sentiment with their broader conceptual views of the past. Nonetheless, the terminology of 'progress' and 'civilisation', and discussion of how cultural, political and material aspects of society might affect one another played an increasing part in historians' repertoire.

One of the significant resources newly available for use in that repertoire was the body of creative thought and colourful information produced by various European encounters with people and societies beyond Europe through exploration, trade and colonial expansion, and later through missionary activity. This included narrative and interpretative writing as well as descriptive accounts or political and commercial pamphlets. Anecdotal accounts of cultures in distant places also included commentary on the 'customs and manners' of 'foreign' peoples and attempts to interpret them and to explain their origins and the differences and similarities between them and European cultures. Depictions of picturesque, or frightening, 'exotic' societies entwined with intellectual endeavours to place them within comparative, historical and social scientific narratives, and to evaluate their suitability for European commerce, colonial rule or Christian conversion. Such narratives took a number of forms, ranging from learned debate and educational texts to accounts of 'customs and manners' aimed at broader publics. The 'modern' disciplines of ethnography and anthropology as well as of sociology and political economy were evolving though use of a growing range of information, images and ideas about peoples, states, religions and communities around the globe. This emerged from the integration of information about peoples around the world into analytical discussions of the structures and histories of human societies. Description and anecdote were deployed or refashioned in historical and comparative accounts of the development of societies over space and time, establishing a global context for history writing which also had important colonial aspects since European overseas colonies were a major source of information and ideas.[27]

Scholarly work on the history writing which emerged in Britain and Ireland after 1750 links it to politico-religious circumstances, to the spread of 'philosophic' (analytical) ideas of social and political institutions, and to the legacies of civic humanist thought.[28] It can also be connected to the larger cultural worlds that were now influencing social thought and establishing interplay between social theory, historical narrative and ethnographical data. The esteemed historian William Robertson's successful history of America (nine editions between 1777 and 1800) used Lafitau's work on the Iroquois, recent texts about Amazonian peoples and accounts of the voyages of Bougainville to the Pacific and Gmelin to Kamchatka alongside archives and early modern material. Edward Gibbon's writing on Muhammad and Islam drew on Pococke and Niebuhr's accounts of Arab societies as well as European translations of Arabic texts. James Dunbar's 1780 *Essays on the history of mankind in rude and cultivated ages* also uses Niebuhr as well as material from Captain Cook's voyages and accounts of Labrador, Cambodia, west Africa and central Asia.[29] The scale of this material enabled those presenting and interpreting it to go beyond the traditions of comparative analysis which went back to classical European authors, modified by European contacts with the wider world since the sixteenth century.

Beyond that, European commentary on that world fed into scholarly theories about the origins, diversity and complexity of human societies created by eighteenth-century thinkers and used in the conceptualising and writing of history. New resources influenced discussions both of social and cultural development and of legal and political systems. Social scientific thought on class and property structures, and on the growth of more complex forms of production, ownership, consumption and exchange, like ethnographic writing on customs and manners, also included reflection on forms of law and government. On the one hand, there was continuing speculation on the social or cultural bases of law and government, and there were attempts to produce systematic accounts of their development. Constitutional and legal forms were analysed in relation to the social hierarchies and relationships which supported them, and which they regulated, as well as in moral or philosophical terms drawn from religious and classical sources. On the other hand, the development of more secular accounts of social structures and social change stimulated arguments which grounded structures of law and government not just in moral and religious principles, but in analyses of human institutions and relationships. This produced complex negotiations between authors' persistent attachment to biblical, classical or civic humanist ideas about states, societies and morals, and innovative and materialist approaches to 'philosophical' politics and history.[30]

Notions of a contract between rulers and ruled which emerged in the work of seventeenth-century English thinkers raised questions about the responsibility and accountability of the former, and the political role of the latter. Arguments that governments should be active sponsors of social improvement and social regulation, developed by 'cameralist' thinkers in German-speaking Europe, redefined rulers and administrators as skilled designers and implementers of up-to-date policies and as agents of modernisation, not just protectors of established regimes or divine purposes.[31] The growing body of thought on natural law and natural rights which developed during the eighteenth century further extended debates on the obligations and duties of rulers and governments, producing new criteria with which to evaluate the virtue and success of particular regimes. This enabled those wishing to analyse, critique or reform existing governments to use rational and philosophic as well as moral frameworks, and buttressed the reforming activities of rulers and statesmen by associating them with social responsibility and progressive agency. From Russia, France and Prussia to Ireland, Britain and its colonies, schemes for reform and improvement were urged on governments by advisers and intellectuals, which energised demands from various subject people and interest groups for inclusion and representation.

Alongside material grievances and political events, such critiques and governmental aspirations shaped the reforms of various eighteenth-century European rulers and the challenges made by European, and American reformers and opponents to existing regimes between the 1770s and the 1830s. Their activism in turn stimulated new debates on reform and revolution, on the importance of social and political order and on the relationships of law and government with social progress and stability. In the United Kingdom Edmund Burke's ideas of the importance of organic institutional development and cultural integrity, Adam Smith's views of markets, morals and progress, and Jeremy Bentham's advocacy of rational (a-historical?) utilitarian approaches to law and government became resources for debate or policy. They were debated in a growing middle-class periodical literature and in the radical press, as well as in the canonical works of those authors.[32] This happened in a context where ideas of religiously sanctioned social and political practice, and of the role of divine providence in that practice, influenced approaches to reform and governance as much as new concepts of markets or government. The growing influence of evangelical views among Anglicans, Methodists and Baptists, and of reforming agendas among Unitarian and Quaker groups interacted with secular trends as well as with practical politics, shaping governance and politics into the nineteenth century.[33] While that story can be told in its own right, the focus here is on how changing perceptions of the role of government, its relationships to social classes and hierarchies and to colonial subjects, and the terminology used to discuss these issues, informed historical accounts of states and peoples. It is significant for this study that such ideas were used as tools for judging the legitimacy or worth of past as well as contemporary rulers, governments and legal systems, modifying older views of the central role of divine or dynastic right, of custom and tradition or of morality.

Discussions of government were linked not only to the specific legal or social arrangements of particular countries, but also to ideas of community, ethnicity and 'nation'. The notion that there were groups of people whose common identity could be defined by reference to shared language, religion, customs and ancestry was well established in European culture. As seen in the previous chapter, terms like 'race', 'nation', 'tribe' and 'people' had been regularly, and often interchangeably, used to refer to such groups in various contexts since classical times. The emergence of a competitive European state system, and of global and colonial dimensions to European state rivalries, between the sixteenth and eighteenth centuries, gave new political relevance to those references. Both rulers and rebels drew on languages of 'people' and 'nations' to mobilise support and legitimise their actions. They might refer to any or all of the criteria of religious difference, of loyalty to rulers and dynasties, and of shared culture and history, in order to emphasise differences between the 'national' community and foreign 'others' or enemies. Examples range from Spanish anti-Jewish and anti-Moorish policies and English or Dutch anti-Catholic rhetoric in the sixteenth century, to English and Dutch anti-French polemic and European anti-Ottoman or Hungarian anti-Austrian discourse in the seventeenth and eighteenth centuries. Appeals to the 'nation' were often designed to legitimise the vested interests of established elites, or those of governments who sought to contain those elites, but they also embedded ideas and images of a 'nation' extending beyond those confines. They became associated with ideas and images of 'national' characteristics, and increasingly disseminated in both visual and written forms to urban and literate audiences.[34] Significantly, the expansion of nationalistic ideas owed much to symbiotic relationships between historical and archaeological work to 'recover' evidence of the ancient past, theories of national identity and political claims to recognition for 'national' demands. Historical practice and nationalist ideals and aspirations fed one another.

In the eighteenth century global and colonial contacts between Europeans and the wider world, and new investigations and specu-lations about the distant past of various European peoples, gave new flavours to the language of 'nation' and 'people'. Existing ideas about kinship and custom as defining characteristics of a 'tribe' or 'nation', or about the influence of the physical environment on human development, were supplemented by other concepts of inherited qualities and abilities developed by natural scientists. Ear-lier views that groups of human beings could be defined by shared physical as well as social and cultural characteristics could be linked to new studies of living species, and to new theories about how their similarities and differences might be explained. In addition, European accounts of the various peoples and cultures which they were now encountering through expanding trade, exploration and colonial settlement provided an enlarged range of ideas, informa-tion and images of human diversity. This opened up two streams of intellectual speculation and imaginative thinking: one drawing on European observations about peoples whom they were encounter-ing around the world, the other on the concepts, researches and theories of natural scientists. The male midwife and anatomist Charles White wrote not only on obstetrics but also on human difference, using his collection of skulls and measurements of different humans acquired through colonial and commercial networks in Liverpool, alongside literary and cultural analysis.[35] As will be seen, historians' references to nations, tribes or peoples often combined language from both these sources, not to replace older forms of expression, whose influence continued, but to supplement them.

The expansion of ethnographic and travel writing, of theories of human difference and development, and of political debate on nation and empire, produced similar expansion in the vocabulary and concepts available for history writing. References to Polynesians, Iroquois or Chinese supplemented the classical and biblical comparisons or models familiar to many writers and readers. Accounts of British or English pasts could now be surrounded and enhanced by a global setting using images and ideas derived from writings on Cook's voyages or interpretations of Chinese, Native American or central Asian histories and societies. Ideas and arguments about English exceptionalism or about multiple cultural influences on English history could be reinforced by this enlarged repertoire of comparisons. More generally, such new resources extended the meanings and associations attached to the terms and images used in historical writing, bringing together the familiar and unfamiliar in their texts. It will be argued that the now-familiar terms 'civilisation' and 'civilised', which came into regular use in the later eighteenth century, were flavoured with ideas, information and assumptions created from a web of global contacts and could be deployed in historical accounts of social and political change and in comparative commentary on such histories.

Perhaps the most influential outcome of these developments affecting history writing was the growing sophistication in narratives and explanations of 'progress' which combined history and social theory. This combination of narrative and theory was well named by practitioners and commentators at the time as 'conjectural history',[36] and is associated with the work of the Scottish intellectuals John Millar, Adam Smith, Adam Ferguson, Henry Home (Lord Kames) and William Robertson. Their work emphasised, albeit in varying ways, the role of social relationships and forms of property and production, as well as custom and culture on the history of particular countries. This analytical treatment of change was linked to an evolutionary account of the 'advance' of at least some humans from 'primitive' and 'uncivilised' savagery to modern 'polite', prosperous and civilised ways of life. By the 1790s it had become normalised in works like Barlow's *General history of Europe*, which frames its narrative within the trope of 'advance from barbarism to civilisation'.[37] It had materialistic and secular implications which were handled differently by different authors, some of whom emphasised the ways in which social structures determined human potential, while others gave greater scope to contingency and individual human agency. Thus the Aberdeen academic James Dunbar in his 1781 *Essays on the history of mankind* emphasised the social nature of man but also criticised over-deterministic or collectivist accounts of the past.[38] William Robertson's materialist ethnographically inflected discussion of medieval western European veneration of the 'Holy Land' is offset by a pious reference to its identity as 'the country which the Almighty had selected as the inheritance of his favourite people, and in which the son of God accomplished the redemption of mankind'.[39] Similar variations emerged among those for whom providence and virtue were important concepts and those who took more sceptical viewpoints. Nonetheless, from the late 1760s, when ideas of the 'stages' of social development and their political and cultural significance were first put forward in this form, they entered into a range of history writing, entwining with the political, providential and patriotic narratives which remained typical of much historical practice.

Empire, state and governance

Such narratives emphasised the long history of the English, and later British, state, and the growth or persistence of the 'liberties' or 'mixed constitution' often said to be uniquely characteristic of England or Britain and 'the most perfect in the world', 'the most perfect system of liberty known among mankind'.[40] While the distinctive experiences and interests of the Welsh, Scots and Irish might be discussed, and even appreciated, in historical texts, such discussions were most often embedded in accounts of the development of English power and political institutions within the 'British' Isles. Those groups may be referred to as 'nations', but it is the subjugation of Welsh rulers or the 'savage' Irish, and competition with the Scots, which are the topics which get attention. Thus Scottish raiders and noblemen, Welsh bards and princes, Irish peasants and rulers make their appearances at points when accounts of the *English* past deemed them relevant to the activities or interests of English governments and people. The invasion of twelfth-century Ireland by Anglo-Norman barons and kings, Edward I's expansionist policies in Wales and Scotland, and the concerns of Tudor or Stuart governments with Scottish neighbours and Irish subjects appear as set episodes in the history of the English state and constitution.[41] The same approach features in much coverage of the seventeenth-century conflicts involving Scots, Irish and English in what is usually labelled the 'English Civil War' and in treatments of political tensions between English, 'native Irish', and Anglo-Irish in the eighteenth and nineteenth centuries. In the 1790s Charles Allen could assert confidently that such tensions would only be solved by union on the same lines as had been beneficial for the Scots in 1707, just as William Robertson saw it as enabling the Scots to achieve political liberties and cultural politeness. Another account saw it as 'a thorough union…happily accomplished'.[42]

Arguably, the story of dominance which is told in these works is one in which notions of 'empire', which had historically been used to describe the power of states or monarchs in quite general terms, come to include an 'imperial' flavour in the modern sense. The absorption of the Welsh under English dominance, and the series of attempts to control and settle Ireland – themes common in histories of England/Britain in this period – were recounted in terms of conquest and authority. Many historical accounts of England/Britain became narratives of the exercise of state power over 'others' within 'Britain' as well as of constitutional progress and the defence of liberty. From Barrow in the 1760s to Grimaldi in the 1820s the conquest of Wales could be presented in terms of ordering and subduing. On the other hand, Cowley, like others, expressed sympathy for Welsh defence of their 'nation' against being reduced to 'slavery', and the disapproving account of Edward I's supposed massacre of Welsh bards was regularly repeated.[43] It should be noted that this trend was countered by texts with different agendas, which indicates a certain instability in ideas of a united kingdom. These might include an interest in specifically Irish, Welsh or Scottish pasts and identities, in contesting Anglo hegemony or in combining positive views of a united 'Britain' with recognition of its composite and contested character.[44]

While Anglo-centric accounts could confidently trace the successes of the English against the Welsh or laudable aspirations to exercise English authority in Ireland, the question of Scottish relations with England was a more challenging topic. Just as uniting the two kingdoms had been controversial in the first decade of the eighteenth century, so English views of those relations as problematic persisted through the century, and it is interesting to compare and contrast the treatment of this theme by Scottish and English writers. Thus William Augustus Allen could comment on the 'gross and ignorant' Scots' inability to decide the succession to the Scottish crown in the thirteenth century, while criticising the 'barbarous' behaviour of Edward I when he invaded Scotland. This is echoed by other authors' comments on his 'unpardonable severity' and 'harsh' conduct, and by the 1830s the whiggish Scot James Mackintosh, in a phrase especially resonant at a time of anti-slavery politics, described Edward's attempts to rule Scotland as 'nothing but submission and slavery'.[45] The repressive policy of Charles II's minister Lauderdale in Scotland was treated in various ways, but all versions present it as a case at best of misgovernment, and at worst of vicious despotism. Hume and Smollett, whose texts remained in use for a century, and who had Scottish backgrounds, give space and force to accounts of attacks on Presbyterian opponents of the restored Stuart monarchy, even if this is accompanied by distaste for their 'fanatic' views and actions.[46] So too did Catharine Macaulay, for whom this condemnation was part of a strongly 'republican' critique of seventeenth- and eighteenth-century politics. In keeping with its general strategy of inclusion and separation, Henry Hallam's 1827 *Constitutional history of England* has a similar account in its chapter on Scotland, prefaced by comments that Scottish religious factions were 'more sanguinary' and public virtues less active than English counterparts. In other texts criticism is briefer and more limited, with Bicknell referring just to the 'rigorous treatment' of the Covenanters, and Russell to the 'cruel and impolitic' actions of Lauderdale.[47]

As will be seen, this arose in part from their ideas of what constituted a 'nation', but it was also about their views of state and governmental power and institutions. The Scottish risings of 1715 and 1745 could be presented as a 'rebellion' by disloyal subjects or adventurers, and as an expression of understandable, if not legitimate, resentments about governance under the union. For the Scot Maria Calcott, writing for children in the 1830s, the 1745 rising, now part of a distant past, was a 'civil war' whose repression was 'cruel', rather than a threat to the British state.[48] It is also worth noting that debates on the problems of court influence and ministerial corruption in the 1760s made use of images of Scottish influence and intrigue in those debates, and compared that practice with circumstances in the early nineteenth century. Hallam's *Constitutional history* had separate chapters on the constitutional history of Scotland and of Ireland, simultaneously distinguishing and incorporating them within his 'English' narrative. Since historians tended to celebrate the English/British state as both the product and guarantor of Protestantism, its relationship with Scottish institutions which included a Protestant (although for some worryingly Presbyterian) church could be portrayed as convergent, and contrasted with the persistent adherence of many Irish people to Roman Catholicism. The negotiated acceptance of Scottish church autonomy in the 1707 Act of Union differed sharply from the political turmoil over the policy of toleration for Catholics within the UK, which was excluded from the 1801 Union with Ireland, and only carried, amid strong controversy, nearly three decades later.

Religious differences between Irish and English had many dimensions, but were an important element in historical depictions of the place of the Irish in the structures of the British/English state. Hallam argued that from the 1640s 'all distinctions of origin have…been merged in those of religion'.[49] Whereas the story of Scotland's incorporation was built on dynastic succession and political negotiation of the union of parliaments and transfers of sovereignty, behind the 1801 union of Ireland with Britain lay a story of conquest, settlement and annexation of property, which can be seen as colonial. The continued use of the seventeenth-century term 'plantations' in eighteenth-century accounts of English settlement in both Ireland and north America suggests acceptance of this parallel. Even more importantly, the English relationship with Ireland produced episodes of direct conflict which became part of the foundation story of the English state as told by eighteenth- and nineteenth-century historians. Accounts of the 1641 Irish rising, often including excessive estimates of massacres of Protestants, fed into narratives of the contest of king and parliament in the civil war of the 1640s, just as the military confrontation between William of Orange and James II and his Irish allies became an episode in the iconic 'glorious revolution' of 1688–91. Hallam suggested that in 1689–91, as in 1641, both sides were engaged in a war of 'self preservation'.[50] For English or Scottish historians the 'problem' of the Irish, and their subjugation to progressive English rule was a constitutive and quasi-colonial theme in the grand narrative of English/British liberties and progress, or, as in accounts of the settlement policy of James VI/I, of a civilising mission.[51] Charles Allen, writing in the 1790s, contrasted Scottish support for William III in 1689 with Irish opposition, and he speculated whether 'incorporation' into Britain along the lines of the 1707 union with Scotland was not the only means to 'civilise' the Irish, deploring the political 'separation' of the Irish parliament in the 1780s. For Russel, William's success in Ireland both 'subjected it fully to the crown and established a 'solid peace' which he considered 'uninterrupted' until the late 1770s.[52] By the eighteenth century the establishment of a property-owning class of Protestant Scots-Irish and Anglo-Irish with legal and political rights distinct from the rest of the population of Ireland might be compared to the growth of similar arrangements in colonial settlements in the West Indies and north America.

As settlers in the British colonies in mainland north America challenged their relationship to the British crown and parliament, using the assemblies that had developed in those colonies, the question of Irish representative institutions also became an issue. Historians' views of the legislative changes which increased the autonomy of the Irish parliament in the 1780s, as a result of pressure from the Anglo-Irish elite, showed awareness of the parallels and concern over potential conflicts of commercial interest between Britain and Ireland.[53] While they might occasionally refer to England, Scotland and Ireland as three 'kingdoms', attempts by Irish or Scots to assert interests of their own, whether Jacobitism in Scotland or the 'unhappy' separation of Irish and British parliaments, were likely to be seen as disruptive.[54] When proto-nationalist movements emerged in Ireland in the 1790s, influenced by the ideals espoused in America and France as well as by Irish conditions and grievances, they were treated as threats to a British state threatened by war and radical politics, and the ensuing union of parliaments was recounted in that context. Calcott suggests that it was the way to end Irish sectarianism and to enable the English to appreciate the Irish, regret their past 'wrongs' to them and 'help the Irish to be better'. Reverend Cooper praises the union's 'utility', calling the parliament which it produced the 'imperial parliament', contrasting it to the violence of the 1798 uprisings.[55] That violence still loomed large in post-union accounts like that of Adolphus; in the 1830s Calcott was telling her child readers that the Irish were still 'not done disputing'.[56] Crucially, the story of the other kingdoms was largely depicted from the standpoint of a hegemonic, even imperial, Anglocentric 'British' state and its institutions and interests. Histories of Wales, Scotland and Ireland which described and celebrated their distinctive pasts also recognised the role of that state.[57]

As with accounts of political conflicts in the seventeenth century, the themes of liberties, rights and tyranny or despotism were deployed in the accounts and interpretations of high politics whose detail dominated the texts produced by most eighteenth-century historians. Two major themes emerge regularly in the histories written in this period. Firstly, strong emphasis was given to the distinctiveness of the English, and later British, states and their institutions. This distinctive pattern was seen to include a balance of power between crown and councils or parliaments expressing the interests of the 'nation', distinctive liberties embodied in law and custom and a 'mixed' constitution which held these elements together in a beneficial relationship. If some historians argued that these features were attained and maintained only through repeated struggle, whereas others emphasised their durability over time, they shared a common perspective that the emergence of Britain as a global power by the eighteenth century was linked to the 'superior' constitutional structures protecting liberty, property and commerce. Secondly, historical writing often argued that these structures had a long history and that while there might be a story to tell about the emergence of 'modern' liberty and a balanced constitution, these valued features of law and government could be traced back over an extended period. Charles Allen declared that the key aim of his *New and improved history* was to 'inspire young minds' with respect for 'the happy state of things under which they enjoy…liberty regulated by law', offering a perspective common to many texts from Mortimer in the 1760s to Mackintosh in the 1830s.[58]

The writers took up ideas about the 'Saxon' origins of English legal and governmental institutions put forward by seventeenth-century writers and used them to depict the distinctively 'English' character of state and politics. In the 1760s Smollett attributed the origins of jury trial to King Alfred, and Gilbert Stuart used Tacitus and Montesquieu to argue that English political institutions, like property laws, social structures and 'national' characteristics, had 'Saxon' beginnings. It is interesting that this is already presented as a narrative of development rather than just of survival, to be taken up in texts like those of Hallam or Palgrave, where they were linked to Whig and philosophical views of 'improvement'.[59] This accorded with established use of references to custom and precedent as explanatory categories, drawing on new interests in the comparative historical analysis of custom and governance, and in the study of the literary and material 'antiquities' of particular peoples. The popular work of Sharon Turner, who had been inspired to the study of Anglo-Saxon texts by reading work on Ossian and Icelandic literature, combined scholarship with celebrations of King Alfred and the Witan.[60] As will be seen, this influenced nineteenth-century views of 'Saxon' cultural or racial identity, but it also established a persistent thread in accounts of the development and virtues of 'English' legal and political institutions.

While these views were sources of English/British patriotism or nationalistic thought and politics, their global and imperial implications also deserve attention. When the term 'empire' is found in historical texts it often retains an older generalised sense of rule and authority. This usage can be found in the 'republican' Catharine Macaulay, in the history of Alexander Bicknell aimed at 'youth' and in the sceptical and 'philosophical' Hume.[61] The term was used to refer to the dominance of a particular monarch, to English rule over other parts of the 'British' Isles, to the rule of 'English' kings in parts of France between the twelfth and fifteenth centuries and later to English/British rule over settlements in America, Asia and the West Indies.[62] It clearly lacked all its later nineteenth-century connotations but embedded the language of empire in the mainstream of discourses of government and state power. Discussions of British military successes in north America during the Seven Years War (1756–63) speak of an 'empire on the Ohio' won from the French, just as discussions of British military activity in India between the 1750s and the 1820s are seen as part of an emergent 'British' empire there. Narratives of conquest and settlement accompanied stories of 'empires of the sea' which emphasised the naval and commercial dominance at the core of British global power.[63] Accounts of Anglo-French rivalry in America or of the clash between American colonists and British government interests, which used comparisons with the Roman and other empires, indicate how the British state and its power beyond the 'British' Isles were understood as imperial. Cooper's reference to the 'imperial crown' suggests this, just as Allen's use of the term 'senate' for the British parliament made a classical and civic humanist connection familiar to many readers.[64]

Here we are moving from thinking about how imperial meanings might be embedded in the language and concepts used to write about the history of the English/British state to considering the treatment of specific 'imperial' topics. The topic which most obviously attracted the attention of historians, like other commentators, was the relationship between the British government and its colonies in North America. The conflicts over imperial taxation and jurisdiction, and over colonists' rights and representation within the empire, which emerged in the 1760s, were conducted to a significant extent in terms of a history of 'English' constitutional and legal liberty and the seventeenth-century struggles to defend and extend them. As Cowley, like others, noted, the dissatisfied American colonists quoted Selden, Locke, Pufendorf and Harrington as well as referring to Magna Carta and the 1689 Bill of Rights.[65] For historians of England this raised interesting questions. Did the 'justice' of the colonists' grievances compromise the story of benign British imperial success, or illustrate important principles of government which were in jeopardy? Did the conflict suggest that possession of empire in itself might threaten liberty and the British constitution? Were the Americans rebellious 'provincials' as they appear in Ashburton's history, and Russel's account of the 1770s, which ends with hopes for a peace based on the agreement of 'mother and sons' and a return to obedience by the colonists? Could comparisons with colonial experiences in the ancient world be useful? Did the conflict suggest that possession of empire in itself might threaten liberty and the British constitution or, as for the conjectural historian Dunbar, offer lessons about the relationships between commerce, progress and empire? Calcott's 1830s story of the conflict for young people could be framed as a tale of government errors, and of the reasonable demands of colonists prosperous and progressive enough to demand and deserve self-government led by a 'great man', George Washington.[66]

Questions of imperial conduct and purpose were posed even more sharply as debate about expanding British rule in India increased during the 1780s, culminating in the impeachment of the governor general, Warren Hastings, and the passing of the 1784 India Act establishing new parliamentary controls on British involvement there. Images of the unchecked and corrupt exercise of British power in India encouraging 'despotic' habits which might be imported into British politics formed a key theme in Edmund Burke's prosecution of Hastings, and in histories of the British in India. They had already surfaced in accounts of British interests in India from two decades earlier.[67] Initially such histories expressed contemporary concerns with the difficulty of balancing the commercial interests of the East India Company, with the British state's military and strategic interests in India, depicting India as a field for British power, profit and prestige. From the 1760s a significant number of memoirs or polemics framed their contemporary concerns in historical accounts of India and of British interests there.[68] However, even accounts of Hastings' impeachment and of the passage of the 1784 India Act in histories published in the 1790s suggest that British expansion raised issues of morality as well as expediency, and by 1826 the Hastings trial was recorded as 'exceeding anything in the history of the world'.[69] Debates in the 1780s and over the renewal of the East India Company charter in 1813 and 1833, and the increasing role of reformers and missionaries in those debates, added concerns with civilising, moral and improving use of British power in the subcontinent. The association of the Evangelical anti-slavery activist Wilberforce with campaigns for missionary access to British-ruled areas of India, and against the religious ritual of widow burning there, exemplifies a web linking politics and religion, reform and empire, the Caribbean, India and the UK, as well as new forms of activism and establishment politics. The extensive reporting of parliamentary debates on India, slavery and the Hastings trial in historical texts shows how those concerns were deemed important for the understanding of the past, even if recent.

If conflict with the American colonists and Indian issues expanded discussions of the English/British past while being assimilated into established philosophic, popular or partisan versions of that narrative, events in France between 1789 and 1815 made an overlapping but distinct contribution. Two aspects of this are worth noting. After initial interest in, and even sympathy for, the emergence of a French national assembly and its attempts at reform, the growth in conflict within France and the war between France and other European powers – including Britain after 1793 – fostered strong links between state policy, patriotic Francophobia and the celebration of English liberty and prosperity. To well-established anti-French views, fuelled by eighteenth-century Anglo-French rivalries, were added new images of 'revolutionary violence' affirming popular and elite support for 'English' institutions against French tyranny, savagery and aggression. Secondly, the period of Anglo-French conflict and the political climate it created had crucial imperial aspects. The convergence of Irish discontent and French policy with French intervention in Ireland in the 1790s, like the Napoleonic expedition to Egypt and Anglo-French conflict in India and the West Indies, linked antagonism to the French with the defence of imperial power and wealth as well as of order and liberty in Britain. At the end of the period of war between 1793 and 1815, the naval, colonial and diplomatic dominance of the new 'United Kingdom' as a world power was a core outcome of the defeat of Napoleon.[70]

Historical narratives produced in this time reflected that process. The suppression of optimistic comments on political change in France in the 1791 version of 'A Lady's' *Geography and history selected...for the use of children* from later editions, and the replacing of them with references to violent, unjust, inhumane republicanism, is indicative. This is echoed in general histories like those by Allen in the 1790s, or Cooper in the 1820s, and in Calcott's children's history in the 1830s.[71] Some extended treatments of events in France in the 1790s reveal a more complex picture. For Reverend John Adam writing in the 1790s, conventional horror at the September massacres and execution of Louis XVI, attributed to the factional contests and republican 'rage' of the French Convention, combined with acknowledgement of patriotic French 'enthusiasm for liberty'. He highlights the French regime's slippage from the high moral ground of its proclaimed principle of non-intervention to expansionist policies, and the relationship between anti-French and anti-reform politics in England.[72] Bicknell's account, ending in 1791, is introduced as the story of the transformation of France from despotism to 'free state', which combines attention to episodes of violent confrontation and crowd action with pictures of the new national assembly promoting reform and producing its declaration of 'the purest sentiments of freedom and the natural rights of mankind'. The narrative in Thomas Lloyd offers considerable sympathy for the French pursuit of liberty, and strong criticism of the British government's joining the war against the French and their manipulation of public opinion in favour of the war and against reform. It gives sympathetic treatment to the politician Charles Fox as the protagonist of liberty and reform and attacks Burke's anti-French 'philippics'. As with other histories, extensive attention to British military actions in the war places emphasis on this global and imperial response to the French Revolution as much as, and often more than, to the issues of liberty and democracy which it raised.[73]

In debates on the war in America, on political developments in France and their consequences, and on the global wars lasting intermittently from the 1790s to 1815 and in Asia into the 1830s and 1840s, the term 'slavery' was in regular use. In historical writing it was deployed to express the sense of associations between 'liberty' and 'British'/'English' identity and history which shaped comparisons between 'Great Britain'/the 'United Kingdom' and other European states, and the sense of mission which came to influence growing British colonial commitments around the globe. It was often embedded in discourses of regime change in 1688–89 and in accounts of that change in texts produced during the eighteenth century, and it continued to be associated with anti-Catholic views in phrases like 'popery and slavery', and sometimes to refer to the Norman conquest or Scottish ward holding. For supporters of 'republican' and reforming ideas of constitutional progress like Catharine Macaulay it could be used to assert links between domestic 'slavery', restrictions on lower-class liberties and an aggressive and 'imperial' foreign policy.[74] What is striking is how the term 'slavery' appears more often in those contexts than in connection with what might now seem the more obvious context of the traffic in, and use of, African people as chattel slaves, which was a key feature of colonial and commercial activity throughout this period. Its regular use in relation to continental European 'despotisms', to views of states and societies in India, Iran and the Ottoman lands, and in stories of liberty and progress in England/Britain, contrasts powerfully with the resounding absence of discussions of chattel slavery. References to a practice which was so integral to global and colonial relations between Europe, Africa and the Americas occurred far less frequently in historical texts than these other uses. The irony of this fact becomes even more powerful in the context of the growing public critique of chattel slavery from the 1770s.

Although the slave trade and plantation slavery were not state enterprises, they flourished within a framework of state support through colonial regimes in the West Indies and, before 1776, in north America, through the legislative protection of the Navigation Acts and the physical protection of army and navy. One of the key factors in British foreign policy in this period was the defence of British possessions in the West Indies, just as one significant activity of the British navy after the abolition of the British slave trade was the prevention of slave trading in various parts of the world.[75] More obviously the British campaign against slave trading and chattel slavery, which emerged in the later eighteenth century, focused on legislative change, invoking parliamentary means to end British trade in enslaved people in 1807 and slavery in the British empire in 1834–38.

What should be noted here are the distinctive, if overlapping, meanings being given to the notion of slavery in history writing. By the 1790s some historians were reporting parliamentary debates on the African slave trade, linking it to sentiments of humanity and morality, and questioning whether 'British' virtue and liberty were compatible with the continued practice of the trade, although many did not mention the topic at all.[76] Those who did so often linked this international issue to virtue in 'British' settings, exemplified by the prominent abolitionist, Pitt supporter, Evangelical, and reformer, William Wilberforce recording in 1787 that 'God Almighty has set before me two great objects, the suppression of the slave trade and the reform of manners.'[77] Thus arguments for abolishing slave trading and slavery were grounded in the reason and humanity of the British, and spoken of as a way for Britons to bring civilisation to Africa. Similarly, attacks on British abuses of power or financial corruption in India voiced concerns for virtuous rule in India and for the danger posed to liberty in Britain by the influence of the exercise of 'despotic' power in the subcontinent, echoing Catharine Macaulay's view of global power. Lloyd's narrative of the Mysore war of the early 1790s concludes with a plea for growing imperial dominance to be matched by a virtuous and civilising relationship with new colonial subjects. Having described the conflict as 'a war which, perhaps, had neither solid justice for its foundation nor sound policy for its object', it continues:

The benefits we may yet communicate to the natives of India remain for time to discover, but certain it is the past history of that country but woefully proves that in those region the British name has been too often dishonoured and our footsteps too often marked with blood…Let us hope that a system of Indian politics founded on justice and equity be adapted and pursued, till science has illumined the inhabitants of those delightful climes: till freedom has erected her standard on the ruins of despotism, and the affection of the people for the British name supersedes the use of arms and the havoc, ruin, and calamities of war.[78]

He floats the idea of providing Indians with the kind of intellectual 'improvement', pleasing to a 'philosopher' and the kind of moral and religious 'renovation' pleasing to a Christian, prefiguring nineteenth-century ideas of imperial mission.

Narratives of state and government linking 'domestic' reform, imperial responsibility and national virtue underpinned cautious but persistent arguments for state action in those areas. They connected the idea of imperial trusteeship put forward by Burke with growing evangelical interest in the reform of manners within the UK and utilitarian interest in improvement through legislative intervention. From the 1760s contemporary controversy over the East India Company was framed in 'historical' accounts of the subcontinent. These included Alexander Dow's supplement to his translation of a Mughal source and the historical section of James Macpherson's argument about East India Company policy in southern India as well as James Mill's influential history and commentary.[79] In this last case it is important to note that Mill's critique of tradition and custom in Indian religion and society supports a parallel critique of British law and government. His narrative of empire and proposals for imperial reform were accompanied by arguments about the relationship between imperial power and unreformed privilege in the UK.[80] The abolitionist Thomas Clarkson not only historicised his 1788 discussion of slavery in the 1780s, reviewing classical and biblical evidence and the reformist role of Christianity in medieval Europe, but was also the first to do the same for the abolitionist movement itself. Jeremy Bentham developed his early ideas on universal law using examples from Bengal and British rule there, drawing on recent histories as well as government papers.[81] Histories of the state thus associated past and future where inherited 'freedom' provided a basis for progress.

Empire, civilisation and progress

The debate on European purchase and use of the labour of enslaved Africans raised questions about the conduct and morals of 'civilised' people. The specific term 'civilisation' was a recent addition to European vocabularies, entering French and English usage in the mid eighteenth century in works by the French political economist Mirabeau and the Scottish thinker Adam Ferguson.[82] By 1772 Dr Johnson was debating its possible use in the fourth edition of his Dictionary with his biographer Boswell. Related terms like 'civility', 'politeness', 'refinement' or 'cultivation' were available for writers who sought to distinguish forms of social life, government, religion or law on a spectrum which was in part a qualitative judgement on their worth, and in part a description of change over time. Certainly the terms 'savage', 'rude' and 'barbarous' were regularly used to describe an opposite state, earlier stage or starting point for human development. This usage drew on Greek and Roman distinctions between their own social structures, political systems and cultural practices and those of peoples whom they saw as lacking them, and also on distinctions between Christian and heathen or heretical cultures used by Europeans since the thirteenth century. More specifically, it drew on seventeenth-century discussions of law and morality which sought a basis for moral conduct which overcame the challenges of scepticism and religious prescription by invoking shared social experiences and relationships encompassed in a reworked notion of 'society', which, they argued, produced and reproduced human morality.[83] This was expressed in Montesquieu's analysis of the 'spirit of the laws', which grounds government in social values, as in Hume's more materialist appeal to sociability (the 'natural commerce and society of men') as an alternative to 'superstitious' belief or nihilistic scepticism about such morality. Humanist uses of classical ideas about the rise and decline of states and societies, and about cyclical, as opposed to linear, patterns in human history as well as continuing debates over the roles of divine providence and human agency were woven into emerging discourses and histories of 'society'. Scottish intellectuals who put forward distinctive views of 'civilisation and 'civil society from the 1750s drew on local traditions of history writing and involvement in European intellectual networks to establish influential accounts of these ideas. Whether or not Tsvetan Todorov is right to term this a process of 'culmination, recapitulation and synthesis, not one of radical innovation', it certainly influenced writers' depictions of the past.[84]

What then was the context for the shifts in historical thinking about human development which took place among 'British' writers on history during the mid-eighteenth century? Often associated with the work of Scottish intellectuals, these shifts established new perspectives on the topic of civilisation or 'civil society', focusing attention on human agency and institutions, and on development over time. Those concerns are very much those which inform historical work, and indeed some of those who theorised about forms of government and social change grounded their arguments in historical narrative rather than just used examples from the past, notably in the work done by various proponents of ideas of the 'stages' of human social and cultural development. This encouraged forms of historical narrative not just of events, of inherent human qualities or of the workings of providence, but of the interaction of various elements within human societies (cultural, material, political) which might stimulate change or conflict. It opened up discussions of the relationships between collective and individual interests and agency, and of comparisons and contrasts between different human communities and their experiences. The views and concepts put forward in this type of work were a varied and complex group rather than a single unified body of thought, but nonetheless provided intellectual tools for the analysis and interpretation of the past by historians.[85] They offered systematic views of the story of material development in human societies through innovations in production, trade and technology, seeing this as a process of advance from less to more productive and sophisticated forms of agriculture, trade and manufacture, and of the social arrangements which supported them. They linked such material advances to advances in the legal or political arrangements defining kinship property, and government. This allowed writers to offer narratives of the human past which were broad conceptual accounts, while including quite specific depictions, and allowed them to make arguments about the connections between material, political and social change. They built on established distinctions of 'savagery' and 'polite society', on humanist and Christian debates about human virtue and progress, and on the use of reason and evidence.[86]

Here were agendas for what these intellectuals called the 'natural history' and/or 'conjectural history' of humanity; history was to be 'natural' in so far as it based explanations of human 'progress' on logical and necessary connections between social, political and cultural developments rather than classical prescriptions or the role of religious providence; it was to be 'conjectural' in that it would offer accounts and analyses of broad patterns or tendencies in human development, and it would demonstrate their universal application rather than emphasising specific circumstances and variety. Above all, they brought the notion of 'society' to the fore in the study of the human past, going beyond philosophic schemes or comments on 'customs and manners', and both describing and theorising its changing character and its effects. They depicted history as a succession of 'stages', each with particular forms of productive activity (hunting, pastoralism, agriculture, commerce), social organisation (bands, tribes, settlements, classes) and legal or political systems, and each with greater material prosperity, political organisation and social sophistication. They proposed various, sometimes conflicting, versions of a 'science of society' examining how social structures, relations and institutions were established, maintained and altered over time. Accounts of such processes might emphasise 'progress'/'improvement' from less to more 'civilised' or 'advanced' forms of material, cultural or political life over time, discussing the growth of trade, literacy, manufacturing skills, organised religion and legal or constitutional systems. They might focus on links between economic, social and political change, looking at connections between economic activity, property ownership, social hierarchy, political organisation and cultural life. As Robert Henry argued in the preface to his large scale *History of Great Britain*, this approach to the past showed that:

> the ingenious scholar who hath enlarged and enlightened the faculties of the human mind; the inventive artist who hath increased the comforts and conveniencies of human life; the adventurous merchant or mariner who hath discovered new countries and opened new sources of trade and wealth; deserve a place in the annals of his country.[87]

Many writers made strong connections between the emergence of 'modern' societies and changes in gender relations, and in family or marital institutions, linking the roles and status of women, sociability among men and women and the growth of 'polite' civilisation.[88] Historians took up these analyses in their work. Robert Henry's comments on the stages of civilisation not only proposed clearly materialist and conjectural links between social development and politics, but used the polite treatment of women and the protection of female 'weakness as benchmarks of difference between barbarism and civilisation. His approach echoed that of Henry Home's *Sketches of the history of mankind*, whose section on 'The progress of the female sex' argued for mutually constitutive links between the treatment of women, levels of civilisation and virtue and the quality of public life. It combined climatic theories of sexuality, with cultural and moral arguments about the influence of education, of 'natural' gender differences and of social and marriage practices, illustrating them from classical and biblical authors, and contemporary material about Hottentots, Ottomans, Lapps and Chinese. Historical notions of 'progress' from savagery to civilisation sit beside claims that gender roles and relations are physically embedded, nationally specific or environmentally determined. Comments and cross-cultural comparisons on the importance of manliness in public life further embedded gendered views of civilisation in historical texts.[89]

Accounts of these issues and of the past, whether 'universal', or European histories or studies of particular countries, combined elements from these varied approaches. They also linked these to existing traditions of history writing, as with William Robertson's linking of Scottish Presbyterian approaches to the workings of divine providence with accounts of social and cultural improvement in his histories of Scotland, of early modern Europe, and indeed of the origins of Christianity. Thus the work of the Protestant leaders Luther and Knox is presented within a historical context, through their personal characteristics, and as manifestation of divine providence. Robertson's analysis looks to the development of social and cultural conditions as a context for the acceptance of increasingly 'advanced' revelations of God's message to humanity and regularly links religious progress to the state of civilisation.[90] The combination of conjectural and materialist ideas with older practices situating the human past within a religious framework can be seen in works like Dunbar's *Essays on the history of mankind*, which offers comparative views of the study of religion while asserting the universal value of Christianity.[91] Whether or not they were set within frameworks of religious belief, such texts developed more secular analyses and narratives of social organisation and social change. When Henry set out a wide (and in some views cumbersome) remit for his *History of Great Britain*, he argued for the links between religion, law and manners, and between the 'political maturity' of any particular state and 'the stage of civilisation' which society has reached, as well as for the influence of laws on culture. A more popular work, Raymond's *New and impartial history of England*, its title signalling a wish to be distanced from partisan history writing, could conclude with a rhetorical invocation of how 'the glories of our country' were made up of a fusion of material progress and scientific and cultural advance.[92]

In addition to offering views of the past which presented social change as progress across time from savagery to contemporary commercial and polished societies, writers often argued that their analyses were universally applicable. As John Millar asserted in the first edition of *The origin of the distinction of ranks*, 'Man is everywhere the same; and we must necessarily conclude that the untutored Indian and the civilised European have acted upon the same principles'. In the third edition he put it more conceptually: 'There is, thus, in human society a natural progress from ignorance to knowledge, and from rude to civilised manners, the several stages of which are usually accompanied with peculiar laws and customs.'[93] It is worth noting Millar's choice of comparison for the opening of his text. His juxtaposition of 'rudeness' and 'civilisation' is not historical but cultural and geographical, contrasting a Native American 'savage' with a 'civilised' European. He went on to discuss the history of marriage and gender relations using a mixture of references to ancient practices drawn from the Bible and classical authors (Herodotus, Strabo, Caesar, Tacitus) and from contemporary travel literature portraying customs in Malabar, Kamchatka, Louisiana, Benin and Formosa.[94] This approach emphasised development over time and the advanced state of (western European) 'society' in the present as opposed to the past. However, while asserting universalist principles, it also emphasised differences among societies in the present. A view of humanity which moved across time was in tension with one which placed contemporary societies along a spectrum of 'savagery' and 'civilisation'. As Adam Ferguson argued,

> It is in their [Arabs or native Americans] present condition that we are to behold, as in a mirror, the features of our own progenitors... If in advanced years we would form a just notion of our progress from the cradle, we must have recourse to the nursery, and from the example of those who are still in the period of life we mean to describe, take our representation of past manners.

He was echoed by a Scottish contemporary, James Dunbar, who wrote that the South Sea island societies of his time 'enable us to glance at society in some of its earlier forms'.[95]

The concepts of social theorists like Millar and Ferguson also found their way into historical writing. Henry's six-volume work has regular references to 'all ages and all countries', 'all nations', all religions', 'all/every people'. While not entirely in the conjectural genre, Barlow's *General history of Europe* referred to transitions from barbarism to civilisation, and the 1791 *Geography and history* linked commerce, government and culture in its dismissal of the Hottentots.[96] Whereas historians writing in the 1750s and 1760s like Blennerhassett and Smollett used terms like 'barbarous' or 'polite' to describe the conduct of individuals or events like massacres or torture, from the 1770s they would be more likely be applied to social practices or political institutions. Charlotte Cowley's *The ladies' history of England*, discussing the pre-Roman Britons in the preface, makes points about universality, change over time and 'savagery' in the contemporary world which recall Millar and Ferguson:

> the whole of their conduct seems to impress us with an idea of those that have been called savage nations *in all succeeding time: for human nature is uniformly and everywhere the same*; it is the polish of education, an intercourse with the world, and all those advantages which arise from refinement of manners, that mark the great line of distinction between our rudest ancestors and ourselves. [my emphasis]

John Adams' *A view of universal history* followed a conventional biblical account of the Flood, and the dispersal of humanity thereafter, with a clear assertion of the centrality of social analysis for history and of the interaction of social, political and cultural 'progress'. Quoting Ferguson, it concluded that 'The arrangements and improvements which take place in human affairs result not from the efforts of individuals but from a movement of the whole society'. It echoed Henry's stress on urban life, commerce and learning as drivers of the civilising process, arguing for the presence of common themes and patterns in all nations, and for attention to be paid to social trends, and not just to prominent individuals, since 'man is the same being all over the world'.[97]

The implications of this view for racial and ethnic thought will be discussed in the next section, but it needs noting here that within the inclusive conceptual frameworks used by conjectural historians were assumptions that the tale of progress they told applied primarily to Europe. While they introduced systematic and analytical approaches to what in the past had been quite generalised interpretations of changes over time or of cultural difference, they perpetuated a problematic overlap between explanations of the former and of the latter. This overlap of comparisons across time and across cultures undercut the universalism of the historical arguments with hierarchical and judgemental views of cultures existing in the present. Crucially, it reinforced a tendency to slip between views of 'progress' or 'civilisation' which showed many human societies around the world improving their productivity, governance and culture over time, and views stressing the distinctive success of Europeans in making such improvements. The 'Lady's' *Geography and history* asserts that Europe is the 'most respectable' part of the earth 'for the politeness of its manners [*i.e.* culture], the policy of its governments, and the wisdom of its laws'.[98] European achievements in global trade, conquest and colonial settlement, and European interest in laws, rights and representative government, provided material evidence for Europeans to use when comparing themselves to states and societies elsewhere.

These comparisons could be nuanced as well as judgemental, recognising the ordered government of the Chinese, contrasting 'savage' American tribes with the 'progress' achieved by the Mexicas and Incas or reflecting on the achievements and limitations of the Mughal empire or Hindu literature. Winterbotham's comments on the probity and effectiveness of judicial and legal processes in China accompany assertions of tyranny and despotism, and the discussion of 'superstition' in religion also acknowledges elements of monotheism.[99] They used culturally inclusive approaches to social and historical explanation, but left the relationship between this universalist agenda and a relativism which ranked societies, governments, religions and 'manners' across the world unresolved. This tension was to feature in much future history writing.

Standards of 'cultivation' and 'advancement' applied to Iroquois, Chinese, Tahitians or Turks (all subjects of social and historical commentary) tended to reflect notions of 'civilised' or 'polite' practices and institutions which Europeans derived from considering their own history. These were used both to evaluate the emergence of modern European societies and to compare them to those elsewhere. By the 1790s works like Barlow's *General history of Europe* and the anonymous 'Lady's' *Geography and history* used this perspective in texts for middle-class circulation, combining them with moralising and patriotic approaches. Such types of comparison relied on the flow of ideas and information generated by the growing quantity of texts by Europeans involved in the wider world as traders, explorers, colonial officials and missionaries. Settlers, entrepreneurs and soldiers in north America, explorers in east Asia, south America, and the Pacific, like visitors and officials (civilian or military) in India, produced descriptions and interpretations of the character, origins and potential of the societies they encountered. This material became a resource for theorists like Millar, Home, Ferguson and Bentham, as for other European intellectuals, but also for the authors of histories such as Robertson and Dunbar, and later Mackintosh. For some, direct involvement in empire directly affected their views of civilisation and English history. Returning from work as an administrator in India in 1811, with a plan to write a history of England, Mackintosh reflected on how appropriate it was for him to be thinking about 'beginning the history of a maritime and commercial empire' while on a British merchant ship crewed by Muslim sailors.[100]

Accounts of 'progress' and 'civilisation' in British or European settings were thus inflected with the global and colonial associations of those terms. Conversely, references to the 'superstition' or 'barbarism' found among non-European peoples were flavoured by the use of these terms in familiar Protestant critiques of Roman Catholicism or debates on the origins and evolution of modern nations from the 'barbarian' peoples supposed to have replaced the Roman empire. In William O'Dogherty's *Epitome of the history of Europe* sixteenth-century Spanish attacks on Dutch Protestants were compared to Muslim anti-Christian 'barbarities'.[101] This language tended to reinforce British perceptions that the achievements of their polite, commercial, globally assertive society, and their 'free', balanced and internationally powerful government, were outcomes of a process of development from a 'barbarous' past to a state superior to that of others. This was often linked to a history of the love for 'liberty', seen as a trait traceable to Saxon or even pre-Roman times according to preference, strengthening over time and distinguishing the British from other Europeans and non-European peoples. Smollett's much reissued *History of England* makes use of 'love of liberty' as a characteristic of ancient Britons, of King Alfred and of seventeenth-century politics. For John Barrow in the 1760s the 'English' of Saxon times were 'tenacious of liberty'.

The Irishman O'Halloran saw 'the cause of liberty' as a prime motivator of English assertiveness in contrast to the mercenary Scots or the pious and patriotic Irish.[102] While the main thrust of historical accounts of English/British political development told of constitutional and legal struggles *within* the Atlantic Isles, featuring Magna Carta, civil war in the 1640s and the 1688–89 'Glorious Revolution', there were interesting imperial corollaries. Many historical texts traced relationships between liberty, property rights and international trade, arguing that progress and prosperity benefited from state support for, but not control of, the global commerce and colonisation undertaken by British settlers and entrepreneurs from the seventeenth century onwards.[103]

Not that interest in empire and civilisation was uncontentious. Several historians reflected contemporary concerns with the unwelcome effects of commercial prosperity and 'luxury', as well as with British governance in India and with the conflict over liberty and authority between British colonists in north America and the government in London discussed already. Alongside political controversy, anxieties about the material and cultural consequences of global involvement also flavoured writing about the past. Added to reflections on the role of luxury in the decline of Rome, historical comments on the Mughals and Ottomans had a contemporary resonance when Edmund Burke was warning his audiences of the threat of eastern habits being imported to Britain. Indeed, use of historical narrative was a central strategy in his political interventions on Indian issues.[104] Anxieties about changing class and gender hierarchies and relations could be discussed in terms of the new consumption of 'colonial' goods (sugar from West Indian plantations, tea and muslins imported by the East India Company) by women and the lower classes. The East India Company could be seen as a selfish vested interest jeopardising the virtuous exercise of politics in a balanced constitution, as well as being the agent of British expansion and success in India, and a source of moral and social challenges in addition to prosperity.[105] Such considerations fed into discussions of English refinement and manners and into debates on government policy.

Significant developments in thought on progress and civilisation emerged in response to debates accompanying the British acquisition of political power in India between the 1750s and the 1780s, and a period of conquest and expansion there from the

1790s to the 1840s. Just as Cowley and others discussed the duty of colonists in America to 'civilise' Native American peoples as an expression and promoter of virtue in English society, so the idea of a reforming 'mission' in India was to be argued as beneficial and virtuous for the British as well as the Indians.[106] While much of this discussion was conducted in texts specifically dealing with India, both the pride and the anxieties provoked by the growth of British power there also surfaced in other historical writing. Concerns about the risks and benefits of reforming intervention in colonial settings were paralleled by the debates over such policies and the activist movements seeking parliamentary reform, Catholic emancipation or social improvements in Britain between the 1790s and the 1830s. It is interesting to track traces of these contemporary controversies, which were social and cultural as well as political, in narratives of British and European history appearing during this period.

As noted earlier, it might well be argued that the impact of the upheavals in France and the post-Napoleonic movements for reform in continental Europe drew attention away from imperial concerns between the 1790s and the 1830s. Comparisons of social order and stability in Britain with disorder and destruction in revolutionary France, or between the tyranny of the Jacobins or Napoleon and the blessings of 'English' liberty and constitutional monarchy became staple features of contemporary commentary and historical writing. However, while supporters and critics of the revolution dwelt on the virtues of the English constitution and European civilisation (in Burke's denunciations) and progress in America and European ideas of rights (in Paine's advocacy), they also referred to savagery, eastern despotism and barbarism. Burke saw the triumphant revolutionaries as more like Native American 'savages' with scalps and captives than 'a civilised martial nation', arguing that, unlike the Mamluks in Egypt, the chivalry of European nobles lifted European societies above those of Asia, and that without it Europeans would be 'sordid barbarians' whose humanity was 'savage'. Paine's text lines up Tipu Sultan, ruler of Mysore, with 'despots' like Catherine II of Russia or Louis XVI, denigrates Muhammad and sees the poverty which affected many in 'civilised' Europe as 'far below the condition of an [American] Indian'. It develops a broad argument about harmful unrepresentative government which juxtaposes 'civilised' European society with 'uncivilised' societies elsewhere.[107]

The reform cause with most obviously colonial connections was the anti-slavery campaign, which, as we have seen, focused attention on the legal rights and liberties of enslaved Africans and the power of government to intervene in the trade, status or treatment of enslaved people. It also raised issues of progress and civilisation, since both pro- and anti-slavery arguments asked whether such people were raised or degraded by their incorporation into European plantation systems. Opposition to chattel slavery included projects to Christianise and educate enslaved or formerly enslaved people as well as campaigns for legal change.[108] Equally interestingly, it raised questions about the virtue and civilised status of Europeans who participated in, or benefited from, plantation slavery. When Dunbar commented that 'in a happier state of society' the British would be able to end chattel slavery, he both sidestepped this debate and linked the slavery issue to narratives of progress and civilisation in Britain.[109] The abolition of the British slave trade in 1807, and of slavery in the British empire in 1834, could be presented as a demonstration of British cultural and moral qualities and commitment to liberty, which were defined as central to British 'national character' as well as politics. Whether narratives of the abolitionist cause emphasised progressive politics, economic rationality or moral and providential virtues, they depicted the self-making of 'Britishness' through a major shift in global and colonial activities and policies.[110]

Empire, race and nation

Associations between 'national character', virtuous improvements and imperial policy threaded through various kinds of historical writing. This was often connected to attempts to explain and celebrate 'national' achievements, rather than to the extensive scientific and philosophical debates on the unity and diversity of the human species which developed between the 1750s and the 1830s. There is a considerable literature examining the emergent use of notions of 'race' to interpret this diversity. It shows that there was no single line of thought leading to later concepts of race, which drew on old views of climatic influence on customs, manners and innate capacities, to ideas of groups with common origins and experiences, to the movements and mingling of 'peoples' and to material presenting and debating information about distant societies.[111]

These could coexist uneasily in a single work. James Adair's *History of the American Indians* included detailed information about the lives and societies of Native Americans, based on his residence in America, with an extended recycling of older arguments for their origin as descendants of the 'lost tribes' of Israel. His role trading and negotiating with Choctaws, Muskegees, Cherokees and Chickasaws is a reminder that European commercial and colonial activities provided opportunities for the collection and reflection on information about peoples encountered in the process of making and maintaining them. Similarly, the section of Rogers' *Concise account of North America* dealing with Native Americans combines reports of the varied customs and manners of different 'nations' with universalising comments on 'Indian' characteristics.[112]

The distinctions and overlaps among the terms 'race', 'nation', 'tribe' and 'people' which engaged natural scientists, philosophers and social theorists in the later eighteenth and early nineteenth centuries had echoes in history writing. In texts of this period dealing with English, British and international history the most frequently used term was 'nation'. It was often deployed to identify people living under a particular regime, but equally importantly to refer to peoples seen as sharing common social forms, origins and temperamental or cultural characteristics. Thus the French, Spartans, Spaniards, Tartars, Dutch or Turks, as well as the English and the Scots, are each described by various historians as 'nations', and Dunbar used the term in a generic reference to groups with common social customs. His discussion of 'nature versus nurture' in human culture is entitled 'Of the hereditary genius of nations'.[113] Their forms of law and government are compared and contrasted, but attention is also given to their 'manners', to the 'liveliness' or 'lightness' of the French, the religiosity of the Spaniards or the 'laziness' and 'cruelty' of Turks. Treatments of 'character', culture and physical characteristics are combined in descriptions and judgements of their identity and roles in past or contemporary history. Such combinations are found in Goldsmith's writing on race and human difference in the 1770s as well as in the more racially focused work of the ethnologist James Prichard at the start of the nineteenth century.[114] Prichard's work exemplifies some of the multiple influences on discussion of race as he critiqued Home's polygenetic ideas, maintained commitment to biblical accounts and developed the new practices of comparative linguistics. Successive rewritten editions of Pritchard's *Researches into the physical history of man* between 1813 and 1855 contained various unstable formations of the roles of environment, culture and physiology.[115]

Prichard's work used comparative approaches to incorporate 'Celtic nations' into the new history of 'Indo-European' languages as well as into a biblical genealogy.[116] It is an interesting feature of English/Scottish views of the Irish, as presented in histories of their relations with the English since the twelfth century, that the Irish are more often referred to as a 'race', or 'people' divided into tribes than as a 'nation'. This contrasts with presentations of the Scots, who are awarded 'nation' status from an early stage, and whose efforts to assert that against English intervention are recounted with some sympathy by English as well as Scottish writers. Treatments of religious and political issues involving Scots or Irish in later periods tended to be set in narratives of specifically English projects of unification and Protestantism. The Irish appear as an uncivilised and superstitious people who would benefit from the introduction of political order and 'civilised' practices (agriculture, primogeniture, private property) as well as proper (Protestant) religion by English and Scottish settlers and rulers. The repeated recycling of praise for James I's settlement of Protestants in northern Ireland uses just these categories.[117] One counterblast to this tendency, suggesting the emergent nationalist outlook of late eighteenth-century Irish intellectuals, is O'Halloran's 1772 historical study, explicitly challenging negative views of the Irish, notably that of Hume, and claiming Irish identity as a 'nation'. Celebrating a long history of Irish valour and culture in the new language of antiquarian learning, it attacks the 'black legend' of the 1641 uprising as recounted by Hume and others, using the term 'race' in a benign context. It locates Irish problems in a history of division (as Catharine Macaulay does) and economic exploitation rather than in race or religion.[118]

More broadly, use of 'the nation' as a standard unit of reference combined with views that different nations might be associated with particular political forms and religious choices, and with suggestions that such associations sprang from the inherent qualities or capacities of particular 'nations'. This could draw on familiar stereotypes from medieval texts such as Gildas and

Isidore of Seville and seventeenth-century polemics like those of Coke and Hawkins. British/English narratives of their own deeply rooted affinity for liberty as against the 'savagery' of the Irish or of French acceptance of despotism, blended with the commitment to Protestantism explored by Kidd and Colley. Thus the text on modern Europe published by 'J.S.' during the Seven Years War stressed the combination of Roman Catholicism and slavery which disadvantaged the French and other Europeans compared to the free and Protestant English, linking it to their 'disposition.[119] Such views also became associated with the 'stages' of development identified by the conjectural historians, so that references to 'rude', 'barbarous', polished' or 'modern' nations abound in histories of England/Britain as well as those dealing with wider histories.[120] While the predominantly political focus of many such histories favoured the projection of ideas of the 'nation' onto those of competing and developing states, regular reference to the 'social' or 'cultural' characteristics or historical origins embedded more ethnic versions of that concept in their narratives. Images of the English/British as free, progressive and commercial were connected to the evolution of state and empire (notably their 'empire of the sea'), but also to their inherent qualities, and to their Germanic/Saxon/Teuton origins.[121]

This theme, found in sixteenth- and seventeenth- century scholarly debate and political argument, was taken up by historians including Catharine Macaulay, David Hume and less noted texts like Russel's 1779 *New and authentic history*, and the anonymous 1771 *New constitutional history*. Celebration of ancient 'free' institutions going back to Saxon times was accompanied by comments on their ethnic and cultural associations with, or differences from, 'Germans', 'Teutons', 'Danes' or 'Dutch'.[122] This set of conventional portrayals was given new force and colour by the expansion of scholarly and literary investigation and interpretation of the 'antiquities' of peoples in the British Isles and elsewhere in Europe. Archaeological enquiry and speculation, as well as discussion of bardic poetry and medieval documents, augmented the familiar use of Tacitus, Caesar, Bede and Geoffrey of Monmouth to portray 'ancient Saxons/Gauls/Irish/Germans/Welsh/Franks/Scots'. Slippages between the terms 'people', 'nation' and 'race' facilitated the extension and intensification of racialised thinking about nations and peoples. This might include using reports of 'savage' peoples met through recent colonial expansion, as when Sharon Turner compared Maori poetry to Saxon equivalents to suggest the 'spirit of active mind, high spirit, fearless boldness, unfeeling cruelty, and barbarous ignorance which distinguishes our ancestors'.[123]

The term 'race', which was frequently used in this period, was given a wide range of meanings. In eighteenth-century texts it was frequently applied to ruling dynasties, but was already being attached to groups supposed to have common origins, cultures, location or kinship (Tartars, Celts, Moors, Saxons, Jews) as well as to Venetian gondoliers, Saxon monks and Sikhs.[124]

This repertoire of references was supplemented by the growing body of ideas and information available in European texts dealing with the wider range of societies, states and cultures with whom Europeans were now involved. Just as depictions of Native Americans, Khoi people, Indians or Tahitians became resources for those theorising the processes of progress and civilisation, so they fed debates about the significance of cultural and physical differences among human groups. This ranged from sceptical comment on climatic theories of racial difference to determinist views on that question, with many texts offering a mixture of ideas. In addition to fuelling social and biological theory, they influenced historical narratives of 'national' identities and origins. While many texts often used the term 'race' to refer to royal dynasties and aristocratic lineages, they also regularly used it to label whole groups who might also be referred to as 'nations'. It was connected to established languages of 'nation' and 'people', but now also to the colonially and globally derived perceptions of peoples in the non-European world – 'mild' Bengali Hindus, 'savage' Hurons or Cherokees, 'barbarous' west Africans, 'corrupt' Orientals or ' unfortunate heathens'.

In 1830 James Mackintosh, former administrator in India and political activist, introduced his *History of England* with ten pages of general discussion of the links between 'race', 'nation' and 'civilisation. He used disparaging comparisons between Druid religion and the 'subservient system of Asia', speculating that love of liberty was 'the peculiarity of the Teutonic race' which would unfold in every nation of Europe and be 'communicated to all mankind'. It was supplemented by discussion of the British 'disposition', 'character' and 'genius' for empire and colonial enterprise which enabled the British to make the most of Britain's climatic and geographical advantages.[125] Racial hierarchy and typology are deployed as the starting point of his narrative of English history. It is linked to religion in his discussion of massacres in the Crusades as a legitimate response to Muslim 'defilement' of sacred sites in Jerusalem, and their expansionist aims for 'universal monarchy', in which religious affiliation becomes an inherent characteristic. This Eurocentric view resurfaces in a comment on how the threat of 'Ottoman barbarians' to 'Christendom' helped to make the 'modern European commonwealth', occluding the role of the Ottoman state as a *European* power and the existence of societies in Ottoman-ruled Europe.[126]

Racialised discourses of religion, nation and empire, which were becoming constitutive of politics and culture in the early nineteenth century, also find their way into historical writing. Authors like Mackintosh, who helped to shape British rule in India, used historical accounts in policy documents and brought experience in politics and administration to their history writing. Thus Mountstuart Elphinstone drew on Bentham in his analysis both of contemporary needs and of past developments, while James Mill's much-quoted hostile treatment of Indian society was linked to his career as an administrator, and to critiques of class and religion in Britain.[127]

If the Benthamite approach to government emphasised universal criteria, much political and historical writing took patriotic viewpoints where empire was rooted in distinctive and inherent 'English'/'British' qualities, and in the support of Providence for English endeavours. This was apparent in how they dealt with the question of British involvement in the trade and use of enslaved people from Africa in America and the West Indies. Goldsmith's 1768 compilation *The present state of the British empire in Europe,* a celebration of imperial success, mentions 'negro' labour in the colonies only in passing, and the slave trade not at all, even in his survey of British bases on the west coast of Africa – perhaps not surprising at a point when the trade and use of enslaved people was not a public issue. Later, the comparative historian Dunbar displaced the issue by stating that the 'race of slaves' in Latin America abused indigenous people under Spanish rule, before mentioning Quaker anti-slavery petitions and deferring the abolition of slavery to 'some happier age'.[128] Use of the old 'black legend' of Spanish colonial misrule and the focus on slavery, race and social conflict in a *non*-British context reinforces the distancing effect of his statement, while discussion of contradictions between ancient Greek slavery and 'democracy' suggests the author's awareness of the problems. In accounts of parliamentary debates on the slave trade and slavery in the 1790s references to universal standards of humanity and to slaves as 'African negroes' maintain both inclusive and racialised viewpoints.[129] However, they centre on the political and moral situation and agency of the British parliamentarians, traders and plantation owners involved with chattel slavery. Reports of the 1790s debates highlight remarks on the moral and religious implications for the British, the capacity of Africans for civilisation or the 'wretchedness' associated with slave trading and slavery. The 'barbarity' of trade in enslaved Africans figures more often in historical texts than their role in the West Indies economy or British imperial power and productivity more generally.[130]

This 'humanitarian' approach is also found in general texts produced between the abolition of the slave trade and the abolition of slavery. In 1826 Reverend Cooper's history spoke of slaves as 'guilty of no offence but of inheriting a colour in their skin differing from that of their oppressors, or of being a few centuries behind them in civilisation', flagging the appearance and culture of Africans, but subordinating those to moral issues. It sets the 1803 Demarara slave rebellion in the context of the civilising role of missionaries among slaves and comment on the likely or desirable end of the 'nefarious domination' of the planters.[131] The blend of racial and non-racial thinking about slavery in historical texts parallels similarly ambiguous depictions of the essential or inherent, as opposed to acquired, characteristics of 'nations'. While strengthening potentially racialised associations between slavery and African origins, most narratives of slavery emphasised the universal categories needed to judge it and its meanings within national political debate in the UK. Listings and comparisons of nations and peoples in Dunbar, Barlow, the 'Lady's' *Geography and history* and Mackintosh's account of nations in the 'European family' likewise move between views of 'nations' as shaped by descent, interest in cultural comparison and desire to place England/Britain at the head of a hierarchy.[132]

The emergence of narratives of the past in which racialised national hierarchies had a visible role set up some interesting contradictions. On the one hand, they expressed forms of essentialism not unlike contemporary arguments for the multiple ('polygenic') character of human species. The superiority of English/British institutions, moral character or material development could be presented both in terms of change over time and of inherent qualities, and anchored in comparison with 'inferior'/'less fortunate' peoples and systems. On the other hand, the narratives were also linked to celebrations of the civilising virtues which they brought to conquest, trade and colonial settlement. Offering the benefits of rational legislation, market forces and ordered government, or of Protestant Christianity, modern education and 'polished' culture to less fortunate people was a mark of the civilised character and inherent qualities and role of British/English entrepreneurs, explorers, administrators or missionaries. Empire offered perspectives on diversity in which the possibility and desirability of 'advancing' and 'civilising' colonial subjects and unbelievers, or indeed inhabitants of the Ottoman empire, sat alongside judgemental denigration of such people. The ambiguity towards these policies expressed by colonial officials, or Evangelical and Baptist preachers had its counterparts in the language and approaches of historians. Goldsmith incorporated accounts of human costumes and differences, whether physical or personal, in his *History of the earth*, a work mainly on natural history. Essentialised treatments of Muslim or Native American 'character' slipped between judging their 'backwardness' or defects in cultural and historical terms and depicting them as inherent characteristics.[133] Alexander Dow's comments on despotism in India suggested that it was rooted in a history of conquest and the influence of religion, but that their effects were 'fixed forever' in Indian society. James Prichard's explorations of ancient history and ethnology combined notions of race and nation to support a religious commitment to the unity of the human species while experimenting with models of racial evolution.[134] Traditions of biblical scholarship persisted alongside interest in recent ethnological and archaeological ideas and information.

Whether or not they included extended treatments of empire in historical accounts of 'England' or 'Britain', historical texts interwove strands of racial and imperial assumption and association with their 'national' stories. Discussions of the 'Irish question', of Africans as chattel slaves, and of 'oriental' peoples and governments, as well as broader interpretations of human history, offered examples of how the stadial notion of human development might be linked to racialised notions of culture and politics.[135] Many texts normalised overlapping notions of 'people', 'race' and 'nation' alongside ideas of civilisation and savagery in their comparisons or narratives of past societies. The effect was to embed all these concepts in everyday thinking about the past, while leaving their exact relationships unresolved, and to create a web of comparative discussion in which British global involvement refigured the cultural repertoire of readers and authors. Here ideas on the character of human difference meshed with emerging views of 'civilisation', 'humanity' and 'progress' as terms available for the discussion of any society, while simultaneously being given specifically European meanings and criteria. Universalism, cultural comparison and ethnicity jostled uneasily in these discussions.

By the time James Prichard was revising his work on the races of man in the 1820s and 1830s, and arguing that ethnological studies should be historical as well as scientific, religious and linguistic, a number of lasting links had been formed between empire and history writing. The shaping of conceptual structures for organising historical narrative and explanation was fleshed out by comparative methods, images and information derived from British imperial, global and colonial involvements. Colonial successes and confrontations in north America, like colonial expansion in India, were points of reference for patriotic reflections on the 'national' story, and for particular interpretations of providence and politics in 'English'/'British' history. Histories of 'English' political institutions and social progress, supported by tradition, contemporary success and antiquarian study, were also becoming flavoured with ideas of ethnic particularity or even superiority, to which imperial as well as European comparisons contributed. Woven in with partisan approaches, Protestant ideals, didactic aims and materialist and conjectural theories, the strand of imperial interest added its visible pattern to the fabric of historical practice.

Notes

1 Edmund Burke to William Robertson, 10 June 1777, in *Correspondence of the Right Honourable Edmund Burke*, 4 vols, London, 1844, vol. 2, p. 162.
2 H. Chapone, *Letters on the improvement of the mind addressed to a young lady*, London, 1773, vol. 2, letter X, 'On the manner and course of reading history', pp. 179–230, p. 198.

3   W. Robertson, *An historical disquisition concerning the knowledge which the ancients had of India*, London, 1794, p. 247.

4   The cosmopolitan context of eighteenth-century history writing is well studied in K. O'Brien, *Narratives of enlightenment: cosmopolitan history from Voltaire to Gibbon*, Cambridge, 1997.

5   J. Mokyr, *The enlightened economy: an economic history of Britain, 1700–1850*, New Haven, CT, 2009; P. Hudson, *The industrial revolution*, London, 1992, 2003; S. King and G. Timmins, *Making sense of the industrial revolution*, Manchester, 2001; M. Berg, *The age of manufactures, 1700–1820*, London, 1994; S. Chapman, *Merchant enterprise in Britain*, Cambridge, 1992, part 1.

6   D. Howe, *The transformation of America*, Oxford, 2007; C. Clark, *Social change in America*, Lanham, MD, 2006; C. Clark *et al.* [eds.], *Who built America: from conquest and colonisation through 1877*, New York, 2000; R. Middleton, *Colonial America*, Oxford, 2002; M. Egnal, *New World economies*, Oxford, 1998.

7   H. Bowen, *The business of empire: the East India Company and imperial Britain, 1756–1833*, Cambridge, 2006; K.N. Chaudhuri, *The trading world of Asia and the East India Company*, Cambridge, 1978; P.J. Marshall, *Bengal: the British bridgehead*, Cambridge, 1987; C. Bayly, *Indian society and the making of the British empire*, Cambridge, 1987.

8   R. Blackburn, *The making of New World slavery*, London, 1997; K. Morgan, *Slavery and the British Empire*, Oxford, 2007; H. Klein, *The Atlantic slave trade*, Cambridge, 1999; D. Northrup, *The Atlantic slave trade*, New York, 1994.

9   N. Thomas, *Discoveries: the voyages of Captain Cook*, London, 2003; O. Spate, *The Pacific since Magellan*, London, 1983, vol. 2; M. Steven, *Trade tactics and territory: the British in the Pacific*, Melbourne, 1983; I. Clendinnen, *Dancing with strangers*, Edinburgh, 2005; A. Atkinson, *The Europeans in Australia*, Oxford, 1997, vol. 1; R. Hughes, *The fatal shore*, London, 2003; A. Lepichon [ed.], *China trade and empire*, Oxford, 2006; M. Rediker, *Between the devil and the deep blue sea: merchant seamen, pirates and the Anglo-American maritime Atlantic world*, Cambridge, 1987.

10 For a general context see C. Bayly, 'The first age of global imperialism', *Journal of Imperial and Commonwealth History*, 26:2 (1998), pp. 28–47.

11 A. Burnes, *Travels into Bokhara* (1834), New Delhi, 1992; W. Moorcroft, *Travels* (1841), Oxford, 1979; A. Lamb [ed.], *The travels of George Bogle and Alexander Hamilton, 1774–7*, Hertingfordbury, 2002; G. Stewart, *Journeys to empire: enlightenment, imperialism and the British encounter with Tibet, 1774–1904*, Cambridge, 2009.

12 F. Nussbaum [ed.], *The global eighteenth century*, Baltimore, MD, 2003; S. Avramudan, *Tropicopolitans*, Durham, NC, 1999; R. Wheeler, 'Limited visions of Africa: geographies of savagery and civility in early eighteenth century narratives', in J. Duncan and D. Gregory [eds.],

Writes of passage, London, 1999; M. Daunton and R. Halpern [eds.], *Empire and others*, London, 1999, chs 2–4, 6–8; S. Huigen [ed.], *Knowledge and colonialism: eighteenth-century travellers in South Africa*, Leiden, 2009; S Schaffer [ed.], *Brokered worlds: go-betweens and global intelligence, 1770–1820*, Cambridge, 2009; G. Hooper, *Travel writing and Ireland*, Basingstoke, 2005; P. Marshall and G. Williams, *The great map of mankind*, London, 1982; B. Melman, *Women's orients*, London, 1992.

13 M. Ogborn [ed.], *Georgian geographies*, Manchester, 2004; J. Gascoigne, *Science in the service of empire*, Cambridge, 1998; T. Ballantyne [ed.], *Science, empire, and the exploration of the Pacific*, Aldershot, 2004; M. Lincoln [ed.], *Science and the exploration of the Pacific*, London, 2001.

14 Mokyr, *Enlightened economy*; P. O'Brien and S. Engerman, 'Exports and the growth of the British economy from the Glorious revolution to the Peace of Amiens', in B. Solow [ed.], *Slavery and the Atlantic economy*, Cambridge, 1991; J. Brewer, *The sinews of power: war, finance and the English state*, London, 1989.

15 C. Shammas, *The pre-industrial consumer*, Oxford, 1990; M. Berg, *Luxury and pleasure in eighteenth-century Britain*, Oxford, 2005; M. Berg, 'Manufacturing the orient', *Proceedings of the Istituto Internazionale di Storia, Economica*, 1998, pp. 385–419; B. Lemire, 'Fashioning cottons', in D. Jenkins [ed.], *Cambridge history of western textiles*, Cambridge, 2003; J. Goodman, *Tobacco in history*, London, 1993; S. Mintz, *Sweetness and power*, London, 1985.

16 L. Colley, *Britons*, London and New Haven, CR, 1992; K. Wilson, *The sense of the people: politics, culture and imperialism*, Cambridge, 1995, chs 2–5; K. Wilson, *The island race: Englishness, empire, and gender in the eighteenth century*, London, 2003, chs 1–3; G. Newman, *The rise of English nationalism*, London, 1987.

17 P. Jenkins, *A history of modern Wales*, Harlow, 1992; D. Smith, *Wales: a question for history*, Bridgend, 1999; P. Morgan, 'Early Victorian Wales', in L. Brockliss and D. Eastwood [eds.], *A union of multiple identities: the British Isles c.1750–1850*, Manchester, 1997; T. Devine, *The transformation of rural Scotland*, Edinburgh, 1994; C. Whatley, *The industrial revolution in Scotland*, Cambridge, 1997; C. Whatley, *Scottish society, 1707–1830*, Manchester, 2000; D. Allan, *Scotland in the eighteenth century*, Harlow, 2002.

18 S.J. Conolly, *Divided kingdom*, Oxford, 2008; D. Dickson, *New foundations: Ireland, 1660–1800*, Dublin, 2000; T. Bartlett, *The fall and rise of the Irish nation*, Dublin and London, 1992; T. Barnard, 'Integration or separation? Hospitality and display in Protestant Ireland, 1660–1800', in Brockliss and Eastwood, *A union of multiple identities*.

19 See D. Walford Davies and L. Pratt [eds.], *Wales and the romantic imagination*, Cardiff, 2010; M. Myrone [ed.], *Producing the past: aspects*

of antiquarian culture and practice, Aldershot, 1999; R. Sweet, *Antiquaries: the discovery of the past in eighteenth century Britain*, London, 2004.

20 See, for example, J. Greene, 'The debate over parliamentary imperial jurisdiction', in P. Lawson [ed.], *Parliament and the Atlantic empire*, Edinburgh, 1995; N. Dirks, *Scandal of empire: India and the creation of imperial Britain*, New York, 2006; K. Teltscher, *India inscribed*, Oxford, 1995.

21 See N. McKendrick, 'The commercialisation of fashion', in N. McKendrick *et al.* [eds.], *The birth of a consumer society*, London, 1982; J. Brewer and R. Porter [eds.], *Consumption and the world of goods*, London, 1993; W. Smith, *Consumption and the making of respectability*, London, 2002; J. de Groot, 'Metropolitan desires and colonial connections', in C. Hall and S. Rose [eds.], *At home with the empire*, Cambridge, 2006; M. Berg, *Luxury and pleasure in the eighteenth century*, Oxford, 2007, chs 1, 2, 4, 6; H. Guest, *Small change: women, learning, patriotism, 1750–1810*, Chicago, 2000, chs 1, 3, 7, 8; E. Kowaleski-Wallace, *Consuming subjects*, New York, 1997.

22 K. Temple, '"Manly composition": Hume and the *History of England*', in A. Jacobson [ed.], *Feminist interpretations of David Hume*, Philadelphia, 2000; K. O'Brien, *Women and enlightenment in eighteenth century Britain*, Cambridge, 2009, chs 2–4, 6; M. Phillips, '"If Mrs Mure be not sorry for poor King Charles": history, the novel, and the sentimental reader', *History Workshop Journal*, 43 (1997), pp. 110–31.

23 R. Henry, *History of Great Britain*, 6 vols, London, 1771, vol. 1, pp. 456–7.

24 S. Tomaselli, 'Woman in Enlightenment conjectural histories', in H. Bodeker and L. Steinbrugge [eds.], *Conceptualising women in Enlightenment thought*, Berlin, 2001; J. Rendall, 'Introduction', to W. Alexander, *The history of women from the earliest antiquity to the present time* (1779), reprint Bristol, 1995; O'Brien, *Women and enlightenment*.

25 K. Wilson, 'The nation without: practices of sex and state in the early modern British empire', in C. Hall and K. McClelland [eds.], *Race, nation, and empire: making histories, 1750 to the present*, Manchester, 2010; O. Equiano, *The interesting life of Olaudah Equiano, or Gustavus Vassa, the African*, London, 1789; N. Rogers, *Equiano and anti-slavery in eighteenth century Belfast*, Belfast, 2000.

26 C. Kidd, *British identities before nationalism*, Cambridge, 1999, p. 287; C. Kidd, *Subverting Scotland's past*, Cambridge, 1993, chs 8, 10.

27 Meek, *Social science and the ignoble savage*; L. Wollff and M. Cipolloni [eds.], *The anthropology of the Enlightenment*, Stanford, CA, 2007, chs 1–3, 5, 6, 15, 16; Ballantyne, *Science, empire and European exploration*, part 3.

28 J. Pocock, 'Between Machiavelli and Hume: Gibbon as civic humanist and philosophical historian', in G. Bowersock *et al.* [eds.], *Edward*

Gibbon and The decline and fall of the Roman Empire, Cambridge, MA, 1977; J. Pocock, 'Gibbon and the shepherds', *History of European Ideas*, vol. 2, no. 3 (1981), pp. 193–202; J. Pocock, *Barbarism and religion*, Cambridge, 1999–2005; O'Brien, *Narratives of Enlightenment*, chs 1, 5, 6; S. Brown [ed.], *William Robertson and the expansion of empire*, Cambridge, 1997, chs by Brown, Phillipson, O'Brien, Lenman, Carnall.

29 W. Robertson, *History of America*, 2 vols, London, 1777, vol. 1, pp. 56, 318, 337, 371, 374, 396, 400 (Lafitau), xii (Gmelin); J. Dunbar, *Essays on the history of mankind*, London, 1781, pp. 191 (central Asia), 192 (Cambodia), 262–4 (Niebuhr), 357–8 (Chandler, *Travels in Asia Minor*), 375–6 (Cook voyages).

30 See the discussion in C. Kidd, *British identities before nationalism*, Cambridge, 1999, pp. 48–51, 54–6.

31 K. Tribe, 'Cameralism and the science of government', *Journal of Modern History*, 56:2 (1984), pp. 263–84; K. Tribe, *Governing economy: the reformation of German economic discourse, 1750–1840*, Cambridge, 1988.

32 See A. Burns and J. Innes [eds.], *Rethinking the age of reform*, Cambridge, 2003; A. Claybaugh, *The novel of purpose*, Ithaca, NY, 2007; W. Thomas, *The quarrel of Macaulay and Croker: politics and history in the age of reform*, Oxford, 2000; J. Dinwiddy, *Radicalsim and reform in Britain, 1780–1850*, London, 1992.

33 See B. Hilton, *The age of atonement: the influence of evangelicalism on social and economic thought, 1795–1865*, Oxford, 1991; G. Ditchfield, *The evangelical revival*, London, 1998; S. Andrews, *Unitarian radicalism: political rhetoric, 1770–1914*, Basingstoke, 2003; R. Watts, *Gender, power and the Unitarians, 1760–1860*, Harlow, 1998; J. Walvin, *The Quakers: money and morals*, London, 1997.

34 Colley, *Britons*; N. Hudson, '"Race"'; R. Wheeler, *The complexion of race*, Philadelphia, 2000.

35 C. White, *Of the regular gradation of man*, London, 1799; L. Cody, *Birthing the nation*, Oxford, 2005, ch. 6.

36 The term was used by Dugald Stuart in his 1793 'Account of the life and writings of Adam Smith' published as a preface to Adam Smith, *Essays on philosophical subjects*, London, 1799, pp. I–CXVIII. Stewart describes the emergence of this distinctive practice in the work of Montesquieu, Smith, Millar and others on pp. XLV–L, naming it 'conjectural history' on p. XLVII.

37 P. Barlow, *General history of Europe*, London, 1791, 'Preliminary discourse', p. 1.

38 J. Dunbar, *Essays on the history of mankind in rude and cultivated ages*, 2nd edn, London, 1781, pp. 5, 258–9, 288, 295–6.

39 W. Robertson, *History of Charles V: with a view of the progress of society in Europe*, 2 vols, London, 1769, vol. 1, pp. 22–3.

40 'A Lady', *Geography and history selected...for the use of children*, 2nd edn, London, 1794, p. 30; W. Russel, *The modern history of Europe*, London, 1784, part 2, vol. 1, p. 492.

41 For example T. Mortimer, *A new history of England*, 3 vols, London, 1764–6, vol. 1, pp. 271–2, 462–8; W. O'Dogherty, *Epitome of the history of Europe*, London, 1788, pp. 98–104; C. Allen, *A new and improved history of England...designed for the use of schools*, London, 1793, pp. 58–60, 98–101.

42 Allen, *New and improved history*, pp. 308–9; W. Russel, *New and authentic history of England*, London, 1777, p. 691; M. Calcott, *Little Arthur's history of England*, London, 1835, pp. 220–2; W. Robertson, *History of Scotland*, 2 vols, London, 1759, vol. 2, pp. 250–60.

43 J. Barrow, *A new and impartial history of England*, 10 vols, London, 1763, vol. 3, p. 148; J. Grimaldi, *A synopsis of English history*, London, 1825, p. 35; C. Cowley, *The ladies' history of England*, London, 1780, p. 133.

44 see C. Kidd, *Subverting Scotland's past: Scottish Whig historians and the creation of an Anglo-British identity, 1689–1830*, Cambridge, 1993; C. Kidd, *Union and unionisms: political thought in Scotland, 1500–2000*, Cambridge, 2008, ch. 4; C. Kidd, 'Gaelic antiquity and national identity in Enlightenment Ireland and Scotland', *English Historical Review*, vol. 109, (1994), pp. 1197–214; J. Hill, 'Popery and Protestantism, civil and religious liberty: the disputed lessons of Irish history, 1690–1812', *Past and Present*, 118 (February 1989), pp. 96–129; C. O'Halloran, *Golden ages and barbarous nations: antiquarian debate and cultural politics in Ireland, c.1750–1800*, Cork, 2004; J. Leerssen, *Mere Irish and Fíor-Ghael: studies in the idea of Irish identity, its development and literary expression prior to the nineteenth century*, Amsterdam, 1986, pp. 67–84, 385–444.

45 W.A. Russel, *New and impartial history of England*, 1777–79, pp. 184, 190; Anon., *New history of England*, London, 1819, p. 51; Reverend Cooper, *A new history of England*, London, 1826, pp. 27–8; J. Mackintosh, *History of England*, 3 vols, London, 1830, vol. 2, p. 261.

46 D. Hume, *History of England*, 8 vols, London, 1778 (the last edition supervised by the author), vol. 8, pp. 51–61; T. Smollett, *History of England*, 3 vols, London, 1757, vol. 3, pp. 467–8, 500–1.

47 C. Macaulay, *History of England*, 8 vols, London, 1763–83, vol. 7 (1781), pp. 93–104; H. Hallam, *Constitutional history of England*, 2 vols, London, 1846, vol. 2, pp. 525–8; A. Bicknell, *A history of England and the British Empire for the instruction of youth*, London, 1791; Russel, *New and authentic history*, p. 515.

48 For example, Mortimer, *History of England*, vol. 3, pp. 280, 465–7; Russel, *New and authentic history*, pp. 625–6, 704–8; Calcott, *Little Arthur's history*, pp. 239–44.

49 Hallam, *Constitutional history*, p. 597.

50 Hallam, *Constitutional history*, p. 591.

51 See Barrow, *New and impartial history*, vol. 6, p. 77; Allen, *New and improved history*, pp. 236–7.

52 Allen, *New and improved history of England*, pp. 299, 308–9; Russel, *New and authentic history*, p. 552.

53 T.A. Lloyd, *The history of England from the peace in 1783 to the present time*, 2 vols, London, 1800, vol. 1, pp. 61–3; Allen, *New and improved history*, p. 399; Mortimer, *New history*, vol. 3, p. 494.

54 Mortimer, *New history*, vol. 2, p. 390 calls Ireland a 'sister kingdom', but vol. 3, p. 11 describes Ireland as 'subject to the domination of England'; Allen, *New and improved history*, p. 434 uses the term 'unhappy'.

55 Calcott, *Little Arthur's history*, pp. 209–10; J. Adolphus, *History of England from the accession of George III*, London, 1817, pp. 148–59; Cooper, *History of England*, pp. 137, 140, 208.

56 Adolphus, *History of England*, pp. 157–8; Calcott, *Little Arthur's history*.

57 W. Warrington, *History of Wales in nine books*, 2 vols, London, 1788, vol. 2, pp. 345–6.

58 Allen, *New and improved history*, preface; Mortimer, *New history*, p. 1; Mackintosh, *History of England*, p. vi.

59 Smollett, *History of England*, vol. 1, p. 147; G. Stuart, *Historical dissertation concerning the antiquity of the English constitution* (1768), 2nd edn, London, 1770, pp. 59–61, 121–2, 154–5; H. Hallam, *View of the state of Europe during the Middle Ages*, London, 1818; F. Palgrave, *The rise and progress of the English commonwealth*, London, 1832; a useful discussion of the shift from antiquarian appeals to 'Saxon' origins to early nineteenth-century 'Whig' accounts of change over time is J. Burrow, *A liberal descent*, Cambridge, 1981, pp. 21–35.

60 See R.J. Smith, *The gothic bequest: medieval institutions in British thought*, Cambridge, 1987; S. Turner, *History of the Anglo Saxons*, 4 vols, London, 1799–1805.

61 Hume, *History of England*, vol. 1, p. 60, vol. 2, p. 360, vol. 4, p. 483, vol. 5, pp. 8, 185, 271, vol. 6, p. 209, vol. 7, pp. 195, 249, 305, 429, 501, vol. 8, pp. 19, 208; C. Macaulay, *History of England*, pp. 60, 73, 177, 310, 360; l.

62 Russel, *New and authentic history*, pp. 78 ('empire of the Anglo-Saxons'), 260 ('empire' of Edward IV); Smollett, *History of England*, vol. 1, pp. 144, 151, 347 ('empire' of Alfred, Edward the Elder, Henry II); A. Bicknell, *A history of England and the British empire designed for the instruction of youth*, London, 1791, pp. 201, 209 (Richard Cromwell, Charles II contending for 'empire', drawing on Hume)

63 Lloyd, *History of England*, p. 88, Mortimer, *New history*, vol. 3, pp. 82, 183, 291, 528, Smollett, *History of England*, vol. 1, pp. 130, vol. 4, pp. 271, 639.

64 Cooper, *History of England*, p. 142; Allen, *New and improved history*, pp. 482, 484.

65 Cowley, *Ladies' history of England*, pp. 581–2.

66 W. Barron, *History of the colonization of the free states of antiquity applied to the present conflict between Great Britain and her American colonies*, London, 1777, ch. 4; C. Ashburton, *A new and complete history of England*, London, 1791–94, pp. 869, 870, 873, 874; Russel, *New and authentic history*, pp. 846, 851, 861, 862; Allen, *New and improved history*, p. 415 suggests that the English saw the conflict as a 'civil war in which, whichever party succeeded, the empire must ultimately suffer'; Dunbar, *Essays on the history of mankind*, pp. 312–14 comparing the removal of constraints on Irish trade in the 1780s with British government commercial policy to the American colonies; this can be contrasted with the short account in 'A Lady', *Geography and history selected...for the use of children*, London, 1794, p. 245, referring simply to the 'war between the Mother country and the colonies' which involved 'the spending of much blood and treasure', leading to the 1783 declaration of the USA as 'free separate and independent states'; Calcott, *Little Arthur's history*, vol. 2, pp. 247–9.

67 E. Burke 'Speech on the impeachment' (of Warren Hastings), in P. Marshall [ed.], *Writings and speeches of Edmund Burke*, 7 vols, Oxford, 1982–2000, vol. 6, pp. 275–6, 277, 345–7 (where Hastings appears as a 'Bashaw [a Ottoman or Mughal governor] of three tails' on p. 346), 353–4, 371; see also vol. 7, pp. 63, 102, 261, 420–1, 427–8, 692; Anon., *A history of the administration of the leader*, London, *c*.1765, pp. 6, 26.

68 For example, R. Orme, *History of the military transactions of the British nation in Indostan*, London, 1763 (many subsequent editions); R. Orme, *Historical fragments of the Mogul empire...and of English concerns in Indostan*, London, 1782–83; R. Orme, *The establishment of British trade at Surat*, London, *c*.1785; R. Sulivan, *Analysis of the political history of India*, London, 1779; J. Bruce, *Historical view of plans for the government of British India*, London, 1793; F. Blagdon, *A brief history of ancient and modern India*, London, 1805; D. MacPherson, *History of European commerce in India*, London, 1812.

69 Allen, *New and improved history*, pp. 428–9, 434–5, 440–1; Lloyd, *History of England*, vol. 1, pp. 44–6, 72–4, 83–5, 93–4; Cooper, *History of England*, p. 128.

70 Colley, *Britons*, pp. 283–91, 308–19, 364–8; M. Duffy, 'Worldwide war and British expansion', in P. Marshall [ed.], *The Oxford history of the British empire, vol. 2: the eighteenth century*, Oxford, Oxford, 1998; E. MacLeod and J. Rendall, 'Women writing war and empire: gender poetry and politics in Britain during the Napoleonic wars', in K. Hagemann *et al.* [eds], *Gender, war and politics*, Basingstoke, 2010; A. Forrest *et al.* [eds.], *Soldiers, citizens and civilians*, Basingstoke, 2008, intro, essays by Kennedy, Linch.

71 'A lady', *Geography*, pp. 61–3; Allen, *New and improved history*, pp. 472–86; Cooper, *History of England*, pp. 129–30; Calcott, *Little Arthur's history*, p. 250.

72 J. Adams, *A view of universal history*, 3 vols, London, 1795, vol. 1, ch. 22, vol. 3, chs 17–19, 24, 29, 33.

73 Bicknell, *History of England*, pp. 408–10, 411–12; Lloyd, *History of England*, vol. 1, pp. 108 (on global impact of developments in France), 111–15, vol. 2, p. 70.

74 Barrow, *New and impartial history*, vol. 7, pp. 100, 164, 166, 170, 181, vol. 8, pp. 56, 129; Smollett, *History of England*, vol. 1, pp. 231, 223 (like Mortimer) quotes Defoe, 'Englishmen are no more to be slaves to parliaments than to kings', also pp. 518–19; Allen, *New and improved history*, pp. 304, 359; C. Macaulay, *History of England*, pp. 36, 142, 182, 221, 350, 396.

75 M. Duffy, *Soldier's sugar and sea power: British expeditions to the West Indies and the war against revolutionary France*, Clarendon Press, 1987; D. Eltis and J. Walvin [eds.], *The abolition of the Atlantic slave trade*, Madison, WI, 1981; L. Bethell, *The abolition of the Brazilian slave trade*, Cambridge, 1970; D. Murray, *Odious commerce*, Cambridge, 1980; W. Ward, *The Royal Navy and the slavers*, London, 1969; C. Lloyd, *The navy and the slave trade*, London, 1968; D. Richardson [ed.], *Abolition and its aftermath*, London, 1985.

76 Allen, *New and improved history*, pp. 459–60, 462–6.

77 R. and S. Wilberforce, *Life of William Wilberforce*, 5 vols, London, 1838, vol. 1, p. 149.

78 Lloyd, *History of England*, vol. 1, p. 205.

79 A. Dow, *The history of Indostan*, London, 1768 (many later editions); J. Macpherson, *History and management of the East India Company since 1600*, London, 1782; J. Mill, *History of British India*, London, 1817 (expanded 1844, 1858).

80 Mill, *History of British India*, 1858, vol. 3, p. 352, vol. 4, pp. 220, 242, vol. 5, pp. 205, 210, 355, 425.

81 T. Clarkson, *An essay on the slavery and commerce of the human species*, London, 1788; T. Clarkson, *The history of the rise, progress, and accomplishment of the abolition of the African slave trade*, London, 1808; J. Bentham, 'Essay on the influence of time and place in matters of legislation', in J. Bentham, *Collected works*, 11 vols, London, 1962, vol. 1, pp. 169–94.

82 The works in question are V.de Riqueti, Comte de Mirabeau, *L'ami des homes, ou, traite de la population*, Avignon, 1756–57; and A. Ferguson, *An essay on the history of civil society*, London, 1767; their use is discussed in J. Starobinski, 'The word "civilisation"', in J. Starobinski, *Blessings in disguise, or, the morality of evil*, Cambridge, MA, 1993; and E. Benveniste, 'Civilisation: a contribution to the history of the word', in E. Benveniste,

Problems in general linguistics, Miami, 1971; see also J. Rendall, 'The progress of civilisation: women, gender and enlightened perspectives on civil society', in G. Budde, K. Hagemann and S. Michel [eds.], *Civil society and gender justice*, Oxford, 2008. Ferguson may have used the term 'civilisation' earlier in a 'Treatise on refinement' produced in the late 1750s.

83 See K. Baker, 'Enlightenment and the institution of society: notes for a conceptual history', in S. Kaviraj and S. Khilnani [eds.], *Civil society: history and possibilities*, Cambridge, 2001, especially pp. 100–5; R. Tuck, 'The "modern" theory of natural law', and I. Hont, 'The language of sociability and commerce: Samuel Pufendorf and the foundations of "four stages theory"', both in A. Pagden [ed.], *The languages of political theory in early modern Europe*, Cambridge, 1987.

84 T. Todorov, *In defence of the Enlightenment* (2006), London, 2009, p. 3.

85 S. Stuurman, 'Can the Enlightenment provide a canon for modernity?', in M. Grever and S. Stuurman [eds.], *Beyond the canon*, Basingstoke, 2007.

86 For the rich field of study and debate which nurtured the work of the 'conjectural' historians see J.G.A. Pocock's multivolume contextualisation of the work of Edward Gibbon, *Barbarism and religion*, Cambridge, 1999, 2003, 2005; M. Phillips, *Society and sentiment: genres of historical writing in Britain, 1740–1820*, Princeton, 2000; Kidd, *Subverting Scotland's past*; D. Spadafora, *The idea of progress in eighteenth-century Britain*, New Haven, CT, 1990; C. Berry, *Social theory of the Scottish enlightenment*, Edinburgh, 1997.

87 R. Henry, *History of Great Britain*, 6 vols, London, 1771–93, vol. 1, p. vi.

88 Rendall, 'Progress of civilisation', and J. Rendall, 'Clio, Mars and Minerva: the Scottish enlightenment and the writing of women's history', in T. Devine and J. Young [eds.], *Eighteenth-century Scotland: new perspectives*, Edinburgh, 1999; O'Brien, *Women and enlightenment*; C. Nyland, 'Adam Smith, stage theory and the status of women', in C. Nyland and R. Dimand [eds.], *The status of women in classical economic thought*, London, 2003, pp. 617–40.

89 Henry, *History of Great Britain*, vol. 1, pp. 208, 456–7, vol. 2, p. 298; H. Home, Lord Kames, *Sketches of the history of man*, London, 1774, pp. 168–219; for universalising views of 'manliness' see pp. 168–9.

90 Robertson, *History of the reign of Charles V*, vol. 1, pp. 46, 63, 70, 81–2, vol. 2, pp. 78–9, 115–17,120–1, 349, vol. 3, pp. 65–7.

91 Dunbar, *Essays on the history of mankind*, pp. 372–3; the issues are well discussed in O'Brien, *Narratives of enlightenment*, pp. 123–8; see also Kidd *Subverting Scotland's pasts*, chs 8–10.

92 Henry, *History of Great Britain*, vol. 1, pp. 89, 159–60, 208; G. Raymond, *A new and impartial history of England*, London, 1787, p. 214.

93 J. Millar, *The origin of the distinction of ranks, or, an inquiry into the circumstances which give rise to influence and authority in the different members of society*, 1st edn, London, 1771, 'Preface', p. iii; 3rd edn, London, 1781, p. 5.

94 Millar, *Origin*, pp. 17–31.

95 A. Ferguson, *History of civil society*, 4th edn, revised and corrected, London, 1773, p. 134; Dunbar, *Essays on the history of mankind*, p. 26.

96 Barlow, *General history*, 'Preliminary discourse', p. i; 'A Lady', *Geography and history*, pp. 5, 26, 122–3, 218, 229, 231.

97 Cowley, *Ladies' history*, p. vi; Adams, *Universal history*, pp. 9–11.

98 'A Lady', *Geography and history*, p. 5.

99 W. Winterbotham, *Historical, geographical and philosophical view of the Chinese empire*, 2 vols, London, 1795, vol. 2, pp. 4, 6–9, 16, 19, 27, 60–4, 65, 68, 71, 74, 75: Robertson, *History of America*, vol. 1, p. 283, vol. 2, book 7.

100 R. Mackintosh [ed.], *Memoirs of the life of the right honourable Sir James Mackintosh*, 2 vols, Boston, 1853, vol. 2, p. 154.

101 O'Dogherty, *Epitome of the history*, p. 293.

102 Smollett, *History of England*, vol. 1, pp. 13, 142, 422, vol. 2, pp. 142, 507, 512, vol. 3, pp. 229, 265, 532, 534, vol. 4, p. 661; Barrow, *New and impartial history*, vol. 1, pp. 145–6; S. O'Halloran, *Introduction to the study of the history and antiquities of Ireland*, London, 1772, p. 297.

103 Barrow's work maintains a theme of British/English commercial capacity and success from pre-Roman Britain to the 1760s; Henry also embeds commerce, civilisation and empire in his narrative

104 Burke, 'Speech on the opening of the impeachment', vol. 6, pp. 307–10, 352–66.

105 S. Mintz, *Sweetness and power*, London, 1985; J. de Groot, 'Colonial desires and metropolitan connections', in Hall and Rose, *At home with the empire*; M. Berg, *Luxury and pleasure in eighteenth-century Britain*, Oxford, 2005, chs 1, 2, 6, 7; M. Berg, 'The rise and fall of luxury debates' and 'Asian luxuries and the making of the European consumer revolution', both in M. Berg and E. Eger [eds.], *Luxury in the eighteenth century*, Basingstoke, 2003; C. Berry, *The idea of luxury*, Cambridge, 1994, part 3 (as evidence of the persistence of ideas, the cover illustration chosen for this recent text is a nineteenth-century European depiction of 'oriental luxury', *Odalisque* by J.-A. Ingres).

106 Cowley, *Ladies' history*, p. 578; R. Rogers, *A concise account of North America*, London, 1769, p. 238.

107 E. Burke, *Reflections on the revolution in France*, 9th edn, London, 1791, pp. 99, 109, 113, 118; T. Paine, *The rights of man* (1791), London, 2008, pp. 16, 264, 267–70, 296.

108 C. Hall, *Civilising subjects*, Cambridge, 2002; M. Turner, *Slaves and missionaries*, Urbana, IL, 1982.

109 Dunbar, *Essays on the history of mankind*, p. 393 (following discussion of racial, historical, ethical and political aspects of slavery on pp. 385–93).

110 S. Drescher, *Capitalism and antislavery*, Oxford, 1987; J. Oldfield, *Popular politics and British antislavery*, London, 1998; C. Brown, *Moral capital*, Durham, NC, 2006; T. Bender [ed.], *The antislavery debate*, Berkeley, CA, 1992, chs 3–8; S. Swaminathan, *Debating the slave trade*, Farnham, 2009; C. Midgley, *Women against slavery*, London, 1992; E. Clapp and J. Jeffrey [eds.], *Women dissent and antislavery*, Oxford, 2011.

111 Discussions of key themes are found in R. Rocher, *The complexion of race*, Philadelphia, 2000; N. Stepan, *The idea of race in science*, London, 1982, chs 1–3; N. Hudson, 'From "nation" to "race": the origins of racial classification in eighteenth-century thought', *Eighteenth-Century Studies*, 29 (1996), pp. 247–64; L. Schiebinger, 'The anatomy of difference: race and sex in eighteenth centry science', *Eighteenth-Century Studies*, vol. 23, no. 4 (1990), pp. 387–405; F. Nussbaum, *Torrid zones*, Baltimore, MD, 1995; P. Marshall and G. Williams [eds.], *The great map of mankind*, Cambridge, MA, 1982; M. Daunton and R. Halpern [eds.], *Empire and others*, Philadelphia, 1999, chs 1–4, 6, 12, 13, 15, 17, 18; N. Leask, *British romantic writers and the East*, Cambridge, 2004, esp. pp. 13–33, 68–120; N. Leask, *Curiosity and the aesthetics of travel writing*, Oxford, 2002, chs 2–5; H. Augstein, [ed.], *Race: the origins of an idea, 1760–1850*, Bristol, 1996, introduction.

112 J. Adair, *The history of the American Indians*, London, 1775, pp. 26–232 presents the 'lost tribes' argument, pp. 233–458 depict the American peoples with whom he had contact; Rogers, *Concise account*, pp. 205–53.

113 For example, Mortimer, *New history of England*, vol. 2, p. 591; Russel, *New and authentic history*, pp. 26, 29, 61–2,191, 204, 338, 557; Smollett, *History of England*, vol. 1, pp. 13 (Silures, Gauls), 49, 131 (Picts), 119, 193, 231, 334, 581 (English), 354, 563, 592, 595 (Scots), 382 (Jews), 602 (French), vol. 2, pp. 6 (English), 23, 59, 151, 150 (French); 'A Lady', *Geography and history*, p. 164 (Arabs); E. Barnard, *New and impartial history of England*, London, 1791, pp. 53, 193, 229, 495 (French), 100 (Jews), 156–61, 483, 661 (Scots), 276 (Swiss); Dunbar, *Essays on the history of mankind*, pp. 381, 418.

114 O. Goldsmith, *An history of the earth and animated nature*, 8 vols, London, 1774, vol. 2, pp. 211–43; J. Prichard, *Researches into the physical history of man*, London, 1848

115 See Rocher, *Complexion of race*, pp. 291–7; H. Augstein, *James Cowles Prichard's anthropology*, New York, 1999.

116 J. Prichard, *The eastern origins of the Celtic nations*, London, 1831.

117 Allen, *New and improved history*, pp. 236–7; Mortimer, *New history*, vol. 2, p. 494; Russel, *New and authentic history*, p. 379; Cowley, *Ladies' history*, p. 302; Barrow, *New and impartial history*, vol. 6, p. 77.

118 S. O'Halloran, *An introduction to the history and antiquities of Ireland*, London, 1772, pp. i, ii, 72, 219, 223, 276–93, 297; C. Macaulay, *History of England*, vol. 2, pp. 172–4.

119 'J.S.', *Modern Europe*, London, 1757, pp. 15–20.

120 Russel, *New and authentic history*, pp. 133–4; Payne, *Epitome of history*, pp. 2, 50, 156; Barlow, *General history*, 'General preface'; Dunbar, *Essays on the history of mankind*, pp. 309–16, 381; Allen, *New and improved history*, pp. 117, 236–7, 309; 'A Lady', *Geography and history*, pp. 5, 218, 229, 231; Russel, *New and authentic history*, 'Preface' (1 page unpaginated), pp. vii, 48, 133–4; Smollett, *History of England*, vol. 1, pp. 59, 83, 130, 150, 336, 368; 'J.S.', *Modern Europe*, p. 12; O'Dogherty, *Epitome of history*, pp. 70, 206, 317; Cowley, *Ladies' history*, pp. vi, 14, 80, 107, 578; Henry, *History of Great Britain*, vol. 1, pp. 113, 115, 191, 208, 229–30, 247–8, 315, 377–8, 390, 435, 438, 470, vol. 2, p. 379, vol. 3, p. 555.

121 Russel, *New and authentic history*, pp. 28, 159–60; O'Dogherty, *Epitome of history*, pp. 13–16, 23; Ashburton, *New and complete history*, pp. 27, 33, 81, 83, 179, Allen, *New and improved history*, p. 10.

122 Thus Ashburton, *New and complete history*, pp. 312–13 debates the elements of continuity and change from 'German' laws or customs to English equivalents.

123 S. Turner, *The history of the Anglo Saxons*, 4 vols, London, 1799–1805 (6 editions to 1836), 1840 edn, vol. 3, p. 154, n. 1.

124 O'Halloran, *History and antiquities of Ireland*, pp. 2, 170, 233 calls both Irish and Saxons a 'race'; 'A Lady', *Geography and history*, prefers to use the term 'people' for many social/ethnic groups but calls the Sikhs a 'race' (p. 173); Payne, *Epitome of history*, uses 'race' for ruling families (pp. 105, 158, 202, 217, 377) but also for gondoliers (p. 351) and all humanity (p. 409); Allen, *New and improved history*, uses 'race' both for ruling dynasties and for the 'British'; Smollett, *History of England*, vol. 1 uses 'race' to describe Danes (p. 172), Saxon monks (p. 161), Welsh (p. 198, 433), and in vol. 3 to describe a merchant (p. 82), while in vol. 2 he criticises Plantagenets as cruel kings who were 'not the friends and fathers but the destroyers of the *human* race' (p. 93 – my emphasis).

125 Mackintosh, *History of England*, vol. 1, pp. 9–10, 29.

126 Mackintosh, *History of England*, pp. 122–4, 378.

127 M. Elphinstone, *Account of the kingdom of Caubul* (1815, four editions to 1849), reprinted Delhi, 1998; M. Elphinstone, *Report on territories conquered from the Paishwa* (1821), reprinted Delhi, 1973; K. Ballhatchet, *Social policy and social change in western India*, Oxford, 1957; Mill, *History of British India*; J. Majeed, *Ungoverned imaginings*, Oxford, 1992; L. Zastoupil, *John Stuart Mill and India*, Stanford, CA, 1994, pp. 7–27; S. Sen, *Distant sovereignty: national imperialism and the origins of British India*, London, 2002.

128 O. Goldsmith, *The present state of the British empire in Europe, America, Asia and Africa*, London, 1768, pp. 280, 308, 332–3, 335; Dunbar, *Essays on the history of mankind*, pp. 411–13.

129 Allen, *New and improved history*, pp. 462–5, 483–8; Lloyd, *History of England*, vol. 1, pp. 15, 147–9, 176–80.

130 For example, 'A Lady', *Geography and history*, pp. 206, 217–18, which focuses on lack of 'civilisation' among Africans but also calls them 'creatures'.

131 Cooper, *History of England*, pp. 128, 232–3.

132 Dunbar, *Essays on the history of mankind*, pp. 185–6, 181, 234, 258, 336, 385–6 refer both to specific nations and tribes and debate what might constitute a nation; essays V, VII, VIII and XIII explore large themes linking 'national character', 'civilisation', nature and nurture.

133 Goldsmith, *A history of the earth*, vol. 2, pp. 211–42 (note the images on pp. 213, 221, 226, 229); 'A Lady', *Geography and history*, pp. 184, 230–1; J. Richardson, *A dissertation on the language literature and manners of eastern nations*, London, 1778 slips between socio-cultural accounts (pp. 2–10, 136–50) and a critique of Montesquieu's determinism (pp. 146–8), comparative analysis (pp. 150–64, 194–208) and essentialist assertions (pp. 144–5, 215); similarly, Rogers, *Concise account of north America* has an extensive section on the Native American 'nations' (pp. 210–64) which homogenises their customs and culture, with occasional essentialist judgements (pp. 214, 220) and some discussion of linguistic variety and political relations among different 'nations'.

134 See Dow, *History of Indostan*, vol. 3, pp. v, xxii; Augstein, *James Cowles Prichard*, pp. 120–2, 135–8.

135 Rocher, *The complexion of race*, pp. 186–90; Nussbaum, *Torrid zones*, p. 10.

❧ 3 ❧

EMPIRE AND HISTORY WRITING
1830s–1890s

It might have been expected that every Englishman who takes an interest in any part of history would be curious to know how a handful of his countrymen, separated from their home by an immense ocean, subjugated, in the course of a few years, one of the greatest empires in the world. (T.B. Macaulay)[1]

In 1866 the publication of an eighth revised edition of William Cooke Taylor's *Student's manual of modern history* brought together two authors whose careers and interests illustrate some key features of history writing in the mid-nineteenth century.[2] Taylor, descended from Cromwellian settlers in Ireland, was a scholar, teacher and journalist in London and Dublin, working with Richard Cobden for the Anti-Corn Law League. He wrote texts on French and Irish history, revisions of Pinnock's and Goldsmith's histories, a defence of the factory system, a life of Robert Peel and a history of Islam, as well as 'student manuals' on ancient and modern history. As 'effective deputy editor' of the *Athenaeum* he contributed to debates on empire, free trade, orientalism and religion, and wrote a history of India for use by British administrators.[3] Originally published in 1838, the *Manual of modern history* had run to five editions by Taylor's death in 1849, and two more before publication of the version revised by Yonge, newly appointed Regius Professor at Queen's College Belfast, which likewise had further editions. Originating from a Devon gentry family, Yonge spent time after university translating classical texts and writing Greek and Latin prose guides for public school use, producing a *History of England* in 1857. He also acted as tutor to the future popular historian J.R. Green.[4] He wrote histories of the navy, of France, of the constitution and of modern

Europe, and lives of Wellington, Walter Scott, Lord Liverpool and Marie Antoinette, as well as a literary history and editions of letters by Dryden, Goldsmith and Horace Walpole. While Yonge may not have shared Cooke's explicit imperial and political interests, both undertook history writing alongside literary, educational and scholarly work, and pursued their careers within an Anglo-Irish setting. An extensive chapter on colonies appeared in both original and revised editions of the *Manual*, since 'colonisation is too important a branch of modern history to be omitted', just as Yonge embedded discussion of Native American and Irish issues in his own explicitly 'English' constitutional history.[5] The *Manual* and its authors are suggestive of the contexts and genres of history writing from the 1830s to the 1890s as a still only semi-professionalised activity undertaken by men and women with diverse roles and interests who were embedded in an imperial world.

Turning to the wider context, it is worth noting how experiences and changes in the later eighteenth and early nineteenth centuries laid down important layers of ideas and practice for use in history writing. As already seen, social and political life in the UK was being reconfigured by urban, commercial and manufacturing growth, by imperial and international expansion and its problems, and by internal political conflicts. Cities like Manchester were transformed into 'Cottonopolis', linking the products of new machine technologies to world markets and capital flows. Rural communities reshaped by commerce and competition for their products, like workers and entrepreneurs responding to the demands of war, expansion and migration, all lived these experiences. This stimulated reforming, democratic, traditionalist and labour movement politics, based in workplaces and homes as well as public spaces, resulting in contests over nation, progress, state and civilisation. The growth of varied forms of organised protest over working conditions or over access to the political sphere was met not just by resistance, but by eloquent defences of the existing order, and by debate about the regulation and management of change. From the 1790s the pamphlet and parliamentary passion of Burke and Paine, the work of plebeian orators and organisers on behalf of social justice and political reform, like the impact of Methodist and Evangelical preachers and secular reformers, added new elements to cultural life in the UK. By the 1830s a wider public were considering issues of economic policy (free trade, workplace regulation), rights and freedoms (for slaves, voters, women, non-Anglicans), social policy (the role of state, market or private philanthropy in dealing with crime or poverty) and imperial affairs (colonial settlement, Irish questions, the treatment of 'native peoples'). These matters continued to occupy public interest and concern through the period.[6]

Such contemporary political debates were buttressed with references to the past in a range of these movements. Anti-slavery activists linked their polemics to historicised ideas of English virtue, liberty and Protestant identity, in controversy over the French Revolution and the 'rights of freeborn Englishmen'. Histories of regime change and radical protest in seventeenth-century England were mobilised in defence of order, or in celebration of liberty and reform. Some reworkings of the story of Henry II's conflicts with Thomas Becket were shaped by the controversies over High Church Tractarian initiatives in the Church of England in the 1830s and 1840s. Thomas Macaulay's celebration of the ordered and unifying resolution of conflict in the polity which emerged from the revolution of 1688–89 invoked ideals which he saw as central to the avoidance of conflict and mob influence in 1832 and 1848.[7] Historical references were also used to argue over the state of progress, materialism, morality and order, as with Carlyle's weaving of images of Saxon and Norman into his 'condition of England' essay on Chartism, and Chartist references to King Alfred. William Cooke Taylor's anti-Corn Law articles likewise used historical references.[8] The 1830s could be seen as a key 'moment' for the movements of preceding decades, with domestic reforms (of religious discrimination, parliamentary and local government, poor relief) and imperial and international change (the abolition of slavery, expansion in China and Australasia, reforms for India, South Africa and Canada). Those movements became points of origin for political initiatives, ranging from 'modern' Liberal and Conservative elite and party politics, to new democratic and labour movements, and single-issue campaigning, all contributing to nineteenth-century culture and politics.

The period from the 1830s to the 1890s could be seen as one in which the consequences and contradictions of earlier upheavals were absorbed and developed. Alongside the turbulence associated with social change and political division, new laws, institutions and practices embedded new versions of reform, order and nation. Changes to the electoral system, to the regulation of banking and trade, as well as to policy on 'humanitarian' problems, normalised notions of 'reform', whether as the redress of abuses or as a process of 'improvement'. The organising of policing, welfare, legal practice and the civil service made a key issue of the presence and effectiveness of state control. Developments in educational and religious policy as well as on Irish and colonial matters were linked to perceptions of the composition and needs of the 'nation'.[9] Questions of social and political inclusion and exclusion, whether associated with electoral representation or with shared cultural and moral values, shaped educational, legislative and social policy and practice, and interpretations of the past as well as debates about present and future. The extension of the franchise, the provision and content of education and the management of social inequality, poverty and discontent were contested as urgent issues of the day, and understood within assumptions about the past and future of the 'nation' or 'people'. Ideas and plans for reform and progress associated with reforming, radical and Chartist movements between the later 1820s and the late 1840s morphed into new languages and alliances in the 1850s and 1860s. Similarly, the approaches, assumptions and aspirations of 'Whig', 'Peelite', 'Radical' and 'Tory' politics, developed new characteristics between the 1850s and 1880s.[10] The cultural and intellectual resources on which they drew reinforced distinctive views of the past and fed into the writing of history.

This blend of influences can be seen in the work of Sir Edward Creasy, frequently reissued during the nineteenth century and thereafter. Creasy's career as the son of a land agent who became professor of history at London University in 1840, and spent fifteen years as chief justice in Ceylon (present-day Sri Lanka) from 1860, illustrates the possibilities of advancement for men of modest origins. It also shows how men like him and the better-known Thomas Macaulay or Henry Maine – who held office in India in the 1830s and 1860s respectively – could combine imperial office with history writing. Creasy wrote on British and imperial history, military history and Ottoman history as well as pamphlets, verses, a novel and a volume of heroic lives, typifying many who wrote in several genres. In Colin Mathew's words, he was 'not an important historian, but...influential'.[11] The 1853 *Rise and progress of the English constitution* endorses and quotes the 'Whig' views of Hallam and Mackintosh, celebrating English capacities to reform without violence or rejecting valuable past practice. It distanced itself both from 'furious Jacobins' and from the 'strange dogma' of Burke 'that the 1688 constitutional settlement bound all future generations'. Referring to his experiences as a special constable in 1848, Creasy evoked the 'true public opinion' which supported 'our thoroughly English-hearted Queen' and the principle of order, rather than the 'misguided' Chartists, and an early version of his text critiqued their 'People's Charter'. Offered as a text for students and 'the public', and in its seventeenth edition by 1907, it set its account of legal and constitutional development within a racial and national narrative of 'Englishness', and of reforms 'adapting themselves to the progress of society and civilisation'.[12] This blended traditions of patriotic history writing with the legacy of Whiggish and eighteenth-century stadial ideas on history. It quotes Thomas Arnold's 'imperial' view of 'this great English nation whose race and language are now over-running the earth from one end to another', and ends by invoking 'this mighty English nation whose language, law, arms and institutions are overspreading every region of the world.'[13] Creasy had already struck an imperial and patriotic note in his inaugural lecture, which used a similar phrase, linking the study of history to 'our duty...to prepare ourselves for the right use of the vast power that England sways, a power over the fortunes of mankind such as no people or potentate ever before possessed'.[14]

References of this kind, like the references to imperial topics in historical texts for children as well as adults, indicate that such matters were now seen as normal if not essential subjects for inclusion in such texts.[15] Beyond the United Kingdom, imperial and international involvements continued to develop. The growth of colonies of 'white' settlement in Canada, Australia, southern Africa and New Zealand created communities seen to be 'British' or 'English', whose links and similarities to communities in the UK became subjects for political and historical analysis. Crises and conflicts in Egypt, Jamaica, India, south and west Africa, China, Ethiopia and the Ottoman empire involved UK governments and armed forces in intervention and conquest to defend or extend 'British' power, interests and security. Unresolved issues posed by Ireland's position within the 1801 union, which had produced conflict over Catholic emancipation in the 1820s and over church organisation in the 1830s and 1840s, continued to do so, with Irish famine, protest and emigration, and from the 1860s with the appearance of Fenian and other nationalistic challenges. Trade, overseas investment, migration and missionary activity spreading from existing networks into new areas and activities during the nineteenth century entwined with colonial and strategic links while also extending beyond them. By the 1880s, the British occupation of Egypt, the 'opening' of China and Japan to European interests, the 'scramble for Africa' and wars in the Ottoman empire, South Africa, Afghanistan and Sudan embedded global concerns in British lives. So too did ongoing British migration, and contests for markets and investment from east Asia to south America.

While the extent of self-conscious or explicit interest in empire within the UK remains a matter of some debate,[16] the human, material and cultural connections bringing imperial and colonial elements into those lives are clearer. Everyday consumption of colonial goods (tea, sugar, rubber, wool), imperial images in advertising and entertainment, imperial themes in school books, fiction and magazines for young people, missionary material in British churches and chapels, and 'colonial' texts (travel accounts, journalism, fiction) available to various reading publics, established empire as an everyday presence. Family links to migrants (some two million left the UK for the empire between the 1850s and 1891, adding to earlier emigration), to members of the armed services and merchant navy and to missionaries, businessmen or colonial officials gave millions of Britons personal connections to that empire.[17] While focused on particular moments and issues, global and imperial concerns regularly featured in party and local politics. Examples range from campaigns over slavery in the USA, east Africa and Egypt, or over international control of prostitution and opium trading, to popular responses to the 1870s Balkan conflicts, to General Gordon's presence in the Sudan, and to Irish issues.[18] Combinations of British, colonial and international involvement in commerce, manufacture and infrastructure similarly entwined colonial elements in working, business and market activities during the period. Colonial goods re-exported to Europe by UK firms, railways, telegraphs and shipping taking colonial, UK and international trade and investment from the Suez Canal to south America and the Chinese treaty ports – like the movement of skills and technology from British mines or workshops overseas – underpinned many British lives and jobs.

With such a range of routes by which experiences, images and ideas of empire might enter politics, society and culture in the UK from the 1830s to the 1890s, their presence in the body of thought which historians used in their work is not surprising. Before examining that work more specifically it will be useful to trace three important themes – race, religion and reform – which developed as complex and diverse intellectual and cultural resources on which all authors might draw. As already seen, the notion of race had been emerging among related ideas of 'people', 'tribe' and 'nation' in the later eighteenth century, incorporating new thought about human differences and social change with biblical and classical models. This thought gained greater range and impact during the nineteenth century, shaped by a number of influences. Existing views of human unity and diversity were affected by expanding scientific and public debate about the roles of language, culture, climatic influence and biological inheritance as sources and markers of human difference, and about whether differences were permanent or capable of alteration. Biblical and philosophical explanations of difference needed to accommodate archaeological, geological, linguistic and ethnographical findings and arguments. The mid-century controversy over Darwin's evolutionary theory was just the best known of the interactions between these contrasting ideas. In the same period, debates on the 'national' or 'racial' character of the Irish (?Celts) contrasted with that of the English (?Anglo-Saxons) blended arguments over migration, physical attributes and culture with the political concerns with order and unity arising from the 1801 union.[19]

These scholarly and general discussions were paralleled by works dealing with British global activity, ranging from tales of conquest to travel narratives and works on slavery, reform, trade, science and missionary work. They established a cultural presence for the exotic and for images and ideas of human difference. They could take the form of heroic portrayals (verbal or visual) of missionary explorers like Livingstone, of military and imperial episodes and figures like Havelock in the Indian 'Mutiny' or the defenders of Rorke's Drift, and of adventurers seeking the sources of the Nile like Burton and Stanley.[20] They might connect 'racial' heritage and 'Englishness' with imperial heroism, as with portrayals of the manly pious Havelock, or Charlotte Brontë's depiction of the heroic missionary 'labouring for his race' in India at the end of *Jane Eyre*. They might offer moral and educational material like the lives of missionaries and accounts of natural history and folklore, or contribute to political controversy over emigration to Australia, and policy in South Africa or Afghanistan. An author like William H. Kingston (1814–80) wrote juvenile fiction on imperial topics, travel books and adult romance, campaigned and wrote on colonial emigration, edited boys' magazines and wrote historical texts. An emergent strand of juvenile fiction, like that set in Africa by Marryat or Ballantyne (author of *The Coral Island*), and others set in India and Australia sat beside works on the history, geology and the 'exotic' cultures of non-European peoples. Novels set in India (*Confessions of a thug*, 1839; *The competition wallah*, 1864; *An Englishman in the harem*, 1877), in Australia (*Martin Beck*, 1853; *For the term of his natural life*, 1875; *Three diggers*, 1889) or in Africa (*The African wanderers*, 1847; *Bush life in Zulu-land*, 1862; *King Solomon's mines*, 1885) sold alongside missionary, scientific and travel writing. The fiction of authors like Henty and Rider Haggard writing at the end of this period, and specialising in 'imperial' topics, continued to be popular into the next century. Combinations of 'scientific' authority for ideas about human difference, the popular appeal of representations of the danger, attraction or inferiority of 'other' peoples, and their use in political debates on nation, empire and reform, established them as familiar elements in nineteenth-century discourse.

This can be recognised in a range of settings. Contests over the abolition of slavery in the British empire, and later the USA, Africa and the Middle East, fuelled analyses of cultural and human diversity, past and present, embedding discussions and depictions of 'race' in learned texts, sermons, journalism, travel writing and fiction. Women's and working-class movements used the language of 'slavery' associated with (racialised) African people in critiques of class and gender inequity. They appropriated it for their own discourses of emancipation while establishing African 'difference'/ distance from the 'freeborn English' among whom women, workers and democrats claimed inclusion.[21] Critics of imperial conquest and expansion combined arguments for international free trade and benevolence to embrace all humanity alike with visions of the spread of 'advanced' civilisation from Europe to 'backward' societies elsewhere.[22] 'Imperial' problems in Ireland, India, Jamaica and the settlement colonies stimulated political contests over 'Englishness' and 'English' global missions in which free traders, moralists and patriots deployed racialised versions of these notions in 'high political' settings, translating them into party political and popular forms. Images of the despotic Turk, the backward African, the Hindu or Muslim fanatic and the uncivilised Irishman were common cultural references, as well as playing more direct roles in reactions to the 1857 uprisings in India, to conflicts in southern Africa, Jamaica and New Zealand, to Irish nationalism and to events in the Ottoman empire. *Punch* cartoons, music hall songs, missionary lectures and the heroic status of David Livingstone, Henry Havelock or General Gordon sat alongside ethnic markers and differences depicted in art and writing, and, like political and learned discourse, had significant cultural roles.[23]

While the precise effects, meanings and extent of the influence exercised by ideas and images of race can be debated, their presence was a visible feature in the nineteenth-century UK. Some historians today argue that notions of nation and civilisation had a more dominant place in culture and politics than ideas of race or empire, and others note how those ideas were entwined with those of gender, class and religion.[24] It is perhaps more useful to understand the pervasiveness of racial images and categories as being based on interaction rather than competition with those other equally important markers of identity and difference. Nervous commentators on labour and democratic protest in the 1840s could describe manual workers as a distinct 'race', and campaigners for women's rights could identify their interests with those of the British race, just as middle-class celebration of British material achievements and progressive influence used racial language. A famous 1890 commentary on English social problems referenced African exploration, anti-slavery and European expansion in its title, *Darkest England*.[25] The cultural and political resonance of these trends were reinforced by biological, anthropological and medical discussions of 'natural', inherent, inherited aspects of human difference which linked visible and measurable physical features to differences in qualities, capacities or 'character'.[26] Existing ideas of established characteristics shared by particular human groups, which had earlier been described mainly in historical or cultural terms, were now flavoured by new ideas of evolutionary biology and 'survival of the fittest'. These featured in the work of scholars and learned societies, media debate and popular images. Categories derived from this approach were used in discussions of criminality, of mental or bodily disability and the deficiencies of the poor, and in arguments over women's fitness for higher education, political participation and professional work, as well as over colonial subjects and the various 'peoples' of the world.

The ideas and images of race established during the nineteenth century were complex and contested rather than 'dominant' in any simple sense. As in earlier periods, slippages between the terms 'race', 'people' and 'nation', as well as the interweaving of racial, class, cultural and gender references, made 'race' an unstable as well as pervasive category. Widespread religious and intellectual views of the 'universal' characteristics and capacities of the human species pulled against equally familiar assumptions about essential human differences, and discourses of difference dealt both with 'English' or 'British' distinctiveness in relation to Europeans, and with non-Europeans. While evolutionist, essentialist and physiological versions of 'race' became prominent in scholarly and popular language, cultural, linguistic and historical approaches to human difference and inequality remained very important. As the 'sciences' of political economy, sociology and professional history expanded in universities, publications and learned societies, existing work on the definition and development of civilisation and on relationships between legal, social and political systems was extended and deepened. Rather than being shaped by antagonisms between the physical and social sciences, it was the combination of the two perspectives which gave racial discourses their prevalence and power. What is significant for the cultural and intellectual context of nineteenth-century history writing is not so much explicit advocacy of racial thought, as in the much-quoted work of Robert Knox, but the way in which racialised discourses blended into many areas of culture and ideas, becoming normal parts of everyday thinking.[27]

If developments in the more secular areas of culture and knowledge shaped the growing presence of racial assumptions and ideas, an equally important influence linking empire and history writing came from religion. UK society and culture in the nineteenth century were marked by active religious debate and change. The Church of England was reshaped by both Evangelical and High Church reform groups; Roman Catholics, Jews and Nonconformists gained civic inclusion; Nonconformist Protestant denominations, notably the Methodists, expanded. Believers of all kinds faced secular intellectual critiques and popular indifference as well as internal and interdenominational controversy. The religious map of England altered further with Irish migration to

English towns through the period, and the arrival of Germans, Italians and later east European Jews in significant numbers.[28] These developments provoked varied responses, from popular and clerical anti-Catholicism and anti-Semitism and sectarian strife, to debates on science and evolution. Various 'crises of faith' shaped cultural and intellectual activity, while social and spiritual change stimulated movements for religious renewal from Primitive Methodism to philanthropic sisterhoods and the Salvation Army. In their different ways, such responses all kept religious issues, ideas and loyalties to the foreground of intellectual and cultural life. Religiously based education and philanthropy were key social forces, and party politics and government policy persistently engaged with religious interests and commitments.[29] Where once historians told stories of the 'decline of religion' in the face of social change, scientific 'advance' or 'modern' secular ideas, the picture is now seen to be much more complex.

Whether in the activism of religious reformers, anti-Catholic and anti-Jewish protest, the role of Sunday schools or the play of religious elements in political parties, religion was a 'modern' element in society rather than a survival from the past, or a barrier to change. Abolitionists in the 1830s, proponents and critics of government policy on education and church reform or the 'Irish question' in the 1860s – like social purity campaigners in the 1870s and 1880s – deployed religious interests, ideas and assumptions. New interactions between patriotic and Protestant beliefs and language reworked established links between them in relation to contemporary concerns with Irish and international politics, and to continued interest in slavery in the USA, the Middle East and Africa. At a more everyday level, the role of all religious denominations in schooling, their efforts to recruit and organise in urban settings, and their prominent part in philanthropic activity, ensured an active religious presence in many localities. These points should be kept in mind when considering nineteenth-century contests between religious and secular ideas of social reform or scientific knowledge, the decline in religious worship and the demonstrable resistance to religious influence among groups from the urban poor to radical activists.[30]

Within this context there were significant links between religion and empire, and, as with other aspects of the history of this period, the connections worked in both directions. Firstly, various religious activities formed a structural part of the British imperial, global and colonial presence. Chapels, churches, priests and ministers met the needs of the settlers, officials, migrants and transients who moved across the empire, and the global networks of business, warfare and politics supporting it. They helped to construct 'British' communities overseas and were a visible manifestation of British authority and virtue, whose British architectural forms physically asserted their presence in colonial settings. The growth of what was seen as a global 'British world', in which Presbyterian Scots, Roman Catholic Irish and Baptist Welsh, as well as Anglican and Nonconformist English, practised their faiths, involved considerable organisation, competition and innovation, establishing religious structures and cultures linking various parts of the empire. The 'imperial' development of various religious denominations within the empire, and their role in settler, governmental and commercial communities, are now studied alongside the more discussed phenomenon of missionary activity.[31]

This latter phenomenon was, of course, a key feature of British imperial expansion, as in other European empires. One distinctive aspect of the renewal of religious commitment and organisation in the UK from the late eighteenth century was the founding of organisations dedicated to sending missionaries overseas. Anglicans and Nonconformists were involved in this process, both together and separately, and by the mid-nineteenth century had established a presence in Africa, India, Australasia, the West Indies and China.[32] This presence had several aspects. Missionary activity was a new development in religious organisation, encouraging the creation of new institutions and structures. The training, funding and management of missionaries required the Christian denominations which sponsored mission work to develop administrative and financial as well as ideological resources to support it. Although quite a middle-class occupation, demand for missionaries drew in recruits from diverse groups (including women, who initially worked alongside male relatives, but from the 1860s were recruited in their own right), thereby shifting the work opportunities available to different classes and genders. Famously, David Livingstone started work as a textile worker, but his career as a missionary, explorer and promoter of British trade in Africa brought public recognition, invitations to lecture at Cambridge and the Royal Geographical Society, and a funeral in Westminster Abbey. His story paralleled that of the jute worker Mary Slessor, who worked as a missionary educator in Nigeria from the 1870s.[33] By the late nineteenth century there were some ten thousand UK missionary workers on four continents, supported by funds about equivalent to those spent on British civil service salaries at that time. As active missionary involvement in heath and educational provision grew alongside the often-unrewarding work of preaching to and catechising potential converts, these workers became increasingly professionalised.[34]

While the complex role of missionary activity in the development of various parts of the British empire has deservedly been much studied, it is its contribution to religion within nineteenth-century British culture and politics which is most relevant to the study of empire and history writing.[35] The reliance of missionaries overseas on the voluntary support of the churches and chapels which financed them from the UK stimulated extensive efforts to celebrate missionary achievements and to describe their work and needs, in order to raise funds and inspire commitment for that work. Missionary pamphlets and magazines, lectures and sermons by returned missionaries, and books about missionary heroes and heroines for both adults and children, brought images of the empire, and of the uplifting of heathen and uncivilised peoples, into homes, churches and Sunday schools on a regular basis. Accounts of their educational activity showed British missionaries as bearers of knowledge and enlightenment; reports of work among Asian and African women foregrounded their role as opponents of women's oppression; stories of difficult missionary lives and deaths emphasised the duty and sacrifice involved in their work. These depictions were accompanied by images of distant scenes and people, ranging from jungles and temples to details of housing, dress and customs, making representations of 'exotic Others' a regular component in the cultures of UK residents. As such material became familiar in the everyday settings of school, home, church or chapel, it established one of the most persistent and widespread means whereby global and colonial experiences and connections were domesticated within the UK.[36] Missionary activity brought the empire 'home' to the UK, helping to entwine ideas of imperial expansion and responsibility with those of the promotion of Christian civilisation in British cultural consciousness.

The development of church and chapel 'missions' in urban areas in the UK to christianise and 'civilise' the under-classes there contributed another link. One response to the material difficulties and moral or political challenges posed to 'respectable' people by the growth of towns with their underprivileged, potentially hostile, 'lower' classes, was for churches, chapels and pious persons to organise programmes of 'poor relief', education, moral reform and 'improvement' aimed at those classes. The language and approaches of believing Britons engaged in such activities overlapped significantly with those used by Britons undertaking similar activities overseas, reinforcing and familiarising perceptions about the importance of class and colonial agendas to improve the 'heathen' ways of slum dwellers and 'natives' overseas. Just as missionaries overseas turned to providing health, welfare and education services alongside, or instead of, calls to conversion, their counterparts within the UK offered similar provision to the poor, sick and homeless, to abandoned children, and to other groups perceived as 'outcast' by 'respectable' sections of society. If the language of 'mission' was in some sense 'secularised' by those seeking material, political or educational improvements in British society, conversely it imported moral and spiritual content and language into governance and social policy in Britain and the empire.

A web of ideas and practices developed for these kinds of 'mission work', and for raising the funds and recruits needed to maintain it, established the value and normality of class-based and colonial relationships. It linked those who participated in that web in exchanges and hierarchies framed by religion and convergent languages of 'mission'.[37] Later nineteenth-century writing on the social problems of the unprivileged in the UK used the imagery of 'savagery', 'darkest Africa' and 'heathen' customs to project reform politics and respectable perceptions of the poor through colonial and racial images. Thus the journalist George Sims, writing about London in the 1880s, described the poor as 'savages alike to the Aborigines and South Sea islanders'. He echoed earlier writers like Henry Dix Hutton, referring to 'the masses whose domestic condition is little, if at all, raised above nomadism, and presents even less than the ordinary comfort and decency of savage life', or the ethnographer and eugenicist Francis Galton, remarking that there was little difference in 'the nature of the lower classes of civilised man from that of barbarians'.[38] It is worth noting that such language appeared in texts by reforming and anti-imperialist authors, indicating that the connected terminology of race and class was accepted language rather than expressing any one political viewpoint.

These assumptions and exchanges were complex and contra-dictory. Some missionaries 'at home' and abroad might become advocates of the interests of the 'poor' or 'natives' with whom they worked, as well as their managers or directors, and so become critics of existing practices and power relations, just as others upheld them. In the early nineteenth century some missionaries were strongly associated with anti-slavery campaigns, continuing to pursue that issue in Africa, the USA, and the Middle East after abolition was achieved within the British empire. They pursued and publicised what they saw as the interests of 'native' colonial subjects, or the evils of the international drink, sex and opium trades, acting as critics of the misjudgements or excesses of colonial regimes and global commerce. Missionaries did not act as agents of empire in any straightforward sense, and missionary activity could complicate imperial power relations, becoming a resource for colonial subjects challenging colonial rule, and sometimes a basis for missionary critiques of imperial practices. The missionary field was a complex arena where relations of power between missionaries, local peoples, colonial administrators or settlers were regularly contested as well as consolidated. While the presence of missionaries often reinforced acceptance of colonial rule and associated behaviours and outlooks, it also contributed to conflicts and debates about colonial aims and practices, and more generally about British global objectives and activities.

Missionary influences thus entwined with other aspirations for 'improvement', moral certainty and reform in imperial and UK politics. If patriotic Britons celebrated the power and prosperity they associated with the growth of distinctively British/English political institutions balancing authority, order and liberty, and of a productive commercialised society trading and investing globally, they also associated them with British support for order and improvement outside the UK. Imperial authority might rest on political and military assertion but it was also underpinned by agendas of virtue and betterment for subject, 'heathen' and 'backward' peoples. This might be exemplified in the legacy of the anti-slavery movements from the 1820s and 1830s and the activism of the Society for the Protection of Aborigines, campaigns over slavery in Egypt, the Sudan, the Gulf and east Africa, or against government abuses in the Congo.[39] It was also visible in the debates among politicians and administrators about relationships between governance and reform, whether in redesigning constitutional arrangements, in New Zealand, Canada and southern Africa, or in the introduction of social and economic changes in India, southern Africa and Egypt. For reformers and governments, as for those who discussed these issues in the media, concern for imperial virtue and for obligations to subject people as constituents of colonial agendas entwined with concerns for material and political advantage.[40] Such relationships linked debate on imperial reform with the discourses of improvement, redress of grievances and pragmatic response to issues or circumstances which came to characterise politics more generally.

These debates, as well as other impressions and ideas about empire, were becoming available to a larger and more varied range of audiences and contributors. By the 1830s the number of histories whose preface refers to the wish to provide accounts of the past which are neither aimed at students nor for exclusively scholarly audiences indicates authors' and publishers' sense of modestly educated but not academic middle-class readerships whom they wished to address. The growth of university and academic historical studies produced a larger body of history writers with claims to scholarly qualifications and encouraged the development of a distinctively academic version of historical writing. As Mitchell and others have noted, the growth of professionalised academic history affected history writing for the young as well as the general public, with informed narrative entwined with, or supplanting, romantic or melodramatic accounts of the past, and increasing interest in 'authentic' as well as picturesque illustration.[41] The expansion of school education and curricula between the 1830s and the 1890s generated demand for books, syllabuses and exam preparation designed for pupils, although subject-specific history teaching or texts remained limited before 1900. Nonetheless, historical material was a key part of general school reading schemes, and by the 1880s publishers like Longmans, already producers of educational texts, were printing some ten thousand history readers a year. Julia Corner's histories of Scotland, England, France, Greece and Ireland sold in tens of thousands in the middle decades of the century.[42]

Literate children were also potential readers of fiction and comics, including historical heroes and dramas – distinctive markets which were clearly being exploited from the 1870s onwards.[43] Such increases in literacy, together with the removal of the duties on the press by the 1850s, opened up new readerships for newspapers and magazines, and new audiences for representations of national and imperial issues and images. Ideas of national virtue, glory, duty, honour or mission were presented as rooted in 'national' history in such publications, as well as in the growing body of historical fiction. These became available to a more diverse audience than read the novels of Walter Scott at the start of the century, and it is an indication of the attraction of this genre that, after a period of decline, sales of his novels rose sharply in the 1870s. Like Corner, other writers for children produced historical fiction as well as narrative histories and school texts for their middle-class readers. While there were new possibilities for depicting the past of nations, states or empires, popular notions of state, nation and empire were themselves influences on the production of history writing.[44]

By the later nineteenth century history writing was part of a significantly altered context in which narratives of national and imperial pasts took a variety of forms. However, there were important continuities in the production of such writing. Reprints and supplementations of historical works by Hume, Goldsmith and Smollett through the century, and continued use of extracts from those texts and more recent work by Mahon, Mackintosh, Hallam and Lingard, ensured that attitudes established in the eighteenth century remained in circulation. William Cooke Taylor's historical work of the 1830s, like his reworking of Pinnock's version of Goldsmith's *History of the earth and animated nature* was being reissued in the 1880s, and John Lingard's *History of England*, first published between 1819 and 1830, was reprinted down to 1902, and in updated forms in the twentieth century. History texts for children like those of Edith Penrose ('Mrs Markham') and Maria Calcott, first published in the 1820s and 1830s, sold in tens of thousands and were still in print fifty years later. Charlotte Yonge, a successful Tractarian author of children's fiction and non-fiction since the 1850s, was rewriting her historical texts, which also sold in tens of thousands, to meet new educational codes in the 1890s. Authors aiming for broad readerships like George Gleig and Charles Knight moved material between 'family', 'popular' and 'school' histories of England, J.R. Green's successful *Short history of the English people* was reworked for school pupils within four years of its publication, as well as reprinting and selling in tens of thousands over the next five decades.[45] History writing was embedded in a web of genres and reissues within which new narratives and analyses made their way. While Macaulay and Mackintosh offered challenges to Hume, as Lingard did to explicitly Protestant patriotic histories, their initiatives flourished within a distinctly varied field.

There were also continuities in the choice and treatment of topics. Partisan debates over turbulent episodes in the English past, and over histories of English involvement in America and Ireland, of church and state and of the constitution, which had developed in the politically charged atmosphere of the 1780s, 1820s and 1830s, continued to resonate in subsequent decades. The convention of presenting the start of the Tudor monarchy as the start of 'modern' history, listing the emergence of monarchical states, European power politics, global exploration and new technologies (print, gunpowder), which went back to eighteenth-century practice, was recycled during the nineteenth century. Accounts of the French Revolution emphasising how violence swamped its early reforming achievements, which were established in the 1790s, continued into the 1870s.[46] Patriotic, imperial and ethnic themes (eighteenth-century victories in Canada and India, Anglo-Saxon political legacies, Irish/English differences and entanglements) acquired new force and character in nineteenth-century texts, restating versions of those themes produced in earlier publications. This combination of newer and established elements in the thematic connections between empire and history writing is the subject of this chapter.

Empire, state and citizenship

The reorganisation of state structures and institutions, both domestic and imperial, which began with the late eighteenth century contests over parliamentary reform, the East India Company and Ireland, persisted during the nineteenth century. The remaking of government at every level from local administration, education and welfare provision, to the refashioning of colonial governance, parliamentary representation, international trade and religious toleration extended from the period of 'reform' legislation in the 1830s to the 1890s. Such governmental changes combined aspirations to inclusion, efficiency, and emancipation with the desire to preserve order, continuity and established interests, and the need to negotiate and therefore compromise on these competing objectives. They also reinforced views that institutional and legislative changes were desirable or at least acceptable means to achieve political and social ends. Arguments for that view, often associated with Utilitarian ideas or policies, were contested from a 'laissez faire' perspective, and from a 'conservative' perspective favouring respect for established customs and practices, and pragmatic rather than planned change. However, this ideological clash was offset by material and political developments whereby even those suspicious of planned reform on occasion saw it as the 'least worst' option, or understood that the achievement of liberalisation required legal intervention. Nineteenth-century governments extended their regulating, surveying and monitoring processes and institutions into a growing number of spheres of life, including global commerce and colonial activities. The growth of the Colonial Office and colonial civil service, like legislation for colonial assemblies, the application of crown rule to India, and for various forms of self-government in Australia, Canada, South Africa and New Zealand, linked colonial power to the rule of law, orderly administration and sometimes representative institutions.

These developments make it possible to understand the strong emphasis given to narratives of constitutional and legal progress, in so many accounts of 'national' history produced at this time. John Edwards' *Concise history of England*, designed for 'studious members of Working Men's Colleges and Mechanics' Institutes', places 'the gradual growth of our free constitution' as its key theme.[47] Stories of the establishment of jury trial, representative institutions, legal security and rights for people and property were made central to the affirmation of a uniquely English achievement, and also to the success of imperial and colonial endeavours. Creasy argued that the social changes which lay behind middle-class demands for parliamentary reform in the early nineteenth century included their interest in 'the concerns of the remotest parts of the empire'. He presented the reformed parliament of 1832 as 'the great organ of the constitution of the British Empire' as well as of England, Scotland and Ireland.[48] Accounts of the 'ordering of affairs', the reduction of crime and disorder, and the establishment of settled government have a central place in histories of politics and government in Britain, Ireland and British overseas settlements and territories, giving these activities a global setting. William Angus in the 1830s, like Sanderson's 1882 *History of the British empire*, speaks of the Scottish Highlands being 'brought under law and order' after Culloden. Birkby wrote of

Ireland 'being rendered completely tranquil' after William III's war there, and Thomas Keightley of Cromwell's 'regulation' of Ireland in the 1650s.[49] In the colonies of British settlement this could be celebrated as the export or recreation of 'English' constitutional rights and liberties in communities increasingly seen as 'Britain [or England] overseas'. In India and the 'tropical colonies' it could be portrayed as the gift of law, order and honest administration to people who had previously only experienced despotism, 'tribal' conflict, anarchy, violence, corrupt rule or theocratic repression.[50] In either case the assumptions and vocabulary linked stories of the emergence of a superior and successful English constitutional and legal system to stories of virtuous empire. Erskine May's *Constitutional history of England* ends by placing that history in an imperial context; 'To the Englishman may it not be said…"having won freedom for thyself, and used it wisely, thou hast given it to thy children who have peopled the earth, and thou hast exercised dominion with justice and humanity"'.[51]

This affirmed English institutions as the best or ideal standard, but embedded them in the rule of difference within the state and the empire. Benign and virtuous authority was considered appropriate for managing those lower classes, colonial subjects or women considered too decadent, backward, unruly or ill equipped to participate in constitutional politics or full legal personhood, just as self-governing status and full legal recognition were right for settler communities with shared 'English' origins. Historians argued that however 'unpopular' the unions between England and Scotland or Ireland might have been, they were productive of order and prosperity. Exponents of this view ranged from the patriotic and conservative George Gleig to texts for students by Yonge and Taylor, and the liberal J.R. Green, who, although he came to support home rule for Ireland, linked the 1801 union to the benefits of free trade and the need for religious toleration.[52] In the case of Ireland particular emphasis was placed on narratives of seventeenth-century English interventions, and later Irish resistance, as showing the violence and absence of security which were overcome by the expansion of state institutions as well as 'plantation'. Disagreements about the grant of civil rights to Roman Catholics as a rational liberal reform or as a dangerous concession, and of Anglo-Catholic trends in the Church of England in the 1830s, flavoured historical accounts of the Irish and the union with

Britain.[53] Like other texts, Goldwin Smith's *Irish history and Irish character* combined sympathy for the Irish experience of English domination with confidence that only within the framework of union could the people acquire education and civilisation.[54]

Questions of Irish home rule and nationalism surfaced in English politics from the 1860s and likewise affected English history writing, in which the beneficial effects of the 1801 union implicitly recognised its contentious character. While it established a clear distinction between Ireland and other overseas territories under UK rule, Ireland was still governed differently, both through different regulation of poverty and education and through the use of coercive responses to protest and conflict there.[55] These ambiguities had effects on history writing as well as political debate. In Macaulay's canonical *History of England* Ireland appears as 'the greatest colony that England had ever planted' but also to be saved and incorporated into the 'British' nation by virtuous Whig reformers.[56] It has been suggested that the revived unionism of the later nineteenth century was echoed in increasingly positive accounts of Oliver Cromwell's attempts to sustain a union of England, Scotland and Ireland in the seventeenth century.[57] J.R. Green's *Short history* closed with an account of the first Gladstone administration, whose Irish policy 'endeavoured to remove' the 'chronic discontent' there, and May concluded that 'freedom, equality, and honour have been the fruits of the union, and Ireland has exchanged an enslaved nationality for a glorious incorporation with the first empire of the world.'[58] Here the ambiguities of Ireland's position within a British empire and the powerful trope of slavery are deployed to present the 1801 union as benign.

The writers paralleled their depictions of the management of order in England (sectarian radicalism in the seventeenth century, Chartist and lower-class protest in the nineteenth) with accounts of comparable actions to control 'disorderly' subjects in the West Indies, Ireland, Canada or India. They portrayed the use of varied blends of authoritarian force, concern for 'legitimate' grievances and improving reforms. Taylor, Yonge and Keightley balanced accounts of the aggressive policies and arguable misconduct of Warren Hastings in India in the 1770s and 1780s with depictions of him and successors as good and concerned administrators as well as imperial conquerors. On the topic of 'improvement' Mrs Markham's much-read children's history linked the anti-slavery work of 'the great and good Mr Wilberforce' with that of John Howard on prison reform in the UK.[59] History writers might, like Creasy and Martineau, write separate texts on imperial topics while also bringing them into their work on English/British history, or like Knight, Taylor, Spencer Walpole and many others, treat imperial topics alongside British/ English or European ones. They might, like Henry Maine, try to create a global comparative framework for discussing law and institutions, linking them to culture, 'tradition, and imperial governance'.[60] They might emphasise order, stability and the organic growth of law and constitutional forms, or stress the importance of conscious reform and improvement informed by principles of reason and justice. Interestingly, they differentiated between peoples suited to have liberty and rights, and those who would benefit from the exercise of enlightened and benevolent authority over them. Such differences were expressed in ethnic and cultural terms and linked discussions of government to views of race and civilisation.[61]

The most frequently used of these links was that which presented the Anglo-Saxon origins of English constitutional and legal institutions not just as some 'ancient' legacy, but as the product of some inherent quality of the Anglo-Saxon 'race' or 'people'. Limited monarchy, communal involvement in local government and judicial processes and the use of consultative assemblies were often associated with the 'spirit' or 'genius' of the Anglo-Saxons. This might support a patriotic view of English 'uniqueness' or be merged into discussion of a supposed 'Teutonic race'. The former can be seen in texts like the *Pictorial history of England*, Edwards' *Concise history*, or Keightley's *History*, the latter in Green's *Short history* and E.A. Freeman's *Constitutional history*. As will be seen, such narratives contributed to the spread of racialised discourses of the 'nation', but they also made legal and governmental institutions specific and central to that discourse. Green's evocation of Anglo-Saxon self-government at the start of his *History* linked it to later parliamentary government able 'to frame laws and do justice *for the great empire* which has sprung from these little farmer commonwealths in Sleswick' (my emphasis).[62] It is worth noting that elements of it appear both in histories aimed at a broad public and in the specialised work of constitutional historians like Stubbs, who argued that 'the history of Germany is bound up with our national *and natural* identity'. Stubbs' use of work by those for whom 'Teutonism' was a key feature of the English constitution, while disagreeing on its exact role, is perhaps less surprising than his linking discussion of medieval states in the eastern Mediterranean to contemporary European relations with 'Asia'.[63] He echoed the more polemical Freeman, whose vehement anti-Turk prejudice informed both his historical treatment of the Ottoman empire and his view of the 'eastern question' in the 1870s.

It can rightly be argued that nineteenth-century writing on constitutional and political history in general does not give much space to imperial or colonial topics. The dominant forms were political and sometimes social narratives of the 'nation', with emphasis on its uniqueness and on developments within the UK. As Catherine Hall has shown in relation to the successful work of Thomas Macaulay, it is the positioning of colonial subjects and 'Celtic' peoples on the margins of accounts of the success and expansion of the mixed constitution and legal liberties associated with 'English' government which is significant. Macaulay's use of the term 'empire' to describe the Scots and Irish components of the UK suggests that Anglocentric but imperial approach.[64] One key aim of histories produced in this period was to present narratives of the English past which would lead readers to appreciate their contemporary material prosperity, political stability, cultural superiority and international success. However, since such accounts of English achievements did associate them with 'greatness' in a wider world, the role of imperial and commercial success was either implicitly or explicitly part of the story. In some cases, international status and success were seen as manifesting the 'advanced' character of British culture and society, but in others it was seen to depend on the strength of good government and institutionalised freedom in Britain, as suggested by May, Creasy, Yonge and Knight.[65] While some commentators, like Congreve and Harrison, posed free trade and peaceful global influence *against* imperial expansionism, the 'patriotic' language of this debate allowed significant overlaps between 'liberal' and 'colonial' perspectives, also found in history writing of the period. Moreover, both supporters and critics of the narrative of the growth of political freedom and representation might celebrate the growth of English power and prosperity in the world. The Whig icon Macaulay, the 'Tory radical' Froude and the radical positivist Harrison responded to the 1857 armed conflict between Indians and their British rulers with robust support of force and imperial control, whether in the name of order or of civilisation.[66]

The story of English constitutional achievement was often told in terms of the growing legal protection for the personal, property and political rights of 'the people', and depicted various forms of belonging to 'nation' or 'society'. As already noted, the changes of the period stimulated fears and debate among the respectable and privileged about the best management of the new forms of group interest and protest. Parliamentary reform, free trade and protection, religious toleration and the relations of church and state – like the grievances of the disadvantaged and excluded – were subjects for polemic, analysis, political controversy and historical reflection. In an era of varied European revolutions, Chartist and labour movements and Irish and colonial protest, questions of political inclusion and control perceptions of those issues could connect to accounts of past 'equivalents', whether the French Revolution, the 1381 English 'peasant revolt', the Levellers, or the 1798 Irish rebellion. J.A. Froude made these connections clear in response to Goldwin Smith's liberal critique of his view of the authoritarian Tudor monarchy in the *Edinburgh Review*, which referenced Irish unrest and the 1848 revolutions.[67] The embedding of a critique of Chartism in Creasy's constitutional history has been noted, and his account of the protection from arbitrary imprisonment conferred in Magna Carta references Gladstone's attack on Neapolitan prisons in 1849. His tone was echoed by Markham's *Children's history*, which asserted that the 'defeat' of Chartism confirmed that 'the principles of order and respect for property are too strong in England to be assailed with success or... possible advantage to any rank or class of society'.[68]

These comments were influenced by the new political and cultural substance given to intellectual and ideological debates over subjecthood, rights and citizenship as a legacy of the American and French revolutions. If earlier accounts of English/British history presented the constitution as an inheritance to be proud of, nineteenth-century versions associated this 'national' achievement not only with the inherent characteristics of the English people, but also with institutions to which there were contested claims. Radical artisans, colonial settlers, Utilitarian reformers and women suffragists all constructed claims to the formal recognition and inclusion of particular groups through citizenship, franchise or property rights – claims which could in turn be countered in the name of order, propriety or reason.[69] In some historical texts commentary on such questions sat beside accounts of the past, just as remarks about the character of Queen Elizabeth I, or Madame Roland, were accompanied by comments or assumptions about 'proper' femininity, an issue contested by some women historians.[70] Edward Creasy's 1848 *Textbook of the constitution* and his 1852 *Invasions and projected invasions of England from Saxon times* were both subtitled 'with remarks on the present political emergencies'. Keightley's *History* concludes with the hope that by encouraging 'love and veneration' for English institutions it will help to avert the dangers of democracy.[71] Conversely, when Goldwin Smith wanted to raise funds for the campaign against Governor Eyre's conduct in Jamaica, he toured England, lecturing on the 'true' British heroes like John Pym, Cromwell and the younger Pitt. When published, his lectures included commentary on the history of freehold rights, empire and parliamentary reform.[72]

From the 1860s the image of colonies of British settlement as communities which took 'English' practices and institutions with them overseas, which went back to Hume, was being deployed in more developed forms. Thus J.A. Froude's celebration of the expansionist role and spirit of Elizabethan explorer-pirate captains sees them as prefiguring English overseas settlement, and itself prefigures his portrayal of that empire of settlement in *Oceana*. The introduction to Charles Knight's 1862 *Popular history* links the island base on which the 'English' state and nation emerged to the unique English capacity to create an empire.[73] In an 1876 lecture, the scholarly historian of the medieval English constitution, Stubbs, argued that English history also belonged to Americans since 'very much of English life was ripe when it was transplanted'. In 1872 Charles Yonge's student text on modern history linked the English adoption of Protestantism, and its political results with the growth of civil liberty in 'every quarter of the globe'. In his 1884 inaugural lecture as Regius Professor of History at Oxford, E.A. Freeman, invoking a predecessor, Thomas Arnold, saw English global expansion not as 'dominion – an eastern despot could do that' but as 'the growth of new lands of Englishmen, new homes of the tongue and law of England'.[74] If the history of British conquest and imperial rule in Asia was a source of patriotic pride, the growth of colonies of settlement could be incorporated into narratives of the global spread of English institutions, established in earlier treatments of north American colonisation.

Already in the 1840s an account of Canada was subtitled *England in the New World*, and this trend strengthened in the later decades of the century. From the 1860s UK politicians faced new European power relations, with the emergence of Germany and Italy, self-assertion in Ireland and in British colonies of settlement, and in changing relations with the USA, which, like Germany, also became an industrial and commercial competitor. Within the UK, reform of the franchise (1867, 1884) and the evolution of party and sectional politics (including labour movements, Irish nationalists, female suffragists and issue-based campaigns) fuelled contention over the rights and roles of subjects. The 'scramble' of European powers for power and territory in Africa, and their competition for influence in China, Latin America and the Ottoman empire, similarly energised controversy over colonial rule and European global competition and intervention. These developments framed several decades of political and intellectual debate over the constitutional structure of the empire which emphasised the colonies of 'white' settlement. Home rule for Ireland, imperial defence policies, relations with the Boers in South Africa, and self-government in Australia and Canada were all issues for debate among politicians and commentators, and were linked to histories of English conquest and settlement.[75]

Many prominent participants in those debates were also writers of history. John Seeley, J.A. Froude, Goldwin Smith and E.A. Freeman were active historians, writing on the past, present and future of the British empire. They were also public intellectuals involved in arguments and organisations committed to various versions of that future. Freeman's lectures on the *History and conquests of the Saracens* were published at the same time as his polemic on the Crimean War (1854–56), and he linked studies of ancient 'federal' states to critical views of contemporary schemes of imperial federation.[76] Goldwin Smith's career as a public intellectual and academic embraced support for university and electoral reform, and for the unionist cause in the American Civil War. He wrote on empire, the history of Ireland and the American colonies, working at Cornell University, and as a public figure in Canada, where he settled in 1871. As with Smith's linking of Irish history and politics, in the 1880s Froude and Seeley produced iconic works on Britain and empire which combined public advocacy and historical narrative.[77] In both cases, history and politics are closely linked. Froude framed an account of his travels in America and the British empire in a combination of historical narrative of British global dominance and the export of the English 'genius' for freedom with a vision of imperial unity as an antidote to threatened decline and degeneration in England. Seeley's lectures on English imperial history frame a historical account of empire and politics in Britain with political reflections on the importance of the empire of settlement as 'Greater Britain'.[78] Just as Smith brought an elite reforming outlook to his political activism and to his version of Irish history, so Seeley's commitment to a study of history which would inform practical politics, and Froude's anxieties about decline, emerged in accounts of the imperial English/British state. Such work was underpinned by institutional as well as textual connections. Smith's tenure as Regius Professor of History at Oxford (1858–65), like those of Freeman (1884–92), and Froude (1892–94), as well as that of Seeley as Regius Professor at Cambridge (1869–95), testified to the imperial connections of establishment writing, politics and academic life.

Empire, civilisation and progress

When Macaulay announced that the subject of his *History of England* would be 'eminently the history of physical, of moral, and of intellectual improvement',[79] he did not describe the actual contents of his narrative of political emancipation very accurately. Nonetheless, the statement signalled a theme which influenced accounts of the past in the nineteenth century, whether in pessimistic views of the fragility of material or political advances, or in optimistic confidence that such advances could be sustained. The legacies of stadial theory and 'philosophical history' might provide a language for discussion of material and cultural change over time, but the anxieties of educated and propertied men confronted by the dislocations of industrial change, social mobility and radical politics were equally important elements in that discussion. A plebeian supporter of liberty and progress, the publisher-turned-author of several histories of England Charles Knight argued that all worthwhile advances had been achieved by 'the union of classes', and that the Chartists represented a violent threat to civilisation (quoting Macaulay's Commons speech against them in his support).[80] Controversy over British relationships with the Irish, and over self-government for colonies of European settlement in the later part of the period, like specific crises in India in the 1850s, Jamaica in the 1860s or Egypt/ Sudan in the 1880s, flavoured English/British pride and confidence in imperial power with comparable conflicts and anxieties. It is in that context that accounts of the past in terms of civilisation and progress were produced.

For all that Macaulay's *History of England* did not deal with imperial matters (despite his significant essays on Indian topics), its partial debt to the Scottish tradition of universalising conjectural history surfaces in its use of exoticising comparisons and images, and of ideas of progress and barbarism. Inhabitants of Dahomey, of the Sandwich Islands, or of Hottentot *kraals*, like Turks, lascars and Native Americans, are used rather arbitrarily as comparators for various English situations. Orientalising terms are deployed to depict the sexual indulgence of Charles II ('flirting with his sultanas'), the absolutist aspirations of James II ('driven step by step to acts of Turkish tyranny') and the hardships of seventeenth-century travel (trains of pack animals as 'caravans'). The cruel transportation of the defeated followers of the Duke of Monmouth in 1685 is declared to have 'equalled to that of the negroes who are now [after British abolition] carried from the Congo to Brazil'. These images sit beside references to the 'mollifying influence of civilisation', to the 'state of barbarism' north of the Trent and to the importance of assessing progress. Specific connections are also made between the seventeenth-century narrative of the *History* and the global power and presence of Britain in the nineteenth century. Military reforms in the 1670s are said to prefigure 'that great and renowned army, which has, in the present century, marched triumphant into Madrid and Paris, into Canton and Candahar', imaging British victories against French, Afghans and Chinese. This picture of military success can be compared with the reference to nineteenth-century markets for Birmingham hardware 'in Pekin and Lima, Bokhara and Timbuctoo'. As the *History*'s much-quoted third chapter on the state of England in 1685 closes with a meditation on how historians might judge progress, it is the abolition of chattel slavery and the custom of *sati* in India which are given as modern examples.[81] The highly Anglocentric project of this work is flavoured with colonial and global associations embedded in ideas of civilisation.

Although, as noted, historical writing on society in England/ Britain was not always overtly concerned with global or imperial issues, it might well have global and imperial contexts. The conclusion to Charles Duke Yonge's *History of England* clinches an account of how the English 'from being an inconsiderable horde of savages has arrived at the height of wealth, power, and of glory which we now enjoy' with a reference to English/British imperial rule.[82] In an earlier generation William Cooke Taylor, who – as noted earlier – saw colonial history as part of modern history, wrote on India and Islam as well as on European, English and Irish history.[83] Cooke's Anglo-Irish Dublin experience, like Yonge's in Belfast, gave him non-metropolitan angles on nation and empire, and in Cooke's case an interest in the 'Irish question'. Spencer Walpole similarly referred to the growth of an English colonial empire in the nineteenth century as 'the true monument of English greatness'.[84] Edward Creasy wrote on the Ottoman empire as well as on English history, imperial and colonial constitutions, military history and English constitutional history, spending fifteen years as chief justice of Ceylon. Froude wrote on Ireland and the West Indies as well as sixteenth-century England, just as the children's author Corner produced histories of China, India and continental Europe as well as the UK. George Gleig, soldier, clergyman and author of *The family history of England* and *The school history of England*, wrote on British activities and leaders in India as well as opposing parliamentary reform and evangelical trends in the Church of England.[85]

Gleig, like many other writers, wove a story about the British/English quasi-colonial presence in Ireland since the twelfth century into the narrative of English/British history. While that story dealt in part with legal or parliamentary links, and with the politics of conquest, settlement and resistance, comparison of the state of civilisation in Ireland and England was a key element in treatments of Irish/British relationships. Many accounts of the invasion of Ireland by Henry II and Anglo-Norman barons in the 1170s began by commenting on the 'savage' or 'uncivilised' character of society in Ireland at the time, recycling views originating from the text of Gerald of Wales, the contemporary Anglo-Norman chronicler. Similar observations accompany accounts of English or Scottish intervention in Ireland in the reigns of Elizabeth I and James I. With the latter the associations of Protestantism, liberty and social progress inflect discussions of politics, law and order, so that, while portrayed in an English setting as a threatening absolute monarch, as a promoter of Scots and English 'plantations' in Ireland and

America, he becomes an agent of civilisation and prosperity.[86] For many authors, views of the different levels of civilisation and of cultural differences between 'native' Irish, Anglo-Irish, Scottish settlers and English rulers and landlords shaped accounts of the Irish uprising of 1798, the union of the kingdoms in 1801 and nineteenth-century Irish campaigns for self-government, religious toleration and land reform. Some acknowledged 'real' material grievances and political complexities, as well as partisan views on home rule, religion and the land question, but whether subtly or simply presented, the theme of difference was depicted in socio-cultural and religious as well as political and 'racial' terms.

A full and complex expression of this view appeared in Goldwin Smith's *Irish history and Irish character*. In this text the narrative of English conquests and politics in Ireland and the 'miserable history of a half-subdued dependency' leads up to a defence of the 1801 union as best for people who 'have never had the advantage of training through which other nations have passed in their gradual rise from barbarism to civilisation'.[87] As befitted an associate of high-minded reformers, Goldwin Smith emphasised the importance of education and right religion (liberal Anglicanism rather than Roman Catholicism) as civilising influences on 'national character'. The failure of the Normans to introduce 'a loftier type of civilisation' in Ireland, as they had done in England, left the Irish 'wild' and barbarous. Praising Macaulay's tale of William III's conquest of Ireland in 1689–90, he regrets the social and religious apartheid created by the Penal Laws. Religious and cultural deficiencies unfitted the Irish for independent nationhood, just as it was the training of the Irishman Burke among English statesmen which enabled him to be a good constitutionalist.[88] Froude's *The English in Ireland* stresses the need for strong English rule in Ireland, but also for the assertive presence of English or Scottish models of industry and Protestantism as offered by the Jacobean and Cromwellian settlers. It deplores the failure of absentee or Hibernicised Anglo-Irish landlords to uphold that model, as well as swings of government policy between coercion and conciliation of Irish grievances.[89] His negative view of the Irish as a 'weaker' degenerate people who would benefit from absorption by the superior merit as well as the superior force of the English was influenced by Thomas Carlyle's thinking on power and critiques of urban industrial society. Although underpinned by the political controversy over the 'Irish question' in the 1870s, Froude's writing echoed popular works from earlier decades, like Keightley's, which associated the Irish with barbarism and superstition.[90] The work of the Anglo-Irishman William Lecky, while also supporting the union, offered a different reading of the damaging roles of religion and colonialism, and of the need for the British to use devolved rule and respect for cultural difference to counter Irish nationalism. It is worth noting that as he became more pessimistic about such an outcome he took the harsher view that 'government rather on the Indian model may become necessary.'[91]

Themes of 'barbarism' and 'civilisation' inherited from eighteenth-century discourse continued to appear in nineteenth-century history writing. From the school- and family-oriented texts of Gleig and Julia Corner to the works of Yonge and Walpole, they are used to describe changes in Russia as well as in Britain and western Europe.[92] This was not just a matter of juxtaposing more or less advanced customs or economic activities, but of a whole range of ethnocentric approaches. These included Taylor's observation that 'nothing of interest' happened in China between the end of the Han dynasty in the early third century CE and the thirteenth-century Mongol invasion, and references to societies and cultures in the Middle East and India in terms separating them from what turns out in practice to be European civilisation.[93] This distinction could be used to connect accounts of the past to contemporary politics, as with E.A. Freeman's depictions of early modern confrontations between the Ottoman state and 'Christian' powers and his Gladstonian views of the Ottomans during the 'Balkan crisis' of 1875–78. His racialised depictions of 'Turks' are combined with arguments that slavery and polygamy were essential and defining social markers of the difference between 'eastern' and 'western' societies, and that language and religion as well as 'blood' ensured that Turks were not, and could not be, Europeans.[94]

The use of references to eastern despotism to stigmatise particular regimes showed the continuing popularity of orient-alising stereotypes, grounded in current British involvement in India, Egypt and the Ottoman empire, as well as earlier cultural assumptions. Macaulay's comment on James II's 'acts of Turkish tyranny', Keightley's description of the elder Pitt acting like the 'vizier of an eastern monarchy' and Yonge's quoting a view of Pitt's language as being such 'as had never been heard west of

Constantinople' are cases in point. Writing of an earlier period, William Cooke Taylor depicts the robust and improving ruler Rollo of Normandy (ancestor of William I) refusing to perform the 'degrading oriental prostration' which French kings required of their vassals.[95] The virtues of English/British civilisation were conveyed by contrasting it with such familiar images, rather like Keightley's sturdy Protestant dismissal of the doctrine of transubstantiation as 'an absurdity scarcely to be paralleled in the Brahmins of India or the lamas of Tibet'. His comparison of a medieval nobleman's romance with an Iranian poetic legend offers readers a more pleasurably exotic analogy, while also making a middle-class gibe at aristocratic manners.[96]

Celebrations of the mission of the British *raj* in India also combined depictions of British interactions with cultures in the subcontinent with their accounts of conquest and governance. They deploy a range of voices depicting a 'protective' mission towards vulnerable subjects and ancient culture as well as a 'civilising' mission to reform 'barbarous' or 'backward' practices. Keightley's commentary on Cornwallis as governor general in India already flags the argument that 'good governance' needed to take account of 'a society totally different from that of Europe', while Edwards associated the *raj* with 'raising the condition of the many millions of India'.[97] Historical texts projected images of benevolence and 'improvement' as well as of military glory and imperial power. Harriet Martineau's *British rule in India*, a title emphasising that theme, also celebrates 'our civilising and dispassionate rule', and argues the importance of free trade and secular education for Indians, praising those who have given up ignorance, superstition and imperial pride.[98] On a broader front, the global reach of British power and influence had significant effects on views of the past of non-European societies and their relations with Europeans, bolstering ethnocentric views of progress and civilisation. James Mill had linked his account of Indian history to comparisons with Iran, Roman Britain, China and the Arabs so as to present images of an 'oriental' world needing the benefits of British rule. Such links also reinforced the pattern of entwining temporal with cross-cultural comparison, found not only in prestigious or scholarly works but in children's histories like *Aunt Anne's history of England*, where ancient Britons are compared to 'Esquimaux', Maoris and Native Americans. Edwards' *Concise history* made similar comparisons, likening Druids to Brahmins; historians compared Scottish Highlanders to Afghans, as others compared them to Native Americans and Zulus, and Sanderson imagined the state of ancient Britain as 'resembling our recent foes the Abyssinians, Ashantis, and Zulus'.[99]

While explicitly stadial models of social progress were not necessarily used in history writing, more general tropes of movement from barbarism to civilisation of oriental cultures and of contrasts between pastoral or uncommercial and 'advanced' societies continued to appear. As with earlier texts, this writing reinforced images of non-European peoples living in an 'uncivilised' present which was compared to the less civilised past of European societies. In Spencer Walpole's *History of England*, which called the growth of colonial empire 'the true monument of British greatness', the movement of 'hordes of civilised Europeans... to savage countries' is contrasted with the 'barbarian migrations' of their ancestors into the Roman empire.[100] More generally, there were important crossovers between the ideas, aims and methods underpinning projects of social reform and social analysis initiated in the colonies and those undertaken in the UK. From census-taking to the regulation of the trade in sexual services, commentators, administrators and campaigners operated in imperial networks linking the UK to other parts of the empire, circulating ideas, images and information in order to lobby, report and make policy.[101] These fed into the assumptions about civilisation and progress available to history writers, so that Taylor's *Student's manual* and Lingard's *History of England* ould make 'the progress of civilisation' a key theme in the history of 'nations' in Europe. Henry Hallam's text on medieval Europe likewise deployed a (quite nuanced) range of uses of ideas of 'barbarism' and 'civilisation, just as Charles Knight's *Pictorial history*, and Julia Corner's book on India dealt with that theme for popular audiences.[102]

A new element shaping historians' discussions of culture, savagery, civilisation and barbarism was the emergent discipline of anthropology. The emergence of new forms of anthropological thinking in the later nineteenth century interacted with the needs and interests of colonial rule, and also flavoured the more general use of ideas about civilisation and progress. Ideas and information about distant societies provided by traders, officials, missionaries and travellers became resources for British writers on society and history, and began to be systematised by thinkers working in the emerging disciplines of ethnology and anthropology. Three new trends are particularly relevant, although, as Stocking shows, they remained entwined with existing thinking about the development and diffusion of culture. Firstly, the physical anthropology which had been influential from the 1830s was offset by new emphases on 'society' and 'culture' as key concepts for comparative study of human groups and institutions. Secondly, historical and quantitative methods in social science were modifying older conjectural, romantic and philosophic approaches. Thirdly, the adoption of the metaphor, if not the concept, of evolution derived from Darwin's work in biology came into use (in various combinations with other approaches) by social thinkers and indeed by historians.[103]

By the 1880s comparative discussions associated with work like that of Edward Tylor and Henry Maine added new dimensions to thinking about difference and progress across space and time. Edward Tylor's comparative reflections on culture, largely based on travel and missionary writing by others, underpinned a version of the stages of progress as a feature of human development centred on human cultural efforts rather than race. His 1881 text *Anthropology* emphasises language, 'the arts of life' and social aspects of 'the study of man and civilization' (his subtitle), which occupy thirteen out of sixteen chapters. His work modified older accounts with ideas drawn from social statistics and evolutionary theory, and used the notion of 'survivals' to explore more complex models of social and cultural change and continuity. His enlarged definition of 'culture' built on earlier definitions of human groups by reference to their language, beliefs and customs, and fed into his work to create academic institutions to support anthropological studies.[104]

Henry Maine, whose background was in legal studies, focused on historical comparisons of institutions and property law, pioneering perceptions of what he called 'traditional' or 'ancient' societies as intrinsically different from 'advanced' societies, rather than examples of earlier stages in European development with the potential to emulate that development. This laid the foundations for views of 'civilisation' in which universalist ideas about paths of progress open to all societies were replaced by an emphasis on inherent cultural difference. In his 1872 *Village communities east and west*, he offered a comparative discussion of 'ancient' law, custom and social organisation in Germanic and Indian villages, but also argued that the potential for change seen in the growth in western Europe of what he called 'feudal' law and social structures, and then of market forces, was lacking in India. The point was further reinforced in his later work that compared what he called 'early institutions', in which he contrasted the dynamic interaction of Roman imperial governance and the practices of incoming 'barbarian' peoples, which generated modern forms of sovereignty and law, with 'the immobility of the East'.[105] He went on to argue that the role of imperial rule should be to protect customary institutions from the potentially destructive effects of the intrusion of modern influences from outside. His dense discussion of differences and similarities between European and Indian communities and cultures portrayed the inherent dichotomies of 'east and west' and argued for informed appreciation of the custom- and status-based institutions of the latter as well as the former.[106]

Maine's work is rightly cited as an influential example of the relationship between imperial administration and the framing of social knowledge. As legal member of the viceroy of India's council (1862–69), he worked on legal reform and land administration issues, and as vice-chancellor of Calcutta University reacted to the presence of educated and politically aware Indian students. Between his return from India and his death in 1888 he continued to offer governments advice on colonial issues.[107] It is also important to note that both before and after his time in India he used Indian material in comparative discussions of the history of English law, challenging not only what he saw as the ahistorical abstractions of Utilitarian thinkers, but also the Teutonism of historians like Stubbs and Freeman. Using analyses of Indian and Roman institutions, he opposed Benthamite views of law as an agent of social change and argued instead for the dominance of historically specific contexts in the shaping of law. He claimed that the study of social organisation (kinship, property law, power structures) was central to understanding surviving 'ancient' societies, and while his specific theories may not have been influential, his views shaped the growth of twentieth-century anthropology and medieval legal history.[108] Maine's colonial involvement and colonial knowledge helped to shape not just thinking on empire, but perceptions and studies of the history of law and society more generally. His influence on arguments for 'indirect rule' as a beneficial as well as practical form of colonial control should be set beside his contribution to the discourses of anthropology and social observation which developed between the world wars. Significantly for the discussions in this book, he also contributed to the decline of the forceful arguments for the inherently 'Saxon' or 'Germanic' character of English constitutional and legal institutions in the work of Freeman and Stubbs, which was to be challenged by early twentieth-century academic historians.[109] Maine's associations with the legal historians Paul Vinogradoff and Frederick Pollock, who developed socio-historical approaches to medieval law and institutions, are one indication of that link, helping to shift the emphasis of medieval studies away from narratives of constitutional 'progress' to one concerned with detailed analysis and criticism.

Two other direct types of association between empire and civilisation were also made in writings on the English/British past. One was the depiction of imperial achievements as evidence of English progress and providence, and as an opportunity for the exercise of moral agency and a civilising mission. Evolving from accounts contrasting the virtuous character of British imperial expansion with the 'black legend' of Spanish imperial rule, or celebrations of global commercial success, nineteenth-century histories showed empire as a manifestation of virtue, and of the benefits of commercial civilisation.[110] They also acknowledged debates on the merits of empire in which the ideal of protecting 'aboriginal peoples' contested arguments about the moral and material dangers of empire, compared with the benefits of free trade and virtuous internationalism. English positivists and advocates of universal ideals of civilisation and progress struggled to combine their ideas of a single human race whose members could all achieve such aims with the view that it was the responsibility of Europeans to spread those very ideals to less fortunate peoples.[111] Similarly, visions of the establishment of imperial order in India or Africa and of needs to defend the empire competed with the claims of overseas 'English'/'British' settlements as extensions of 'Britain'/'England beyond the UK.

The growth of colonial settlements in Australia, Canada, New Zealand and South Africa was seen not only as evidence of British power and influence, or as territorial gains materially beneficial to the UK, but as the expansion of English/ British civilisation globally. With the development of political, legal and cultural life and institutions derived from British/English originals in the settlement colonies came perceptions of these societies as replications or transplants of England/Britain overseas. These might parallel eighteenth-century views of British settlements in north America, but also represented a particular shift in ideological and historical viewpoints after 1850. From the mid-century, improvements in communication facilitated the flourishing of imperial networks and the ending of convict transportation to Australia, and the opening up of greater material opportunities there and in South Africa and New Zealand encouraged positive views of those settlements.[112] Debates on the value of colonial migration and settlement or on problems of imperial defence, as well as ideas of the colonies of settlement as part of a global British cultural, social and moral presence, shifted attention from British rule in India to that 'British world' in Australia, Canada, South Africa and New Zealand. Reactions to the 1857 uprising in India, the 1865 Morant Bay rising in Jamaica and the Zulu and Afghan wars reinforced tendencies to refocus interests and aspirations on those parts of the empire.

In that context the influential writings of Charles Dilke (*Greater Britain*, 1868, *The problems of Greater Britain*, 1890), John Seeley (*The expansion of England*, 1883) and J.A. Froude (*Oceana*, 1886) gave explicit voice to ideological, but also historicised, views of a global and imperial British civilisation. As discussed below, this involved 'racial' and evolutionary approaches to 'Anglo-Saxon' qualities, and it also established and maintained a view which blended social, constitutional and cultural perspectives on the growth and success of 'English/British' civilisation in the UK and overseas. Froude emphasised the role of empire in regenerating or replacing the damaged culture of modern materialist Britain in its overseas settlements. Dilke backed his racial thinking on 'Greater Britain' with materialist analyses of labour, and references to the export of 'British' civilisation to America as well as British colonies. Seeley reassessed the notion of the 'civilising' mission while urging English people to think more about the colonies of settlement than about British rule in India. Their depictions of the colonies of settlement made reference to character and customs as well as to laws and 'racial' descent.[113]

Empire, race and nation

In celebrating the 'Greater Britain' of colonial settlers who established and maintained British/ English institutions and practices in Africa, Australasia and Canada, distinguished by descent and culture from the other inhabitants, commentators and historians clearly linked empire and nation. Their grounding of 'Englishness' in racialised accounts of distinctive, perhaps inherent, Anglo-Saxon attributes passed down through time and nurturing distinctive institutions extended that link to the varied ideas of race which played a part in nineteenth-century culture and politics. While mid-nineteenth-century politicians tended to rank 'imperial' considerations against or behind domestic, European or international concerns,[114] it is also useful to consider how they were interactive and interwoven as well as competing or incompatible. British views of both imperial and European 'others' often deployed comparable assumptions of racialised identity expressed in historic links between descent, culture and political development. Thus the supposed 'Tartar' origin of the Russians (seen as both European and imperial rivals) was connected to their 'despotic' form of government and 'backwardness'. Racial terminology was used both to differentiate 'English' from other European 'peoples' and to distinguish them from non-Europeans, creating an elaborate spectrum and a complex field of debate and representation. Learned discussion of diversity and identity, like colourful stereotypes of particular races/nations/peoples, brought the language of race to a wide range of audiences.

It is often argued that the nineteenth century saw the emergence and flourishing of racial thought and opinion in particularly powerful forms. Scientific debate on the plural as opposed to unitary character of the human species and the development of evolutionary theories culminating in the impact of Darwin's work and its use by social scientists – like the growing influence of beliefs in inherent 'national' characteristics – are key elements in that argument. The debate around it has evolved in a number of ways since it was developed in the 1970s and 1980s, questioning whether ideas of nation and civilisation were as racialised as has been claimed, and linking notions of race to those of gender, class, religion, criminality and illness (mental or physical).[115] These debates discuss continuities and changes in ideas of race over the period, with some interpretations emphasising their persistent if shifting role during the century, others stressing shifts to more explicit 'racial' views from the 1860s. They also include diverse interpretations of the importance of scientific, cultural and social scientific discourses on racial ideas, although, as Lorimer observes, 'The ambiguous linkages between race and culture were the source of the power and utility of Victorian and Edwardian racial discourse.'[116] Some focus specifically on overlapping meanings of 'nation', 'race' and 'people' in the imperial context of the nineteenth-century UK with its four resident 'nations'/'peoples'. Rather than repeating such arguments, which have extended understanding of all these categories, it will be useful to consider how ideas of race entwined with many other elements in presentations of 'nation' and 'empire' in accounts of the English/British past.

It has already been seen that the terms 'race', 'people' and 'nation' could be used by historians, like other writers, to describe a range of different and sometimes overlapping phenomena, a trend which persisted from the eighteenth into the nineteenth century. For historians of England/Britain, the 'English', and sometimes the Scots or Irish, could be a 'people', 'nation' or 'race' on different pages of the same text.[117] Such ambiguities might reinforce arguments that the role of race in nineteenth-century thinking has been overemphasised or misinterpreted, but also suggest that it was well embedded in thinking about human differences and human institutions. Certainly, references to the 'Anglo-Saxon race', or to the 'Teutonic race' of which Anglo-Saxons were said to be a part, were commonplace in accounts of the early period of English history. Together with comments on their place as the core element of the contemporary 'English', they were typical in most types of historical text. Charles Dickens' *Child's history*, the detailed *Pictorial history*, Green's *History of the English people*, like the works of Keightley or Freeman, vary in their approach, intended readership and indeed their view of 'race', but their regular use of the term normalised it as a way to categorise particular groups of humans. There were important slippages and nuances in this usage, as well as actual controversies over its meanings, but its ubiquitous presence in popular and learned texts made it familiar and acceptable.

From the point of view of historical writing, one of the most important overlaps in this extensive practice was that between ideas of 'race' and of 'nation' – terms often used interchangeably in the nineteenth century, as they had been earlier. It brought ideas about inherited and/or inherent characteristics, whether cultural or biological, which were associated with race close to ideas associating state and political sovereignty and 'peoples' with a supposed common history and, increasingly, to representation in government. By the mid-nineteenth century this overlap had been reinforced by campaigns and debates over political representation in Europe, Latin America, Asia and the Caribbean in which the 'emancipation' of 'natives' was linked to the achievement of enfranchisement of key sections of the population. Historians influenced by this cultural climate could project images of 'nations' as entities whose inherited qualities and political identities might be traced back to the movements of peoples in the fourth and fifth centuries CE, and whose fortunes over subsequent centuries they could recount. They might continue to associate nationhood with religion – as when Taylor wrote of 'Muhammedan nations', and other authors defined the Irish as both 'Celtic' and (superstitiously) Catholic – or with particular institutions, as with 'Turkish' despotism or French 'feudalism' and 'absolutism'. However, these established practices were increasingly combined with references to the inherent 'spirit', 'genius' or indeed deficiencies of particular 'nations', used as tools of historical explanation. From narratives of the French Revolution to descriptions of Flemish merchants in medieval London, or 'the strife between Aryan and Semitic man' in eleventh-century Sicily, race was invoked in this way.[118]

One expression of 'national genius' which could be treated in racial terms was imperial expansion. The nation–empire link was presented in three principal forms. As already noted, imperial and colonial achievements could be presented as evidence of English/British virtue and progress, often linked to notions of inherent national 'spirit' and 'character' which were part of a racialised vocabulary. If earlier authors had contrasted the 'black legend' of Spanish (Catholic) exploitation oppression and enslavement to narratives and celebrations of Protestant Britishness, nineteenth-century texts linked this both to recent material and moral progress, and to depictions of 'Anglo-Saxon' qualities. As Yonge put it when lamenting the failure of Spanish colonialists to follow the 'humane' example of Cortez, 'England is the only nation which has shown a genius for colonisation.' This is echoed by Froude's celebration of Elizabethan seamen and Seeley's statement about 'the natural aptitude for colonization and a faculty for leadership in our race'.[119]

By the mid-nineteenth century political intellectuals like J.S. Mill were also arguing that the possession of a legacy of 'freedom', rule of law and the ability to progress rationally and moderately fitted the 'English'/'British' to be imperial rulers. This argument was established by reference to the *un*fitness of some 'races'/'nations'/'peoples' to rule themselves, just as male propertied political entitlements were justified in terms of the 'unfitness' of the uneducated lower classes, or women, for such entitlements.[120] As Creasy put it in his historical text, *Imperial and colonial constitutions of the Britannic empire* (significantly, including discussion of Ireland), Hottentots, Esquimaux, and Australian aborigines were 'rightly considered' unfit for the franchise. A generation earlier, Keightley (implicitly criticising the reform programme attempted in India in the 1830s) asserted the importance of recognising the unsuitablility of European institutions for the Indian subjects of the British *raj*.[121] This approach combined a negative positioning of colonial subjects in relation to their English/British rulers with a positive affirmation of the benefits to those subjects of strong but virtuous British rule. Dilke made this theme central to his highly racialised reflections on 'Greater Britain', in which inherent qualities separated Britons from (inferior) Maoris or Indians, even if education might benefit the latter. His points reappear in a number of historical texts.[122] This development was not associated with any one political position or philosophy. The 'advanced liberal' J.S. Mill, the avowedly non-partisan Creasy, the 'conservative' Keightley or the supporter of political economy and Cobdenite Taylor all concerned themselves with the fitness of particular 'races' to rule or be ruled. Mill's *Considerations on representative government* distinguished between governmental arrangements suitable for those of British 'blood' and language, and those appropriate for 'others' who lacked it.

Even before the well-known writings of Dilke and Froude on the 'Greater Britain' of white settler colonies, images of the virtue and value of English/British communities overseas were part of narratives of the British past. In his 1853 *Child's history*, Dickens commented both that 'Saxon blood remains unchanged' wherever modern descendants of the Saxons settle, and that 'wherever that race goes, there, law, and industry and safety for life and property and all the great results of steady perseverance are certain to arise.'[123] Mid-nineteenth-century discussion of institutions which might express the distinctive relationship and character of settler colonies, and benefit those communities and the empire, included contributions by writers who wrote historical material as well as being observers or players on the contemporary political scene. Seeley's *Expansion of England* lectures are grounded in the argument that the study of the history of 'Greater Britain' was an essential moral and intellectual basis for future politics, a theme central to his own academic and intellectual career. He describes the colonial empire as 'a mere normal extension of the English race into other lands', 'sharing' population ('of our own blood') as well as institutions, and he considers the relevance of family metaphors (child–parent, mother–stepmother) to describe colonial connections. Froude, who had brought a racialised outlook to his work on English rule in eighteenth-century Ireland, turned to organic plant and tree metaphors and to the image of marriage and divorce to debate the future of relations between the UK and its colonies of settlement. His vision of colonial space as the terrain on which the British race might create lives unspoilt by materialism and industrial exploitation used bodily as well as cultural and spiritual images.[124]

If social and political anxieties of the first half of the century expressed the fears generated among 'respectable' opinion formers by revolutionary politics in France, or popular protest in England and Ireland, later global competition with Germans and Americans stimulated different concerns. In both periods it can be argued that European rivalries had imperial and global dimensions, but from mid-century the specific role of the settler colonies was given greater importance. While there were pragmatic and political reasons for this both in the United Kingdom and in settler colonies, one significant element in the discussion was a specifically historical argument about kinship and nationhood which affirmed the connections between settlers and British/ English institutions and history. As Froude argued, Britons could no longer rely on material supremacy and should shape imperial policy around a sense of their organic racial identity rather than around a cash nexus.[125] Twenty years earlier, Charles Dilke used his travels through the empire to argue for empire as a 'racial' mission, throwing up complex challenges to the dominance and survival of the 'English' or 'Teutonic' race. He mapped racial narratives onto colonial policy, concluding that the well-being of 'our race... as a whole' lay in the just government of Irish and Indians, the strengthening of English colonies of settlement and the planting of English 'free institutions' in Asia and Africa.[126] The threads which linked the empire were understood as being made up of ancestry, qualities and practices carried from Britain overseas and reproduced in Australia, Canada, South Africa or New Zealand. As conflicts in India and Jamaica challenged commitments to universal ideas of civilisation, ideas of inherent racial difference and uncrossable boundaries gained in appeal. For Dilke, 'love of race' was more important than either narrow British patriotism or the 'childish absurdities' of universalist humanitarianism, and manifest in English law and government [127]

Here the narrative of empire and the narrative of the 'British/ English nation' intertwine within mid-nineteenth-century history writing. The story of how 'our nation, from being an inconsiderable horde of savages has arrived at the height of wealth, of power, and of glory' was presented through extensive reference to the mingling, ranking and distinctiveness of the 'race' or 'races' thought to make up the 'English' or 'British'.[128] The effect of early evolutionary thought can be seen, for example, in Goldwin Smith's 1862 argument that 'In the primeval struggle of races for the leadership of humanity the Keltic race, for the most part, ultimately succumbed.' Spencer Walpole linked his comments on the spread of European civilisation to 'savage' societies to remarks about the triumph of the fittest.[129] Many texts focused quite straightforwardly on the supremacy and superiority of Anglo-Saxon ancestry, character (courage, love of freedom, strength, good sense) and institutions (local governance, royal councils, the rule of law for all). Some, like Creasy in his *Rise and progress of the English constitution*, emphasised the importance of fusion between 'British', 'Saxon', 'Danish' and 'Norman' elements in constituting the traditions and qualities of the 'English' – a trope frequently repeated elsewhere. Others sought to distinguish and rank these elements. Depictions of the beneficial combination of 'Celtic' and 'Saxon' features in an enhanced 'English race' or 'nation' were a typical feature of this approach.[130] Historical practice was thus neither homogeneous nor consistent, but whatever perspective was taken tended to affirm relationships between 'racial' characteristics (however understood), forms of government and 'national' achievements in empire building.

These 'racial' characteristics were still presented as a many-sided phenomenon. At the core of depictions of the 'distinctive nature' of 'Saxons' or English were references to ancestry, descent and blood, which spoke of qualities passed down the generations as a biological inheritance. This was as much a discourse of family kinship as of 'scientific' racial theory, and the 'inherited' features pointed out by historians were a mixture of cultural, character and physical traits, associating both 'nature' and social environment with 'racial' or 'national' identity. Such discourses were, of course, often used in conversations about resemblances between children and parents, or in discussion about whether 'aristocratic' or 'underclass' characteristics passed from one generation to another, making this approach to the past a familiar one. It echoed a long-established set of depictions of colonial migrations and settlements as the spread of a 'family', and of emergent self-government in such colonies (whether the independent United States in the 1770s or the constitutional changes of the 1850s and 1860s) as the coming of colonial 'children' to maturity. Discourses of empire-as-family thus combined ideas of a racial identity shared by the English/British and settlers in the colonies with notions of an empire as a 'family' of settlements and dominions institutionally connected to their English 'mother'.

Racial or familial images also had a cultural dimension in which social habits or religious beliefs were included among the inherited qualities seen as distinctively English'/'British'. The association of English/British identity and superiority with Protestantism, established in eighteenth-century history writing as well as in politics and popular culture, was understood as a factor in national character not just a matter of historic religious affiliation. Imaginative depictions of the legacy of Saxon institutions and racial qualities were accompanied, and in some cases overshadowed, by portrayals of the contribution made by English Protestantism to the formation of English and sometimes Scottish character. There might even be a reverse polarity whereby some accounts of the dissident fourteenth-century English religious preacher and writer John Wycliffe suggested both that he prefigured the sixteenth-century Reformation and that he demonstrated a congenital English affinity for Protestantism.[131] The 'providential' development of Protestant practice and institutions, and its central role in the political changes of the seventeenth century, could be linked to a story of national/racial 'advance' to prosperity and global power in which those achievements were presented as the product of religious values embedded in the 'national character'. This might be seen in relatively undefined terms, or linked to support for broad church Anglicanism, or for more evangelical Protestantism, but in either case linked divine providence with imperial destiny.

The association of religious and racial attributes added its own element to accounts of empire and more generally to the language of historical writing. Such an association allowed Hindu and Muslim Indian, or Catholic Irish and French Canadian subjects to take their place under the improving and moral authority of a (Protestant) empire. Just as 'free', 'just' and 'constitutional' government was seen as an expression of 'English' qualities, so Catholicism and Islam had been viewed as formative of Indian or Irish character (superstitious, weak, degenerate violent, corrupt, subservient) and favourable to 'despotism' since the seventeenth century. For some, British shock at the violent opposition of Indians to British rule in 1857 could be compared to English reactions to violence in Ireland in 1641.[132] For some historians, the benefits and duties of British imperial rule might include the provision of opportunities for 'native' subjects to learn and 'progress' under English/British tutelage, but the role of the 'superior' race as models, guides, tutors and judges of that 'progress' was intrinsic to that process. For others, the intrinsic and inherent character of these subjects simply meant that they were best off under the benevolent authority of an 'advanced' race. The interconnections between historically minded commentators on India and Ireland like Froude and Fitzjames Stephen, like those between administrators and politicians, bonded 'race', 'nations' and 'empire' within historical writing and political debate.[133]

Associations between ideas of race and civilisation are clearly in play in discussion of a 'Greater Britain' extending across the world, and of the 'Irish question' which intermittently but persistently preoccupied commentators and writers of history as well as politicians from the 1860s. The politics of land issues, of nationalist and unionist controversy, and of religious or parliamentary partisanship, all surfaced in historical writing, which in turn was deployed to argue such politics. In her presentation of two volumes of document transcripts dealing with the uprisings and killings in Ireland in 1641, demonstrating the role of the 'native Irish', the historian Mary Hickson claimed descent from 'O'Donnell's and O'Sullivan's' as well as 'Saxon' origins. Like Froude, who wrote an enthusiastic preface to the work, Hickson linked her attempt to rebalance views which emphasised British 'crimes' and downplayed Irish 'atrocities' to the ongoing politics of Irish nationalism in the 1880s. While challenging the 'demagogues' and historians of their own times who looked at wrongs done to the 'native Irish' rather than their violent behaviour, they framed the controversy over 1641 in racial terms. Hickson argued that 'the Ireland of today is the Ireland of the mixed race,' exemplified in her ancestry, and in a sympathy for Irish interests comparable to Lecky's, noted by Froude as greater than his own. This allowed her to lambast 'sentiment and sorrow' over Irish wrongs, and to celebrate how British settlement in Ulster created 'the Ulster of today...the garden of Ireland filled with the sturdy industrious freedom loving men of the mixed race'.[134] If the work of Carlyle, Goldwin Smith, Stephens and Froude established British versions of this relationship, as Macaulay had done earlier, Lecky – like his predecessor Cook Taylor – expressed more complex Anglo-Irish perceptions.[135]

Growing interest in colonies of settlement after 1860 reinforced links between race, legal and political institutions and civilisation in ideas and images of the 'English'/'British', whether within the UK or in the empire generally. These ideas might well be flavoured with anxiety and uncertainty as much as confidence, so that Dilke's celebration of 'Greater Britain' dealt as much with the threats to 'British' hegemony posed by Indian, Irish or 'negro' groups as with the superiority of the 'British race' over others. His contemporary polemic, underpinned by references to the history of the British in the USA, India and elsewhere, is similar to views expressed in explicitly historical texts. While increasing use of the term 'race' with biological or phenotypical connotations is a feature of the last third of the nineteenth century, this was not accompanied by the disappearance of established political and cultural usages for 'race' or 'nation'. More significant is the complexity and instability of discourses about the 'racial' or 'national' identity of the constituent peoples of the UK and of the empire as a whole. The racial 'otherness' of the Scots and Irish within the UK might appear differently when they were depicted undertaking imperial activities beyond it, just as differences between groups of Europeans might be central to some historical depictions, but less so in global discussions. The shift towards greater interest in the colonies of 'English'/'British settlement did not so much replace interest in India as set it in new depictions of empire and establish parallel discussions, as seen from the space devoted by Dilke and Seeley to the British *raj*.

Conclusions

In reflecting on the role of empire in history writing in the nineteenth century it can be argued that empire shaped important trends within the diversity of that writing. The work of Mandler and Porter offers useful correctives to any simplistic picture of the 'pervasiveness' of empire in nineteenth-century cultures or politics within the UK. It is a reminder that UK writers and their readerships were as concerned with the local, the immediate and the specific as with the patterns of global and imperial connection which influenced their lives over the century. It also reminds us that the meanings of 'nation' and 'patriotism' were multiple and shifting, and, as Robert Colls has shown, could combine local and imperial elements.[136] However, other work has built a powerful case for the interactive and mutually constitutive relationships between developments within the UK and those in its imperial and global domains. While these developments have been shown to play a part in material life, in religious activity, in elite and popular cultural production and in party political activity, it is the traces of such interactions within history writing which have been the concern of this chapter.

Building on the practices and patterns established by predecessors, nineteenth-century texts were comfortable with the inclusion of imperial topics in their 'English' or 'British' narratives, and a growing number of them took imperial subjects as their specific topic. They also used notions of 'civilisation', 'progress, 'race' and 'nation' which were inflected by global and colonial associations. What was added to those repertoires during the nineteenth century was patriotic and imperial confidence in the moral and mental qualities of the 'English'/'British' which made global primacy not just the manifestation of power or material success but of virtue, liberty, Protestantism and reason. Critics of colonial expansion and expenditure were as likely to express their views in those terms as were supporters of imperial rule and reform. The 'English' or 'British' might be seen as beacons of progress enlightening others, or as actively managing colonial subjects, whether to raise them up to 'English' standards or to defend those standards against barbarous or decadent threats. These different roles were depicted in historical accounts as well as in contemporary commentaries.

Englishness, global mission and patriotism became entwined in the messages sent to school pupils, general readers and students by narratives of UK history. Historical understandings of empire as an ethnically as well as politically English project made their contribution to, and drew on, increasingly racialised discourses in politics and daily life. However, as Mandler has argued for racial thought in general, historical accounts of nation and race relied on ideas of civilisation as much as on biology or anthropology, and they combined universalist views of human history with a sharp sense of human difference.[137] They were also shaped by, and shaped, the discourses of class and gender developing in response to demands by popular, women's and labour critiques of exclusionary versions of citizenship or membership in the 'nation' (and its empire). Issues of inclusion and governance within the UK were pursued in accounts which juggled manliness, racial hierarchy and class attributes in histories of Chartism, Irish politics and colonial crises, flavouring patriotic narratives of the 'British'/'English' past with these elements. It is within this complex set of practices that empire established its place.

Notes

1 T.B. Macaulay, 'Sir John Malcolm's life of Lord Clive', in T.B. Macaulay, *Critical and miscellaneous essays*, 5 vols, London, 1841, vol. 3, p. 85 (original used here).

2 W. Cooke Taylor, *The student's manual of modern history: containing the rise and progress of the principal European nations, their political history and the changes in their social conditions, with a history of the colonies founded by Europeans*, 8th edn, revised and edited by C. Duke Yonge, London, 1866.

3 See H.C.G. Mathew, 'William Cooke Taylor', in *Oxford Dictionary of National Biography*, Oxford, 2004; P. Maume, 'The orientalism of William Cooke Taylor', in R. Blyth and K. Jeffery [eds.], *The British empire and its contested pasts*, Dublin, 2009.

4 A. Brundage, *The people's historian: John Richard Green and the writing of history on Victorian England*, Lanham, MD, 1994, p. 14.

5 Taylor, *Student's manual*, p. v; C. Duke Yonge, *Constitutional history of England*, London, 1881.

6 Studies exploring these issues include C. Hall, K. McLelland and J. Rendall, *Defining the Victorian nation*, Cambridge, 2000; R. Liedtke [ed.], *The emancipation of Catholics, Jews and Protestants: minorities and the nation state in nineteenth-century Europe*, Manchester, 1999; M. Poovey, *Making a social body: British cultural formation, 1830–1864*, Chicago, 1995; J. Parry, *The rise and fall of Liberal government in Victorian*

Britain, New Haven, CT, 1993; J. Parry, *The politics of patriotism: English liberalism, national identity, and Europe, 1830–1886*, Cambridge, 2006; A. Howe, *Free trade and liberal England*, Oxford, 1997; E. Biagini, *Liberty retrenchment and reform*, Cambridge, 1992; E. Biagini, *British democracy and Irish nationalism, 1876–1906*, Cambridge, 2007; M. Finn, *After Chartism: class and nation in English politics*, Cambridge, 1993; C. Hall, *Civilising subjects*, Cambridge, 2002; R. Bellamy [ed.], *Victorian liberalism*, London, 1990.

7   C. Simmons, *Reversing the conquest: history and myth in nineteenth-century literature*, Brunswick, NJ, 1990, pp. 125–33; C. Hall, 'Macaulay: a liberal historian?', in S. Gunn and J. Vernon [eds.], *The peculiarities of liberal modernity in imperial Britain*, Berkeley, CA, 2011; C. Hall, 'At home with history: Macaulay and the *History of England*', in C. Hall and S. Rose [eds.] *At home with the empire*, Cambridge, 2006; C. Hall, *Macaulay and son*, New Haven, CT, 2012.

8   T. Carlyle, 'Chartism' (1839); the Chartist poem is quoted in C. Hill, 'The Norman Yoke', C. Hill, *Puritanism and revolution* (1958), London, 1968.

9   Hall *et al.*, *Defining the Victorian nation*; Parry, *Politics of patriotism*; Gunn and Vernon, *Peculiarities of liberal modernity*, chs 1, 5, 7, 10, 11; J. Lawrence, *Speaking for the people: party, language and popular politics in England, 1867–1914*, Cambridge, 1998; Bellamy, *Victorian liberalism*.

10 P. Mandler, *Aristocratic government in an age of reform: Whigs and liberals, 1830–52*, Oxford, 1990; M. Taylor, *The decline of British radicalism, 1847–60*, Oxford, 1995; Finn, *After Chartism*; J. Vernon, *Politics and the people: a study in English political culture, 1815–67*, Cambridge, 1993; J. Vernon [ed.], *Re-reading the constitution: new narratives in the political history of England's long nineteenth century*, Cambridge, 1996; Parry, *Rise and fall of Liberal government*; Biagini, *Liberty, retrenchment and reform*.

11 H.C. Mathew, 'Edward Shepherd Creasy', in *Oxford Dictionary of National Biography*, Oxford, 2004.

12 E.S. Creasy, *The rise and progress of the English constitution*, 3rd edn, London, 1856, pp. vii, 2, 3, 10, 27.

13 Creasy, *Rise and progress of the English constitution*, p. 354.

14 E.S. Creasy, *The spirit of historical study*, London, 1840, pp. 15, 30; see T. Arnold, *Introductory lecture on modern history*, London, 1843.

15 V. Chancellor, *History for their masters: opinion in the English history textbook, 1800–1914*, Bath, 1970.

16 See the debates in B. Porter, *The absent-minded imperialists*, Oxford, 2004; P. Mandler, '"Race" and "nation" in mid-Victorian thought', in S. Collini *et al.* [eds.], *History, religion, and culture: British intellectual history, 1795–1950*, Cambridge, 2000; D. Cannadine, *Ornamentalism*, London, 2002; *Journal of Colonialism and Colonial History*, 3:1 (2002), special issue 'From Occidentalism to ornamentalism: empire and

difference in history'; A. Burton, 'Rules of thumb: British history and imperial culture in nineteenth- and twentieth-century Britain', *Journal of Women's History*, vol. 3, no. 1 (1994), pp. 483–501; A. Burton, 'Who needs the nation? Interrogating British history', *Journal of Historical Sociology*, 10:3 (1997), pp. 227–48.

17 M. Harper and S. Constantine, *Migration and the British Empire*, Oxford, 2010; C. Bridge and K. Fedorowich [eds.], *The British world diaspora*, London, 2003; K. Fedorowich and A. Thompson [eds.], *Empire, identity, and migration in the British world*, Manchester, 2010; R. Woodman, *History of the British merchant navy*, 5 vols, Stroud, 2008–10, vol. 3; H. Streets, *Martial races: the military, race, and masculinity in British imperial culture*, Manchester, 2004; D. Killingray and D. Omissi [eds.], *Guardians of empire*, Manchester, 1999, chs 1, 3; I. Land, *War, nationalism and the British sailor*, Basingstoke, 2009; M. Conley, *From Jack Tar to Union Jack*, Manchester, 2009.

18 Parry, *Politics and patriotism*; A. MacFie, *The eastern question*, Harlow, 1996; M. Kovic, *Disraeli and the eastern question*, Oxford, 2011; R. Harrison, *Gladstone's imperialism in Egypt*, Lanham, MD, 1995; R. Price, *Making empire*, Cambridge, 2008; R. Bickers, *The scramble for China*, London, 2011; J. Onley, *The Arabian frontier of the British raj*, Oxford, 2007.

19 See R. Young, *The idea of English ethnicity*, Oxford, 2008, ch. 4.

20 G. Dawson, *Soldier heroes*, London, 1994; H. Adams, *The weaver boy who became a missionary*, London, 1867; J. Roberts, *The life and explorations of David Livingstone*, London, 1874; F. Williams, *General Havelock and Christian soldiership*, London, 1858; J. Marshman, *Memoirs of Sir Henry Havelock*, London, 1860; T. Spruzen, *The battle of Rorke's Drift and other poems*, London, 1880; E. Pfeiffer, *The fight at Rorke's Drift*, London, 1879; H. Little, *Henry Morton Stanley*, London, 1890; A. Brice, *Henry M. Stanley, the African explorer*, London, 1890; C. Beke, *The sources of the Nile*, London, 1860; on the work and fame of Richard Burton as an explorer see D. Kennedy, *The highly civilised man*, Cambridge, MA, 2005, chs 3, 4; and M. Lovell, *A rage to live*, New York, 1998, chs 8, 9, 14–16; W. Frith, *General Gordon, or the man of faith*, London, 1884.

21 For example C. Hall *et al.*, *Defining the Victorian nation*, Cambridge, 2000; C. Midgley, 'Bringing the empire home', and J. Rendall, 'The condition of women', in Hall and Rose, *At home with the empire*; A. Burton, '"States of injury": Josephine Butler on slavery, citizenship and the Boer War', in I. Fletcher *et al.* [eds.], *Women's suffrage in the British Empire*, London, 2000; R. Gray, *The factory question and industrial England*, Cambridge, 1996, pp. 37–47; M. Cunliffe, *Chattel slavery and wage slavery*, Athens, CA, 1979.

22 For example, the essays in R. Congreve [ed.], *International policy: essays on the foreign relations of England*, London, 1866; Congreve, the leading

UK promoter of Auguste Comte's 'religion of humanity', also wrote against British rule in India, Gibraltar and Ireland, the Ashanti war and the annexation of the Transvaal.

23 Dawson, *Soldier heroes*; S. West [ed.], *The Victorians and race*, Menston, 1996; J. Kember *et al.* [eds.], *Popular exhibitions, science, and showmanship, 1840–1914*, London, 2012, chs 6, 10, 11; H. Waters, *Racism on the Victorian stage*, Cambridge, 2009; B. Lindfors, *Africans on stage*, Bloomington, IN, 1999; N. Al-Taee, *Representations of the orient in western music*, Aldershot, 2010; N. Tromans [ed.], *The lure of the east*, New Haven, CT, 2008; J. Sweetman, *The oriental obsession*, Cambridge, 1988; S. Mathur, *India by design: colonial history and cultural display*, Berkeley, CA, 2007; A. Coombes, *Reinventing Africa*, New Haven, CT, 1994; E. Edwards [ed.], *Anthropology and photography*, New Haven, CT, 1992; U. Mukherjee, *Crime and empire: the colony and nineteenth-century fictions of crime*, Oxford, 2003; J. Codell [ed.], *Imperial co-histories: national identities and the national and colonial press*, London, 2003; F. Driver and L. Martins [eds.], *Tropical visions in an age of empire*, Chicago, 2005.

24 P. Mandler, '"Race" and "nation" in Victorian thought', in S. Collini *et al.* [eds.], *History, religion and culture: British intellectual history, 1750–1950*, Cambridge, 2000 takes a sceptical view; other perspectives can be found in M. Sinha 'Gender in the critiques of colonialism and nationalism', in J. Scott [ed.], *Feminism and history*, Oxford, 1996; M. Sinha, *Colonial masculinity*, Manchester, 1995, introduction; J. Epstein, 'Taking class notes on empire', in Hall and Rose, *At home with the empire*; C. Hall, *White, male, and middle class*, Cambridge, 1992; C. Hall, '"From Greenland's icy mountains"…ethnicity, race and nation in mid-nineteenth-century England', *Gender and History*, vol. 5, no. 2 (1993), pp. 212–30; M. Ferguson, *Subject to others: British women writers and colonial slavery*, London, 1992; J. Walkowitz, 'The Indian woman, the flower girl and the Jew', *Victorian Studies*, vol. 42, no. 1 (1998), pp. 3–46.

25 W. Booth, *Darkest England*, London, 1890; on this theme see J. Marriott, *The other empire: metropolis, India and progress in the colonial imagination*, Manchester, 2003.

26 N. Stepan, *The idea of race in science*, London, 1982; D. Lorimer, 'Race, science, and culture: historical continuities and discontinuities 1850–1914', in West, *Victorians and race*.

27 C. Kidd, *The forging of races: race and scripture in the Protestant Atlantic world, 1600–2000*, Cambridge, 2008, chs 5, 6; G. Stocking, *Victorian anthropology*, New York, 1987.

28 S. Gilley and W. Sheils [eds.], *A history of religion in Britain*, Oxford, 1994, part 3; S. Brown, *Providence and empire*, Harlow, 2008; J. Livingston, *Religious thought in the Victorian age*, London, 2007; D. Hempton, *Religion and political culture in Britain and Ireland*, Cambridge,

1996; D. Bebbington, *Evangelicalism in modern Britain*, London, 1989; H. McLeod, *Religion and society in England, 1850–1914*, London, 1996.

29 R. Brent, *Liberal Anglican politics*, Oxford, 1987; J. Parry, *Democracy and religion: Gladstone and the Liberal Party, 1867–75*, Cambridge, 1986: G. Machin, *Politics and the churches in Great Britain, 1832–1868*, Oxford, 1977; G. Machin, *Politics and the churches in Great Britain, 1868–1921*, Oxford, 1987.

30 C. Brown, *The death of Christian Britain*, London, 2000; McCleod, *Religion and society in England 1850–1914*, Basingstoke, Macmillan, 1996.

31 H. Carey, *God's empire: religion and colonialism in the British world*, Cambridge, 2011, parts 1, 3; R. Strong, *Anglicanism in the British empire*, Oxford, 2007; J. Wolffe, *Religion in Victorian Britain, vol. 5: culture and empire*, Manchester, 1997.

32 A. Porter, *Religion versus empire: British Protestant missionaries and overseas expansion*, Manchester, 2004; J. Cox, *The British missionary enterprise since 1700*, London, 2008; H. Carey [ed.], *Empires of religion*, Basingstoke, 2008; N. Etherington [ed.], *Missions and empire*, Oxford, 2005.

33 For example, H. Adams, *Life and adventures of David Livingstone*, 22 edns, 1867–90, 51,000 copies sold by 1881 plus four other lives running to several editions; J. Moffat, *The lives of Robert and Mary Moffat*, 10 edns, 1885–90; *Memoirs of Mrs Rebecca Wakefield*, London, 1876, 1879; E.R. Pitman, *Heroines of the mission field*, London, 1880, 1897.

34 A. Porter, 'Religion and empire', *Journal of Imperial and Commonwealth History*, vol. 20, no. 2 (1992), pp. 370–90; R. Bickers [ed.], *Missionary encounters*, London, 1995, chs 1, 3, 7, 9; R. Semple, *Missionary women*, London, 2003.

35 S. Thorne, 'Religion and empire at home', in Hall and Rose, *At home with the empire*; and S. Thorne, *Congregational missions and the making of an imperial culture in nineteenth-century England*, Stanford, CA, 1999.

36 Marriott, *The other empire*; M. Roberts, *Making English morals*, Cambridge, 2009; K. Lawes [ed.], *Paternalism and politics*, London, 2000; P. Murray, *Poverty and welfare, 1830–1914*, London, 1999; A. Summers, *Female lives, moral states*, Newbury, 2000.

37 A. Twells, *Civilising missions and the English middle class*, Basingstoke, 2009; E. Breitenbach, *Empire and Scottish society*, Edinburgh, 2009.

38 G. Sims, *How the poor live; and, horrible London*, London, 1889 (a collection of articles originally published 1879–83), p. 3; H. Hutton, 'England and the uncivilised communities', in R. Congreve [ed.], *International policy: essays on the foreign relations of England* (1866), 2nd ed, London, Chapman and Hall, 1884, (a set of essays advocating approaches to international and colonial policy shaped by the positivist and humanitarian ideas of the French thinker Auguste Comte), p. 311; on Congreve, the positivists and anti imperialism, see G. Claeys,

Imperial sceptics: British critics of empire, 1850–1920, Cambridge, 2010, pp. 21–45, 58–83, 97–124; F. Galton, 'Hereditary talent and character', *Macmillan's Magazine*, vol. 12, 1865, pp. 157–66, 318–27.

39 J. Heartfield, *The Aborigines Protection Society, 1836–1909*, London, 2011.

40 J. Fisher and A. Best [eds.], *On the fringes of diplomacy*, Aldershot, 2011; J. MacKenzie, 'Passion or indifference: popular imperialism in Britain', in J. MacKenzie[ed.], *European empires and the people*, Manchester, 2011; Codell, *Imperial co–histories*; D. Finkelstein and D. Peers [eds.], *Negotiating India in the nineteenth-century media*, New York, 2000; S. Potter, *News and the British world: the emergence of an imperial press system*, Oxford, 2003, chs 1, 3, 5.

41 R. Mitchell, *Picturing the past: English history in text and image*, Oxford, 2000, pp. 57–60, 63–5.

42 S. Heathorn, *For home, country and race: constructing gender, class and Englishness in the elementary school, 1880–1914*, Toronto, 2000, pp. 7–11, 226; A. Briggs, *A history of Longmans*, London, 2008.

43 K. Castle, *Britannia's children: reading colonialism through children's books and magazines*, Manchester, 1996; Mitchell, *Picturing the past*.

44 Julia Corner (1798–1875), a printer's daughter, wrote and adapted histories of areas of the world from Ireland to China as well as novels, children's religious and educational texts, plays and fairy tales, between the 1830s and the 1870s.

45 C.W. Tait, *Analysis of English history*, London, 1878.

46 For example, G. Gleig, *The family history of England*, London, 1836, pp. 111–15, W. Angus, *History of England*, Glasgow, 1837, pp. 211–14; C. Yonge, *History of England*, London, 1857, pp. 708–9; T. Birkby, *History of England*, London, 1870, pp. 266–8; E. Thompson, *History of England*, London, 1878, p. 300.

47 J. Edwards, *A concise history of England*, London, 1860, pp. vi, 359.

48 Creasy, *Rise and progress of the English constitution*, 4th edn, London, 1892, p. 347.

49 T. Keightley, *The history of England*, London, 1839, pp. 25–30; T. Birkby, *History of England*, London, 1870, p. 210; E. Sanderson, *History of the British empire*, London, 1882, p. 309; W. Angus, *History of England*, London, 1839, p. 199.

50 See, for example, Yonge, *History of England*, 1871, pp. 694–5, 743–4, 767, 813.

51 T. Erskine May, *Constitutional history of England*, 2 vols, Boston, 1864, vol. 2, p. 546; see also Yonge, *History of England*, 1871, pp. 78–9, 98–9, 245–6, 252, 352, 406–8.

52 G. Gleig, *The family history of England*, 3 vols, London, 1836, vol. 2, pp. 330–2; vol. 3, p. 171; Taylor, *Student's manual*, pp. 413–14, 452–4; Yonge, *The history of England*, 1857, p. 726; J.R. Green, *Short history of the*

English people (1874), London, Folio Society reprint, 1992, pp. 822–6, 828.

53 J. Wolffe, *The Protestant crusade in Great Britain, 1829–1860*, Oxford, 1991; Machin, *Politics and the churches, 1832–68*; on Roman Catholic emancipation see Gleig, *Family history*, vol. 3; Angus, *History of England*, pp. 256–7; Keightley, *History of England*, p. 519; H. White, *History of Great Britain and Ireland*, London, 1850, pp. 396–7; Edwards, *Concise history*, p. 238; Yonge, *History of England*, p. 806.

54 G. Smith, *Irish history and Irish character*, London, 1861; see also M. Calcott, *Little Arthur's history of England*, London, 1835, p. 210, Gleig, *Family history*, vol. 3, pp. 93, 171.

55 C. Kinealy, At home with the empire: the example of Ireland', in Hall and Rose, *At home with the empire*; T. Mcdonough [ed.], *Was Ireland a colony?*, Dublin, 2005.

56 T.B. Macaulay, *History of England* (1849), 6 vols, London, 1913, vol. 4, p. 2082.

57 See B. Worden, 'The Victorians and Oliver Cromwell', in Collini *et al.*, *History, religion, and culture*, pp. 134–5; T. Lang, *Victorians and the Stuart heritage*, Cambridge, 1995, p. 190; R. Samuel, 'Grand narratives', *History Workshop Journal*, no. 29, 1990, pp. 120–33.

58 Green, *Short history*, p. 857; May, *Constitutional history*, vol. 2, pp. 508–9.

59 Taylor, *Student's manual*, pp. 532–4; Keightley, *History of England*, vol. 3, pp. 461–5; Green, *Short history*, vol. 4, pp. 1709–11, 1740–1; Mrs Markham, *History of England...for the use of young persons* (editions from 1827 to 1891), London, 1872, pp. 445–6.

60 H. Maine, *Village communities east and west*, London, 1872, pp. 231, 271; K. Mantena, *Alibis of empire: Henry Maine and the ends of liberal imperialism*, Princeton, 2010, chs 2, 3.

61 Creasy, *The imperial and colonial constitutions of the Britannic empire*, London, 1872, pp. 36–7; see also Yonge, *Constitutional history of England*, London, 1882, pp. 427–9.

62 Green, *Short history*, pp. 3–4.

63 W. Stubbs, *Constitutional history*, 3rd edn, Oxford, 1876; W. Stubbs, *Seventeen lectures on the study of modern and medieval history*, Oxford, 1887, 'Introduction', p. 70.

64 C. Hall, 'Macaulay's nation', *Victorian Studies*, 51, no.3 (2009), pp. 505–23; Hall, 'At home with history'; C. Hall, 'Macaulay: a liberal historian?'.

65 See C. Knight, *The popular history of England*, 8 vols, London, 1856–62, introduction; Yonge, *History of England*, p. 841.

66 J.A. Froude 'The *Edinburgh Review* and Mr Froude's *History*', *Fraser's Magazine*, September 1858, pp. 359–78, the key passage is on pp. 375–7; Macaulay is quoted in G. Trevelyan, *Life and Letters of Lord Macaulay*, 2 vols, 1876, vol. 2, pp. 359–60; Harrison's views are quoted in Claeys, *Imperial sceptics*, pp. 83–4.

67 G. Smith, 'Review of Froude's *History of England*', *Edinburgh Review*, July 1858, pp. 206–52; Froude, 'The *Edinburgh Review*'; Smith responded in *Edinburgh Review*, October 1858, pp. 586–94.

68 Creasy, *Rise and progress of the English constitution*, pp. 339–40, 207; Mrs Markham, *Children's history*, 1851, p. 547, Edwards, *Concise history*, p. 243; T. Birkby, *History of England*, London, 1870, pp. 327–9; Yonge, *Constitutional history*, 1882, pp. 352–4.

69 Hall *et al.*, *Defining the Victorian nation*.

70 See Mitchell, *Picturing the past*, ch. 6.

71 Keightley, *History of England*, p. 328.

72 G. Smith, *Three English statesmen*, London, 1867 (still in print fifteen years later).

73 Knight, *Popular history*, 8 vols, 1862, vol. 1, p. 2; J.A. Froude, 'England's forgotten worthies', published in J.A. Froude, *Short studies on great subjects*', London, 1867 (reprinted regularly through the century and in the twentieth century); J.A. Froude, *Oceana, or, England and her colonies*, London, 1886 (five editions that year, more subsequently).

74 Stubbs, *Seventeen lectures*; C. Yonge, *Three centuries of modern history*, London, 1872, p. 78; E.A Freeman, *The methods of historical study...with the inaugural lecture of the office of the historical professor*, London, 1886, p. 9.

75 See D. Bell, *The idea of Greater Britain: empire and the future of world order, 1860–1900*, Princeton, 2007; J. Kendle, *Ireland and the federal solution*, Ontario, 1989; Hall *et al.*, *Defining the Victorian nation*.

76 Bell, *The idea of Greater Britain*; E. Freeman, *History and conquests of the Saracens*, London, 1876.

77 Froude, *Oceana*; J.R. Seeley, *The expansion of England*, London, 1883.

78 Froude, *Oceana*, pp. 2–16, 385–8; Seeley. *Expansion of England*, pp. 1–16, 293–308.

79 Macaulay, *History of England*, 1913, vol. 1, p. 2.

80 C.Knight, *School history of England*, London, Bradbury & Evans, p. 881; compare J. Corner, *History of England*, London, 1870, pp. 297–8; Taylor, *Student's manual*, pp. 473–6.

81 Macaulay, *History of England*, 1913, vol. 1, pp. 1, 23, 112–13 180, 191 276, 284, 296, 301, 332, 339, 362, 365, 418, 423.

82 Yonge, *History of England*, 1857, p. 842.

83 W. Cooke Taylor, *The history of Mohammedanism*, London, 1834, 1839, 1851; W. Cooke Taylor, *A popular history of British India*, London, 1842; W. Cooke Taylor, *Memoir of the first centenary of the earliest Protestant mission at Madras*, London, 1847; W. Cooke Taylor, *Ancient and modern India*, London, 1851, 1857.

84 S. Walpole, *A history of England from the conclusion of the great war in 1815*, London, 1878, p. 433.

85 G.R. Gleig, *Life of Sir Thomas Munro late Governor of Madras*, London, 1830, 1831, 1849; G.R. Gleig, *History of the British empire in India*, 4 vols,

London, 1830–35, G.R. Gleig, *Memoirs of the life of Warren Hastings*, London, 1841; G.R. Gleig, *Sale's Brigade in Afghanistan*, London, 1846, 1861, 1879; G.R. Gleig, *Life of Robert, first Lord Clive*, London, 1848, 1861, 1869, 1907; G.R. Gleig, *History of the British colonies*, London, 1851; G.R. Gleig, *India and its army: an essay*, London, 1857.

86 Gleig, *Family history*, 1836, vol. 2, pp. 135–6; Angus, *History of England*, 1839, p. 113; Keightley, *History of England*, vol. 2, pp. 317–18; Corner, *History of England*, 1840, p. 192; an exception is Calcott, *Little Arthur's history*, p. 149.

87 Smith, *Irish history and Irish character*, pp. 1, 194.

88 Smith, *Irish history and Irish character*, pp. 5, 19, 33, 56, 60–1, 88–91, 99–100, 120, 134.

89 J.A. Froude, *The English in Ireland in the eighteenth century*, 3 vols, London, Longmans Green, 1872–74, vol. 1, pp. 68–70, pp. 120–35; vol. 2, pp. 398–400, 486–9; vol. 3, pp. 1–5, 558.

90 Keightley, *History of England*, vol. 3, p. 523; S. O'Siochain [ed.], *Social thought on Ireland in the nineteenth century*, Dublin, 2009 has discussions of Martineau, J.S. Mill, Froude and Maine.

91 Quoted in D. Macartney, *W.E.H. Lecky, historian and politician*, Dublin, 1994, pp. 98–9.

92 Yonge, *Three centuries of modern history*, 1872, pp. 330–8, 355.

93 Taylor, *Student's manual of modern history*, p. 562.

94 E. Freeman, *The Ottoman power in Europe*, London, 1877, pp. 11–13, 54–68.

95 Macaulay, *History of England*, vol. 2; Keightley, *History of England*, vol. 3, p. 431; Yonge, *History of England*, p. 655; Taylor, *Student's manual*, 1866, pp. 53–4.

96 Keightley, *History of England*, vol. 1, pp. 409, 417.

97 Keightley, *History of England*, vol. 1, p. 465; Edwards, *Concise history*, p. 245.

98 H. Martineau, *British rule in India*, London, 1857, pp. 333, 184–5, 287–91, 355; E. Freeman, *The chief periods of European history: six lectures read in the University of Oxford*, London, 1885, pp. 5–6.

99 *Aunt Anne's history of England on Christian principles*, London, 1849, p. 4; Edwards, *Concise history of England*, pp. 3–4; G. Craik, *Pictorial history of England*, 7 vols, London, 1854–58, vol. 4, p. 838; E. Sanderson, *History of the British Empire*, London, 1882, p. 14.

100 Walpole, *History of England*, vol. 5, pp. 453, 68–9.

101 see Marriott, *The other empire*; R. Phillips, *Sex, politics, and empire: a postcolonial geography*, Manchester, 2006; A. Lester, *Imperial networks: creating identities in nineteenth-century South Africa and Britain*, London, 2001; D. Lambert and A. Lester [eds.], *Colonial lives across the British empire*, Cambridge, 2006; P. Levine, *Prostitution, race, and empire: policing venereal disease in the British empire*, London, 2003.

102 Taylor, *Student's manual*, p. v; Gleig, *Family history*, vol.1, pp. 140–2, vol. 2, p. 147; J. Lingard, *A history of England from the first invasion by the Romans*, 10 vols. 3rd ed. London, Mawman, 1825, vol. 1, pp. 12–13, 86–7, 103, 478; J. Corner, *India: pictorial, descriptive and historical*, London, 1834, pp. 6, 30–1; G. Craik [ed.], *Pictorial history of England*, 4 vols, London, C. Knight, 1838 (later versions ran to 9 volumes), vol. 1, pp. 134–6, 262, 658–9; vol. 2, pp. 318; vol. 4, p. 838; H. Hallam, *A view of the state of Europe in the Middle Ages*, (1826), new ed., 3 vols, London, 1878, vol. 1, pp. 269–70, 393–4; vol. 2, pp. 36, 38, 104, 115, 123, 141–2, 321, 351; vol. 3, pp. 269, 307, 374–5.

103 The densest single treatment of these themes is Stocking, *Victorian anthropology*, chs 3, 4–6; see also D. Lorimer, 'From natural science to social science: race and the language of race relations in late Victorian and Edwardian discourse', *Proceedings of the British Academy*, 2009.

104 Stocking, *Victorian anthropology*, pp. 156–64, 190–7, 300–20; J. Leopold, *Culture in comparative and evolutionary perspective: E.B. Tylor and the making of primitive culture*, Berlin, 1980.

105 Maine, *Village communities east and west*, London, 1872, pp. 3–62, 103–28, 175–201; H. Maine, *Lectures on the early history of institutions*, London, 1874, 3rd edn, 1914, ch. 13.

106 Maine, *Village communities east and west*, 1876, pp. 26–8, 181.

107 Mantena, *Alibis of empire*; C. Dewey, 'The influence of Sir Henry Maine on agrarian policy in India', in A. Diamond [ed.], *The Victorian achievement of Sir Henry Maine*, Oxford, 1991; K. O'Brien. 'Empire, history and emigration: from enlightenment to liberalism', in C. Hall and K. McLelland, [eds.] *Race, nation and empire*, Manchester, 2010, pp. 47–51.

108 Maine, *The early history of institutions*, 1875, p. 361.

109 Maine, *Village communities east and west*, pp. 9–12, 124; P. Vinogradoff, 'The teaching of Sir Henry Maine' (inaugural lecture 1904) in his *Collected papers*, 2 vols, Oxford, 1928, vol. 2, pp. 173–89.

110 Walpole, *History of England*, vol. 1, p. 109 still uses the 'black legend'; Yonge, *History of England*, 1871, p. 767 celebrates British rule in India as 'greatly to the advantage of even the natives whom it had subdued', echoing Edwards, *Concise history*, p. 245.

111 J. Pitts, *A turn to empire*, Cambridge, 2007; Claeys, *Imperial sceptics* deals with positivist and socialist anti-imperialism; see also F. van Holthoorn and M. van der Linden [eds.], *Internationalism in the labour movement*, Leiden, 1988.

112 R. Grant, *Representation of British emigration, colonisation, and settlement*, Basinstoke, 2005; J. Belich, *Replenishing the earth: the settler revolution and the rise of the Anglo world*, Oxford. 2009; J. Belich, *Making peoples: a history of the New Zealanders*, Honolulu, 1996.

113 Seeley, *Expansion of England*, pp. 4–8, 222–6, 251–3; Froude, *Oceana*, pp. 109–23; it may be noted that Dilke's text inspired a children's

version, E. Bulley, *Great Britain for little Britons*, London, 1881, which ran to six editions by 1906.

114 E. Ingram, *Britain's Persian connection*, Oxford, 1992; E. Ingram, *The British empire as a world power*, London, 2001; contrast C. Bayly, *The birth of the modern world*, Oxford, 2004.

115 N. Stepan, *The idea of race in science*, London, 1982; D. Lorimer, *Colour, class and the Victorians*, Leicester, 1978; and D. Lorimer, 'Theoretical racism in late Victorian anthropology', *Victorian Studies*, vol. 31, no. 3 (1988), pp. 405–30; West, *The Victorians and race*; D. Pick, *Faces of degeneration*, Cambridge, 1989, chs 6, 7; C. Hall, *Civilising subjects*, Cambridge, 2002; R.C. Young, *The idea of English ethnicity*, Oxford, 2008; P. Mandler, '"Race" and "nation" in mid-Victorian thought'.

116 D. Lorimer, 'From natural science to social science: race and the language of race relations in late Victorian and Edwardian discourse', in D. Kelly [ed.], *Lineages of empire: the historical roots of British imperial thought*, Oxford, 2009.

117 Gleig, *Family history*, vol. 1, pp. 29, 32 (on Saxons); Keightley, *History of England*, pp. 3, 5 (Celts), 84 (Anglo-Saxons), 157, 161 (Irish); Craik, *Pictorial history*, vol. 1, pp. 138, 154, 262–5 (Saxons, Danes), 659–60 (Danes, Normans), Yonge, *History of England*, pp. 3–4, 6 (Saxons, Danes); Taylor, *Student's manual*, pp. 1–2, 24 (Goths, Saxons), 21, 45 (Arabs), 106 (Spain); Thompson, *History of England*, pp. 1, 5 (Anglo-Saxons, Scots, Irish).

118 Freeman, *Methods of historical study*, p. 23.

119 Yonge, *Three centuries of modern history*, 1872, p. 50; Seeley, *Expansion of England*, p. 295.

120 J.S. Mill, *Considerations on representative government*, London, 1865; U. Mehta, *Liberalism and empire*, Chicago, 1999, J. Pitts, *A turn to empire: the rise of liberal imperialism in Britain and France*, Princeton, 2005; B. Schultz and G. Varouxakis [eds.], *Utilitarianism and empire*, Lanham, MD, 2005; C. Hall *et al.*, *Defining the Victorian nation*, Cambridge, 2000.

121 Creasy, *Imperial and constitutional history*, p. 36; Keightley, *History of England*, vol. 3, p. 465.

122 Dilke, *Greater Britain*, 2 vols, London, 1868, vol. 1, p. 126, vol. 2, p. 407; Seeley, *Expansion of England*, pp. 222, 234; Sanderson, *History of the British empire*, p. 14; Freeman, *Methods of historical study*, p. 9.

123 C. Dickens, *Child's history of England* (1852) vol. XII in *The centenary edition of the works of Charles Dickens*, London, 1910, p. 17.

124 D. Wormell, *Sir John Seeley and the uses of history*, Cambridge, 1980, pp. xxx; Seeley, *Expansion of England*, pp. 296–8, 301, 308, 311; Froude, *English in Ireland*; Froude, *Oceana*, pp. 383–96.

125 Froude, *Oceana*, pp. 387–8.

126 Dilke, *Greater Britain*, vol. 1, p. 318, vol. 2, pp. 157, 403–7.

127 Mantena, *Alibis of empire*, pp. 21–55; Dilke, *Greater Britain*, vol. 2, p. 403.

128 Yonge, *History of England*, p. 842.

129 Smith, *Irish history and Irish character*, 1862, p. 8; Walpole, *History of England*, p. 69.

130 Creasy, *Rise and progress of the English constitution*.

131 J. Lingard, *History of England*, 3rd edn, London, 1825, p. 267; J. Mackintosh, *History of England*, 3 vols, London, 1830, vol. 1, p. 320; Gleig, *Family history*, p. 250; Keightley, *History of England*, p. 320.

132 Green, *Short history*, p. 544 made an imagined comparison of the uncertain knowledge of events in Ireland in 1641 with the rumours surrounding the massacre at Cawnpore in 1857.

133 G. Peatling, 'Race and empire in nineteenth century intellectual life: James Fitzjames Stephen, James Anthony Froude, Ireland, and India', *Eire/Ireland*, 42:1–2 (2007), pp. 157–79; G. Peatling, 'The whiteness of Ireland under and after the Union', *Journal of British Studies*, 44 (2005), pp. 115–33; J. Garnett 'Protestant histories: James Anthony Froude: partisanship and national identity', in P. Ghosh and L. Goldman [eds.], *Politics and culture in Victorian Britain*, Oxford, 2006.

134 M. Hickson, *Ireland in the seventeenth century, or, the Irish massacre of 1641–2*, 2 vols, London, 1884, vol. 1, pp. 15, 165–6; the 'preface' by Froude is pp. v–xiii.

135 Garnett, 'Protestant histories'; Peatling, 'Race and empire'; Macartney, *W.E.H. Lecky*; Lecky's ambivalences are seen in his *Leaders of Irish public opinion*, 1861 (reissued regularly to 1912); Froude's views are expressed in *Ireland and the Irish land question*, 1870 and in *The English in Ireland in the eighteenth century*, 1872 and later editions.

136 R. Colls, *The identity of England*, Oxford, 2002.

137 Mandler, '"Race" and "nation" in mid-Victorian thought'.

4

EMPIRE AND HISTORY WRITING
1890s–1950

The civilization of Europe has been made the civilization of the world. (Ramsay Muir).[1]

In 1940 Ramsay Muir, a former professor of history in both England and India, as well as an activist and writer for the Liberal Party, produced a text entitled *Civilisation and liberty*. It was a sweeping historical treatment of those themes, whose publication was subsidised by the Association for Education in Citizenship. Written in the atmosphere of the Second World War, it linked Muir's professional expertise in academic history, his liberal political ideals and assumptions and the practice of historical writing for wide audiences, made affordable by that subsidy. Like his earlier work on European expansion, on histories of the British empire/commonwealth, and on contemporary politics, it linked democratic politics and liberties with western dominance, arguing that the convergence of 'liberty' and 'civilisation' in Europe was 'to give vitality to western civilisation and ultimately to win for it the leadership of the world'. While this view was explicitly posed against the 'totalitarian' regimes and cultures of Nazism, communism and fascism which the empire/commonwealth was resisting in 1940, it echoed views expressed by Muir over twenty years earlier. In *The expansion of Europe* he had argued that European political changes were 'implicit in, or...result from the conquest of the world by western civilisation'.[2] One way to understand the cultural climate of history writing in this period is to track challenges, responses and alternatives to the liberal and imperial outlooks which had been consolidated during the nineteenth century, and which Muir and others continued to put forward during and after the First World War. Reactions to that war, to new developments on the left and right of the political spectrum, and to changing patterns of academic and popular history writing, affected those outlooks and many historical texts published after 1920, but they provide supplementary voices rather than replacing the existing ones. Michael Bentley has argued one aspect of this case in his discussion of the persistence and transmutation of the so-called 'Whig' tradition of history writing, and wider aspects will be explored in this chapter.[3]

Muir's 1940 text offers a broad, secular and idealistic account of the growth of ideas of 'liberty' (defined as freedom of thought, expression and public action) and of 'civilization' (defined as the social and technological means for a better life). It expresses confidence in, and commitment to, a liberal and imperial vision of the world, based on the global spread of European influence, and a combination of self-governed settlement colonies with 'trusteeship' for 'backward peoples' under British rule. These would ensure the rule of law, peace and a civilising process, as understood by Europeans.[4] This vision combined ideas of virtuous empire with a new universalism, grounded in a refigured liberal internationalism damaged but not ended by the 1914–18 war, nor by the undermining of one embodiment of that internationalism, the League of Nations, in the 1930s. The definition of a new 'mandate' form of European colonial control and the resistance of the League to dealing with emergent anti-colonialism show the two faces of the liberal imperial vision in the interwar period. Despite its sharp sense of the confrontation between 'liberal' and 'totalitarian' ideals and agendas in the 1940s, Muir's book embodied narratives which had been produced since the start of the century. Commitment to 'liberal' aims (free trade, internationalism, the civilising mission), linked with belief in the unique capacity of Europeans to achieve such aims for themselves and for others, was a theme in these and other texts by Muir. It also appeared in works by historians like the more conservative J.A.R. Marriott, or the explicitly Christian V.T. Harlow.[5]

This suggests that discussion of British history writing between the supposed 'high watermark' of empire at the turn of the twentieth century and the era of decolonisation after 1945 should be attentive both to particularities of that period and to its links to the past. That high watermark is associated with passionate political debate for and against empire as well as with elite and popular portrayals of imperial service and adventure. It is often contrasted with the 'Little England' outlook, and 'European' concerns (communism, fascism, the League of Nations) often said to characterise the interwar period, but both worldviews influenced narratives of British history produced between the 1890s and the 1940s. The fact that active Liberals like Muir, and Conservatives like Marriott, as well as academics like Harlow and Newton, produced texts affirming the role of empire in various tones for diverse readerships in the 1930s and 1940s indicates that this theme continued to appeal. Since the time of Macaulay, narratives of English/British pasts had set stories of progress 'at home' in the context of imperial and international achievements overseas, binding empire, nation and social change together. In the period between 1890 and 1950 the practice of specifically imperial history was announced in research projects, student curricula and publications. Both 'conservative' and 'liberal' versions of patriotic/imperial assumptions and arguments were repeated and modified in the twentieth century, as more secular and defensive moods, as well as anti-colonial challenges, had their cultural and political impact. One significant topic in this chapter will be the challenges and adaptations to the dominant views of history and empire which had been woven into history writing since the 1830s. Consensus around such themes came under significant pressure, while also showing considerable tenacity, in the period being discussed, with consequences for history writing in which both tenacity and pressure can be seen.

In material terms the effects of colonial and commercial competition in the late nineteenth century were reinforced and redirected with the decline of established staple industries and international economic difficulties during the 1920s and 1930s, and the effects of war in the 1940s. The period after 1918 saw significant unemployment and deprivation, which have shaped many familiar images of the interwar depression, but there were also shifts in the composition of the workforce and the emergence of new industries.[6] Whereas unemployment averaged 4.8% annually between 1881 and 1914, it averaged 14% annually between 1921 and 1939, with employment in the old 'staple' industries of mining, cotton textile production and shipbuilding halving between 1920 and 1938. However, rationalisation of old industries and the growth of new ones enabled the share of manufacturing in output to increase as a result of domestic demand and imperial protection. After the difficulties of the early 1930s total civil paid employment rose from its 1921 total of 19.5 million to 21.8 million in 1939, involving the expansion of white-collar as against manual jobs, and the growth of new areas of work in car production, utility industries and, after 1945, in the public sector. White-collar workers formed 25% of the paid workforce in 1940, and 39% by 1951, compared with 18.7% in 1911, while numbers of car workers and electrical engineers more than doubled to nearly three-quarters of a million between 1920 and 1938. These UK statistics conceal important regional and social inequities, as do figures on falling infant mortality, improvements in diet and new housing. Patterns of reliance on imported foodstuffs and on overseas markets, established in the later nineteenth century, altered, as Indian textiles and German-engineered goods competed with British products and were affected by international trading and monetary fluctuations or by new demands for oil and rubber in the twentieth century.[7]

In this context overseas migration, government colonial economic policies and global trade, consumption, investment and influence had both explicit and indirect resonance in the UK.[8] The material relationships shaping empire between the 1890s and the 1940s were varied, uneven and entwined with a wider range of international connections and influences, as had been the case in the past. Industrial development in the USA, Germany and later in Japan challenged British positions in imperial as well as in wider global exchanges, although trade between Britain and the rest of the empire, which had been 27% of the total before 1914, rose from over 30% to over 40% in the period between the world wars.[9] British migration to the colonies was some 60% of total migration, even before US restrictions on immigration in the 1920s, and rose to some 82% of that total in the later 1930s, continuing to create personal and professional networks and flows of remittances to and from the UK, as it had in the nineteenth century.[10] While indicating the material significance of imperial connections, this can only be fully understood in the context of the continuing importance of British links with the USA, Europe and south America, and the limited place of colonial commerce within those links. Decisions about tariffs, investments and trade agreements were made in that context, so that rather than acting as a buffer or bolthole for entrepreneurs and policymakers, imperial markets, opportunities and resources were assessed competitively, and, as Cain and Hopkins argue, politically. If British products struggled in the new global setting, British bankers and diplomats shaped new roles and defences for British financial and imperial interests, ensuring their survival if not success into the 1950s.[11] The political, economic and international difficulties of the 1930s and 1940s gave a sharp edge to this process.

The demands made on the UK state by the world wars, the instabilities of the interwar period, and commitments to direct government social and economic involvement after 1945, were met by a blend of conventional and innovative response. New patterns of party politics with the rise of the Labour Party, its consequences for liberalism, and the arrival of the full adult franchise, entwined with rather than replacing existing practices. Thus elite Utilitarian and liberal traditions of reform, and legacies of nineteenth-century popular and labour politics, were reconfigured in twentieth-century Fabian, municipal or campaigning activism. This held true of imperial issues as well as others. The Fabian Colonial Bureau's 1940s discussions about improving the lot of colonial subjects in Africa combined commitment to a civilising mission with the confidence in the benefits of British rule which had characterised nineteenth-century policymakers, albeit a modernised technocratic/managerial version. It was paralleled in the official language of colonial civil servants and advisers in the 1930s and 1940s.[12] Searle has argued that concern with 'national [and imperial] efficiency', a political preoccupation between the 1890s and the 1914–18 war, left its legacy in the authoritative/authoritarian expertise with which reformers approached imperial policy issues in the 1930s and 1940s.[13] The idealistic liberal imperialism of Muir, or Reginald Coupland, like the critical views of empire put forward by Leonard Woolf or H.N. Brailsford in the interwar period, owed much to patterns of liberal internationalism and critiques of finance capital going back to the mid-nineteenth century. The blend of imperial and 'Little England' views which grew within the Conservative tradition in the later nineteenth century supported not just the imperialist advocacy of the Round Table group or the populist politics of the Tariff Reform League, but the more limited and cautious engagement of Stanley Baldwin with dominion politics and Indian nationalism in the 1930s.[14]

It would indeed be mistaken to argue that imperial issues dominated politics or government between the 1890s and the

1940s. The explicit and public debate and activism around imperial tariffs and the 1899–1902 war in South Africa, the imperial display associated with George V's succession in 1910 and conflict over the Irish question were quite specific features of the period before 1914. Thereafter new issues arising from international conflict and concerns with social reform and economic difficulty within the UK which had already emerged before 1914 were central to political debate and government action. Nonetheless, between the 1910s and the 1940s imperial issues continued to affect political life, through debates on governance and economic relations in old and new spheres of imperial power and influence and the need for UK governments to mesh colonial policy with other international concerns. Conflicts in the Middle East, Africa, Afghanistan and Ireland during and after the 1914–18 war, and in south-east Asia, the Pacific, India, the Middle East and Africa during and after the 1939–45 war – like the continuing impact of Irish, Middle Eastern and Indian nationalisms – were direct reminders of the 'imperial' aspects of UK life. Conflicts over imperial taxation and customs systems, and over relationships between the UK and the rest of the empire, played their part in party politics.[15] The politics of patriotism, of 'national efficiency' and of social reform had imperial dimensions and were pursued by those with imperial experience and connections. These included the Fabian Sidney Webb, a former Colonial Office civil servant, the romantic conservative Winston Churchill with his Indian, South African and Sudan exploits, and the academic and administrator William Beveridge, son of parents with careers in India.

Such politics may have been conducted predominantly in elite metropolitan and educated settings, but generated various activities, publications and organisations which reached other audiences. These initiatives included both official or organised ventures and self-conscious reliance on imperial images and associations by cultural and commercial bodies. Promotion of imperial awareness in youth groups and public broadcasting (with talks from established empire historians like Reginald Coupland), like the promotion of Empire Day and empire exhibitions, are instances of the former.[16] In addition to more obvious forms of publicity for colonial trade, the Colonial Marketing Board sponsored the 1939 publication of *The story of the British colonial empire*. Away from officialdom, the use of imperial themes and images in advertising and for product names or locomotives, alongside their appearance in various popular media, flavoured leisure activities and public culture.[17] Of course, as Thompson has argued, there are important differences between the existence or visibility of such efforts and their measurable impact, but their presence in the cultural landscape is worth noting.[18] The millions who visited empire exhibitions in London in 1924–25 or Glasgow in 1938 very likely treated them as opportunities for entertainment and diversion, just as most school pupils may have disregarded the promotion of imperial messages in the classroom. Such endeavours are more usefully understood as presenting and normalising the empire within the public awareness, rather than as successful means for converting people to 'imperialist' views.

The public rhetoric which proclaimed imperial connections through support for Empire Day and commemoration of colonial participation in the world wars disseminated images of empire, as a benign international project, or as central to British power and prosperity. This was done through radio talks and paralleled in film, radio and popular fiction.[19] Imperial images, settings and references appeared regularly as background context or as central features in boys' papers, in romantic and adventure novels and in other forms of fiction. The continued popularity of Henty's novels and the boys' comics with imperial adventure stories, demonstrated in a 1.3 million readership for the latter and high sales of the former, was a significant legacy from the period before 1914. Themes used by Henty in the 1880s were still visible in the boys' stories produced in the 1930s by Frank Richards, who was also the author of reminiscences of imperial soldiering. Authors like Kathlyn Rhodes, Maud Diver and Gertrude Page set successful romances in eastern deserts (Rhodes, with twelve novels between 1908 and 1944), India (Diver, with fourteen novels between 1907 and 1934) and Rhodesia (Page, with ten novels between 1907 and 1921), as well as writing school stories, non-fiction and pieces for girls' comics. The presence of the retired Anglo-Indian officer, or the problem of colonial investments, in the cosy English settings of Agatha Christie mysteries, the imperial adventures of air ace Biggles, or John Buchan's heroes, like colonial themes in novels by Diver or Page, signalled the normalcy of imperial references in British settings.[20] The appeal of such material was also manifest in the dozens of British and American films on imperial subjects produced by mainstream studios between the 1920s and 1950s, the period when cinema-going became a widespread activity. By 1938 some five thousand cinemas received around 987 million visits, and by the 1940s one third of the population went to the cinema at least once a week. Celebrations of 'heroes' like Cecil Rhodes, Clive 'of India' or David Livingstone, adaptations of imperial fiction or putting a popular 'Lancashire lass', the singer/actress Gracie Fields, into a story set in the South African goldmines brought such subjects to audiences across the UK.[21]

As in the nineteenth century, the extent of interest in imperial matters among ordinary people can and should be questioned. In the late 1940s a Mass Observation questionnaire and a survey of public opinion on colonial affairs suggested that less-privileged or less-educated people had little knowledge of the empire.[22] Historians of literature like Alison Light have argued that in the interwar period the sense of Englishness became flavoured with a 'less imperial more inward looking' quality, which she associates with a particular version of conservative feminism. A number of historians suggest that a domesticated, ruralised version of England, which celebrated 'English' qualities, landscapes and traditions, arguably worked against any imperial elements in notions of 'Englishness' during that period.[23] One impact of the 1914–18 war may have been to reduce the appeal of more militarised versions of imperial patriotism, with discussions of national interests or identity in the 1920s and 1930s focusing on internal rather than global issues. However, it may also have contributed to the shift from militaristic to developmental ideals and images of imperial rule. It has also been suggested that explicit external concerns were as likely to focus on UK responses to developments in Europe or on the League of Nations as on the empire. In a context of major domestic material difficulties and changes after 1918, and of a political system which enfranchised many for whom those difficulties took priority over the management of global and colonial power, the popular political appeal of imperial issues was likely to be limited. This was as true for social reformers opposing deprivation, inequality and mismanagement as it was for politicians like Baldwin, for whom the rhetoric of 'Little England' provided a means to draw varied political views and aspirations into support for National/Conservative governments.[24]

It is perhaps less useful to pose imperial and non-imperial readings of culture and politics against one another than to reflect on the complex relationships between them. As well as taking account of overlapping or interacting gender, class or regional differences in views of empire, it may be useful to consider how these elements might coexist, and how far newer features combined with or replaced older ones. Thus the web of missionary influences which had linked UK residents to missionary endeavours overseas, or in urban slums since the mid-nineteenth century still played a role in disseminating ideas and images of empire, albeit in a climate of declining formal religious participation. The publication of Sunday school material and missionary stories continued to flourish, as evidenced by the production of hundreds of missionary memoirs, biographies, plays and Sunday school texts between 1920 and 1950. Missionaries supplemented written material on empire with the use of film and photography to inform and motivate their audiences. As in the past, heroic lives of missionaries like Mary Slessor, Livingstone, William Carey, Bishop Colenso, Irene Petrie, Robert Moffat and others were retold for both adults and children, and tales of missionary endeavour combined exotic travel and adventure with tales of moral, social and spiritual improvement. Evidence about how such material was received may be limited, but the regular republishing of some of these works indicates that the market for them persisted.[25] In the 1920s Stanley Baldwin linked service to the empire with service to social harmony and moral improvement in public addresses to the Church Army and other religious groups as well as in speeches dealing explicitly with service, democracy and disarmament. In a patriotic speech of 1924 he moved from a characteristic evocation of rural England to its projection in the dominions, bracketing 'home' and empire.[26] The significance of this is less that a leading politician expressed these particular views, but that he calculated or assumed that such references would appeal to, or at least be recognised by, his audiences.

It should not be argued that positive forceful depictions of imperial success or ambition were typical of British cultures in general, since different social groups responded differently to such depictions. Awareness of empire, where it existed, included doubts and criticisms as well as interest or enthusiasm. The patriotic imperial material in Robert Roberts' school in Salford in the 1910s may well have been an oddity to be remembered or resisted rather than an inspiration (Roberts himself became a pacifist).[27] For readers of detective novels, romances and adventure stories, the presence of exotic and colonial settings just added an element of glamour, authenticity or excitement, enhancing enjoyment of their favourite reading. Young people might accept such settings as one flavour in the comics or fiction which they enjoyed. Studies of electoral politics and public opinion since 1920 suggest that for the majority of inhabitants of the UK immediate circumstances and difficulties loomed much larger than imperial or international affairs, despite the continuing concern with imperial issues.[28] If enthusiasm for empire had played a distinctive role in particular lower middle-class, female and youth groupings before 1914, there is evidence that – while not disappearing – it was refigured and combined with other influences after the war. The imperial orientation of the early Boy Scout movement modulated into empire-flavoured internationalism between the wars, just as arguments linking women's imperial roles to claims to citizenship before 1914 blended with other approaches.[29] Issues of class difference shifted in the period, stimulating divisions and accommodations among established professional, newer technocratic and managerial, 'skilled' and 'unskilled' workers and their lifestyles, affecting ideas of Britishness or Englishness, and their imperial or patriotic settings.[30] Moreover, writings on imperial topics during the first half of the twentieth century primarily addressed niche readerships defined by education or specific interests (missionary, party political or issue based) and competed with work on other social and political questions.

In this context, the presence of imperial elements in the political and cultural fabric is best treated as a contingent and variable, but nonetheless normal and identifiable, feature of the worlds of inhabitants of the UK in this period. For schoolchildren, cinema-goers, journalists or fiction readers, as well as those with political interests, empire was part of their cultural fabric if not always the object of particular attention. The view that explicit interests in empire were confined to, and reached, only limited sections of society does not do justice to the presence of imperial ideas, contacts and images within everyday experience regardless of individual opinion or interest in imperial issues. The 'insular' patriotism often seen as typical of the interwar period arguably expressed English hostility to continental Europeans (Bolsheviks or fascists) rather than rejecting ideas of a 'Greater Britain' which included British settlements overseas established in the later nineteenth century. The ability to combine imperial and domestic approaches in popular texts can be seen in the varied works of the self-made editor and writer Arthur Mee between the 1900s and the 1940s. These included evocations of English regional landscapes, and multivolume works on science, literature and world history, published in weekly series, combining 'Little England' with 'imperial' patriotism, and shaped by Nonconformist and commercial enthusiasm for popular educational texts.[31]

From the end of the nineteenth century onward the production of academic and educational history writing and discussion of empire took increasingly organised and explicit forms. The formalisation of university history teaching and research, and the spread of school and adult teaching and study of history, opened up opportunities for the production of texts, syllabuses and professional careers, and for formal and informal interest in the past. Between 1890 and 1903 the proportion of elementary schools teaching history rose from under 2% to around 98%, a 'turning point' in the development of school-based history. The number of secondary school pupils taking School Certificate exam in history more than trebled between 1918 and 1938, although it is important to note the scale and effects of all these increases were uneven and limited.[32] This can be set beside political changes arising from the extension of the franchise, the growth of organised party activity, of popular and polemical depictions of empire, and of organisations promoting 'imperial' aims. If the number of 'history titles' published in the UK rose between 1870 and 1910 and then fell between 1915 and 1940, the first half of the twentieth century nonetheless saw the launch of various kinds of historical texts which stayed in print sometimes into the post-1945 era.[33] These included school and student texts and multivolume series covering English history from the Roman occupation to the world war, as well as European and imperial history.[34] There was also work in what were becoming identified as the distinctive fields of economic and social history, and biographies like Arthur Bryant's successful three volumes on Samuel Pepys (1935–38, still reprinting in the 1960s). At the scholarly end of the spectrum the appearance of volumes of printed archival material on British, European and imperial history indicated the growing commitment of historians to archival as well as narrative achievement. Such work reinforced the increasingly dense structures of professional history, like the Historical Association for history teachers, the Institute of Historical Research for the formation of researchers or the development of research training and career paths for academic historians in universities. It offset earlier 'whiggish' traditions which continued to play their role in historical practice, where, as Feske and Bentley suggest, there were tangled connections and disjunctions between that legacy, new scholarly expectations and changed politico-cultural conditions.[35]

Tensions between patriotic narratives of progress and the growing authority of professional practice were offset by new relations between historical practice and other scholarly fields. During the later nineteenth century the work of scholars like Maine created links between legal history and forms of cross-cultural comparison which were being constructed as the domain of anthropology.[36] Paradoxically, British anthropologists' move away from conjectural histories of diffusion or evolution towards concern with functions and meanings in 'primitive' societies influenced historians' own shift from dramatic narrative to close investigation and interpretation of contexts. In each case there was a move away from grand theory and linear narrative to more focused and contextualised accounts of particular communities (in the case of anthropologists) or past situations (in the case of historians). Medievalists like Power and Postan drew on opportunities for contact with anthropologists like Raymond Firth at the LSE in developing their approaches to socio-economic history, recalling the earlier links between Maine, Pollock and Vinogradoff.[37] Another element of changing historical practice was the emergence of economic history as a distinct field organised around publications, academic posts and a learned society. Grounded in a search for more rounded approaches to the past, and critiques of neo-classical economics and Whig views of politico-constitutional history, it embodied that professionalism and the interface between contemporary concerns and work on the past. Texts by Tawney, Clapham and the Hammonds, and the controversies around them, were influenced by current views on state intervention and the economic depression, and the tensions between Fabian and liberal thought, as well as by scholarly considerations.[38]

History writing was shaped by new conditions in its fields of production (education, publishing, professional formation, readerships) and by a political and cultural climate in which concerns about nation, empire and democracy had their historical dimensions as well as contemporary urgency. We can consider the realignment of the 'liberal' G.M. Trevelyan towards patriotic Baldwinite conservatism, reflected in revisions of his historical texts, or the echoes of interwar concerns with materialism and morality in Tawney's texts on the sixteenth century. Tawney, indeed, explicitly affirmed the relevance of links between past and present within historical practice in a 1933 piece on economic history.[39] His role in the Workers' Education Association exemplified the commitment of professional historians across the political spectrum to the presentation of their subject within a developing arena of popular culture. The notable predominance of history courses within the Workers' Education Association programme suggests the demand for such material and the transforming tradition of links between history, inclusion and citizenship.[40] Tension between the aspirations of 'modern' historians to transcend the whiggish narratives of their predecessors, their development of the scholarly practices inherited from those predecessors and the appeal of teleological narrative shaped historical writing in this period.

Empire, state and citizenship

The title of Arthur Mee's series celebrating the English counties, *The king's England*, published in the late 1930s and 1940s and still being reprinted twenty years later, captured the refigured place of the monarchy in English culture, rebranded over previous decades. This included the making of links between monarchy and empire, amongst them royal titles and visits to dominions and colonies, royal radio broadcasts to UK and empire and royal jubilee or coronation celebrations.[41] Some historians note that this both reinforced and altered people's sense of 'Englishness' (or 'Britishness') between the 1890s and the 1940s, while others link empire and crown in an argument that attachment to the former was 'really' loyalty to the latter. Miles Taylor has argued that these links were emerging in the mid-nineteenth century, and David Cannadine has considered how the use of royal/aristocratic codes and rituals cemented imperial power.[42] Whether or not it increased enthusiasm for empire, the link to monarchy did normalise it in everyday understandings of state and government, as well as cultures of patriotism and shared identity. Historical texts offered arguments over financial, constitutional or military arrangements among the constituent parts of the empire/commonwealth, and over shared loyalty to, and pride in, monarchy and empire as entwined institutions. The historian and public intellectual G.M. Trevelyan drafted the silver jubilee speech of George V to parliament, and by 1947 a history textbook could assert that the king was 'the one bond of empire'.[43] References to 'our empire' continued to be scattered through historical writings of all kinds.

What impact, if any, did the significant changes affecting the British state during the period under discussion have for history writing? Between 1884 and 1928 the franchise was extended by stages to include nearly the whole UK population aged over twenty-one, and from 1906 new forms of state welfare provision also added new dimensions to citizenship. The growing political presence and impact of organised labour opened other avenues of public activity. As a result, issues of political rights and participation, raised earlier by upheavals in America in the 1770s, France in the 1790s and the UK from the 1820s to the 1840s, as well as by the parliamentary reforms of 1832 and 1867, continued to flavour accounts of the English/British past in the decades after 1890. If nineteenth-century texts had distanced their accounts of parliamentary progress from the challenge of Chartism, and later on from the effects of the widened male franchise after 1867, those produced in the early twentieth century could incorporate those elements into a less anxious narrative. By the 1890s Sanderson's school history could describe the Chartists as 'ahead of their time' in asking for what is 'right and just', and Marcy's 1920s exam text, like that of Glew and Plaskett in the 1940s, noted that their demands were now accepted. An Edwardian text like that of Arthur Innes might still note that they were unacceptable in their time, referring to Chartists 'terrorising' the authorities, but, like others, he could set Chartism within a narrative of later reform.[44] Such issues could be imperial as well as 'domestic', since notions of being a subject or citizen discussed in history books were often inclusive of some at least of the inhabitants of territories outside the UK under British rule. Just as Creasy in 1853 had located parliament at the core of the British empire, not just of the UK, William Reddaway in the 1901 *Evolutionary history of England*, offering explicit support for imperial unity, depicted it as the precursor of 'a parliament of the whole British empire'. Texts like those of Sanderson and the Pitman *Complete history* and *Introductory history* repeated this framing device.[45]

Debates on imperial federation, Irish independence or tariff reform, and the emergence of notions of 'dominion' and 'commonwealth' to describe relationships between the UK and its overseas possessions added an imperial element to changing understandings of inclusion, citizenship and subjecthood.[46] These shifts gave a new flavour to depictions of government and democracy, both past and present, a development which nevertheless took time to have an effect, not least because the shelf life of popular and educational history books was a long one. Reissues of J.R. Green's influential *Short history of the English people*, which went to five printings in the twenty years after publication in 1875, continued regularly over the following forty years. Like Edgar Sanderson's histories of England and of empire, Gardiner's *Student's history of England*, first published in the 1890s, was being reissued with updates in the 1920s, just as texts by George Guest from before 1914 were being reissued in the late 1930s. More sophisticated texts by Innes, Marriott and Trevelyan, first published before 1914 in the Methuen *History of England* edited by the Oxford academic Charles Oman, were still in print in 1950, and the Oxford histories which first came out in the 1930s were still being reissued in the 1970s. School texts like the *Royal England readers*, first published in 1889, or the *Abbey history readers* and the *Complete history readers*, first published in 1902, continued in use unrevised for decades. Ideas about the past formed in the later nineteenth century were thus disseminated to subsequent generations of readers and pupils alongside recent publications produced to meet growing demand.[47]

'Imperial' approaches to the presentation of British and European history which emerged before 1900 had an extensive life thereafter. Idealistic and confident depictions of empire as an achievement in which the British could and should take pride as a benefit to them and to colonial subjects continued to be available. In a post-1918 climate of anxiety over international affairs, domestic depression and social or political change, ideas of 'imperial' Britain or of Britain as the centre of an empire could have a reassuring effect, reinforced by the role played by the 'white dominions' on the UK side in the 1914–18 war. In the decade before 1914, history books cited dominion support for the British against the Boers in the 1899–1901 war in South Africa as evidence of the bonds linking Britain to 'white' settlers overseas, and the role of the dominions and other colonies in the 1914–18 war was used to reinforce positive views of empire in the post-war decades.[48] Enthusiasm for the 'empire of settlement' generated in the work of Seeley, Dilke, Froude and Freeman a generation earlier appeared in texts which reached wider audiences during the twentieth century, and in depictions of the 1914–18 war from school textbooks to the novels of John Buchan. When Scottish/British/South African Richard Hannay takes on the German enemy in Buchan's patriotic adventure tales he is supported by an Afrikaner and an American as well as a T.E. Lawrence-like Anglo-Scottish aristocratic adventurer, and a Glasgow worker.[49] The empire propagandists Philip Kerr (later Marquis of Lothian), an active member of the elite Round Table group working with Lord Milner and Leo Amery to influence politicians and ministers on imperial issues, also wrote a popular short illustrated text, *The growth of the British empire* (1911). Taking a view going back to Froude, it provided a celebratory narrative of that empire starting in the sixteenth century, presenting its growth as a triumph of self-government for white settlers, and of justice and progress under British rule for other colonial subjects. C. Ellis' 1947 *England and the modern world*, if more positive towards Indian self-government than earlier texts (unsurprising on the eve of Indian independence), still described the 'white' dominions as 'first in importance'. Muir's 1920 *Short history of the British commonwealth*, still in print in 1949, and aimed at both teachers and students, labelled Indian nationalism as 'discontent', but affirmed liberty and progress as key features of imperial success. It called the empire 'the glorious fellowship of free peoples', in an interesting erasure of those colonial subjects denied political participation or equal treatment.[50] Both the Conservative Kerr and the Liberal Muir made settler colonies and imperial institutions central to their accounts.

As the title of Muir's work suggests, narratives of the British state written after 1900 began to present the growth of a 'commonwealth' of British dominions, colonies and other territories as the key trajectory of empire history. Notions of imperial rule as trusteeship, and of the growth of self-governing colonies as central to the story of empire, came out of nineteenth-century debates on colonial responsibility, and narratives of empire depicting the links between 'Britain/England' and 'British' settlements overseas. While some of these relied on cultural and racial elements, as will be seen, they also emphasised institutional connections and the sometimes tricky relationships between colonial self-government and the structures and needs of imperial power (legal, military or political). In the late nineteenth century pride in these connections became as important to accounts of empire as pride in British rule in India, or missionary work in Africa. From 1900, arguments previously aimed mainly at educated or political audiences appeared in texts for schools and general readerships. Nineteenth-century moves to self-government in Canada and Australia, like the creation of the Union of South Africa in 1910, became markers in the story of the British empire. The contentious issue of imperial federation and its relationship to self-government in those parts of the empire, which engaged politicians between the 1890s and 1930s, was also presented in Pitman readers.[51] Scholarly histories of empire published after 1920 often emphasised constitutional and administrative aspects, presenting empire in terms of governance, law and state formation, and linking it to British legal, constitutional and administrative history.

This was reinforced by the development of studies of military and organisational aspects of the 1914–18 war, within which imperial defence and contributions were embedded. The Royal Colonial Society sponsored a multivolume series on the topic, edited by an Oxford academic, former colonial administrator and author of imperial histories, which appeared between the 1880s and 1930s, matching the official volume on the subject.[52] John Buchan, an active politician as well as successful writer who became governor general of Canada, turned his multivolume commentary on the war, including its imperial aspects (published from 1915 to 1919), into a book, and wrote a specific history of South African contributions to the war. Similar histories of other colonial involvements in the 'Great War' appeared during the interwar period. As this became 'history', affirmation of the links and tensions between 'British' and 'colonial' wartime involvement modified, and continued, some of the political advocacy of Round Table enthusiasts like Buchan, and of imperial reformers as well as their opponents.

There were wider aspects to this approach. The institutions of the 'white settler colonies' and their supposedly organic relationship to the United Kingdom are presented as achievements in themselves and as north American, South African or Australasian projections of the state established there. The lack of constitutional precision, and the pragmatic governmental compromises, involved in the emergent British commonwealth in the twentieth century were seen to exemplify and parallel the pragmatism and 'unwritten' forms of limited monarchy and representative government previously developed in the UK.[53] The history of UK governmental institutions could be entwined with the history of empire, as in Muir's *Short history of the British commonwealth*, where the story of imperial expansion and development is embedded in extended accounts of political, social and cultural development within the UK. Arthur Innes' 1923 *Class book of the British commonwealth* likewise interspersed the imperial narrative with accounts of developments within the UK. Conversely A.F. Pollard, a historian whose own interests were in Tudor England, still gave space to imperial developments in the narrative of parliamentary history under the title 'The British realms in parliament'.[54] This typical practice of placing separate chapters on 'imperial ' issues within general histories of England/Britain echoes the *Evolutionary history of England*'s statement that 'The three greatest gifts that England...has given to the world are her Empire, her literature, and her Parliament.' This text also argued that the existence of the secret ballot in the UK affected 'countless millions who live under the protection of the British flag'.[55] Like the *Evolutionary history*, other popular or educational texts combined specific treatments of empire with inclusion of empire links within their broader narratives. Stories of parliamentary reform in the UK become an imperial story too, as with Ellis' framing of his history of England as an account of how Britain became 'the founder and centre of the British Commonwealth of nations'. Trevelyan's generally Anglocentric account of the reign of Queen Anne opens with the claim that this is 'no parochial theme' but a story visiting the West Indies, Gibraltar, and Newfoundland.[56]

In the period after 1918 there may have seemed to be a possibility that the island of Ireland might be included in that commonwealth, as when the Empire Marketing Board promoted trade with the Free State.[57] Conflict among British politicians over home rule for Ireland, and rising Irish nationalism and Ulster unionism from the 1880s, produced confrontations, British repression, civil war among Irish nationalists and the emergence of an independent Irish state alongside six Irish counties which remained within the UK. To some extent, this reframed British presentations of Irish history, whether as a discordant note in a national British story, as a tale (sympathetic or critical) of specifically Irish nationalism, or as a variant colonial relationship. Twentieth-century treatments of that history shifted from narratives of the difficulties experienced by British governments in Ireland, to critical, even apologetic, accounts of British 'mistakes and misunderstandings'. In the early 1920s Muir's treatment of sixteenth-century Ireland, embedded in an imperial and British narrative, observes that it left 'manifold seeds of ill from which the whole British Commonwealth still suffers', and denounced the discriminatory settlement of the 1690s. Unlike the robustly Tory/Unionist treatment of the 'ungrateful' and 'disloyal' Irish in 1798 by Fletcher, Muir goes on to treat the uprising as a 'tragedy' and the Act of Union as a 'well meant measure' undertaken under 'unhappy auspices'.[58] A school history like Miller's might make links between 'traitorous' nationalists, Germany and Roger Casement's role in the 1916 rising, but, as in earlier texts, also noted the ill effects of Cromwell's actions in Ireland, the Penal Laws and the failure to combine the 1801 union with rights for Roman Catholics. Historical texts were now sceptical of Protestant exaggerations of casualties in the 1641 'Catholic' rising. Arthur Innes, a historian of British involvement in India and lecturer at the School of Oriental and African Studies with an Anglo-Indian background, as well as being an author of educational texts, compared them with the sensationalised figures for the 1857 'Mutiny'.[59]

Accounts of Irish nationalism can be compared with those dealing with newer nationalisms in Egypt, India and later in Palestine. For the liberal Muir, Indian nationalism could be treated as reasonable, provided it was 'moderate', but not given priority over the maintenance of peace and justice. He emphasised the narrow, perhaps undemocratic, base of educated Indian nationalists.[60] Miller's 1921 *Beginners' history of England*, reissued in 1936, still emphasised the violent aspects rather than the political issues involved in the history of Irish nationalism, but did not even acknowledge the reality of nationalist aspirations in Egypt or India, placing that term in quotation marks to signal its dismissive view.[61] This can be contrasted with Glew and Plaskett's more neutral account of British–Irish relations since the 1801 Act of Union, or Ellis' tracking of Irish grievances and what is portrayed as a long-standing north–south divide among the inhabitants of Ireland.[62] The multipart pre-1914 *Harmsworth history of the world* dealt with Indian nationalists as a source of unrest, sedition, unlawful association and anarchist conspiracy. It provided a fuller account of the killing of an Anglo-Indian official in 1909 than of the nationalist politics surrounding it, making comparisons between this assassination and that of the Chief Secretary for Ireland in 1882. Interestingly, as late as 1947, Ellis' text presented Gandhi as a just a campaigner on behalf of Indian 'untouchables', and not as a prominent anti-colonial nationalist.[63] The implicit or explicit judgements of Irish nationalism made in the texts can be linked to the (limited) degree to which Irish as well as British views of the so-called 'Irish question' were presented or acknowledged. While recognising the specific economic grievances of Irish peasants, or the religious concerns of Irish Roman Catholics, there was continued acceptance of the need and even the benefits of the 1801 union.[64] Daniel O'Connell, who tended to appear as an artful demagogue in nineteenth-century histories, can be presented as an effective if troublesome politician in later accounts.[65] Such views could still be linked to discussion of whether there was a place for independent Ireland within the commonwealth.[66] It seemed difficult to let go of perceptions of Ireland as an 'imperial' topic.

This strand of continuity could also be seen in the handling of other 'four-nations' aspects of the history of the 'British' Isles. In the 1940s Glew and Plaskett, like Airy fifty years earlier, presented Edward I's conquest of Wales as a solution to 'troubles' caused by the Welsh, with no 'Welsh' perspective. Like Miller or Gardiner, most Edwardian history readers celebrated the 1707 union with Scotland in terms similar to those used in nineteenth-century texts.[67] Anglocentric and imperial perspectives on the evolution of the United Kingdom remained typical of much historical writing. In the *Evolutionary history* the incorporation of Scots and Welsh, as well as that of the Irish, into the UK is recounted as part of the section on 'The expansion of the empire'. Authors of school texts and popular histories like Arthur Innes might include appended summaries on Scottish and Irish history in their texts, simultaneously recognising and subordinating the different 'national' elements in their narrative, alongside summaries of Indian, colonial and church history.[68] Conventional snapshots of William Wallace, Scottish Covenanters or 'troublesome' if brave Welsh 'rebels' confronting English kings with an admirable or at least understandable wish to control them made regular appearances in narratives of 'English' history. Accounts of seventeenth-century conflicts over crown, parliament, and religion presented the Scots and Irish as bit players, even intruders, in 'English' struggles, as well as the mistaken or pitiable victims of the policies pursued by Strafford, Cromwell, Charles II or William III.[69] Macaulay's practice of placing non-English peoples at the margins of the 'national' story of the English was alive and well nearly a century after his history first appeared

Revived interest and controversy over state-led social reform from the 1880s, associated with 'social' or new' liberalism, reinforced bonds between involvement in empire and questions of government and citizenship. In a 1901 speech the liberal imperialist politician Asquith asked, 'What is the use of talking about empire if here, at its very centre, there is always to be found a mass of people, stunted in education, a prey of intemperance, huddled and congested beyond the possibility of realising in any true sense either domestic or social life?'[70] If some conservative imperialists saw British law and loyalty to the crown as the key bonds of empire, liberal, Fabian, paternalist and socialist supporters of empire associated it with programmes for social reform and rational progress in which they argued that the state should have a key role. By the mid-1930s a comparative and partly historical survey of European imperial expansion and policies sponsored by Chatham House set economic development squarely in the imperial picture, stating, 'The development of the wealth of the country must march…with the progress of self government.'[71] Links between the Fabian Webbs, who promoted imperial reform, and tariff reformers like the conservative academics L. Knowles and W. Hewins, at the London School of Economics, and imperial politics spanned intellectual and political activity. Hewins wrote on seventeenth-century imperial mercantile policy as well as undertaking imperial tariff policy work for Chamberlain and Balfour, and Knowles opened up the fields of imperial, overseas and comparative economic history. While early twentieth-century celebrations of empire emphasised shared English/British legal and constitutional freedoms and institutions, by the 1940s ideas of government-led economic reform, a key political issue in the interwar years, became colonial as well as a 'domestic' topics of concern. A 1940 secondary school text noted the value of new thinking on the benefits of state involvement in the management of industry and competition, contrasting it with early nineteenth-century approaches.[72]

As some colonial subjects began to challenge British dominance, accounts of colonial rule outside the 'white' dominions developed themes of the need for the British colonial authorities to provide protection and material development for those they ruled, rather than engaging with demands for representation or independence. Ellis' 1947 text still opened its section on the empire/commonwealth by asserting that the latter was 'the greatest organisation of its kind in the world'.[73] Building on the nineteenth-century discourse of trusteeship, history writers took it in new directions, perhaps echoing the growing influence of 'social' approaches on historical writing. Some general accounts remained focused on political authority and administrative progress, but in others themes of social reform or material improvement initiated by colonial rulers became part of narratives of imperial politics.[74] They sidestepped the difficult issues raised by opposition to colonial power, prefiguring the emergence of 'development studies' as a tool for depicting societies which experienced colonial rule, and linking questions of governance to narratives of material change. Newton's imperial history explicitly argued that attention to 'social and economic distress' in Jamaica was more important than dealing with 'agitations for self government'.[75]

This modified the dominant administrative or political accounts of empire while buttressing the role of colonial government. The narrative of British rule in Egypt and nationalist opposition to it provided by Glew and Plaskett stresses the 'progressive' material reforms enacted by the British (the Aswan dam, railways, ending forced labour). It associates nationalism not with the grievances understandably produced by colonial rule, but with the 'decline' of the British administration after the departure of its long-serving leader, Lord Cromer, referring to Egyptian views as 'prejudices'. Muir's view of that administration, in a text which embeds its narrative of British history within that of the whole commonwealth, similarly praises its promotion of material development, associating Egyptian nationalism with religious 'unrest' and 'Muslim' resentment at European dominance.[76] This can be compared with the portrayal of the 1882 British occupation of Egypt and Egyptian nationalism in the mainly politically oriented *A hundred years of the British empire*, first published in 1940. The account of Indian nationalism in the same text juggles references to extremism, terrorism, 'fanatics' and violence with those to 'moderate' support for 'practical steps' which might meet 'legitimate aspirations of responsible Indian public opinion'. Glew and Plaskett called nineteenth-century British rule in India an efficient 'despotism' while giving a very cautious account of the clashes between the *raj* and Indian nationalists and the 'problem' of Indian self-government.[77] A liberal wish to find acceptable and safe stories of reform (the theme of progressive change without conflict, going back to Macaulay) struggled with defensive reactions to anti-colonial nationalism.

The anxieties provoked by more confrontational challenges to established colonial rule had counterparts in responses to what the distinguished medievalist T.F. Tout called the end of middle-class ascendancy.[78] Writing in 1900, he dated this to the passing of the 1867 Reform Act, but the effects of an expanded franchise and education system, the role of new media and new electoral and campaigning tactics of parties or unions kept the issue alive over the whole period discussed in this chapter. Wider democracy, new forms of communication and challenges from educated colonial subjects, like the appeal of new mass media or the growth of suburbia, could be experienced as threats by those who dominated politics or acted as gatekeepers to culture and knowledge. With hindsight, it can be seen that they would find many ways to adapt to, and indeed manage, these changes, but in the interwar period that outcome might seem uncertain. It is worth noting that historical discourses were used to address that uncertainty, deploying both 'domestic' and 'imperial' elements. The historian and politico-cultural activist Arthur Bryant used historical pageants to project a new version of patriotic 'one-nation' conservatism. These events celebrated the local and domestic but also the history of empire at the 1932 Empire Tattoo and the 1933 Greenwich Pageant.[79] Bryant's linking of Englishness to empire included depictions of London combining images of Fleet Street and Bow Bells with the vision of 'a great cosmopolitan nation forged by imperial ties', and praise of the naval commander beside the country gentleman as English heroes.[80] One response to the perceived threats of democracy and modernism was to turn to the 'English' rural or historic hinterland, but empire too was a space where anxiety could be contained. Muir's and Newton's affirmations of possibilities for orderly progress in colonial reform upheld whiggish traditions, as did the vision of English virtues implanted overseas and evoked in

Bryant's view that the British navy had enabled the British to 'give law to the lawless and justice to the oppressed'. Similarly, Marriott's study of the commonwealth in its international setting linked nineteenth-century British pioneering of trusteeship with the post-1919 'opportunity that the empire offers for service to mankind'. Muir spoke of the imperial contribution to 'the enlargement of justice and freedom in the world', and Newton ended his volume on the empire by invoking Christian values as the underlying purpose of empire, echoing Seeley's links between spiritual and colonial purposes.[81]

The expression of such views in the 1940s suggests that the interest in moral agendas associated with 'Victorian' politics and history writing survived the modernist turn to critical scholarship and detached commentary as core elements of historical practice. Diplomatic and international history became a terrain on which a new style of professional historians developed their practices and their careers, but also one where contemporary debates on peace, empire and democracy were echoed in historical texts. Hopes or suspicions about the League of Nations and debates over the role of the UK and empire/commonwealth after the 1914–18 war linked imperial questions to more general concerns with the role of the UK as a great power. This was visible in the influences on the founding of the Institute of International Affairs (Chatham House) where imperial perspectives on the outcomes of the 1914–18 war were bonded to those concerns.[82] Whether seen as a matter of interests, of loyalties or of ideals, British perspectives on the international scene combined global, European and western elements. Muir's history presented empire as 'a part of the greater commonwealth of Western Civilisation', and, like Newton, linked European colonial competition in Africa to threats of universal war'.[83] Rather than losing interest in imperial aspects of the UK state, it seemed that historical texts were relocating them.

Empire, progress and civilisation

A well-known story recounts that when the Indian nationalist and reformer 'Mahatma' Gandhi visited England in 1931 he was asked about his view of western civilisation, and he answered that he thought that it would be an excellent idea. Apart from showing the wit and adroitness appropriate for an experienced political

activist and Middle Temple-trained lawyer as well as a commitment
to Hindu culture, his reply reminds us that notions of 'civilisation'
can usefully be understood as relative. Such uncertainties are
not typical of historical treatments of those themes in the period
under discussion. The themes of continuity and adaptation
identified earlier offer a useful starting point for a discussion of
the associations between 'civilisation', 'progress' and empire
expressed in history writing between the 1890s and the 1940s.
At a time when notions of the 'modern' were regularly used in
social or cultural commentary, in advertising, in popular culture
and in political discourse, the persistence of long-established
views of the difference between 'savage' and 'civilised' societies
and their practices was a notable feature of this writing. Marcy's
1925 *Examination history of England,* and Miller's 1936 *Beginners'
history,* like their eighteenth- and nineteenth-century predecessors,
and the Edwardian Pitman's school histories, introduced the
inhabitants of Britain at the time of the Roman invasions as
'savages' and 'barbarians'. As late as 1950, Neolithic settlements
in England were imagined as African *kraals.* In a similar manner
tenth-century Slavs or Magyars and eleventh-century Seljuq
Turks were called 'savage tribes', just as Muir and Trevelyan used
tribal metaphors and comparisons with Africa in discussion of
seventeenth-century Highlanders and sixteenth-century Welsh.[84]
The 1909 serially published multivolume *Harmsworth history of the
world* offered judgements and descriptions of 'civilisation' based
on long-established assumptions. These volumes used narrative
conventions derived from the 'stage' model of social development,
repeating the notion that 'backward' contemporary societies were
unchanging survivals from a remote past. Thus an account of pre-
Columbian cultures in central America was illustrated with pictures
of twentieth-century indigenous Americans making pottery or
cultivating crops, captioned by the familiar remark that they 'must
be' living and working in the same ways as supposed forebears from
five centuries earlier.[85]

Macaulay's great-nephew G.M. Trevelyan made his own
contribution to progressivist history in his *English social history,* and
in a successful *History of England,* combining social and political
analysis in a fluent and sweeping narrative, taking readers from
ancient settlements to 1918. In the latter text he uses the old tropes
of civilisation and barbarism to rank Irish people behind English

or Scots, and to judge Roman Christianity over other traditions, as well as paganism. He offers a stadial argument to situate feudal institutions and medieval western Christianity in his story of progress and English Protestantism, observing:

> Primitive societies, if they are ever to move on towards knowledge, wealth, and ordered freedom, are obliged to travel in the first instance not along the path of democratic equality, but along the path of aristocracy, kingship and priesthood.[86]

The two approaches are brought together in his summary of social and political change in the later Middle Ages, when 'barbarism' grew into civilisation, but decidedly not along the path of liberty and equality. He deployed similar categories in comments on the social context of nineteenth-century reform politics. The mass movement of Irish people for Catholic emancipation is disparaged by comments on 'ill educated peasants' with the 'instincts of herd morality', contrasted with the humanitarian morality of the contemporary movement for the abolition of slave trading and slavery.[87]

The legacies of older conventions of categorising 'civilisation' were equally manifest in works like Ramsay Muir's 1940 *Civilisation and liberty*. Like Bryce's text of forty years earlier, it subscribed to well-worn conventions associating 'Muslim' societies with despotism, doctrinaire religion and cultural stagnation. It also labelled Chinese civilisation as backward looking, authoritarian and placing low value on human life, and Indian culture as dominated by caste, subservience and Brahmin influence. In just nine pages these civilisations are compared to European civilisation, which is argued to have 'the guidance of human destiny' since only 'western peoples' had the potential for liberty. This was supposedly rooted in ancient Greek commitment to critical thought, Roman respect for the rule of law and Christian ideals of the equal value of all human individuals. The alleged absence of liberty in Indian, 'Muslim' or Chinese civilisations was seen as more important than their governmental, religious and intellectual achievements or their sophisticated art and culture. The views in Muir's text echo the blend of concern for progress of all humanity with a clear picture of a hierarchy of civilisations, and a vision of a 'western' mission to lead human progress, dating back to the mid-nineteenth century. It leads to his vision of the inclusive but hierarchical 'civilisation' which acknowledged 'the rights of the humble and poor and of the simple ad backward peoples to a full share of the boons of civilized life' being defended from Nazism in 1940.[88]

This approach reinforced perceptions of cultural hierarchy and linear development as essential elements in accounts of civilisation or progress, but there was also interest in the diversity of human cultures which incorporated both pleasure and power. Such interest drew on established cultural and consumer associations between the exotic, the saleable and the desirable, but also on new approaches to cultural relativities and hierarchies. Not only were there successful scholarly works which deployed images of cultural diversity, but also popular works such as the *Harmsworth history* and missionary texts made use of colourful detail and visual images of exotic 'others'. Images of 'African', 'oriental', 'savage' or 'native' practices had roles in advertising, film or fiction, and enhanced discussions and depictions of the past. Reviews of anthropological work in generalist journals, and sales of texts like Frazer's *Golden bough*, as well as radio broadcasts featuring anthropological material and specialists, illustrate crossovers which brought cross-cultural topics to wider audiences.[89] While reinforcing the liberal tradition exemplified by Muir, they also supported a reading of culture which reversed the story of 'progress' spreading to all peoples (by self-development or colonial intervention) to imagine the 'primitive' beneath the rational 'modern' surface of 'modern' British civilisation. Whether arguing universalist views of human needs which transcended culture and history, or exploring threats to the fragile structures of what educated privileged men saw as 'civilisation', they used the framework of cultural relativism rather than formulaic versions of stadial history. Miller's *Beginner's history* followed its hostile reference to the Seljuqs with comment on the growth of Crusader respect and tolerance for their 'Saracen foes' as a civilising influence on European culture.[90]

The emergence of anthropological thinking in the later nineteenth century interacted with the structures and interests of colonial rule, and also flavoured the more general use of ideas about civilisation and progress. During the nineteenth century ideas and information about distant societies provided by traders, missionaries and travellers, which were resources for British writers on society and history, also began to be systematised by thinkers working in the emerging discipline of anthropology. In the twentieth century British anthropology became professionalised as well as intellectually reshaped. Three new trends are particularly relevant: firstly, the physical anthropology which had been influential from the 1830s was offset by new emphases on 'society' and 'culture' as key concepts in the comparative study of human groups and institutions; secondly, historical and quantitative approaches to social science were modifying existing conjectural, romantic and philosophic approaches; thirdly, the adoption of the metaphor, if not the concept, of evolution derived from Darwin's work came into use and debate by social thinkers. From the 1890s comparative and historical study of religion, law and social structure, associated with earlier work by Edward Tylor and Henry Maine, added new dimensions to thinking about difference and progress across space and time.[91] Subsequent work perpetuated and challenged the evolutionist tradition in which Tylor had worked. James Frazer's popular text on comparative religion kept an evolutionist approach, tracing human thought from savagery to civilisation, but also used cultural relativism to claim that 'savage' ritual 'had the imprint of reflexion and purpose stamped on it just as plainly as any actions of civilised man'.[92] New approaches to the study of communities and cultures in the non-European world developed new emphases on relativism, and on the 'function' of kinship and religion, rather than stadial analyses, although the influence of evolutionary thought continued. Efforts to develop distinctively 'anthropological' concepts and methods, often distant from conventional historical narrative, led to growing emphasis on 'fieldwork' and the closer relations between imperial and anthropological interests resulting from that.[93]

Tylor's work had laid foundations for the professionalisation of anthropology but also began to unhook the interpretation of non-European cultures from simple linear or evolutionist models. It reinforced the work of commentators like Mary Kingsley, who brought experience of travel and observation of peoples in west Africa into discussions of cultural difference and campaigns on colonial policy. She drew on ideas of racial polygenism to fashion arguments for cultural relativism in support of a critique of missionary efforts at 'improvement'. She stressed the specific character of African cultures, which she distinguished from 'Asiatic' as much as from 'European' culture, arguing that it was the responsibility of colonial rule to protect them from dilution or intervention, rather than to reform them. Her writings on west Africa were taken up by advocates of 'indirect rule', by liberal critics of imperialism and by anthropologists turning from studying ancient African artefacts to looking at African social and cultural organisation.[94] Her critique of reformist interventionism reinforced views of empire which deployed images of the wise management of native peoples whose customs and practices were understood by colonial rulers. It prefigured mutually constitutive relations between anthropologists and colonial administrators which shaped fields of knowledge and authority over 'native' peoples.[95] It was echoed in popular historical treatments like the 1920 edition of S.R. Gardiner's *Student's history of England*, where comments on the 1857–58 Indian uprisings argued that cultural relativism and caution about reform were the best policies for colonial government. Muir's more liberal view presented the rising as a stimulus to better government. In 1940 Glew and Plaskett's *History of England* presented the post-1920 mandate system as being for the 'protection' rather than the improvement of 'native peoples'.[96] They repeated familiar nineteenth-century maxims about colonialists needing to 'understand' the peoples they ruled, but with enhanced confidence in a growing body of anthropological work.

One effect of the new forms of anthropology which shaped the practice of those who studied non-European peoples and the organisation of research and teaching in that field from the 1890s was to intensify distinctions between such studies and study of the European past. Some of these distinctions, as will be seen, fed into twentieth-century ideas of 'race', but were also organised around ideas of 'culture' and 'civilisation', as they came to be used by scholars like Rivers, Malinowski and Radcliffe-Brown. These ideas emphasised function and structure rather than change over time as explanatory tools, combining the view that culture was the expression of timeless and universal human needs and characteristics with rationalist and observation-centred approaches to 'primitive 'societies. [97] Unlike the well-studied links between anthropology and the structures of empire, their influence on history writing needs some clarification. As Stocking has argued, a substratum of evolutionary or stadial thought continued to underpin the 'new' anthropology, sustaining some overlapping areas of interest between its practitioners and historians. More relevant from the perspective of this text is the question of the influence, if any, of anthropological work on historical practice. It is interesting to note that by the interwar period much socio-economic historical work on colonial societies was being done by scholars who identified themselves as anthropologists as well as by former colonial officials.[98] This division of labour between those scholars and the 'historians' who focused on constitutional, political and legal accounts of colonial history reflected the focus of the former on materialist field-based approaches to culture and the attentiveness of the latter to political concerns with empire. Historical writing on areas where 'white' settlement and rule brought them into contact with other societies, polities and cultures certainly addressed cultural difference in terms which drew on the work of anthropologists as well as invoking established notions of 'custom' and 'tradition'.

One interesting case is that of Eileen Power, whose comments on India and south-east Asia combined conventional comparisons of modern India with medieval Europe, experiments with cultural relativism and distinctively gendered readings of eastern 'difference'.[99] Not only did she deploy experiences of travel in lectures on Asian and world history, but that experience allowed her to add comparative perspectives to her work on medieval European history.

Significantly for this discussion, anthropological work contributed to the decline of arguments for the 'Saxon' or 'Germanic' character of English constitutional and legal institutions found in the work of Freeman and Stubbs, now being challenged by academic historians.[100] Maine's connections to the historians Paul Vinogradoff and Frederick Pollock, who developed socio-historical approaches to medieval law and institutions, were an early indication of that link. They helped to shift the focus of medieval history from narratives of constitutional 'progress' to concern with close textual analysis and criticism, placing sources in their specific context rather than in any grand narrative. Although Vinogradoff, Pollock and Maitland were critiqued for an overly 'legal' focus by those who argued that the 'social' and contextual should be central to the study of medieval English history, both sides in that debate contributed to a general shift of emphasis.[101]

Periods in the past were interpreted through accounts of social change and struggle, as with the Hammonds' work on early nineteenth-century labourers, R.H. Tawney's *Religion and the rise of capitalism* or histories of Chartism and the trade unions. More generally, social and economic subjects increasingly became specific topics for historical texts. From the 1890s growing numbers of treatments of specifically 'social' or 'economic' aspects of the past were published for both general and scholarly readers, and, interestingly, a noticeable number of these dealt with the economic development of the dominions and their role in the 1914–18 war.[102] The famously best-selling *English social history* by Macaulay's great-nephew G.M. Trevelyan, first published in 1942, was just the best-known example of an established approach to social history which now competed with other variants.[103] These included broad introductions to social and economic development, colourful 'period' texts like *The social history of Mr and Mrs Warren Hastings* and scholarly studies of mining, trade, textile production and manorial land, as well as textbooks, teachers' guides and bibliographies for schools. The pioneering work of George, Clark, Philpotts and Pinchbeck opened up important fields and drew on a variety of methods in social, economic and anthropological analysis. The publication of collections of documents on social and economic history by Stenton or Tawney, and the scholarly surveys of Clapham, Postan and Power consolidated the field.[104] While works of political, diplomatic and administrative narrative, as well as historical biographies, were the staple forms of historical writing in the first half of the twentieth century, the genres of social and economic history, and specific research and teaching in those fields, also became established areas of historical practice.

The emergence of 'social' and 'economic' narratives as a distinct subset of historical writing marked a shift from older treatments of 'manners' and stadial accounts of social development while incorporating existing assumptions. While Bentley has argued that the persistence of established 'whiggish' approaches and assumptions should not be underestimated, other narratives of progress were also coming into use. Some works offered Marxian variants of the stadial account of transitions from one form of socio-economic organisation to another, focused on conflicts of interest, exploitation and the dynamic working-out of contradictions in economy and society. Others built interpretations of social and economic change based on the close analysis of data and sources and attention to complexity and diversity rather than strong narrative. The Hammonds' books had focused on the contentious issue of the human costs of industrial and commercial change in the later eighteenth and early nineteenth centuries without sacrificing notions of 'progress' in their arguments. In challenging prevailing accounts of urban and industrial change as 'advance' they still saw the possibility of progress, but looked to its coming when those disadvantaged by those changes redressed the damage caused by capitalist industrialisation – views consonant with their commitment to social liberalism. Their 'pessimist' account was to be challenged by economic historians of the 1920s and 1930s using quantitative regional and enterprise-based sources to offer 'modern', 'non-partisan' analyses, which in turn stimulated debate over quantitative and qualitative assessments of 'well-being' or 'improvement'.[105] Such accounts of 'progress' focused much more precisely on technical innovation, socio-economic structures and material change but retained familiar ethnocentric and linear frameworks for presenting them, with the story of western European development remaining the template.

One of the shifts in notions of 'civilisation', and their imperial associations, during the interwar period was rooted in gloomy responses to the 1914–18 war and its aftermath. Awareness of new levels of destructive warfare, the collapse of long-established European governments into violent or unstable successor regimes, and real and imagined threats of social conflict, stimulated various pessimistic assessments of the human condition. The idealism associated with support for the League of Nations and for internationalism, or with hopes for social advance among advocates of reform and social justice who had campaigned on such issues since the 1880s, was challenged by new forms of confrontation and uncertainty. While the hostile or gloomy critiques of 'modern' society produced during the interwar years can clearly be linked to new circumstances, it should also be noted that they continued a pattern of both 'left' and 'right' critiques of modern civilisation going back to Carlyle, Ruskin, Arnold, or Morris. One strand in interwar discussion echoed older opposition to what was seen as class conflict materialism and social inequity, but developed and used nostalgia for 'Merrie Englande' or 'olden times' which had emerged during the nineteenth century. Certain kinds of medievalism could be used either to condemn the oppressive and squalid conditions of the deprived and unprivileged, or to lament the disintegration of community and order, both associated with industrialism and urbanisation. Tawney's work on sixteenth-century England was flavoured by critiques of unrestricted individualism and materialism inherited from nineteenth-century Christian socialism, and by forms of ethical and collectivist thought which were shaping the Labour Party.[106]

Older forms of pessimism intertwined with newer concerns about the emergence of mass society, of trends to secularism, and of what were seen as expressions of 'barbaric' behaviour or culture in what should have been 'civilised' (that is, European) societies. The decline of social deference, or of reasoned approaches to the world, or of established beliefs, cultural practices and values could be interpreted not so much as threats to the political order, but as evidence of decay in the social fabric. This kind of anxiety and anger might take the form of attacks on jazz music or cinema going, of fearful consideration of the power of 'vulgar' views and preferences and of the 'decline' of 'civilised' social relationships and established social structures. In some cases this included anxieties about colonial 'others' After 1918 the growing consolidation of the distinctive aspects of both middle-class and working-class identity was expressed in defensive, sometimes adversarial, forms, ranging from party politics to everyday lifestyles, intensified by economic difficulties and changes in the interwar period. The emergence of a Conservative Party based on cross-class appeal as an anti-socialist party, and of the Labour Party as the main alternative party, linked to the trades unions and various traditions of social reform, was perhaps less important than the growing organisation of housing, education and leisure patterns around 'class' differences. The anxieties and antagonisms provoked by these developments underpinned a pessimism which could be reinforced by reflections on conflict and violence, whether of 'left' or 'right' on the international scene. Selfish employers or fascist sympathisers, confrontational left-wing activists, destructive revolutionaries or financiers and a sense of material or political changes beyond the control of any groups or individuals became familiar images or associations.

Such themes should also be considered as influences on the use of ideas of progress and civilisation in history writing, and the presence, or absence, of imperial influences on those ideas. The theme of progress might still be given prominence, as in C.S.

Higham's 1929 *Pioneers of progress: stories of social history, 1750–1920* (reissued in 1952) or R. Lambert's *Pioneers of social progress* talks, broadcast and then published by the BBC in its 'Aids to Study' series in 1928. A 1927 pamphlet on *Christian reformers of the nineteenth century* included the socialists Keir Hardie and William Morris alongside Florence Nightingale, Wilberforce and Dickens, signalling overlaps between different reforming traditions. This range of publications offered positive accounts of change and celebrated the 'progressive' work of scientists and reformers, and also of 'imperial' figures like David Livingstone, Francis Drake and Robert Clive. More books were published on Cecil Rhodes than on Clive in this period, perhaps showing a shift of interest to African empire building and 'white' settlement, but we should also consider whether imperial influences continued to flavour historical writing on society more generally. One strand of influence might be personal, whether in Arthur Innes', H.A.L. Fisher's and Tawney's family links to reform, law and education in India, or in Power's travels in India and China. Internationalism and history writing intersected when Tawney's visits to China as a League of Nations education adviser in the 1930s enabled him to bring his work on sixteenth-century England to bear on his 1932 *Land and labour in China*. Lawrence Hammond's early journalistic activity in liberal pro-Boer and home rule politics resurfaced in his last historical work on Gladstone and Ireland, and Innes held a post at the School of Oriental and African Studies while writing school histories of England.[107] Other strands were formed by the interaction of social scientific and historical studies in particular texts, and through academic links within institutions such as developed at the London School of Economics and Cambridge. Those who were defining themselves as economic historians did so partly by negotiating boundaries and alliances between their activities and those of economists on the one hand and historians on the other. Nonetheless, most UK historians remained distanced from, or sceptical about, the systemic and structural approaches of social scientists.

Progress was coming to be seen as not just a matter of ideals and missions but one of material and technocratic improvement both for empire and for home. While promoting empire trade, the Empire Marketing Board used images of prosperity and benevolence as the underpinnings and outcomes of the production of Sudanese cotton, Ceylon tea or Rhodesian tobacco in the colonies, as well as in the UK.[108] Regardless, accounts of empire continued to present stories centred on moral as well as material improvement. Reginald Coupland's work on imperial politics and institutions was buttressed by studies of missionaries and anti-slavery reformers and general accounts of empire which foreground progress and virtue. His more contemporary pieces were on imperial questions. Set in an explicitly Christian context (he wrote for the *Christian Science Monitor* among other publications), his writings looked to the combination of humanitarianism and business sagacity in the African colonies and new imperial partnerships with educated nationalists in India.[109]

What is worth considering further here is the remaking of views of 'civilisation' or 'progress' over the first half of the twentieth century. On the one hand, knowledge of trench warfare or Nazi extermination camps acted as a counterweight to any overconfidence in 'western civilisation'. On the other hand, belief in having engaged in war to defend civilisation was a strategy for managing difficult contradictions or memories, and for sustaining patriotic thinking and feeling. The conviction expressed by historians like Muir and Newton that the empire/commonwealth was still an inspiring agent for good indicates their wish to convey such beliefs and the influence of the more 'optimistic' responses to world war. For the former this took the form of secular idealism about liberty and civilisation, while the latter used the Christian reference 'do as you would be done by'. Concluding an officially sponsored account of the empire/commonwealth in the 1940s, Vincent Harlow emphasised British responsibility to 'set each colony on a sound economic footing' with education, legal and healthcare provision and the professionals to run them. This responsibility required the continuation of the British imperial presence, on which colonial people 'must rely' for some time to come. At the end of this period the image of an imperial civilising mission was still underpinning historical narrative.[110]

Empire, race and nation

If nineteenth-century history writing was flavoured by newly acquired perspectives on racial and national differences and characteristics, the period from the 1890s to the 1940s was one in which these perspectives were consolidated and normalised.

The matter-of-fact use of these terms in history writing during this period can be contrasted with the apparently more dramatic shifts which had taken place earlier, or those in the era of decolonisation and postcolonial debate after 1950. Much early twentieth-century history writing worked with understandings of 'nation' or 'race' established over previous decades. Interchangeable and imprecise references to 'German', Mongol, 'French Canadian', 'African', 'British', 'Boer', 'Indian' or 'Irish' nations or races continued to be typical of many texts.[111] When Ellis wanted to distinguish the inhabitants of Abyssinia/Ethiopia from other peoples in Africa in the 1940s, he deployed accounts of 'racial' origins and characteristics already familiar in popular and academic discourse. It is worth noting that both Ellis and Miller did this in the context of discussion of Mussolini's attack on Abyssinia in 1936 which challenged liberal faith in League of Nations principles.[112] Eugenic and evolutionary views of human difference still combined with differentiation on the basis of history or customs and assumptions about racial hierarchy which had long been taken for granted. The overlaps, inconsistencies and differentiations between 'race' and 'nation' established during the nineteenth century continued to influence twentieth-century history writing.

The historical work of James Bryce (1838–1922), a successful campaigning liberal education reformer and internationalist, MP and government minister, as well as academic lawyer and historian, illustrates these influences at the start of the period. His writings on American government, and his internationalist campaigning, have had more attention than those of his texts which linked legal history with reflections on racial and national character, or discussed the role of race in history. However, one of his earliest and often reissued works, a *History of the Holy Roman Empire* (thirty-three reprints between 1870 and 1950), flagged questions of imperial federation or devolution which also influenced his treatments of Irish and colonial issues. A typical 'advanced' liberal of his times, he combined commitment to humanitarian and universalist ideas and causes with unquestioning views of racial hierarchy. His socio-cultural and comparative analysis of the historic links of law and religion included references to something he termed 'the Muslim mind', and ethnographic anecdote rather than intellectual analysis in his discussion of Azhar University in Cairo. His lecture *The relations of the advanced and the backward races of mankind*, following the arguments of Ernest Renan, distinguished between the supposed homogeneity of 'races' and the 'mixed' composition of 'nations'. It also presented arguments for racial segregation, and for excluding non-white colonial subjects from self-government, appealing to the best interests of humanity and social order and to familiar views about inherent racial differences and inequalities.[113] These texts expressed liberal and moral concerns with justice and humanity alongside statements about miscegenation and racial characteristics, and airbrushed some of the violent episodes in colonial history. A prominent critic of genocidal attacks on Armenians in the 1890s and in 1915, Bryce wrote of how the indigenous inhabitants of Tasmania 'died out', and not of the role of British settlers in their disappearance, and he described the enforced removals of Native Americans from their lands by US governments as 'peaceable'.[114] His writings on the USA emphasised the importance of 'white' colonial ethnicity and institutions as in the earlier work of Freeman and Goldwin Smith, and advanced by twentieth-century advocates of imperial or 'commonwealth' federation.

Racial thinking was transmitted from nineteenth- to twentieth-century history writing via a web of influences and assumptions linking public life, academic and professional practice and wider cultural experience. Bryce's public career began in the 1860s and ended with his endorsement of the 1921 Irish treaty, but the connections he embodied were not exclusive to his generation. Many practitioners of imperial and colonial history between the 1920s and 1950s brought to it experiences in colonial administration and policy, and in turn developed their history teaching and research in conjunction with the training and education of colonial administrators. 'Empire historians' like Egerton and Lucas, and later Coupland, Perham, Harlow, Keith and Hancock, and critics such as Leys, Olivier, Woolf and Barnes combined scholarly work with activities as colonial officials, as educators of officials and as advisers on colonial questions. Their contemporary activities in India, the Sudan, Sri Lanka, the Caribbean or sub-Saharan Africa informed their depictions of nation and empire in the past, and provided a distinctive authority for their historical knowledge and judgements. Authors like Bryant or Marriott (a strong Unionist) might be less close to imperial matters, but brought experience of politics, public debate and journalism, including debate on empire, to their historical writing. Arthur Innes, whose father and grandfather served in India, lectured at the School of Oriental and African Studies as well as writing popular and school histories, and Ramsay Muir worked as an academic in both India and the UK.

Racialised language was still part of the repertoire of history writing, if also somewhat different in its patterns. Depictions of the early history of the 'British' Isles in Edwardian school readers, and also in later histories and school texts, continued to refer to Celtic, British and English 'races' in their narratives of the movements, conquests and cultures of different groups in the 'British' Isles.[115] In the 1920s Marcy called the eleventh-century invaders of Palestine a 'wild tribe of Mohammedans', and referred to Disraeli's 'eastern love of pomp', just as Glew and Plaskett labelled Mongols, Ottomans and Aztecs as 'races' in the 1940s.[116] Marcy used the idea of 'degeneration', in use since the late nineteenth century, to describe the effects of Roman rule on the 'brave and warlike race' of Britons. Historians like Muir also maintained a convention going back to the eighteenth century whereby from later medieval times the 'English' and 'Scots' are called 'nations', supposedly blended from different 'races'. G.M. Trevelyan's *History of England* made the 'mingling of races' the organising theme of the history of England up until the conquest, but then presents the 'mingled' English as themselves a 'race'.[117] The early modern and modern population of Ireland were often called a 'race' (or 'races' if 'Ulster' matters were discussed). Trevelyan maintained a 'racial' perspective and terminology for the Irish throughout his *History* from the medieval period to nineteenth century.[118]

Dissident Scots might be labelled as a 'brood' or 'race', as in Innes' and Gardiner's accounts of the 1690 massacre of the Macdonalds in Glencoe. Interestingly, distinctions began to be drawn between the 'racial' views of the Irish taken by seventeenth-century English people and twentieth-century ideas.[119] As in the past, the French, Spanish, Germans, not to mention the 'Saxons' and 'Angles' who figure in early medieval history, or South African Boers in the nineteenth century, could be named as both 'races' and 'nations', indicating the persistence and prevalence of racial thought, and its lack of clarity. Muir's history of the commonwealth, which is critical of British rule in Ireland, also sees it as 'a system of racial dominion', with the privileged place of the Church of Ireland before disestablishment a 'sign and token of racial ascendancy', also echoed in Trevelyan's *History*. Muir's account of the formation of the English 'nation' emphasised institutions not race, but he proclaimed the twentieth-century commonwealth as 'the glorious fellowship of the free peoples she [*i.e.* Britain] has bred, and of the ancient peoples she has roused from stagnation, and of the simple peoples whom she has brought under her tutelage'.[120]

Similar confusion was evident in the various discussions of English 'national character', and its history found in journalism, books and broadcasting in the 1920s and 1930s. From one perspective such discussions contributed to inward-looking affirmations of an identity seen as challenged domestically by class conflict and modernising reform, and/or internationally by totalitarianism, decline and competition. Historians have drawn attention to how interwar depictions of 'Englishness' embedded it in 'historic' settings ('ancient' villages, landscapes or buildings) threatened by encroaching suburbs, or in patterns of life and work under attack by modernisers and reformers or by economic decline. Presentations of 'national character' both historicised and essentialised that character by emphasising a view of 'English' identity as being shaped by past experience, from Saxon settlement to Georgian rural prosperity, but also somehow being unchanging or persisting over time. Alongside such depictions of a long-established, picturesque 'Englishness' (usually *not* 'Britishness') were images of the modern suburban 'Englishman' centred on his solid domestic lifestyle and unassertive respectability, not high public, political or military virtues.[121] In addition to the domestic and softened features of this reworked identity, and the iconic figure of the modest 'little man', it is also worth noting the ethnographic and culturally based construction of this persona with its emphasis on habits, history and customs rather than grand moral qualities. In some ways these depictions of 'Englishness' used an approach and language not dissimilar to that familiar in portrayals of 'foreign' peoples.

Alongside celebrations of 'deep history' embodied in landscape and customs, another way of conveying 'Englishness' in the interwar period was reports of 'journeys into England', in books, articles or radio broadcasts. Their anthropological tone echoed the convention of travellers' tales of Africa or India. Educated observers constructing accounts of rural life, or of poverty in areas of declining industry, organised their accounts around ideas of the 'national' or the 'English', in which the historical, the nostalgic and the ethnic played visible roles. Their key purpose was to address current social or cultural questions. This applied to the leftist agenda of former Burma police officer George Orwell's now famous, though initially little read, *Road to Wigan Pier*, the rural Christian nostalgia of H.V. Morton's best-selling *In search of England*, and the ambivalent populism of J.B. Priestley's *English journey*.[122] While these texts evoked the distinctive localised 'character' and contemporary condition of 'the English', that 'character' was presented using methods with imperial antecedents. As with earlier notions of 'darkest England', models of exotic travel writing and colonial style ethnographic depictions of 'others' influenced the accounts of the 'English' people with whom Orwell, Priestley or Morton wished readers to identify. After the 1914–18 war 'Englishness' might not be celebrated in the direct imperial terms typical of preceding decades, but the more domestically centred views of the period offered an 'ethnic' view of the 'English', whose style and method drew on imperial experiences of interpreting 'others'.

This combination of history, ethnography and empire is tellingly presented in the published version of a set of radio lectures given in 1933 by the popular historian and cultural politician Arthur Bryant on *The national character*.[123] Defining the notion of 'England' as a composite of 'place', 'history' and 'people', it discusses 'character' in terms of race, geography and climate, celebrating the rural virtues of 'home', and a blend of 'races' varied enough to prevent stagnation but without too much 'alien inflow'. While evoking Yorkshire moors and Cornish harbours, and celebrating rural settings and people, it asserts that English attributes include an aptitude for colonisation, and it quotes imperialist Cecil Rhodes' praises of the English as 'the first race in the world'.[124] Home, character and empire are intertwined, whether by imagining 'imperial' heroes like Clive fighting for 'home' in India, or envisaging national decline as 'the last British flag lowered from the seven seas'. The self-assurance seen as central to national character accounts for English ability to 'absorb under its rule something like one third of the habitable globe' and for their difficulties ruling 'intellectual races like the Irish or the Hindus'.[125] Two-thirds of the text explores that character through seven 'types' – an approach reminiscent of anthropological discourse, although delivered in tones of the nostalgic, the picturesque and polemic critique. As well as 'the gentleman', 'the parson', 'the housewife' and 'the yeoman farmer', these include 'the merchant' and 'the adventurer'. These last two are both associated with global and imperial achievements via references to exotic imports, to the East India Company, Captain Cook, Rhodes and Clive, as well as Livingstone and the nineteenth-century *raj* soldier hero John Nicholson.[126]

Bryant's major historical work of the 1930s, a biography of Pepys which despite wartime conditions had sold over thirty thousand copies by 1948, was intended to challenge anti-monarchical 'whig' accounts of the reign of Charles II. It emphasised Pepys' role as a loyal and patriotic servant of the crown and 'saviour of the Navy' (the title of the third volume), setting his story within England's emerging naval and imperial destiny. In *National character*, Bryant explicitly linked the naval revival of the 1670s, in which Pepys had played a role, to the nineteenth-century 'heroic' exploits of Nicholson in India and Gordon in the Sudan. Bryant built on the work of J.R. Tanner, who had lectured on Pepys and the navy, and in the preface to volume 2 of his own work stated that Pepys' work had begun the process which 'gave his country dominion of the seas and the empire of more than a quarter of the world'. Pepys' naval reforms are called 'a course being charted which led through the shoals of Quiberon and the deeps of Trafalgar to sea dominion and empire'.[127] This echoed concerns with empire and navy prevalent in Bryant's youth and connected him to historians with imperial interests such as Keith Feiling, who served in India and had passed Bryant the Pepys commission since he himself was working on a study of Warren Hastings. Bryant sets Pepys at the start of an imperial trajectory, as 'a pioneer of bureaucracy in a young empire', observing the decayed empire of Spain, who when in Tangier has yet to learn to 'disbelieve natives' in order to 'grasp …imperial destiny'.[128] The text continued the 'empire of the sea' tradition in history writing found in Froude, and Bryant's work generally, like that of other interwar commentators, voiced the anti-industrialism of Froude's *Oceana* while adding a new kind of anti-modernist, anti leftist argument. Trevelyan's history likewise incorporated the theme of sea-and-empire and nostalgic images of pre-industrial England in accounts of industrialisation and urbanisation, criticising the latter developments even while arguing their benefits.[129] It is worth noting the convergence of sympathies between these two prominent historians troubled (Trevelyan as an old style liberal, Bryant as an active Tory) by the changes they saw in interwar Britain.

One shift in the ethnic terms and assumptions used in history writing in the twentieth century was the decline in the explicit 'Teutonism' typical of nineteenth-century texts. Developments in anthropological and archaeological thought, critical archival work by historians of medieval England – and perhaps a legacy of anti-German views associated with the 1914–18 war, and later Nazism – each contributed to undermining this perspective on the English past. The account of medieval government in Tout's *Short analysis of English history* focused more on the conflict between the crown and 'feudal party', and dated the 'definition of the constitution and national character' (an interesting pairing) to the reign of Edward I. This emphasis was found in authors less steeped in medieval administrative history than Tout, with many textbooks still heroising Alfred, but more inclined to discuss Edward I and Magna Carta in modified versions of a story going back to Hallam.[130] They offered more nuanced depictions of Anglo-Saxon culture, and in Feiling's 1948 text it is Christianity rather than Germanic political traditions which is said to have united the Anglo-Saxons – a view propounded by Innes forty years earlier. This might partly express Feiling's own interest in the history of Toryism with its strong association of church and nation, but continuing presentation of Saxons, British and Irish as 'races' was now often detached from legal or constitutional accounts.[131]

Racial references in historical texts of the interwar period presented a paradoxical picture. These texts shared the general cultural acceptance of 'race' as a term at a time when scholarly anthropologists were testing and complicating that term as a useful category, while working with ideas of the 'primitive' and the 'half-caste'.[132] What is striking about them is the persistence of established usage of the terms 'people', 'race' and 'nation' as interchangeable labels for groups supposed to share cultural, political and perhaps physical characteristics – a usage going back to eighteenth-century practice. Like nineteenth-century predecessors, Innes could still write of the 'British race' as the free and law-abiding creators of 'the greatest empire in the world'. The soberly professional editors of the *Cambridge history of the British empire* could root the growth of the empire in the 'sea instinct' of fifteenth- and sixteenth-century explorer/entrepreneurs.[133] This might be contrasted with the emphasis placed by Muir on the equally well-established notion of 'civilisation' – albeit, as has been argued, a Eurocentric one – as the unifying category for liberty and progress. He too, however, set this notion against one of the 'backward races' who might be uplifted by European imperial influence.[134] It seems that while historical practice in this period included many distinctive and inconsistent variants of ethnic and racial discourse, much of it operated from 'within' a racialised and ethnicised culture shared by historians and their readers alike.

Notes

1 R. Muir, *The expansion of Europe*, 2nd edn, London, 1917 (reprinted 2006), p. 4.

2 R. Muir, *Civilisation and liberty*, London, 1940, p. 24; Muir, *Expansion of Europe*, p. 6.

3 M. Bentley, *Modernising England's past: English historiography in the age of modernism*, Cambridge, 2005, pp. 5–10.

4 Muir, *Civilisation and liberty*, pp. 194, 242, 282.

5 see A.P. Newton, *A hundred years of the British empire*, London, 1940, 1947; V.T. Harlow, *Origins and purpose of the British commonwealth and empire: a handbook*, London, 1944, J.A. Marriott, *Commonwealth or anarchy*, London, 1937.

6 K. Laybourn, *Britain on the breadline*, Gloucester, 1991 emphasises the former, C. Cook and J. Stevenson, *Britain in the depression*, London, 1994 the latter; another perspective is M. Glucksmann, *Women assemble*, London, 1990.

7 M. Daunton, *Wealth and welfare: an economic and social history of Britain, 1851–1951*, Cambridge, 2007 unpicks the story of decline and contrasts global and insular capitalism; B. Alford, *Britain in the world economy since 1880*, London, 1996.

8 A useful summary is D. Fieldhouse, 'The metropolitan economics of empire', in J. Brown and W. Louis [eds.], *Oxford history of the British empire: the twentieth century*, Oxford, 1999.

9 P. Cain and A. Hopkins, *British imperialism: decline and deconstruction*, London, 1993, pp. 36–40; A. Thompson, *The empire strikes back?*, Harlow, 2005, pp. 168–75.

10 B. Tomlinson 'The contraction of England: national decline and the loss of empire', *Journal of Imperial and Commonwealth History*, vol.11, no.1, 1982, pp. 58-72, and 'The British economy and the empire 1900-1939', in E. Wrigley [ed.], *A companion to early twentieth century Britain*, Oxford, 2008; Thompson, *The empire strikes back*, pp. 56–63, 156–62; A. Thompson, *Imperial Britain*, Harlow, 2000, ch. 6; S. Constantine [ed.],

Emigrants and empire: British settlement in the dominions between the wars, Manchester, 1990.

11 Cain and Hopkins, *British imperialism,* pp. 40–8.

12 H. Kuklick, *The savage within: the social history of British anthropology, 1885–1945,* Cambridge, 1991; G. Stocking, *After Tylor: British social anthropology, 1888–1951,* London, 1995, ch. 8; D. Mills, *Difficult folk: a political history of social anthropology,* London, 2008, chs 1, 3, 5, 6.

13 G. Searle, *The quest for national efficiency,* Oxford, 1971, pp. 30–1, 70–1, 260–2.

14 P. Williamson, *Stanley Baldwin: conservative leadership and national values,* Cambridge, 1999, chs 1, 2, 8; Thompson, *Imperial Britain,* ch. 7; W. Garside, 'Party politics, political economy, and British protectionism 1919–32', *History,* vol. 83, no. 269 (1998), pp. 47–65; G. Claeys, *Imperial sceptics: British critics of empire, 1850–1920,* Cambridge, 2010.

15 P. Rich, *Race and empire in British politics,* Cambridge, 1990; Thompson, *Imperial Britain.*

16 J. Springhall, 'Lord Meath, youth, and empire', *Journal of Contemporary History,* vol. 5, (1970), pp. 97–112; J. English, 'Empire Day in Britain, 1904–58', *Historical Journal* vol. 49, no. 1 (2006), pp. 247–76; T. August, *The selling of empire: British and French imperial propaganda, 1890–1940,* Westport, CT, 1985.

17 A. Ramamurthy, *Imperial persuaders: images of Africa and Asia in British advertising,* Manchester, 2003; H. Casserley, *British locomotive names of the twentieth century,* London, 1965, pp. 19–21, 59, 79–80, 97, 122; J. MacKenzie [ed.], *Imperialism and popular culture,* Manchester, 1986.

18 S. Constantine, *Buy and build: the advertising posters of the Empire Marketing Board,* London, 1986; A. Warren, 'Citizens of the empire: Baden-Powell, Scouts and Guides', in MacKenzie, *Imperialism and popular culture,* Thompson, *The empire strikes back,* pp. 1–8.

19 J. Richards [ed.], *Imperialism and juvenile literature,* Manchester, 1989; J. Richards, *Film and British national identity,* Manchester, 1997; J. Richards, 'Ireland, empire and film', in K. Jefferys [ed.], *An Irish empire?* Manchester, 1996; J. Richards, 'The sun never sets: *Sanders of the river*', in J. Richards and A. Aldgate, *Best of British,* London, 1999; A. Jenkinson, *What do boys and girls read?* London, 1946; W. Webster, 'The empire answers: imperial identity on radio and film, 1939–45', in P. Buckner and R. Francis [eds.], *Discovering the British world,* Calgary, 2005; J. MacKenzie, '"In touch with the infinite": the BBC and empire', in MacKenzie, *Imperialism and popular culture;* S. Nicholas, '"Brushing up your empire": dominion and colonial propaganda on the BBC Home Services, 1939–45', *Journal of Imperial and Commonwealth History,* vol. 31, no. 2 (2003), pp. 207–30; K. Dunn, 'Lights…Camera…Images of Africa and Africans in western popular films of the 1930s', *African Studies Review,* vol. 39, no. 1 (1996), pp. 149–75.

20 Christie travelled the empire in 1922 promoting the British Empire Exhibition, see A. Christie, *Grand tour: letters and photographs from the British Empire exhibition*, [ed. M. Prichard] London, 2012; Page lived on an estate in what was then called Rhodesia; Rhodes travelled in British-ruled Egypt in 1908; Diver grew up in an army family in India; one view of romance and imperial settings is in R. Anderson, *The purple heart throbs*, London, 1974, pp. 182–94; see also C. Duder, 'Love and the lions: images of white settlement in Kenya in popular fiction', *African Affairs*, vol. 90, no. 360 (1991), pp. 427–38.

21 R. McKibbin, *Classes and cultures, 1918–1951*, Oxford, 1998, p. 419.

22 Quoted in J. Rose, *The intellectual life of the British working classes*, New Haven, CT, 2010, pp. 363–4.

23 A. Light, *Forever England: femininity, conservatism and literature between the wars*, London, 1991, p. 8; D. Bivona, *British imperial literature*, Cambridge, 1998.

24 Williamson, *Stanley Baldwin*, chs 3, 4, 7; R. Colls, *Identity of England*, Oxford, 2002.

25 Library data show that this material was regularly republished as well as gaining new titles.

26 S. Baldwin, *On England*, London, 1926 (collected speeches 1923–26), pp. 7–8, 17, 71–2, 200.

27 R. Roberts, *A ragged schooling*, London, 1971, p. 142; Rose, *The intellectual life of the British working classes*.

28 See Rich, *Race and empire in British politics*; R. Whiting 'The empire and British politics', in A. Thompson [ed.], *The British experience of empire in the twentieth century*, Oxford, 2012; McKibbin, *Classes and cultures*; Thompson, *The empire strikes back*, chs 6, 8; N. Owen, 'Critics of empire in Britain', in W.R. Louis [ed.], *Oxford history of the British empire, vol 4: the twentieth century*, Oxford, 1999.

29 Warren, 'Citizens of empire'; J. Alberti, *Beyond suffrage*, Basingstoke, 1989, ch. 7; J. Alberti, *Eleanor Rathbone*, London, 1996, ch. 6; S. Pedersen, *Eleanor Rathbone*, New Haven, CT, 2004, pp. 241–65; A. Burton, *Burdens of history*, Chapel Hill, NC, 1994; A. Burton, *At the heart of the empire*, Berkeley, CA, 1998.

30 A. Thompson, *The empire strikes back*, chs 1–4; McKibbin, *Classes and cultures*.

31 D. Smith, 'Englishness and the liberal inheritance after 1886', in R. Colls and P. Dodd [eds.], *Englishness: politics and culture, 1880–1920*, London, 1986; J. Hammerton, *Child of wonder: an intimate biography of Arthur Mee*, London, 1946.

32 D. Cannadine *et al.*, *The right kind of history: teaching the past in twentieth-century England*, Basingstoke, 2011, pp. 18–19, 44–6, 50–5, 86–96; H. Hendrick, *Children, childhood, and society*, Cambridge, 1997, pp. 63–78.

33 The pattern of decline is noted in P. Mandler, *History and national life*, London, 2002, pp. 64–5; his calculation does not include historical biographies, and it is unclear whether it includes textbooks.

34 Longman, Macmillan and Oxford University Press all offered multivolume series on England, and Cambridge University Press its European and imperial histories. Longman, Nelson and Cassell published school textbooks.

35 V. Feske, *From Belloc to Churchill: private scholars, public culture, and the crisis of Victorian liberalism*, Chapel Hill, NC, 1996; Bentley, *Modernising England's past*.

36 G. Stocking, *After Tylor: British social anthropology, 1885–1951*, London, 1995; Kuklick, *The savage within*, chs 2, 3.

37 M. Berg, *A woman in history: Eileen Power, 1889–1940*, Cambridge, 1996; E. Miller, 'Postan, Sir Michael Moissey', *Proceedings of the British Academy*, vol. 69 (1983), pp. 543–57.

38 Bentley, *Modernising England's past*, pp. 120–8; T.C. Barker, 'The beginnings of the Economic History Society', *Economic History Review*, vol. 30, no. 1 (1977), pp. 1–19; P. Blaas, *Continuity and anachronism*, The Hague, M. Nijhoff, pp. 44–50; Feske, *From Belloc to Churchill*, ch. 3.

39 B. Schwartz, 'Englishry: the histories of G.M. Trevelyan', in C. Hall and K. McClelland [eds.], *Race, nation and empire: making histories, 1750 to the present*, Manchester, 2010, pp. 119–22, 130 n. 19; R. Tawney, 'The study of economic history', *Economica*, vol. 39 (Feb. 1933), pp. 1–21 (his inaugural lecture as Professor of Economic History at the London School of Economics), pp. 9–10.

40 L. Goldman, *Dons and workers: Oxford and adult education since 1850*, Oxford, 1995, p. 62; Rose, *Intellectual life of the British working class*.

41 D. Cannadine 'The context, meaning, and performance of ritual: the British monarchy and the "invention of tradition"', in E. Hobsbawm and T. Ranger [eds.], *The invention of tradition*, Cambridge, 1983; F. Prochaska, *The republic of Britain, 1760–2000*, London, 2000, pp. 156–77.

42 Colls, *Identity of England*; Colls and Dodd, *Englishness: politics and culture*; R. Hyam, *Britain's declining empire*, Cambridge, 2006, p. 2, n. 4; M. Taylor, 'Imperium at libertas', *Journal of Imperial and Commonwealth History*, vol. 19, no. 1 (1991), pp. 1–23; Cannadine, 'Context, meaning and performance of ritual'; D. Cannadine, *Ornamentalism: how the British saw their empire*, London, 2002.

43 C. Ellis, *England and the modern world*, London, 1947, p. 275.

44 E. Sanderson, *The story of England: a reading book for students*, London, 1892, pp. 190–1; W. Marcy, *Examination history of England*, London, 1925, p. 168; D. Glew and H. Plaskett, *History of England*, 3 vols, London, 1940, vol. 3, pp. 158–9; A. Innes, *History of England for use in schools*, London, 1907, 1908, 1912 1926, pp. 468–72; E.W. Miller,

The beginner's history of England (1921), London, 1936, pp. 232–3; *King Edward history reader*, London, 1901, pp. 163–4; E. Conan and E. Kendall, *A short history of England for schools*, London, 1902, p. 405.

45 Creasy, *Rise and progress of the English constitution*, p. 360; O. Browning, *The evolutionary history of England* (a Pitman reader), London, 1901, p. 157, Sanderson, *Story of England*, p. 210.

46 R. Holland, *Britain and the commonwealth alliance, 1918–39*, London, 1981; J. Gallagher, *The decline, revival, and fall of the British empire*, Cambridge, 1982; D. McMahon, *Republicans and imperialists: Anglo-Irish relations in the 1930s*, New Haven, CT, 1984; R. Coupland, *The empire in these days*, London, 1935; a useful summary is J. Darwin, 'A third British empire: the dominion idea in imperial politics', in and Louis, *Oxford history of the British empire, vol. 4*.

47 Cannadine, *The right kind of history*, pp. 80–1.

48 For example *King Edward history reader*, p. 204; Browning, *The evolutionary history of England*, p. 215; C.E. Dawes, *King Edward's realm*, London, 1902, pp. 210–11; P. Kerr, Lord Lothian, *The growth of the British empire*, London, 1911, pp. 143, 155, 176–7; S. Gardiner, *A student's history of England*, 3 vols, London, 1920, vol. 3, pp. 978, 1004; R. Muir, *A short history of the British commonwealth*, 2 vols, London, 1923, vol. 2, pp. 717, 781–8; Ellis, *England and the modern world*, pp. 275, 285; Newton, *A hundred years of the British empire*, pp. 314, 360–6.

49 J. Buchan, *Greenmantle*, London, 1916 (nine editions by 1920, reprints to 1952, school version published 1937); J. Buchan, *Mr Standfast*, London, 1919 (reprints to 1952).

50 Ellis, *England and the modern world*, p. 275; R. Muir, *A short history*, vol. 2, pp. 787, 789.

51 Innes, *History of England*, pp. 531–3, *King Edward history reader*, pp. 209–10; see too Browning, *The evolutionary history of England*, p. 157 hoping for 'a Parliament of the whole British empire'.

52 C. Lucas [ed.], *The empire at war*, 5 vols, Oxford, 1921–26; HMSO, *The military effort of the British empire in the Great War*, London, 1922.

53 Newton, *A hundred years of the British empire*, pp. 355–6 uses the motifs of pragmatism and organic/flexible adaptation conventionally used in accounts of English constitutional change to depict the development of imperial links in 1900–1914; the point is also made in Glew and Plaskett, *History of England*, vol. 3, p. 340.

54 A. Pollard, *The evolution of parliament*, London, 1920 (reprinted until 1964), pp. 359–79.

55 Browning, *Evolutionary history of England*, p. 119 (in the section on 'Parliament' by W. Reddaway).

56 Ellis, *England and the modern world*, pp. xv, 273; G.M. Trevelyan, *England under Queen Anne*, 3 vols, London, 1930–34 (republished until 1965), vol. 1, p. 1; p. 10 links England to the colonies in 'New England; pp.

286–7 discusses the advantages of 'British' (rather than 'English')
empire; pp. 381–3 deals with the West Indies and naval power.

57 Manchester Art Gallery, *Empire Marketing Board posters, 1929–33*,
Manchester, 2010; C. Fletcher, *Pocket history of England*, London, 1911,
p. 252.

58 The phrase is from Ellis, *England and the modern world*, p. 280; Muir,
Short history, vol. 1, pp. 333, 587–90, vol. 2, pp. 202–12.

59 Miller, *Beginner's history*, pp. 155–6, 172, 265, 280–1, 213–15; *King
Edward history reader*, p. 112; Innes, *History of England*, pp. 260, 276,
301–3, 337, 424-6; his Mutiny comparison echoes J.R. Green, *Short
history of the English people*, London, 1874 (I have used the Folio Society
reprint, 4 volumes in 1, London, 1992), vol. III, p. 1126; G. Guest,
Military and imperial history of England, London, 1915, p. 81; Gardiner,
Student's history, vol. 3, pp. 831–5; Marcy, *Examination history*, pp. 150–1;
Browning, *The evolutionary history of England*, p. 249 (in a section on
'The expansion of empire'); Muir, *Short history*, vol. 1, p. 437.

60 Muir, *Short history*, vol. 2, pp. 668–72, 747–50, 787.

61 Miller, *Beginner's history*, pp. 214, 265, 280–1, 282–3.

62 Ellis, *England and the modern world*, pp. 280–2; Marcy, *Examination
history*, p. 82 explicitly links sectarian division in Ireland to seventeenth-
century Scots and English settlement.

63 A. Innes and A. Mee, *Harmsworth history of the world*, London, 1909, pp.
6362–5; Ellis, *England and the modern world*, p. 278.

64 Innes, *History of England*, pp. 425–6; Guest, *Military and imperial history*,
p. 118; Gardiner, *Student's history*, vol. 3, pp. 840–2; Marcy, *Examination
history*, pp. 151, 160; Miller, *Beginner's history*, p. 215; Ellis, *England
and the modern world*, pp. 166–7; Browning, *The evolutionary history of
England*, pp. 250–2.

65 Innes, *History of England*, p. 470; Glew and Plaskett, *History of England*,
vol. 3, p. 215; in the Pitman *King Edward history reader*, pp. 192–4
O'Connell and the Fenians are bracketed together as 'agitators'; G.M.
Trevelyan, *England in the nineteenth century*, London, 1922, p. 218; Muir,
Short history, vol. 2, p. 333 speaks of O'Connell's 'extraordinary gifts'
and non-revolutionary politics.

66 Miller, *Beginner's history*, p. 294, O.Airy, *Textbook of English history from
the earliest times*, London, Longmans, 1891, p. 95; Ellis, *England and the
modern world*, p. 282; Gardiner, *Student's history*, vol. 3, pp. 685–6.

67 Glew and Plaskett, *History of England*, vol. 1, pp. 167–8, vol. 2, pp.
178–9; Miller, *Beginner's history*, pp. 178–9.

68 Innes, *History of England*, pp. 516–33.

69 Sanderson, *Story of England*, p. 107; Guest, *Military and imperial history*,
pp. 10–14; Marcy, *Examination history*, pp. 33–4, 91–6, 114; Miller,
Beginner's history, pp. 82–6; Glew and Plaskett, *History of England*, vol.
1, pp. 167–8, 172–6, vol. 2, pp. 115–28, 150–3; K. Feiling, *A history of*

England, London, 1948, pp. 128, 188–220; T. Tout, *A short account of English history*, London, 1900, pp. 34–6, 88–94.

70 Quoted in S. Webb, 'Lord Rosebery's escape from Houndsditch', *The Nineteenth Century*, 50 (September 1901), pp. 366–86, at p. 276. Webb's policy-making role for the 'Liberal imperialists' linked social reform in the UK to imperial progress via state power.

71 Royal Institution for International Affairs, *The colonial problem*, London, 1937, p. 198; chs 7–11, 14–18 deal with trade, finance, land issues, investment and labour questions.

72 Glew and Plaskett, *History of England*, vol. 3, pp. 287–8, 328; see also criticism of nineteenth-century laissez-faire views as a block to social reform in Ellis, *England and the modern world*, p. 112.

73 Ellis, *England and the modern world*, p. 273.

74 For the former see Miller, *Beginner's history*, pp. 191–201; for the latter see Glew and Plaskett, *History of England*, vol. 3, pp. 54, 162–5 (reform in India).

75 A.P. Newton, *A hundred years of the British empire*, p. 388.

76 Glew and Plaskett, *History of England*, vol. 3, p. 269; Muir, *Short history*, vol. 2, pp. 657–8.

77 Newton, *A hundred years of the British empire*, pp. 249–51, 257–9, 385–7 (Egypt), pp. 323–30, 367–77 (India); Glew and Plaskett, *History of England*, vol. 3, pp. 258, 341–3 (where the names of Amritsar and Gandhi, interestingly, are misspelt).

78 Tout, *A short account*, p. 132.

79 J. Stapleton, *Sir Arthur Bryant and national history in twentieth-century Britain*, Lanham, MD, 2006, pp. 52–4.

80 A. Bryant, *The spirit of Conservatism*, London, 1939, p. 141; *idem*, *Macaulay*, London, 1932, p. 102.

81 Muir, *Short history*, vol. 2, p. 788; Newton, *A hundred years of the British empire*, p. 403; A. Bryant, in *Illustrated London News*, 14 February 1942, quoted in Stapleton, *Bryant*, p. 54; Marriott, *Commonwealth or anarchy*, pp. 218–19.

82 P. Williams, 'A Commonwealth of knowledge: empire intellectuals and the Chatham House Project', *International Relations*, vol. 17, no. 1 (2003), pp. 35–58; A. Bosco and C. Navari [eds.], *Chatham House and British foreign policy, 1919–1945*, London, 1994.

83 Muir, *Short history*, vol. 1, p. xx, vol. 2, p. 601; Newton, *A hundred years of the British empire*, pp. 231–9, 252–60; see also A. Zimmern, *The third British empire*, London, 1926.

84 Marcy, *Examination history*, pp. xx, 24; Miller, *Beginner's history*, pp. 9, 10, 17, 67; Trevelyan, *England in the reign of Queen Anne*, vol. 2, pp. 216–18; G.M. Trevelyan, *Social history of England*, London, 1941 (editions to the 1960s), pp. 149, 151; Feiling, *History of England*, 1950, p. 5.

85 Innes and Mee, *Harmsworth history of the world*, vol. 5, p. 3694 (Magyars), vol. 8, p. 5700 (Pueblos); Marcy, *Examination history*, p. 6 (Seljuqs).

86 G.M. Trevelyan, *History of England*, London, 1926 (reprints to 1956), p. 48

87 Trevelyan, *History of England* pp. 31–3, 41, 48, 55, 65, 133, 146, 164, 200–2, 207, 359–62.

88 Muir, *Civilisation and liberty*, pp. 63–71, 282.

89 See Kuklick, *The savage within*, pp. 8–14; Stocking, *After Tylor*, p. 148 notes that *The golden bough* sold tens of thousands between the wars.

90 Miller, *Beginner's history*, pp. 67, 74.

91 Stocking, *After Tylor*, pp. 3–14 sets up Tylor's work as a starting point for modern British anthropology.

92 See R. Jones, 'Robertson and Frazer on religion', in G. Stocking [ed.], *Functionalism historicized*, Madison, WI, 1984, quoting Frazer on p. 39; Stocking, *After Tylor*, pp. 126–51.

93 See Stocking, *After Tylor*, chs 5–7; Kuklick, *The savage within*, chs 3, 4.

94 M. Kingsley, *Travels in west Africa*, London, 1897, appendix 1; M. Kingsley, *West African studies*, London, 1899, pp. 313, 318, 323; see also D. Birkett, *Mary Kingsley: imperial adventuress*, London, 1992; Rich, *Race and empire in British politics*, pp. 27–49.

95 See T. Asad, 'Afterword', in G. Stocking, *Colonial situations: essays on the contextualisation of rthnographic knowledge*, Madison, WI, 1991.

96 Gardiner, *Student's history*, vol. 2, pp. 954–5, Glew and Plaskett, *History of England*, vol. 3, p. 327; Muir, *Short history*, vol. 2, pp. 549–56.

97 Stocking, 'Radcliffe Brown and British social anthropology', in Stocking, *Functionalism historicized*, especially pp. 150–6; H. Kuper, 'Function, history, biography: reflections on fifty years of the British anthropological tradition' in Stocking, *Functionalism historicized*, pp. 197–200; H. Kuklick, '"The sins of the fathers": British anthropology and colonial administration', *Research in the Sociology of knowledge, sciences, and arts*, 1 (1978), pp. 93–119.

98 A.D. Roberts, 'The British empire in tropical Africa', in R. Winks [ed.], *Oxford history of the British empire, vol. 5: Historiography*, Oxford, 1999, pp. 463–5; C. Ambler, 'East Africa' in Winks, *Oxford history of the British empire, vol 5*, pp. 500–3; N. Tarling, 'The empire in South-east Asia', in Winks, *Oxford history of the British empire, vol 5*, pp. 404–7.

99 Berg, *Woman in history*; M. Berg, 'The first women economic historians', *Economic History Review*, vol. 45, no. 2 (1992), pp. 308–29; B. Melman, 'Under the western historian's eyes: Eileen Power and the early feminist encounter with colonialism', *History Workshop Journal*, no. 42 (1996), pp. 147–68.

100 See P. Vinogradoff, 'The teaching of Sir Henry Maine' (inaugural lecture in Oxford, 1904) in P. Vinogradoff, *Collected papers*, 2 vols, London, 1928, vol. 2, pp. 173–89.

101 Bentley, *Modernising England's past.*

102 There were eleven printings of Tawney between 1926 and 1951.

103 Mandler, *History and national life*, p. 71 states that it sold 100,000 copies in its first year and 500,000 by 1952.

104 D. George, *English social life in the eighteenth century*, London, 1923; D. George, *London life in the eighteenth century*, London, 1930; D. George, *England in transition*, London, 1931; A. Clark, *The working life of women in the seventeenth century*, London, 1919; B. Philpotts, *Kindred and clan in the middle ages and after*, London, 1913; B. Philpotts, *The Elder Edda and Scandinavian drama*, London, 1920; B. Philpotts, *Edda and Saga*, London, 1931; I. Pinchbeck, *Women workers and the industrial revolution*, London, 1930; R. Tawney, *The agrarian problem in the sixteenth century*, London, 1912 (reprints to 1961); R. Tawney, *English economic history: select documents*, London,1913 (reprints to 1937); R. Tawney, *Tudor economic documents*, London, 1924 (reprints to 1965); R. Tawney, *Religion and the rise of capitalism*, London, 1926 (reprints to 1964); F. Stenton, *Documents on the social and economic history of the Danelaw*, London, 1920; F. Stenton, *Introduction to the survey of English place names*, London, 1924 (reprints to 1980); F. Stenton, *The Danes in England*, London, 1927 (reprints to 1957); F. Stenton, *The first century of English feudalism*, London, 1929 (reprints to 1979); J. Clapham, *Economic history of modern Britain*, 3 vols, London, 1926–38 (reprints to 1968); J. Clapham, *Concise economic history of Britain to 1750*, London, 1949 (reprints to 1967).

105 Feske, *From Belloc to Churchill*, pp. 109–33; S. Weaver, 'The bleak age: J.H. Clapham, the Hammonds, and the standard of living in Victorian Britain', in M. Taylor and M. Wolff [eds.], *The Victorians since 1901*, Manchester, 2004; E. Hobsbawm, *Industry and empire*, London, 1969.

106 See S. Collini, 'Moral mind: R.H. Tawney', in S. Collini, *English pasts*, Oxford, 1999; W. Lamont, 'R.H. Tawney, "Who did not write a single word that can be trusted"', in W. Lamont, *Historical controversies and historians*, London, 1997; A. Wright, *R.H. Tawney*, Manchester, 1987.

107 S. Weaver, *Thfe Hammonds: a marriage in history*, Stanford, CA, 1997; Wright, *R.H. Tawney*; Berg, *Woman in history*; Feske, *From Belloc to Churchill.*

108 Manchester Art Gallery, *Empire Marketing posters*; Constantine, *Buy and build.*

109 R. Coupland, *Wilberforce*, London, 1923, 1945; R. Coupland, *Raffles*, London, 1926; R. Coupland, *Kirk on the Zambesi*, London, 1928; R. Coupland, *The British anti-slavery movement*, London, 1933; R. Coupland, *The British empire*, London, 1933; R. Coupland, *The exploitation of east Africa*, London, 1939; R. Coupland, *Britain and India, 1600–1941*, London, 1943, 1946, 1948; R. Coupland, *Livingstone's last*

journey, London, 1945, 1947; references to Coupland's journalism and lectures are from the collection *The empire in these days*, pp. 137, 261.

110 Muir, *Short history*, vol. 2, p. 789–90; Newton, *A hundred years of the British empire*, p. 403; V. Harlow, *Origins and purpose: a handbook of the British Commonwealth and empire*, London, 1944, 1949, p. 117.

111 *King Edward history reader*, p. 200; Tout, *Short analysis of English history*, p. 1, 34, 85; Innes, *History of England*, pp. vi, xxx, 9; Gardiner, *Student's history*, vol. 3, pp 687, 758, 885; Guest, *Military and imperial history*, pp. 8–9, 43; and Guest, *Social history*, London, 1929, p. 13; Marcy, *Examination history*, p. 8; Trevelyan, *England in the nineteenth century*, p. 415; Trevelyan, *England under Queen Anne*, vol. 2, p. 201; Trevelyan, *Social history of England*, pp. xi, 32; Miller, *Beginner's history*, p. 9; Glew and Plaskett, *History of England*, vol. 1, pp. 2, 20, 22, 46, 224, vol. 2, pp. 1, 9, 13, 51, vol. 3, pp. 42, 171, 208, 245; Ellis, *England and the modern world*, pp. 214, 227, 276, Feiling, *History of England*, pp. 27, 33, 43, 45, 56.

112 Ellis, *England and the modern world*, p. 227; also Miller, *Beginner's history*, p. 291.

113 J. Bryce 'Law and religion' (lecture XIII), *Studies in history and jurisprudence*, 2 vols, Oxford, 1901, vol. 2, pp. 638–68 (pp. 655–8 deal with Al-Azhar; p. 660 labels 'Turks' as 'a race intellectually sterile'); J. Bryce, *The relations of the advanced and the backward races of mankind*, Oxford, 1902, pp. 12–26, 35–9.

114 Bryce, *Relations of the advanced and backward races*, p. 11.

115 Tout, *Short analysis of English history*, p. 1; Innes, *History of England*, p. 1; Browning, *The evolutionary history of England*, pp. 7, 223, 224, *King Edward history reader*, pp. 5, 17, 34; Miller, *Beginner's history*, p. 9.

116 Marcy, *Examination history*, pp. 24, 176, Glew and Plaskett, *History of England*, vol. 1, p. 19, vol. 2, pp. 9, 13; Guest, *Military and imperial history*, p. 43 (Ottomans).

117 Muir, *Short history*, vol. 1, pp. 28, 35, 81, 113–15; Trevelyan, *History of England*, book 1 is entitled 'The mingling of the races' and the argument set out on pp. 1, 6, 43; the 'English race' appears on pp. 132, 597, 658.

118 Trevelyan, *History of England*, pp. 201, 361, 422, 485, 688, 696.

119 Innes, *History of England*, p. 323; Gardiner, *Student's History*, vol. 3, p. 655.

120 Muir, *Short history*, vol. 2, pp. 89, 595, 789.

121 A full recent account of these images is in P. Mandler, *The English national character*, New Haven, CT, 2006, ch. 5; see also R. Colls, *Identity of England*; J. Baxendale, '"I had seen a lot of Englands": J.B. Priestley, Englishness, and the people', *History Workshop Journal*, 51 (2001), pp. 87–111.

122 G. Orwell, *The road to Wigan Pier*, London, 1937; H.V. Morton, *In search of England*, London, 1927 (thirty-nine editions by 1949); J.B. Priestley, *English journey*, London, 1934 (reprints 1935–49).

123 A. Bryant, *The national character*, London, 1934; a recent sympathetic account of Bryant and his work is Stapleton, *Bryant*; see also the comments in S. Collini, 'Believing in England: Arthur Bryant, historian as man of letters', in S. Collini, *Common reading*, Oxford, 2008.

124 Bryant, *National character*, pp. 4, 6, 9, 12, 23–5.

125 Bryant, *National character*, pp. 5, 13, 17–19.

126 Bryant, *National character*, pp. 102–5, 116, 120, 123.

127 A. Bryant, *Samuel Pepys*, 3 vols, London, 1933, 1935, 1938 (quotation on vol. 3, pp. 99–100 of the 1949 edn); Bryant, *National character*, p. 124.

128 Stapleton, *Bryant*, pp. 85–91; Bryant, *Pepys*, vol. 3, pp. 22, 50–4.

129 Trevelyan, *History of England*, pp. 295, 340–4, 425–8, 527–8, 601–14; the titles of books 2, 5, and 6 of his text include the term 'sea power'.

130 Tout, *Short analysis of English history*, pp. 28–34; Marcy, *Exam history*, p. 26; Miller, *Beginner's history*, pp. 77–9; Glew and Plaskett, *History of England*, vol. 1, pp. 144–5.

131 Feiling, *History of England*, pp. 52, 151; Innes, *History of England*, p. 9.

132 See, for example, disclaimers about race as a 'scientific category' in J. Huxley *et al.*, *We Europeans*, London, 1935,1939, pp. 20–6, 90–3 and chs 1–3 generally, discussed in E. Barkan, *The retreat of scientific racism*, Cambridge, 1992, pp. 296–302; a contrasting example would be C. Seligman, *Races of Africa*, Oxford, 1939 (many reprints), discussed in Barkan, *Retreat* pp. 30–4.

133 Innes, *History of England*, p. vi; E. Benians *et al.* [eds.], *Cambridge history of the British empire*, 8 vols, Cambridge, 1929–36, vol. 1, p. 5.

134 Muir, *Expansion of Europe*, p. 127.

✹ 5 ✹

EMPIRE AND HISTORY WRITING
SINCE 1950

It's our cultural bloodstream, the secret of who we are, and it tells us to let go of the past, even as we honour it. To lament what ought to be lamented and to celebrate what should be celebrated. And if in the end, that history turns out to reveal itself as a patriot, well then I think that neither Churchill nor Orwell would have minded that very much, and as a matter of fact, neither do I. (Simon Schama)[1]

they're all leaky categories, history, nostalgia, memory, heritage. They're not hermetically sealed categories, and when they stray into each other you get some quite interesting things happening. Lola Young

the Empire isn't out there in the past, this material can help us now. (Judith Brown)[2]

At the start of a new millenium, empire, history and identity are still in the public eye. A prime minister invokes 'national' identity and 'Christian'values against 'multicultural' and 'terrorist' threats; films like *The queen*, and *The king's speech* repackage the monarchy (again), while others explore the multicultural lives which he denigrates.[3] New media play their role in creating and disseminating transformed versions of these views.Simon Schama, academic presenter of the 2002 TV series *A history of Britain*, including two programmes on empire in its thirteen episodes, links it to a patriotism about which he suggests there is little choice, since 'it is our cultural bloodstream' (note the use of 'our'). A historian (Judith Brown) and a cultural analyst (Lola Young) involved in another TV series broadcast in 2002, *The British empire in colour*, argue that the past plays various cultural, political and psychological roles in the present. BBC and commercial TV programme-makers found it worthwhile to produce images of the 'British' past for education, entertainment and profit, with book and DVD spin-offs from both series. They offered imperial material alongside the ever-popular topics of Nazis, Tudor monarchs, warfare, glamorous adaptations of Austen and Brontë novels or a costume drama series like *Garrow's law*, with its references to eighteenth-century empire and slavery. Whether using the deterministic biological image of blood to denote cultural transfer over time, or acknowledging the complex links of feeling, memory, past and present, the makers of these narratives produced and recognised the constitutive role of empire in their accounts of the past, and feelings or imaginings about it. At a time when awareness of the British empire was arguably low and declining, they share a concern with the 'afterlife' of the past, including the colonial past, in twenty-first-century culture and politics.

This afterlife, and its place on the map of UK history and history writing in the last half of the twentieth century and beginning of the next, has a number of striking and not always consistent features. Many historians' views of the key material features of the period have been shaped by the themes of 'decline' and 'reconstruction'.[4] Changes in the UK's global economic position, beginning in the early twentieth century, and intensifying after 1945, involved growing competition for British producers and traders from competitors, and the reconfiguring of economic activities and relationships. Post-war reconstruction and social reform have been associated with a period of 'austerity' followed by 'rising affluence' in which low levels of unemployment, rising living standards and wider but unequal access to health, welfare and education altered life for many UK residents. So too did lack of modernisation in industry, the expansion of jobs in services and the public sector, rather than manufacturing, and the impact of immigration notably from South Asia and the Caribbean. Contradictions between structural economic difficulties and rising standards of living and consumption continued through turbulent conditions in the 1970s and 1980s. At that point the 'Butskellite' consensus of the previous two decades was challenged by global pressures and domestic conflict and pushed aside by neo-liberal economic practices, continued during the 1990s and into the first decade of the next century.[5] The period was characterised by deregulation, high unemployment, technological and financial innovation, sales of council housing and public utilities and legal restrictions on trades union activity. It also saw a property boom, followed by new forms of public–private investment in health and education. Through all these developments UK entrepreneurs, like their American and European counterparts, faced the emergence of other centres of economic power: in Japan from the 1970s, Korea from the 1980s and India and China from the 1990s.[6] By 1979 the UK, which in 1950 had still produced 22% of the world's exported manufactures, produced just over 9% of that total.

The shift of material emphasis from commonwealth to European connections began in the 1950s and came to reshape UK trade and investment, as did the 1980s deregulation which opened London financial markets to new global influences. By 1970, despite absolute increases in quantity, exports from the UK to the commonwealth and South Africa had fallen from a 47.7% share of all UK exports to 24.4%, while exports to the European Community rose from 28% of the total in 1954 to 32.5% in 1965, and 44% in 1980.[7] Former colonies and dominions diversified their trade and investment away from the London-dominated sterling area, and government attempts to manage economic relations with the commonwealth in the 1950s and early 1960s could not outweigh structural and global constraints and domestic weaknesses.[8] Material relationships between the UK and what was becoming its former empire diminished or changed in significance, just as migration from south Asia and the Caribbean to the UK, or from the UK to Australia and southern Africa, which was significant in the 1950s and 1960s, diminished for both economic and political reasons thereafter.

These material developments should be set beside the political complexities of the UK global position between the 1940s and the 1980s. The demands of the Second World War provided a temporary lease of life for empire/commonwealth solidarity and involved the active British deployment of imperial power, but also challenged the empire in Asia. Ultimately it drained UK governments of both political and material resources for maintaining its existing imperial roles. This had contradictory implications for the UK, combining international, domestic and colonial elements. On the international front three key features of the early post-war era were the emergence of the USA as the dominant world power, the Cold War between the 'free'/US and 'communist'/Soviet blocs and major anti-colonial movements in Asia and Africa. For UK governments between the 1950s and 1980s this entailed acting as a US ally in the Cold War, which preserved aspects of their global role while embedding them in dependency on their ally. They could not ignore US influence on UK finances, or US views of decolonisation and development and their links to Cold War politics, any more than they could ignore the growth of international challenges to European colonialism or 'third world' voices in the United Nations (UN).[9] UK relations with the European Community (later European Union) were as central to UK politics from the 1970s onward as other global concerns, if not more so. Governments faced domestic practical and political pressures to devote effort and resources to social and economic issues and problems within the UK, and to protect the new global interests of domestic and overseas investors. They also faced divisive views of UK links with Europe, and electorates for whom imperial issues were rarely a priority.[10]

The global position and priorities of the UK were further changed with the unravelling of the Soviet empire, and its impact within Europe and on Cold War approaches to international relations. Together with events in Iran and Afghanistan from 1979, whose importance to Afghans and Iranians was matched by their regional and international effects, the collapse of the Soviet bloc changed British and American perceptions of the global threats and interests which they feared. The real and imagined presence of 'Muslim terrorism', and Anglo-American responses to it in the Gulf, Afghanistan and Iraq, as well as domestically, played into a new global politics in which governments and media drew on historic prejudices and new fears about Muslims 'at home' and abroad. The expansion of the European Union to include eastern as well as western Europeans altered patterns of investment and migration, and British approaches to the EU. Anglo-American involvement in former Yugoslavia used familiar forms of liberal interventionism in the name of high ideals, as they did in Sierra Leone. The Anglo-American invasions of Afghanistan in 2001 and Iraq in 2003 were backed by arguments about making the world safe familiar from the Cold War, by appeals to current liberal concerns with human rights and gender discrimination and by images of fanatical Muslims dating back centuries. A further element was contributed by radical domestic challenges to British post-imperial policies during the 1970s and 1980s, whether against the apartheid regime in South Africa, US intervention in Vietnam or the siting and potential use of nuclear weapons in the UK.[11] Such challenges revealed contention over the role of the UK as a former colonial power, over the Anglo-American alliance as a prop to UK global status and over British relationships with so-called 'third-world' countries. They were strengthened by convergences between anti-racist, leftist, student and third-world activism.

This activism was in part the product of a particular configuration of radical movements grounded in the presence of articulate ethnic minorities, of new types of university student and of 'new left' critiques of Stalinism and labourism. It also expressed changing perspectives on Englishness in a global post-imperial setting. As parts of the UK were transformed by new communities of migrants, many from former colonies, key material and cultural questions of inclusion, assimilation, discrimination and cultural identity were linked to racialised discussion of what it might mean to be 'British' or 'English'. The politics of race prejudice and immigration challenged the practices of the trade union movement, of the welfare and education systems and of policing, as well as fuelling confrontations between the activists of left and right.[12] The revival of Welsh and Scottish national self-consciousness, and campaigns for and against devolution, also contributed to debates on nationality. They were reinforced by the re-emergence of the 'Irish question', as issues of civil rights and nationalist or unionist politics engaged government and public in Northern Ireland, and in Britain.[13] While public interest in the specifics of policy was limited, protest over race discrimination and immigration issue expressed continuing uncertainties around 'national identity'. So too did media images of 'Britishness' in relation to Ireland, the Falklands war, the European Union or white settlers in Africa, as well as to 'race' issues. Such internal debates were paralleled by contests over the role of the UK in the wider world 'after empire'. The attractions of links to the USA competed with those of being a benign presence in the 'third world', via the British Council, business, the BBC and development initiatives, or of forming a 'bridge' between American and European interests and a key player in European politics.

These debates suggest that empire no longer had much of a part in British international concerns. Yet disengagement from empire was a prolonged process, extending from UK withdrawal from Palestine, Jordan and the Indian subcontinent in 1946–48 to acquiescence in Zimbabwe's independence in 1980, and the 1984 agreement to end British rule in Hong Kong in 1997. Within that long withdrawal there were periods of intense change in the later 1940s when UK rule was dismantled in its main centres in Asia, and in the 1960s when the same happened in much of Africa and the Caribbean. Since British colonial power had always been entwined with 'informal' international involvements based on commercial, diplomatic, military and cultural influence, disengagement was approached as an exercise in the reshaping of that broader set of UK global interests and power. This had the effect of maintaining both actual and imagined imperial issues and assumptions within the mindset and policy of UK governments long past the sell-by date of colonial rule. If explicit celebration of, or attacks on, empire had limited political resonance, assumptions about the importance of the commonwealth or the global influence of the UK via the North Atlantic Treaty Organization (NATO) alliance and the UN Security Council preserved a post-imperial, rather than non-imperial, construct of the UK's international role. The Blair government's interest in UK ability to 'punch above its weight' in the early twenty-first century showed the persistence of such an approach decades after the end of empire.

Debates over 'national' identities and interests involved questions of cultural influence and diversity, not just political divisions over immigration, devolution, UK involvement in European institutions, and what British politicians liked to see as a 'special relationship' with the USA. Concerns with 'decline' or social change were often expressed through arguments about undesirable (often 'foreign') influences on popular culture, about the content and organisation of education or about cultural 'authenticity'. The contested character of trans-Atlantic links was seen in divergent responses to Anglo-American exchanges in film, fashion and popular music dating back to the 1920s, and in television from the 1950s. The doubts and prejudices of intellectuals and opinion formers contrasted sharply with popular enthusiasm for rock and roll, American TV programmes, blues and westerns. From the 1960s, the adoption by working-class teenage boys of aspects of Italian fashion (suits, scooters), like middle-class interest in 'Continental' art-house cinema, or the spreading consumption of wine and pasta dishes signalled new European elements in daily life. This was paralleled by the presence of strong Afro-Caribbean musical influences within

UK popular music since the 1960s and the success of fusions of bhangra, rock and hip-hop music in the 1980s and 1990s. These were rooted in historical connections between empire, migration to post-war Britain and encounters between different musical agendas. The late twentieth century saw the spread on UK high streets of curry houses established by migrants from south Asia, Chinese restaurants run by migrants from Hong Kong and kebab shops set up by those from Cyprus. In 2001 a government minister described 'chicken tikka masala', an Indo-British dish served in 'Indian' (in fact largely Bengali) restaurants and takeaways, as having become the 'national dish'.[14] This post-colonial remaking of lifestyles among various sections of UK society stimulated both warm endorsement of cultural pluralism and negative comment on the 'dilution' or 'debasement' of 'national' culture, in each case incorporating reference to former colonial connections.[15]

As with discussion of other periods there is a debate to be had about the level of explicit interest in empire within the UK in the second half of the twentieth century. It is regularly and understandably argued that, with the exception of specific moments (Mau-Mau in Kenya in the 1950s, Suez in 1956, the Falklands war in 1982), issues of colonial rule and decolonisation were of little concern to the wider public, and that the end of empire was managed by small numbers of politicians, officials and opinion formers. The lives of most UK residents and the energies of those who were politically active were focused elsewhere. The decline of Empire Day and the failure of its replacement, Commonwealth Day (instituted in 1958) would be one indication of the weakness of official invocations of imperial or post-imperial connections. Falls in migration to the former empire, and new legal, economic and cultural links with continental Europe redirected business interests, political debate and leisure activities. Just as trade and investment were directed into Europe from the 1980s, more UK residents ate Italian food, drank Czech or German lagers and travelled to continental Europe as holidaymakers or football fans.

Yet in this period there were 'post-imperial' presences which signalled imperial antecedents as well as the disjunction between empire and decolonisation. The growth of organisations and discussion that were focused on 'third-world development' encompassed the old reform agendas associated with benevolent colonial rule, the new internationalism of bodies like the UN, the Food and Agriculture Organisation (FAO) or World Health Organistion (WHO) and aspirations to autonomous progress and prosperity in former colonies. Those involved in non-governmental organisations (NGOs) and development studies often offered radical critiques of imperialism and its legacies and supported postcolonial aspirations, as well as the autonomy of producers and policymakers in the 'third world'. They were also heirs to universalising views of progress and civilisation which had shaped European approaches to the non-European world, and to reforming ideals for two centuries, juggling such views with relativistic knowledge of the complex varieties of structure and experience in societies around the world. Development programmes and research thus contained tensions between the certainties and universal validity of engineering, social scientific or medical expertise and recognition of indigenous localised equivalents. As with abolitionist or humanitarian movements in earlier generations, the development specialists of the later twentieth and early twenty-first centuries sought to bring the disadvantaged into an inclusive domain of human advance and well-being with somewhat ethnocentric confidence in 'knowing' what was best to achieve that end. This troubled relationship between knowledge and power, the construction of 'third-world' societies as the objects of external expertise and analysis, and the transmission of languages of 'development' from their earlier forms in the policy making of colonial planners to postcolonial settings, established certain continuities.

Such continuities altered over time. The early generation of development specialists were close to, and in some cases actually transferred from, work in colonial contexts. By the 1970s they were recruited from those without such connections, who often had critiques of colonialism developed within the social scientific and historical scholarship of that period. They worked with third-world partners who brought their own experience, insights and agendas to development issues. Ideas of empowerment, local knowledge and autonomy, and the need to challenge dependency, became influential alongside technocratic views and approaches. While some relationships and assumptions linking late twentieth-century views of 'third world' and development issues to the colonial past preserved echoes of empire, the circumstances of the postcolonial world and new international order disrupted such links.

If aid and development activities sustained only tenuous connections to empire, the demands, debates and difficulties associated with what came to be called race relations kept legacies of empire more obviously alive within culture and politics in the UK. Just as movements of migrants from the Caribbean and south Asia, and later of east African Asians, to the UK raised questions of citizenship within the commonwealth, so the presence of those groups in UK towns and cities raised questions of discrimination, cultural diversity and national identity. While such issues had also been raised by earlier Irish and east European Jewish migrations, the colonial context of post-1950 migration was one of its most distinctive features.[16] Early initiatives for the study and management of newly arrived migrant groups from the Caribbean and south Asia were closely linked to policy networks concerned with the UK's global position (the Royal Institute of International Affairs) and to colonial experience. The first director of the Institute for Race Relations, which undertook key work on migration and race issues in Britain in the 1950s and 1960s, was a former Indian administrator, and the institute's formation was supported by missionary and British South African interests. His replacement by those with views and policies grounded in awareness and experience of new migrant communities and interests signalled an important wider shift.[17] As with discussions of 'development', colonial linkages were eroded by a new generation of policymakers, scholars and opinion formers, by pressure to embed race relations work in politics and research rather than 'official' practices, and by challenges from intellectuals and activists from migrant and leftist backgrounds.

Contests over the position of migrants and their descendants in the 1950s and early 1960s focused on their 'outsider' position, on liberal policies of 'educating' existing communities to accept these 'strangers' and on encouraging migrants to assimilate to local norms and expectations.[18] From the later 1960s pressure from migrant communities themselves, from external critics and from sharper public opposition to immigration redirected attention to substantive discrimination and to the experiences and views of what were becoming labelled 'ethnic minorities'. Demands for full social, legal and economic inclusion and equal treatment of those minorities opened up further contests over national identity and diversity, as they asserted themselves and sought respect and recognition for their distinctive cultures. By the 1980s and 1990s arguments for pluralism and relativism formed part of 'anti-racist' politics alongside opposition to the 'structural discrimination' of institutions (schools, police, local authorities), and critiques of communal and cultural separatism.[19] In addition to challenging governments, anti-racist politics also took on the labour movement, the media and gender aspects of racism. This was expressed not just in oppositional activism, but also in creativity and self-organisation ranging from theatre groups to refuges for abused women, and from music and journalism to legal advice centres. It should be noted that campaigns and contests over these issues within the UK were sometimes linked with colonial and postcolonial questions, whether apartheid in South Africa and Zimbabwe, the politics of Palestine/Israel or 'anti-colonial struggles' more generally. Although the history of UK race politics became increasingly internal to the UK, and was significantly influenced by its American counterpart, it also bore traces of its historical global and colonial connections. In the view of analysts like Simon Gikandi and Stuart Hall the emergence of new forms of racialised politics, associated with the figure of Enoch Powell, in the 1970s was partly shaped by concern with relationships between the imperial past and the contemporary nation.[20]

One way to understand this would be to set it among the varied responses of different groups in the UK looking back at the imperial past. Direct contact with that past was maintained by migrants from former colonies who kept contact with families and communities there, and by those who had worked as colonial officials, missionaries, military personnel or professionals and returned to the UK with memories, opinions and material objects. It was also maintained by development specialists, missionaries or businessmen, who continued to work in former colonies, pursuing reforming, entrepreneurial and philanthropic activities. In a context where former colonies changed significantly after independence, where British economic focus had shifted away from the former empire, and where the privileged place of British interests in business or development had been undermined by others, too much should not be made of such contacts. However, just as policymakers could work with an imagined picture of the UK's continuing world role, so a picture of benign post-imperial interests and relationships could be produced and projected through the ongoing movements and activities of aid and charity volunteers and development experts between former colonies and the UK.

The stories, ideas and images which emerged from these contacts became part of a varied set of depictions of empire which were part of UK culture in the twentieth and early twenty-first centuries. In the 1950s feature films depicted empire (for example, *Kim*, 1950; *Bengal Rifles*, 1954; *Bhowani Junction*, 1956; *Northwest frontier*, 1959) and resistance to anti-colonialism (*The planter's wife*, 1952, set in emergency Malaya; *Simba*, *Safari*, 1955 and *Something of value*, 1957, set in Kenya during the Mau-Mau uprising). From the 1960s films on imperial topics (*Lawrence of Arabia*, 1962; *Zulu*, 1964; *Guns at Batasi*, 1964; *Khartoum*, 1966; *The long duel*, 1967; *The man who would be king*, 1975; *Conduct unbecoming*, 1975; *Zulu dawn*, 1979) offered more nuanced, sometimes critical, perspectives on empire in which images of manly heroism, romance and adventure in exotic settings refigured but also perpetuated imperial images. Empire nostalgia and exoticism coexisted with 'sympathetic' portrayals of anti-imperial nationalism and critiques of empire (*Gandhi*, 1982; *Heat and dust*, 1982) and lush location settings which commodified and glamorised as well as challenging it. As Australian and Indian filmmakers began to produce films on imperial subjects (*The chess players*, 1977; *Breaker Morant*, 1980; *Gallipoli*, 1981; *The home and the world*, 1984; *The light horsemen*, 1987; *The making of the Mahatma*, 1996; *Lagaan*, 2001) they added voices and views from other parts of the colonial and postcolonial experience to existing images and ideas of empire. The ability of films to convey negative or ambiguous messages about the empire enhanced rather than undermined its appeal as a topic, and liberal accounts of the weaknesses of empire and benign versions of its end, as in *Gandhi*, bolstered comforting views of decolonisation. The ongoing use of imperial topics, from Burton's explorations in Africa to the British suppression of banditry in India by UK and US filmmakers – including film versions of 'imperial' writing (*King Solomon's mines*, *Kim*, Elspeth Huxley on colonial Kenya, 'Indian' novels by Rumer Godden and John Masters) – indicates their continued marketability. Three of the seven film versions of A.E.W. Mason's 1902 novel *The four feathers*, depicting British imperial exploits in the Sudan, appeared in 1955, 1977 and 2002.

The cinematic presence of empire had its written counterparts. Leaving scholarly writing on imperial history for later discussion, it is worth noting that fictional and memoir treatments of empire were a means whereby the pleasures of nostalgia and the exotic, together with interrogations of the meanings and problems of the imperial past, were made available to varied audiences. The success of John Masters' novels during the 1950s and 1960s, of Paul Scott's '*raj*' novels since the late 1960s, or M.M. Kaye's *Far pavilions* (15 million copies sold in the quarter-century after its publication in 1978, TV version in 1984, radio dramatisation in 2011) indicates the potency of this subject matter, in book, film and TV forms. Masters' 1951 'adventure story' version of the 1857 'Mutiny' uprising in India, *The nightrunners of Bengal*, sold 300,000 copies in the first six months, and the same topic featured in many popular and 'serious' novels. These ranged from M.M. Kaye's romance, *Shadow of the moon*, or an ironic postcolonial treatment in J.G. Farrell's *Siege of Krishnapur*, to V.A. Stuart's swashbuckling Sheridan series and Julian Rathbone's gendered approach. This was paralleled by the use of Second World War settings in Burma and Malaya, maintaining a link between the mythologies and nostalgia associated with the war and empire, created both by the threat to empire manifest in the war in Asia, and by the imperial solidarity with Britain in the fighting. Nevil Shute's successful 1950 novel, *A town like Alice* (reprints 1950–2009, film in 1956, TV series in 1981), linked wartime Malaya to post-war Australia through an English heroine, celebrating public school values and Greater Britain. Stars like Kenneth More and John Mills, who were familiar to UK audiences for roles in films celebrating British wartime heroism, also played roles in 'imperial' films, as did Virginia McKenna, who starred in the 1956 version of *A town like Alice*. If this emotive bond of empire to wartime faded in the late twentieth century, the empire continued to have attractions as a glamorous and exciting location for mass-circulation romances and family sagas,[21] for crime thrillers[22] or for war-and-adventure stories,[23] as well as an imaginative terrain for 'serious' fiction.[24]

These developments can be seen from several contrasting perspectives. One feature of imperial subject matter was its consumability, and like the use of Indian or African products or motifs in home furnishings or fashion, the use of empire settings and plotlines could benefit sales. This was connected to the appeal of the exotic, which could enhance tales of passion and adventure, just as Indian fabrics might glamorise clothes and African carvings or the widely sold *Green Goddess* (a bestselling fantasy depiction of a woman in east Asian dress) enhance the décor of a room. As in the imperial past, this was more than a mere marketing device, and commodified imperial images and themes continued to domesticate the exotic and exoticise everyday life. As expressions of nostalgia, as refigured post-imperial products or as prompts to rethinking colonial histories, these images and themes were accessible as popular cultural choices, and as means to come to terms with, or commercially appropriate, an imperial past. Fictions of empire became sites for the presentation of gendered pleasures (war, romance) and for self-conscious reflection on the implications of empire by 'white' British writers as well as a growing number of authors from colonial and postcolonial backgrounds. The public success of writers like Salman Rushdie, Caryl Phillips, Amitav Ghosh, Andrea Levy, Hari Kunzru and Zadie Smith projected new perspectives on empire and postcolonial legacies. Authors like Saul David or Noel Barber shifted from journalistic, travel or historical writing to the production of fiction, or like Philip Mason and Elspeth Huxley moved between the two. Texts often combined memoir, storytelling and argument, or engaged ironically and confrontationally with colonial pasts from the perspective of former colonial subjects as well as of colonial rulers and their agents.

There were important cultural dimensions to the politics of nostalgia and of post-imperial change in 'multi-ethnic' Britain. Contests over the teaching or recognition of religious diversity in schools (and, as will be seen, the teaching of history) over dress codes (Sikh turbans, dreadlocks, 'Muslim' head or face coverings) and over the content of children's fiction gave colonial legacies and postcolonial experiences a visible and audible public presence. These were, of course, more expressive of tensions in a UK society undergoing significant changes from the 1960s onwards than they were of consciousness of empire, but they did contain a colonial legacy. When television company ITV ran a series on the end of empire in 1985, or Channel 4 invited an established academic to front a series on empire in 2003, programme makers and planners built on earlier successful broadcasts of dramatisations of Paul Scott's *Jewel in the crown* novels and Elspeth Huxley's *Flame trees of Thika*. Images of the colonial past were consumed as popular sit-coms (*It ain't half hot mum* – a comic war-story/colonial hybrid) or as 'serious' and creative documentary programmes, as well as drama. Growing interest in versions of the past which recognised the role of slavery and its legacy in the UK as well as the empire lay behind programmes like *The British slave trade* (Channel 4, 2000),

Mary Seacole (Channel 4, 2005), *The slavery business* (BBC2, 2005) and *Empire's children* (Channel 4, 2007). These were never more than a small proportion of broadcast material, but they persisted in changing modes across the post-war decades.

The broadcasting of a successful professional historian Niall Ferguson's forceful case for the beneficial legacy of empire in 2003 signalled a new turn in debate on empire, challenging the liberal or anti-colonial critiques which had flourished since the 1970s. It gave expression to the contests which had emerged in academic and political settings in the later twentieth century. These involved reflections on the significance of empire for descendants of colonial subjects and for descendants of colonial rulers and their agents, and were associated with concerns about racism and cultural diversity. Clashing memories of colonial rule and New World slavery among the descendants of colonial subjects and rulers, uncertainties about how or whether Asian and Afro-Caribbean residents in the UK 'belonged' and what demands they might legitimately make for recognition or 'difference' surfaced in media and political controversy. Debate and creativity were shaped by the appeal of 'empire nostalgia' on the one hand, and by powerful articulate 'postcolonial' voices bringing the views and experience of former colonial subjects into UK political life (diplomacy, race politics) and culture (media, fiction, fashion) on the other. Criticism and celebration, anxiety and advocacy, arguments for the inclusive 'nation', for non- or trans-national forms of connection, or for more narrowly defined national boundaries (cultural or political) all had their voices.

Nowhere was this more evident than in arguments over the 'national narrative' of the 'British' past which might be told to TV audiences or school students in the UK which developed in the UK in the 1970s and 1980s. In school settings this debate was linked to controversy over comprehensive secondary education and 'traditional' teaching methods, but it also focused on curriculum content.[25] This included concern about what would now be the appropriate view to take on empire as part of the 'national' story, and about the value of versions of that story told from the viewpoints of subordinate or marginalised groups. Should studies of the UK's global position acknowledge the end of empire by situating it within broader studies of world affairs? Did attention to the experiences and activities of subordinate groups enhance or 'fragment' the national story by introducing accounts of unequal power, exclusion or conflicts of interest? Did recently arrived residents need to learn the established versions of the national story rather than revised accounts (Magna Carta, the Civil War, nineteenth-century reform, rather than the conquest of Ireland, plantation slavery and the Amritsar massacre)?

Public debates on empire and its legacies can be connected to the dynamics of professional history as it transformed over this period. During the 1960s and 1970s new approaches to social and economic history moved practices within the discipline along some new paths. One such approach emphasised the experiences and agency of unprivileged or subordinate groups rather than the sweep of impersonal 'trends' or the role of elite groups and dominant institutions. Adapting and sometimes abandoning established practices in social and labour history, new studies of slaves, workers, communities and families, and of 'subaltern' groups of poor people, women or colonial subjects, treated them as historical actors and sought to remove them from what one practitioner of this approach called 'the enormous condescension of posterity'.[26] Another approach sought to extend or deepen investigations and interpretations of the past by using concepts and methods developed in the social sciences. The use of ideas of 'deviance' or 'subculture' to study crime, workplaces or youth groups, of 'social structure' to study families, work relations or neighbourhoods, or of anthropological insights into religion or communal relationships, could also support study of such phenomena in the past. Rather than offering atomised anecdotes of 'society', they embedded and supported accounts of specific topics within larger conceptual frameworks. Keith Thomas' work on early modern magic, like the historical explorations of protest, culture and class from a range of perspectives, illustrates such work in the 1970s.[27] The 'turn' to social history also included approaches which emerged from Oxbridge historical traditions rather than from leftist or social scientific practice. This stimulated work on nineteenth-century social relations and cultures of respectability which were neither anecdotal nor grounded in structural or materialist analyses, preferring to consider attitudes and values rather than ideologies.[28]

Yet another approach critiqued the complacency or narrowness of conventional analyses by drawing attention to the exclusions and unquestioned ideological assumptions underpinning key historical narratives constructed in the earlier part of the century. Critiques of gender-blind analyses of 'work' or 'politics', of ethnocentric views of 'civilisation' or 'progress' or of official ideas of 'disorder' or 'conflict' showed that histories of 'subaltern' groups challenged the actual terms used to construct accounts of the past, rather than just adding to them.[29] Histories of labour and popular communities and politics, and of gendered and raced class formation, like analyses of the racial and gender dynamics of imperial formations, had reconfigured existing concepts of class, family and empire as well as adding to knowledge. Such rethinking of practice could be found in texts on topics ranging from plantation slavery and medieval mysticism to histories of missionary activity and household labour.[30]

From the 1980s the exploration of social life and social action, which had produced a wide range of scholarship, was further modified by new concerns and contests over the notion of culture. Expanded notions of what might be included in the field of culture (popular music, literature or media, fashion, everyday objects and activities) and new approaches to the study of culture, developed to consider aspects of contemporary life, stimulated new approaches to the study of such phenomena in the past. Examinations of politics during the French Revolution, of culture and power in seventeenth-century aristocratic households or of gender and colonial rule in India under the British *raj*, all explored the potential of these approaches.[31] Analytical discussion of the links between knowledge, ideas and social or political power, and of how words and images convey or create meaning, opened up different ways of thinking about how to understand texts, images and behaviour and their connections, both past and present.[32] Some historians applied these approaches to the study of past cultures and societies, whether rethinking histories of medicine, linking race, citizenship and slavery, or developing new views of the history of modern labour patterns. They enabled them to develop analyses of the slippery, complex and contradictory features of social and political affiliation or activism with approaches which neither relied on grand oversimplified narratives, nor collapsed into atomised detail.[33] Other historians saw these 'cultural' and 'linguistic' turns as irrelevant to 'real' history, as 'theoretical' distractions from the need to give due attention to substantive, rather than ephemeral, aspects of past life, or as tilting at the windmills of grand theory which had never mattered much to 'good historians' anyway. They often defended practices which themselves had been innovative in the 1970s, but now could be defended as established practice, or dismissed as the failed initiatives of embarrassing progressives.[34]

This is not the place to unpack, let alone adjudicate over, these debates, but rather to note their impact on narratives of nation, society and empire. In the UK they grew within an academic culture in which trends towards professionalisation and recruitment from aspirant as well as established groups, which had begun before the Second World War, were reinforced by the expansion of secondary education and later of post-school education. Between the 1960s and the end of the twentieth century the proportion of young people going to university rose from under 10% of the age group to around 40%, and the number of postgraduates in humanities and social sciences rose, supported by the availability of state-funded grants for university study from the mid-1960s until the 1990s. There was a major shift in the gender balance of students (women increasing from 33% of the student population in 1970 to 57% in 2004–5) and growth in the proportion of students from manual worker families. This rose from 4% to 19% of the student population between the 1960s and 2001, although, significantly, the proportion of students from non-manual worker families grew from 27% to 50% in that period. By 2001, over 20,000 undergraduates and over 5,000 graduates were studying history in colleges and universities.[35] The pool for researchers and academic historians was enlarged by these changes, by the new demand for postgraduate qualifications for entry into academic posts and by the demand for jobs in higher education. The context of academic history provision was changed by the addition of new kinds of higher education institutions (polytechnics, new provision for mature students, colleges of education) to the previously limited range, and by new curricula and structures for teaching and research (area studies, cross-disciplinary and thematic programmes). While established practices and views of history writing continued to flourish, those studying, researching and writing history could also more easily encounter and explore, or contest, ideas and methods from a range of intellectual and academic traditions, and bring a range of experience and insight to their work.

Some of the energy behind the development of the range of possible history writing came from the convergence of this growth and diversification of university experience with the political radicalism associated with anti-war, leftist and anti-racist movements. For some radicals, especially those on university campuses, it was important to connect their concern with these public issues to critiques of the study of societies past and present. This critical edge was found in a range of work published in the 1960s and 1970s, reformulating established approaches to the history of slaves, women, colonial subjects and workers. Such work proposed new analyses [36] or opened up the history of marginalised groups.[37] Their contributions were contentious, both because they challenged existing historical practice and because they were associated with the politics of the period, whether new versions of leftist politics or the emergent politics of gender and race, and therefore suspect as scholarly contributions. Their effects on history writing were complex, stimulating some scholars to follow their lead, others to strengthen their commitment to existing practices, and yet others to develop practices which distanced themselves from politics while exploring new perspectives on social and political history. The pursuit of these varied approaches combined with the expansion of advanced historical training and proliferation of research degrees and was reinforced by the adversarial and competitive approaches favoured in academic practice. This ensured that historical writing over the following decades developed multiple voices and preoccupations. It can be illustrated by studies of the French Revolution and Chartism, of workplace and urban communities, and of sport or crime.[38] For some historians the turn to culture and deconstruction threatened and misrepresented the value of 'proper' social and political history. From the opposite perspective, such history was limited by the refusal of its defenders to recognise the constructed character of their own practice and knowledge and, as will be seen, it spilled in to the debates on empire which emerged in the 1990s.[39]

One way in which the diversified presentation of 'national' history was manifest was in the multivolume series on the history of England and of Europe, following precedents set earlier in the century by the Oxford and Cambridge histories, or the Methuen series edited by Charles Oman. Longmans and Nelson, which had been publishing school readers and textbooks since the 1870s, now produced series aimed at new student and public readerships emerging through the education system, with paperback publishers like Penguin, Paladin and Fontana following suit. They used established academic authors and offered readers new kinds of social history and historiographical viewpoints as well as conventional political narratives. Oxford University Press was sufficiently confident in the format to launch a *New history of England* series in the1990s following their earlier series which had been reprinted and revised from the 1930s into the 1980s. Historians who had been building their careers from the 1960s replaced the generation who produced the earlier series, many of whom had been intellectually formed in Edwardian or interwar culture.[40] The flourishing of such series into the 1980s and their subsequent decline raises important questions about changing demands and assumptions and the competition from other media. In schools the use of video, electronic and interactive technologies reduced or reframed the demand for textbooks, just as the popular market for history books turned towards military history and colourful social themes rather than sustained multivolume narratives.[41]

However, other media were becoming more dominant than books in depicting and shaping views of the past. As television became an omnipresent medium in the 1960s and diversified from the 1980s, the pre-war educational and cultural missions of BBC broadcasting were recast by new ideas and assumptions within wider society, and by the technical stimulus and demands of the medium itself. While history programmes were only a small part of TV output, they established a niche where established forms of 'lecture' and 'documentary' programmes on history were supplemented and cross-fertilised by interactive and 'reality TV' programmes, and 'edutainment' aimed at multiple platforms and markets. Events, people, nations and empires could be visualised as well as depicted in words, with varied narratives and images of the past being offered to TV audiences. These included re-run film footage of world wars, docu-dramas on 'heroic' figures, documentary series with 'characterful' presenters, ancestry programmes, re-enactments in 'period' houses or streets, and 'human interest' treatments of colourful individuals or sexy and sensational tales of cross-racial intimacy. Viewers could choose a biopic of Cecil Rhodes, a documentary about Indian troops on the western front in the First World War, reality TV reconstructions of Victorian pharmacies or an educational narrative accompanying gorgeous images of Norman conquests in England and Sicily.

Interactions of glamorising, educational and entertaining versions of the past in accessible broadcast forms added images of the past and 'historical' topics to other subjects of docu-drama, 'reality' TV, drama series and documentary broadcasting. Traditional educational versions of the past for school or Open University students sat beside sex-and-violence dramas about Tudor rulers, 'human interest' explorations of ancestry (including colonial ancestry) and the attractions of watching re-enacted life in 'period' kitchens, streets, or farmhouses. Creative fusions between these genres as well as their diversity embedded history programming within the varied types of broadcast entertainment.

Empire, state and citizenship

As UK residents debated the relationship of law and government in the UK and the European Union, the devolution of Scotland and Wales and UK laws on immigration and citizenship for new arrivals from the Caribbean, south Asia and Africa since the 1960s, they turned to history to support their varied views. Notions that laws could or should define, connect or limit various historically formed identities influenced state regulation of rights and institutions in the period after 1950, as it had earlier – as seen in laws on immigration and citizenship, and on the new differences and overlaps between UK, commonwealth and European institutions. These connections were manifest in the 1965 unilateral declaration of independence (UDI) in what was then called Southern Rhodesia, in revived conflict over the legacies of the 1922 partition of the island of Ireland from the 1970s, Scottish and Welsh devolution politics since the 1980s, and a series of redefinitions of UK or commonwealth citizenship over the period. Changes in UK relations with the redefined commonwealth, and with what became the European Union, as well as the growth of 'transnational' human rights legislation were constant, and for some troubling, reminders that the concept and boundaries of 'state' and 'nation' were unfixed and contentious. Awareness of, and sometimes resistance to, such ongoing shifts in the legal organisation, authority and definition of such categories nurtured an interest in their history.

The main concern here is with the role of ideas of state and citizenship in history writing, and its connections, or lack of them, to empire. As already seen, historians' preoccupations with government policies and institutions had shifted with the emergence of new social and cultural histories, but the continuing appeal of established practices, and the possibilities for bringing new perspectives to administrative and political history, ensured that those themes continued to be important. Among the multiple accounts of the past produced over the period since the 1960s were new analyses of medieval state formation, of the dynamics of party political or monarchical power and influence, and of interactions between government, economy or religion.[42] Thus, while many historical texts were now organised around 'social' or 'cultural' themes, the framework of royal reigns, political parties in office and legislative change, inherited from the past, continued to shape much history writing, research and teaching. Individual monographs, historical series and teaching materials all made use of such frameworks. Moreover, growing interest in historical studies which linked cultural to political issues stimulated new approaches to thinking about state, empire and 'high politics'. By the 1990s there was much reactive thinking about the 'national' or 'imperial' meanings of moments of political change such as the Reform Acts of 1832 and 1867, the union of England and Scotland, and the American Revolution. Armitage, Hall, McLelland, Rendall and Taylor drew on the historiography of social movements and on cultural politics to offer new insights into such conventional high points of political narrative.[43]

In the 1960s A.J.P. Taylor could dismiss questions of 'England's' place in a 'British' state by arguing that notions of 'England' and 'Britain' could, and should, be collapsed into one another.[44] By the 1990s this picture had changed. Interestingly, an early challenge to the Anglocentric collapsing of the diverse pasts of Scottish, Welsh and Irish peoples into accounts of 'English' history came from a New Zealand historian concerned about the threat to commonwealth links posed by the UK's 1975 entry into the EEC. Equally interestingly, his intervention was rebuffed both by Taylor and by historians of the 'Celtic fringe'.[45] It may be noted that 'new British history', which recognised the differences and interactivity among the various parts of the 'British' Isles, was more often taken up initially by historians who focused on Ireland and Scotland than by those whose central interests were English.

From the 1980s historians have acknowledged, and sometimes emphasised, the composite, constructed and changing character of the 'English' state and its successors since the thirteenth century, and the roles of conquest and colonial power in the formation of state institutions and policies. Between the late 1980s and the first decade of the new millennium single studies and collections of essays began to present versions of that story as a plural process in which 'English' state making and politics interacted with developments among the Welsh, Irish or Scots. This was also acknowledged by contributors to the new *Penguin history of Britain* (not England), and by the inclusion of Irish and Scottish chapters in studies of the seventeenth-century 'English' civil war.[46] More specifically, historians have paid growing attention to the dynamics of relationships between the English, Scottish and Irish polities, and their wider imperial connections, since the sixteenth century. This might involve the disaggregation of stories about England/ Britain/the United Kingdom in order to trace the distinctive pasts of what became seen as the constituent nations of the UK.[47] It might involve rethinking those pasts by considering them from Welsh, Irish or Scottish viewpoints, and exploring shifting patterns of dominance and resistance. General histories and collections took a similar 'four nations' perspective.[48] It might open up studies of interactions between the distinctive 'nations' or constituent elements of the UK, notably in work on the seventeenth century. The 'English' civil wars of that period could be rethought as overlapping wars involving Scots, Irish and English, and the emergence of 'nationalistic' thought and politics in Scotland or Ireland be explored as interactive as well as adversarial processes.[49]

One theme which emerged from work on the early modern period was that of an 'Atlantic world' in which an 'Atlantic archipelago' (a term introduced by Pocock) was the location for experiments in state building, settlement policy and governance which might be seen as prototypes for the more explicitly 'imperial' practices of later times. The work of David Armitage, Nicholas Canny, Jane Ohlmeyer and others offers accounts of such experiments, exploring seventeenth-century intersections of policies and people in Ireland, England and the Americas as constituents of an emerging 'British' polity, including its global and colonial interests.[50] Interest in the distinctive histories of the Scots, Irish and Welsh in later periods, and in their relationships to histories of the English stimulated work on Irish, Scottish and Welsh involvement in an undoubtedly 'British' empire and the paradoxes of power, subordination and opportunity which this created. Historians now study how the role of soldiers and administrators from all 'four nations' in imperial governance, and the need for governments to consider the interests of settlers and missionaries from those backgrounds, affected the British state and colonial policy, cross-fertilising new views of UK and imperial history.[51]

In addition to expressing professional debates and searches for new fields to explore and explain, these approaches reflected the wider context where questions of citizenship, devolution and UK connections to the USA, Europe and former imperial territories regularly surfaced in politics and the media. In that sense the tensions between historical analyses of the subordination and partnerships of the Welsh, Irish or Scottish within the UK, and those of their contribution to 'British' imperial dominance, paralleled contemporary debates about autonomy and inclusion at UK and other levels of government. They encouraged the growth of powerful arguments that imperial developments had been constitutive of state formation, politics and government in the UK, which gained influence in the 1990s, and, as will be seen, reshaped some historians' approaches to the study of national and ethnic identities and divisions. Of course, such arguments coexisted with many versions of national and imperial pasts which continued to treat them as discrete stories and were comfortable with unitary depictions of 'Britain' and the UK, and indeed fostered controversy over the merits of alternative approaches. The 2010 edition of the *Oxford history of Britain* spoke of claiming back the cohesiveness and continuity of 'British' history in a country where key institutions and cultural unity were under threat, echoing the Palgrave history despite its partial acceptance of a plural view of the UK. Similar thoughts on British continuities now under threat appear in the volume edited by J.C.D. Clark.[52]

One interesting aspect of recent scholarship is its interest in the distinctively imperial elements which shaped the disparate experiences, activities and identities of Welsh, Scots or Irish people. While these elements can be examined as stories of social and cultural development shaped by religion, migration or global exchange, historians also analyse them as shaping and shaped by connections to state structures and citizenship. On the one hand, the imperial activities of 'English', 'British' or UK governments could be shown to have drawn on contributions from Irish, Welsh and Scottish administrators, soldiers and politicians, who might thus gain acceptance as citizens, albeit from supposedly subordinate parts of the kingdom.[53] On the other hand, historians have also shown how, perhaps more paradoxically, self-consciously Scottish, Irish or Welsh identities were developed and expressed through imperial service, as well as by social and cultural means to be discussed later. Contributions to colonial wars and administration are thus being shown to play an integral role both in the incorporation, or even subordination, of the peoples of the 'Atlantic' isles within imperial projects, and also in the forming and reforming of the distinctive identities of each of these peoples. Discussion of the distinctive organisation and celebration of Irish or Scots regiments, or demonstrations of specifically Scottish/Irish/Welsh versions of 'imperial' loyalty suggested that they signalled the inclusion of those who were identified in that way within the empire/commonwealth, while marking their 'difference' and perhaps junior status in the imperial partnership. Moving beyond studies of migration and histories of the Irish, Welsh or Scots in parts of the empire outside the Atlantic isles, some studies considered the influence of imperial participation on the development of conscious assertions of their interests back in those isles, as well as on their material and political achievements. They have suggested that through the twentieth century those who claimed fuller recognition of the place of the Welsh, Scottish or Irish in the UK might draw on stories of past contributions to the empire, as had nineteenth-century predecessors.

This could create historiographical as well as political tensions. As Stephen Howe and Steven Ellis have shown, historians of Ireland have pursued the conflicts which were a legacy of British rule in that island in their accounts of the Irish past and its relationship to empire.[54] Stories of conquest, exploitation and resistance to the British are contested by narratives of involvement in empire, and of the complex affiliations and interests which shaped the politics and culture of different sections of the Irish population in relation to Britain, to empire and to each other. Alongside debate over Ireland's position as a 'colony' or some other kind of component of the UK and its empire, relationships between Catholic soldiers or policemen, Anglo-Irish officers and colonial subjects – like those between Indian nationalists or Boers and Irish counterparts, or those between Irish settler politics and colonial, British and Irish politics – have become subjects of scholarly study.[55] The contentious character of the 'British' state and its imperial dimensions, like the contested versions of citizenship and inclusion associated with them, emerge in particularly sharp forms if seen from an Irish perspective, but are also illuminated when the viewpoint is Welsh or Scottish. Recent historical work has explored how Welsh as well as Irish patriotisms and political demands might be bolstered by military or missionary activities in the empire. Similarly, work on the Scottish dimensions of imperial power illustrates how involvement in empire contributed to the shaping of Scottish interests and identities and to the embedding of a Scottish presence in British and English politics and society, as Scotsmen parlayed colonial success into English estates, businesses and parliamentary patronage.[56] The imperial deeds of Irish, Welsh or Highland regiments, like parliamentary arguments over the shared or diverse political rights and duties of 'British' colonial settlers, could be seen as inclusive or as divisive by historians at the end of the twentieth century, in ways which might reflect contemporary debates or uncertainties about 'Britishness'. If Hancock and Coupland in an earlier generation had linked the 'unity' of the United Kingdom to that of the empire, more recent work has expressed, whether with enthusiasm or concern, the current climate in which devolution and plurality are familiar terms for discussing state, citizenship or governance.

However, not all discussion of empire took a 'four nations' approach. A modernised version of a collective chronologically based history, the *Oxford history of the British empire*, offered a 'companion volume' on *Ireland and the British empire* and single chapters on Ireland in the chronological volumes – a recognition of the distinctive character of Irish roles. Otherwise its political and administrative chapters took a largely UK/British state perspective.[57] General histories of empire by Lloyd, Judd and James take state and governance within 'Britain'/the UK to be centred on Whitehall and Westminster, with the 'official mind' interacting with 'public opinion', and circumstances or pressures in other parts of the empire.[58] This depiction of an empire with a central focus was not, of course, homogeneous, and Darwin's recent study argues that the British/UK state at best attempted to manage, and at worst merely reacted to, events or processes within a 'system' which it neither created nor controlled.[59] There were also important variations between accounts which emphasised politics, war and government – thus keeping the state prominent, whether reactively or proactively – and those with other perspectives. These included Ferguson's broad thematic sweep, and that of Levine, which gave less space to the role of government, choosing to consider the experiences of colonial subjects and socio-cultural themes.[60] Darwin embedded his politically oriented narrative of the empire within a 'British world system' where politicians and administrators juggled the requirements of settler colonialism, diplomatic and 'informal' influence, world monetary and commercial interests and direct or indirect rule. Taking this a step further, some historians seek to locate the work of the UK state in the century after 1860 in 'transnational' analyses, linking core state functions (policing, censorship, legislation) to wider activities and ideas around international organisation, or universal rights and standards. Transnational approaches, first developed to rethink the histories of migration and cultural plurality, could be applied to accounts of the 'British' past and its global and imperial features. They could support arguments that histories of Britain's empire could usefully be decentred and treated comparatively alongside those of other empires.[61]

Yet much history writing in the UK, whether in detailed monographs or general accounts, most often handled histories of the state as stories of a distinctive phenomenon evolving within the Atlantic archipelago. It shifted from a dominant focus on 'great ideas' such as 'reform', 'stability' or ideologies, and indeed on leaders (despite the continued popularity of historical biography among general readerships), towards a greater concern with process and complexity, and scepticism about linear narratives. In such writing 'empire' might at most be a discrete chapter or brief reference in texts focused on court or party politics, on the evolution of government institutions or on the UK polity within the archipelago. Powerful 'national', or UK-wide perspectives remained the typical framework, or unit of study and analysis, whether or not modified by 'four nation' or regional additions. By the early twenty-first century some historians mounted polemical defences of the value of 'national narrative' against what they saw as 'damaging' fragmentation consequent upon the use of regional, global or postcolonial frameworks, whether social, political or cultural. Even those who did not engage in sharp debate reflected on the present and future of the UK state in relation to devolution, the Anglo-American 'alliance' in the post-Cold War era, and the European Union. These issues fed into depictions of the 'decline' of the UK.

Empire, civilisation and progress

For some late twentieth-century historians at least, accounts of the British/UK state and its imperial aspects had evolved into sophisticated narratives and analyses of their development and inter-relationships. If the question of the 'four nations' had stirred controversy, and shifting UK government structures encouraged rumination on uncertainty, empire remained marginal, if never wholly invisible, in such narratives. This was evidenced by the imperial elements in edited volumes of narrative or of thematic history and by the analyses and popular volumes on the politics of empire.[62] However, the evolution of social history over the second half of the twentieth century generated a more turbulent historiography. The disaggregation of 'society' or 'nation' by analyses of distinct and sometimes antagonistic groupings (regions, classes, communities, genders, subalterns) and of deconstructions of power and meaning challenged narratives of progress or reform. Miles Taylor has argued that accounts of 1960s social history which stress the influence of leftist or social scientific ideas ignore important debts to existing historical practice and to 1950s political thought. Michael Bentley has shown that the 'modernist' forms of history writing which dominated UK practice between the 1920s and 1970s developed interactively with, rather than in opposition to, the influential 'whiggish' approaches of earlier periods.[63] Both texts offer careful analyses of shifts in historical practice and question the sharpness of those shifts, although arguably they sidestep substantial discussion of the serious intellectual and political challenges posed by subaltern or post-structural alternatives. Their polite and thoughtful arguments should not obscure the force of those challenges, and of their ripostes to them, and whatever view is taken of the merits of challenge or riposte, the discussion signalled important differences.

Two of the key themes at issue, universalism and power, were directly relevant to the approaches being taken to notions of 'civilisation' and 'progress' deployed or critiqued by historians. Social histories offered accounts of the past experiences of less privileged or subordinate groups, depicting their distinctive responses to, and experiences of, change. Such accounts implicitly or explicitly challenged homogenising versions of 'the Reformation', 'industrialisation' or the seventeenth-century civil wars. Whether by taking local or regional perspectives or by drawing attention to the activities and relationships arising from the specific and sometimes conflicting interests of the powerful and powerless, they produced more complex stories of social and political change. From accounts of gender divisions of labour and industrial change and of conscription and poverty during the French Revolution, to depictions of gender politics in Reformation Augsburg or of subaltern anti-colonial politics, conventional views have been significantly altered by more diverse approaches.[64] This was not just a matter of including new material and narratives, but of their impact on the organising ideas used to shape history writing. Notions of 'industrialisation', or 'religious reformation', or 'political protest' need to be refigured once it is recognised that they incorporate varied and conflicting experiences and relationships into analysis as well as description. If Joan Kelly's 1977 question, 'Did women have a Renaissance?', or Ranajit Guha's call for 'subaltern' histories of the British *raj* in India,[65] had a provocative, even polemical, edge, they expressed substantive challenges to historians' familiar terminology, stimulating serious work which questioned and refigured established categories. Presenting divergent and subaltern views of particular social, cultural or political processes challenged unreflective uses of the labels which historians were used to applying to them, although, of course, many historians chose not to respond to such challenges.

What is interesting about these challenges is that they set up not binary oppositions between powerful and powerless, exploited and exploiters, but many-sided encounters of different forms of dominance or subordination. Their interest was in exploring combinations of gender and class in the medieval sex industry, or nineteenth-century popular radicalism, of class and ethnicity in modern nationalist movements or early modern colonialism, and of class, ethnic and gender aspects of New World slavery, Roman republicanism or apartheid.[66] Such approaches kept a focus on issues of power but also showed its contradictory strands, and its contested and unstable forms. They investigated and interpreted unequal power relations but also explored and evaluated their plural and shifting relations. They could show how women whose opposition to slavery expressed liberal or religious humanitarianism, class and gender aspirations and visions of a civilising imperialism enacted both privilege and subordination. They could trace the blends of patriarchal authority, class power and heterosexual masculine anxiety involved in the regulation of same-sex sexual encounters on urban streets or in colonial settings. They could explore gendered and ethnic elements in the language and practices of modern popular or class politics, tensions of gender power and social hierarchy in the dynamics of medieval rule and governance.[67] In all these instances what can be seen as skilful academic treatment of complexity can also be understood as combining social, cultural and political analysis to investigate the making of and resistance to power relations, and the agency of subordinate as well as dominant groups.

Some historians ignored or opposed that concern with power, concentrating on the academic treatment of complexity. One scholar's response to the 1987 appearance of a distinguished and detailed study of gender and class formation, *Family fortunes: men and women of the English middle class, 1780–1850*, was the revealing comment, 'Excellent social history, shame about the feminism'.[68] Similarly they sidestepped or denounced arguments about knowledge and power, and the problems with large overarching interpretations which emerged from thinkers on historical practice, and on history as a form of knowledge. These arguments emphasised: (a) the dubious value of overarching schemes of narrative or explanation; (b) the textual and discursive nature of material from the past, seen as 'documentary representation' rather than 'evidence'; (c) that accounts of the past are the creative constructions of historians rather than reconstructions; and (d) the difficulty of making 'objective' judgements between different versions of the past.[69] They met with vigorous challenges from critics. The strength of such responses came from assertions that historians' core relationship with original sources gave them a practical familiarity with context-specific, competing and multiple voices and viewpoints, needing no support from theory. Among UK practitioners this was reinforced by a well-established view that concepts and theories were not very important tools in their professional kit, or were actual obstacles to 'good historical work'.[70] If historical practice was fragmented in many directions by the opportunities and insights pursued by professional and popular historians, it was also divided by these arguments.

Such arguments are relevant for a discussion of how notions of 'civilisation' and 'progress', which had informed history writing in the first part of the twentieth century, were used, abandoned or refigured subsequently. Three trends modified historians' acceptance of a single agreed understanding of 'civilisation', which of course had never been universal or unquestioned in any case. The expansion of scholarly work on the specifics of life and ideas in various periods and places in the past shifted attention towards the diverse and distinctive ways in which particular societies and ruling regimes organised and presented themselves.[71] This normalising of variation and specificity was part of the wider professional fragmentation of historical research and writing already noted as a core feature of historical practice. It is also linked to a second trend where comparative discussion of particular past societies supported relativist views of what might or might not be labelled 'progress' or 'civilisation'. Influenced by a growing range of publications about different 'civilisations' and of work on societies where archaeologists used and analysed material rather than written evidence, pluralistic uses of the term became familiar in both learned and popular texts. A third trend arose from academic fragmentation, and from interest in the experiences and views of 'subaltern' groups, as described earlier. It stimulated study of 'subgroups' and 'subcultures' (religious dissidents, rural settlements, female reform networks, young urban males) which likewise disaggregated notions of culture and civilisation.

In the past 'civilisation' was typically understood either as an overarching set of practices and values relevant to, if not shared by, all members of society, or as a criterion for assessing any society. In a classic formulation offered to millions of TV viewers by the cultural mandarin Kenneth Clark in his successful 1969 art historical series on *Civilisation*, this term was to be distinguished from the idea of 'culture'. This latter might be associated with medieval Norse carvings or an African mask but was not in the same league as the achievements of the ancient Greeks and Romans, or Renaissance Italians.[72] Past debates had often centred on how, when or if, 'others' (dissidents, the unprivileged, non-British people) would be capable of progressing to a 'civilised' state, and what the civilised or privileged might do to assist or resist that progress. Turbulent Irish, uneducated labourers, women, colonial subjects and suburban villa dwellers had all been commented on from this perspective in the nineteenth and twentieth centuries, just as economic, political and social institutions around the world had been evaluated according to their degree of 'civilisation'. However, there were also traditions of comparative and descriptive analysis which supported more relativistic views of different societies, and contests between more and less universal hierarchies of 'civilisation' were a feature of historical debate. In the later decades of the twentieth century the sense that 'western civilisation' faced problems and challenges stimulated discussion among historians as well as media and social commentators, and also provoked more specific discussion about what was happening to 'civilisation' in the UK. Historical writings were flavoured by changing perceptions of 'civilisation' as a global phenomenon. Between the 1950s and the 1980s this might take the form of controversy over European–north American cultural relations (fellow defenders of western civilisation, as well as Cold War political allies? A dangerous dilution of that civilisation?). Thereafter it was more likely to focus on the non-western alternatives to European/north American 'civilisation' emerging in China or India, or the new menace (real and imagined) of 'Muslim' challenges within and outside 'western' countries.[73]

Pessimistic themes, which had already surfaced in earlier decades, now appeared repeatedly in general histories of England/Britain. They differed from the optimism of the conclusion to A.J.P. Taylor's *English history, 1914–1945*, which contrasted the decline of jingoistic patriotism ('few now sang "Land of hope and glory"') with social progress and wartime achievements ('England had risen all the same').[74] T.O Lloyd's 1970 volume on the twentieth-century history of the UK in the *Oxford history of the modern world* series (interestingly titled *Empire, welfare state, Europe*) closes the 2002 fifth edition with reflection on the brief life of the democratic reform politics signalled by the coming of adult suffrage and the creation of a welfare state. In keeping with the volume's emphasis on UK-level high politics, it argues that the brief moment in the 1940s when politicians seemed to have the capacity to lead 'a secular transformation of society' was just that, and was followed by a decline in the relations between political parties and voters.[75] The closing section of J. Black's *History of the British Isles* refers to the weakening and obscuring of 'Britishness', linked to the decline of established institutions (parliament, churches, monarchy, 'national independence'), and of 'a culture of liberal viable alternatives'. Its final appeal is to the value of history as the provider of 'a sense of place and time that provides identity and helps maintain social values'.[76] Kenneth Morgan's framing of the collectively authored *Oxford history of Britain* likewise sees historical awareness as a potential source of understanding and social solidarity, and it suggests that recent changes to 'an ancient country' threatened social coherence and unity. Echoing ideas put forward by Tawney, it posed the decline of 'social citizenship and the public realm' against the force of individualistic consumerism.[77] As will be seen, these views say much about historians' perceptions of national and ethnic identity, but merit mention here for their expression of social as well as ethnic or patriotic pessimism.

There is, of course, quite a gap between such pronouncements and professional accounts and debates about the past, although it could be argued that the relativism referred to above reinforced historians' avoidance of bold pronouncements on progress and civilisation. Since the early twentieth century, depictions of social and material change had been influenced by interactions between social scientific thought, empirical work on particular past societies and the presentation of distinctively historical ideas about change. If social scientists grounded ideas about what came to be called 'modern society' in historical narrative, historians wrestled with tensions between their professional investment in the study of specificity and the appeal of larger narratives and concepts which might frame them. The extensive literature on European and global socio-economic transformations since the sixteenth century, variously labelled industrialisation, take-off, development and modernisation, illustrates some of the continuities and changes in notions of civilisation and progress. In an interesting postcolonial development, one type of text blended existing accounts of changes in manufacture, commerce and urban growth with concepts created by specialists in the field of development studies which emerged from the 1950s to plan and analyse the economic development of 'third-world' societies, often former colonies.

Such specialists used models of 'development' which often assumed that it was appropriate to apply the 'successful' model of European and north American experience to those societies – an assumption which was questioned from the 1970s. This influenced the work of historians who transferred such models back to their work on the European and north American past. They applied the terminology of 'factors' and 'structure' to accounts of investment, technology and trade or production systems in the past; sometimes they sought to establish ways of identifying 'necessary' conditions for material transformation by adapting the predictive methods of social scientists in historical writing. It is worth noting that while this was a 'modern' approach to the analysis of change, it also replicated older interest in the uniquely 'leading', 'unique', 'successful' experiences of Europeans. It thus recast familiar associations between Europe, progress and civilisation, contrasted with the deficiencies of other areas of the world. This can be seen in accounts of western development, but also in recent writing about why and how western societies 'succeeded' where others did not. The latter recast older views in which 'civilisation' was associated with European 'achievements', contrasted with the limited or backward practices of others. From the quantitative analyses and comparative studies of Maddison and Pomeranz to the popular works of Diamond and Ferguson, narratives of world history in these terms continued to present this dichotomy. Where they differed was in their emphasis on technological/scientific factors, on contingent circumstances or on inherent capacities and/or inherited practices and institutions as underpinning explanations of their Eurocentric accounts. [78] By the 1980s this Eurocentrism was confronted by various comparative, anti-colonial and indigenist or subaltern views of development past and present. It was also confronted by new forms of 'world history' in which transnational and interactive accounts of material change and power relations replaced 'national' approaches. From the 1990s some historians were arguing for a pluralistic account of different paths to material development in which Europe would be 'provincialised'.[79] By the turn of the new millennium awareness of the material dynamism of China, India, Brazil and south-east Asia raised further questions of western 'decline' or limitations.

Such influences can be seen in the more specific context of writing about socio-economic changes in the UK in the eighteenth and nineteenth centuries. The growing technical and analytical sophistication of the tools available to post-1950 historians of what had once been called the industrial revolution [80] stimulated scrutiny of those changes which modified and diversified narratives while confirming some of their established content. More dramatic notions of sudden 'take-off' were replaced by depictions of a cumulative set of changes, and close technical analysis, but the story of a 'great discontinuity' survived in a modified form. It is worth noting how earlier accounts of the 'progress' associated with industrialisation, and debates over 'pessimistic' as against 'optimistic' views of its impact, came to be replaced by less judgemental terms like 'change' and 'growth'. Historians dealing with social and economic topics remained more invested in narratives of some kinds of 'progress' or at least 'modernisation' than those with more political or cultural interests. Some began to consider the global and interactive elements (Chinese connections, the Atlantic economy) feeding into the early British adoption of industrial innovation.[81] Nonetheless, general studies like Bartlett's *Medieval panorama* maintained the view of the late fifteenth century as the opening of 'modern' times which went back to Hume, although its emphasis was more on print and Protestantism than on the new humanism.[82]

The bundle of changes usually associated with that viewpoint, of course, includes the shift in European relations with the wider world following the so-called 'voyages of discovery' and subsequent colonial expansion. Like other fields this shift is now the subject of detailed professional scholarship and analysis, but is also charged with controversy about the nature and impact of European imperial and global dominance, and its American successor. Here notions of progress and improvement loom large in contested narratives of the British *raj* in India, colonial settlement in Canada or Australia, the Atlantic slave trade and the partition of Africa. One tendency has been to use accounts of the agency of Zulus, Bengalis, Maoris or enslaved African labourers to create interactive stories of 'imperial social formations', but controversy over the benefits and costs of empire for colonial subalterns still fuels historical debate.[83] Studies of the 'British world' of settler colonies have shown the complex webs of conflict and attachment which linked Australians, Canadians or South Africans of 'British' origin to the UK and contributed to the emergence of autonomous societies with their own imperial/racial features. Those arguing for the benefits of empire tend to set aside political aspects of colonial power and its exclusionary practices to emphasise material or cultural opportunities created and benefits bestowed in contemporary variants of the 'civilising mission' story of empire. Those focusing on indigenous agency revealed the conditional and contested conditions for the making and maintenance of imperial power and activity and the hybridity of colonial relationships, modifying binary interpretations of that power and its subordinates.

There are a number of ways to understand the changed connections between notions of empire, civilisation and progress in recent history writing. One view would be that the large quantity of close studies of the complexities of empire has dismantled analyses of unequal power and advantage. Another would be that such studies have deepened understanding of colonial inequalities by demonstrating their workings more fully. Yet another would note how work on the 'empire at home' has inflected social and cultural histories of the UK, and indeed other European countries with colonial histories. More generally it might be noted that controversy over the extent of the effects of 'empire', whether in the metropole or outside it, has enlarged discussion of civilisation and progress, while also creating antagonisms around implied moral or political judgements embedded in historical texts.

Empire, race and nation

While it may seem relatively easy to follow the impact of imperial decline and of changes to the ethnic composition and politics of the UK on social and political life there, their effects on history writing are a more complex matter. Historians of the twentieth-century UK could not fail to deal with those developments in one way or another, but the question of any larger impact on history writing is more challenging. Despite the interactions between historical and social scientific scholarship already mentioned, this was in part a function of the professional confidence and distinctiveness with which history was practised in the second half of the twentieth century. From the perspective of many practitioners, the concerns with contemporary developments which shaped the work of observers and policymakers were not relevant to those concerned with the investigation and interpretation of the past. One of the central tenets of historical practice in this period was indeed to maintain the distinction of past and present. Such views were frequently buttressed by the use of L.P. Hartley's remark that 'the past is a foreign country' – a literary and psychological insight into memory and change rather than a piece of professional advice.[84] This much-repeated commitment to the empathic and informed depiction of past situations 'in their own terms' existed in tension with the equally well-established commitment to creating narratives which linked past and present in accounts of the development of institutions or social structures over time. By the 1970s it also faced critical arguments about the importance of connectedness, relevance and inclusion in the teaching and writing of history, whether from curriculum reformers or radical scholars. It is within this framework that history writing has engaged with questions of race and nation over the last fifty years.

Debate about history writing focused in particular on the content and narrative of the history of the UK itself. By the 1980s some historians argued that the coherent stories of the growth and continuities of freedom, liberty and distinctive 'English' national institutions and culture had been damaged by distracting attention to the conflicts of interest and the disruptions or shifts which were part of such stories. The durability and value of key trends and institutions had been obscured by 'fashionable' (a favoured term of abuse) concern for their excluding or exploitative features. The unpacking of the class, colonial or gender dynamics of social or political reform or of economic change threatened to distort narratives of progress, or overestimate the negative aspects of valued institutions and the significance of challenges to them. Just estimations of the durability of constitutional monarchy or the Church of England should not be misled by too much attention to dissidence, secularism or radical protest. Respect for contingent and specific elements in historical narratives or past situations was undermined by structural or analytical accounts of change which used social scientific models with their dubious leftist or whiggish associations. These arguments might be polemical or scholarly, or combine the two, and if strongly flavoured by the political climate of the 1980s and 1990s (as the 'new' social histories had been flavoured by that of the 1960s and 1970s), they also reframed important debates and research questions.[85]

Just as these issues had affected discussions of civilisation and modernity so they affected the use of terms like 'race' and 'nation' in historical writing. The period after 1950 saw some paradoxical developments, as certain types of racialised discussion of the past became less acceptable or useful, while concern with 'race' as a social, political and cultural issue in the late twentieth-century UK intensified. Work by Brah, Gilroy, Stuart Hall, Gikandi and Schwarz has interrogated the history and politics of migration and diversity in the UK in the twentieth century, as Catherine Hall, Kathleen Wilson and Antoinette Burton have done for earlier periods.[86] One way in which this paradox was negotiated by other historians was through discussion of 'national ('English'? or 'British'?) identity which figured interestingly, and often negatively, in many summaries of twentieth-century UK history. If some ended their surveys with references to relative global decline in material and diplomatic power, and to internal political difficulties, others considered the dangers to such an identity. The 2010 multi-authored *Oxford history of Britain* edited by Keith Robbins ended with questions about the 'challenge' to 'national coherence' posed by devolved government, migration and cultural pluralism, and the pressures of globalisation. This echoed Jeremy Black's comments on the destruction of hitherto essential props to 'national identity' at the end of his 2003 *History of the British Isles*.[87] From a liberal perspective Hugh Kearney argued for a multinational and non-racialised approach to the history of the 'British' Isles, while from a gloomier viewpoint J.C.D. Clark considered the threats of religious and national conflict and federalisation within the UK. They linked the role of memory and of practices of history writing to what they saw as threats and opportunities for establishing and maintaining 'national identity'.[88] More open ended and constructive, if optimistic, was Robert Colls' *Identity of England* with its vigorous analysis of the new conditions in which that identity might be remade in the twenty-first century, and its confidence in the 'English' capacity for mutual trust which would enable them to do so.[89]

These conclusions to history texts locate themselves in the circumstances of the UK in the late twentieth and early twenty-first centuries, and hence among media and political debates over migration, cultural diversity and social inclusion or cohesion. In this sense, historians responded to contemporary concerns, but if social scientists had been the first investigators and analysts of 'racial' phenomena in the twentieth-century UK, by the 1980s and 1990s these had also become subjects for historical writing. The work of historians such as Hall, Webster, Young, Midgley and Walvin contributed to discussions of the social, political and cultural legacies of empire, or absence thereof, in the twentieth century and earlier. Notions of race and nation gained chronological depth as historians revisited early modern, medieval and eighteenth-century uses of the term, just as they reinforced contention over more cultural as against more political or materialist readings of ethnicity and empire.[90] This contributed to controversy over how far, if at all, investigation or interpretation of the past should recognise, explicitly or implicitly, its grounding in present conditions, since the emergence of this work was stimulated by, and sometimes directly referred to, contemporaneous arguments on race and colonialism. The kinds of anxiety about social solidarity expressed in the texts referred to above was paralleled by the to and fro of debate among social analysts, journalists and politicians over the dangers and possibilities of multiculturalism and assimilation. Historians who have pursued the study of 'race' and 'nation' in various parts of the past have faced criticism for 'finding' or exaggerating these phenomena, just as they in turn have criticised the unwillingness of others to acknowledge or examine them adequately.

Indeed, one of the important shifts in historical practice has been the move from treating 'race' or 'nation' as self-evident categorisations for particular groups of people, or as unchanging phenomena, to exploring past uses and developments of such categories. Assumptions about the inherent or persistent character of 'racial' or 'national' groupings have given way to historical inquiries into the social, cultural and political resources which might have been used to create and maintain such labelling in given places and periods. Studies of nationalist and ethnic ideas in the sixteenth century as well as the nineteenth century, of racial and ethnic dimensions of ancient Roman as well as modern imperial policy or of the persecution of Jews in the twelfth as well as the twentieth century have changed discussions of these terms.[91] They open up the possibility of using them productively to understand a range of past situations, and also enrich work on their role in the more familiar settings of modern history. As studies of specifically 'national' or 'racial' policy or ideas were connected to those on popular and consumer cultures, or on religious and commercial activity, concepts of 'race', 'nation' or 'ethnicity' could be seen to be many-sided and problematic. They also provided useful tools for historical writing and analysis. Ideas of race and ethnicity were compared and contrasted across periods and cultures, and questions of national identity, material life, political organisation or cultural influences were used in discussions of 'Englishness', or 'Britishness', as their historic relationship itself became a subject for study.

The recent historiography of 'Englishness', 'Britishness' and ethnicity can be seen as a response to contemporary debate, as opening up a rich seam of research and analysis, and as a continuation of older interests in ethnicity, themselves now a topic for historical writing. It can be argued that the professional assumptions leading 'good' historians to focus on such themes in their work, while distancing themselves from the 'politics' and 'ideology' of race or nation as 'contaminating' concerns, were understandable and appropriate. It might then be said that it would be inappropriate to look for awareness of empire and ethnicity in studies of fourteenth-century government, or sixteenth-century religion, or eighteenth-century crime. Yet it might also be suggested that continued interest among historians in identifying distinctively 'English' features of medieval institutions and of early modern religious reform linked careful academic examination of the specifics of 'English' history with long-standing assumptions about the existence of something called 'Englishness'. For the most part the former approach predominated, underpinned by various sophisticated understandings of particular histories, by the uses of comparative approaches and by interest in how Englishness might have been created and understood in different times or by different people in the past. In a similar way, the study of the 'Irish', 'Welsh' or 'Scots' has engaged with political and cultural negotiations between such groups and 'English' rulers, settlers and rivals, and with the ambiguous and even intimate relations of the 'four nations' has both critiqued and considered notions of 'race and 'nation'.[92]

Popular presentations of the story of 'Englishness' as a medieval development, thus giving it an extended history, have survived and evolved in recent accounts of both English and indeed British history. Some historians link the emergence of effective structures of administration in church and state in tenth- and eleventh-century England to a form of 'national' self-identification and to ideas of 'Englishness'. Others make similar links for the fifteenth and sixteenth centuries, or turn to the history of conflict within the 'Atlantic Isles' or between English rulers and the papacy or their French counterparts, to argue for various forms of 'English' identities and attachments.[93] Not surprisingly this has led to debates about the content of 'Englishness' (shared practices, common loyalties, a common language or a differentiation from 'others'?) and about its purposes and proponents (government propaganda, literary creativity or vested interests?). This served both to reveal complex and changing connections between political, cultural and social aspects of stories of 'Englishness', and to revive or reinforce interest in that phenomenon. If the historical discussions of the topic during the last few decades have not taken the racialised forms so striking in earlier periods, they have deepened and consolidated the seriousness with which it is taken by scrutinising, unpacking and modifying it.

Some of the issues which historians now explore when they write on race and nation can be seen through a comparison of two recent texts in which they play a significant part. Robert Colls' *Identity of England* is an exploration of the role of government, culture and politics in shaping 'how the English thought of themselves', flagged inside the cover as a necessary reassessment to stimulate a new sense of identity.[94] It narrates histories of elite and popular politics and culture across an extended period of time and goes on to explore a set of themes which are shown to have contributed to various views of 'Englishness'. In particular it emphasises various ideas of 'belonging' (in a place, in a culture, in a 'community'), expressed in activities and in words, as constituents of Englishness entwined with histories of the state and of politics in the nineteenth and twentieth centuries. Catherine Hall's *Civilising subjects* is formed by concern with the historic links between Englishness and colonialism since the eighteenth century and investigates and interprets 'Englishness' as a specifically racial, or racialised, formation in the middle decades of the nineteenth century. It explores the role of British involvement in Jamaica in the shaping 'English' selves between the campaigns for slave emancipation and the first parliamentary reform act to that of the suppression of the Morant Bay rebels in Jamaica in 1865 and the passing of the Reform Act of 1867. It looks at missionary activity in Jamaica and abolition and reform politics in Birmingham in order to explore gaps and links between the UK and its West Indian colony, between enslaved Africans or their descendants and English men and women, and between colonial rulers and their subjects.

If the core theme of Colls' text is of complex and changing insular and indigenous developments, touched at times by war and empire, that of Hall's work is of the making of Englishness through global and colonial experiences and imaginings. The former draws on the rich post-1960 tradition of analyses of (largely male) popular culture and politics, and their involvement with, and effects on, more official and privileged versions of 'Englishness'. The question of race only enters into discussion in the context of post-1945 Afro-Caribbean and south Asian migration, with questions of 'Anglo-Saxon' and 'Celt' dealt with separately. The central tensions around identity are presented as centring on class and region and on 'popular' as against 'establishment' views of 'Englishness'. In its concluding review of the various strands of identity, 'the English' are said to have gone through empire without losing all their decency. It praises a history of openness to 'other' cultures, regretting the replacement of 'core' identities based on heartfelt conviction and love of past and place with more plural and negotiated versions.[95] Hall's account of the reimagining of Englishness in the mid-nineteenth century, like that of Colls, with its centre of gravity rather later, understands the making of identity in terms of power relations, but draws on recent race- and gender-aware scholarship as well as on concern with class. It argues that some aspiring and reforming middle-class men and women in England empowered themselves by espousing the cause of slaves and heathens in ways which combined inclusive universalising ideals with the moral confidence and authority which they wished to exercise in the UK and its empire. It places racial and colonial issues at the centre of a shift towards less inclusive versions of reforming missions (religious or secular) and clearer imaginings of differences and distinctions between 'English' and 'negro' characteristics or capacities, and of forms of colonial authority which controlled and directed as well as civilised colonial subjects. Thus imperial involvements and experiences (of governance, of religion, of political activism) are presented as constitutive elements in UK social, political and cultural history.

It is interesting to compare these two politico-cultural studies of 'Englishness' with Linda Colley's earlier work on the emergence of 'British' patriotism between 1700 and the 1830s. The text focuses on how global war and the adaptation of established institutions (religion, monarchy, aristocracy) both contributed and responded to changing circumstances, playing a role alongside newer social and political influences in the creation of a 'British' nation.[96] It combined an analysis of high politics with an examination of the cultural and social contexts within which such politics took place to provide a multifaceted account of the making of a 'British' identity. This identity is presented as expansionist, Protestant and inclusive of elite concerns and populist views, and of Scots and Welsh as well as of commercial and reforming interests. Imperial aspects of this identity are regularly acknowledged, but largely through their connection to themes which are seen as more central – notably global warfare, the drawing in of Scots and Irish into some sort of affiliation with 'Britishness' and the power of anti-French sentiments. While there are important discussions of artistic depictions of colonial subjects, and of the role of anti-slavery campaigns as expressions of shared national virtue and superiority to others, mutually constituent aspects of empire, ethnicity and nation making in the period are not highlighted.[97] The text registers colonial expansion and conquest without foregrounding them, and pays little attention to ethnicity or to eighteenth- and early nineteenth-century racial thought and images. Colley's assertion in her introduction that 'the British are not an insular people in the conventional sense...they have had more contact with more parts of the world than almost any other nation' captures this form of recognition.[98]

Hall's creative, and contentious, emphasis on mutually constitutive relationships between UK and imperial history, and on accounts of modern UK history as one element of a web of global connections, places the work within a distinctive revival of imperial history, where questions of race were central. One historiography saw imperial issues as developing 'over there' in Africa or India or Australia, and having little interest or meaning for residents of the UK. It includes studies which emphasise that imperial policy was the concern of enthusiasts and specialists, rather than a broader political issue, and those which show how imperial policy was shaped at least in part by the interests and activities of indigenous subjects as well as of settlers, traders or European competitors.[99] Another historiography emphasises the penetration of information, images, involvements and ideas derived from imperial involvements and experiences into the social political and cultural worlds of many groups in the UK, and their movement between empire and metropole. It includes studies of racial and colonial strands in religion, politics and social practices in the UK going back to the eighteenth century, and of the connections as well as changes between the long-established patterns and present concerns with assimilation, exclusion and 'Englishness'. If the former historiography sees disjunctions between long and coherent stories of 'Englishness' and the disruptive effects of change since 1945 (immigration, links to Europe, loss of imperial and global primacy), the latter is attentive to the links between a long history of global and colonial dominance and present debates and difficulties, and to the plural and contested character of 'Englishness' over a long period.[100]

There is an interesting and difficult dialogue to be had between views that 'race' is a recent and disruptive element in narratives of 'Englishness' and views which place ethnic and racialised elements within such narratives, alongside other contests over difference and identity. It is a dialogue about how ideas of ethnicity and identity change, about links between material and institutional aspects of society and about the politics and cultures which shape and are shaped by them. It also deals with what Stuart Hall has called 'the unstable point where the "unspeakable" stories of subjectivity meet the narratives of history, of a culture'.[101] Historians now examine the inequities, oppressions and confrontations which made and maintained ethno-racial differences, and their entwining with those of class and gender, and also consider the uncertainties and contradictions which complicated them. From work on modern masculinities in class, European or anti-colonial nationalist settings to explorations of the combinations and tensions of gender, religion and class in anti-slavery or feminist politics, many studies of 'Englishness' incorporate such approaches.[102] However, other studies maintain approaches in which national or patriotic identities are associated with attachment to particular versions of the 'English' past and to state institutions. These studies are reminiscent of eighteenth- and nineteenth-century accounts of 'Englishness'. Arguments for the importance of religion have been refurbished, presenting it as a marker of long continuities in 'English' identities and of English/British patriotism and its imperial flavouring. It has been posed against what some dismiss as 'fashionable' concerns with ethnicity, class or gender. In the work of J.C.D. Clark this takes the form of asserting the continued importance of a British *ancien regime* including the Church of England, very different from Colley's wider examination of relationships between Protestantism and patriotism in the eighteenth and nineteenth centuries.[103] Interestingly, the title chosen by Clark for his recent edited survey of the history of the 'British Isles' since Roman times is *A world by itself*.

The growth of contemporary debates and anxieties over English' and/or 'British' identity was a point of reference for history writing which opened up the complexities of these categories in different times and contexts. This might be a way to assert the difference between current and past circumstances, and to locate ethnicity as a 'modern' issue. It might equally be a way to trace continuities and changes in the composition of ethnic identities which connect as well as distinguish present and past. Studies of responses of existing residents of the UK to new migrants, might compare and contrast recent with older episodes, or suggest that the long history of migration to the British Isles provides warnings, examples or inspiration for the present and future.[104] Historians were also willing to draw more general messages for the future of 'Englishness' from their analyses of past developments. They might express fears of future religious conflict between Muslims and Christians, or hopes for 'a more pragmatic and generous form' of 'British' identity, or appeal for the retention of 'the sense of place and time that provides a sense of identity and maintains social values'.[105]

These comments, like those of Colls, are a reminder that history writing is itself one of the resources which can enter the repertoire of those constructing, critiquing or maintaining views of ethnicity, nationality or identity. The arguments over school curricula which engaged politicians, historians and teachers in the 1980s concerned the content and ownership of the national story, its role in making citizens (?'Britons'), and who might be included within that story. John Seeley in the 1880s argued that the study of history was a key element in the formation of statesmen and administrators; Charles Allen in the 1790s thought that it should help pupils understand and accept their lot in life; similarly governments and educationists in the later twentieth century debated the relevance, coherence and patriotism of the historical narratives provided for school pupils, students and various reading/viewing/listening publics. If Seeley focused on the responsibilities of empire and Allen on social order and progress, recent debates have been flavoured by contests over whether to defend or modify 'national' narratives in a world of new cultural diversities and practices. Should historical work seek to draw everyone regardless of background and outlook towards an established version of the national story (monarchy, progress, Englishness), or open up alternative, multiple, even conflicting versions? Should delight in detail, and empathy for past social experiences, take priority over narrative or over critical understanding of the larger contexts and structures within which specific experiences take place, and indeed critiques of the notion of 'experience' itself?[106] In these debates racial, national and imperial legacies were brought into play.

Notes

1 Simon Schama in the closing episode of his TV series *A history of Britain*, broadcast by the BBC in June 2002.

2 Lola Young and Judith Brown, interviewed about *The empire in colour* series in 2002 at the British Film Institute.

3 David Cameron, speech at a European security conference 5 February 2011; speech in Oxford 16 December 2011; examples of feature films exploring ethnic and multicultural aspects of the post-1950 UK include *Ghosts* (2006), *Wondrous oblivion* (2003) *Dirty pretty things* (2002), *Rage* (1999), *My beautiful launderette* (1985) and *Babylon* (1980).

4 For debate on these categories see G. Bernstein, *The myth of decline: the rise of Britain since 1945*, London, 2004; D. Reynolds, *Britannia overruled: British policy and world power in the twentieth century*, Harlow, 2000; N. Crafts and C. Woodward [eds.], *The British economy since 1945*, Oxford, 1991; B. Tomlinson, 'The contraction of England: national decline and the loss of empire', *Journal of Imperial and Commonwealth History*, vol. 11, no. 1 (1982), pp. 58–72.

5 See, for example, the headings for chs 10–15 in T. Lloyd, *Empire, welfare state, Europe: history of the United Kingdom*, 5th edn, Oxford, 2002.

6 A stimulating brief account is D. Harvey, *A brief history of neoliberalism*, Oxford, 2007, chs 2–4.

7 D. Fieldhouse, 'The metropolitan economics of empire', in J. Brown [ed.], *Oxford history of the British empire, vol. 4: the twentieth century*, Oxford, 1999, p. 104.

8 see J. Darwin, *The end of the British empire*, Oxford, 1991, ch. 3; P. Cain and A. Hopkins, *British imperialism: decline and deconstruction*, London, 1993, vol. 2, part 4.

9 W.R. Louis, *Ends of British imperialism*, London, 2006; W.R. Louis and R.E. Robinson, 'The imperialism of decolonisation', *Journal of Imperial and Commonwealth History*, vol. 22, no. 3 (1994), pp. 462–511; R.F. Holland, *The pursuit of greatness: Britain and the world role, 1900–1970*, London, 1991.

10 See W. Louis, 'The dissolution of the British Empire', in Brown *Oxford history of the British empire, vol. 4*; Darwin, *End of the British empire*, ch. 2;

J. Darwin, *Britain and decolonisation*, Basingstoke, 1988, pp. 5–33, chs 4, 6; J. Darwin, 'Fear of falling: British politics and imperial decline since 1900', *Transactions of the Royal Historical Society*, 5th series, vol. 36 (1986), pp. 27–43; S. Howe, *Anticolonialism in British politics*, Oxford, 1994; R. Weight, *Patriots; national identity in Britain, 1940–2000*, London, 2002.

11 R. Fieldhouse [ed.], *Anti-apartheid: a history of the movement in Britain*, London, 2005; M. Veldman, *Fantasy, the bomb, and the greening of Britain*, Cambridge, 1994, part 2; I. Welsh, *Mobilising modernity: the nuclear moment*, London, 2000; J. Liddington, *The long road to Greenham*, London, 1989, parts 2, 3; G. de Groot [ed.], *Student protest: the sixties and after*, London, 1998, chs 1, 5, 12, 14; B. Campbell and A. Coote, *Sweet freedom*, Oxford, 1987; H. Graham *et al.* [eds.], *The feminist seventies*, York, 2003; S. Rowbotham, *The past before us*, London, 1989.

12 J. Solomos, *Race and racism in Britain*, Basingstoke, 2003; P. Rich, *Race and empire in British politics*, Cambridge, 1990; R. Hansen, *Citizenship and immigration in Britain*, Oxford, 2000; P. Gilroy, *There ain't no black in the Union Jack*, London, 1987; P. Fryer, *Staying power: the history of black people in Britain*, London, 1984; R. Visram, *Asians in Britain*, London, 2002; K. Paul, *Whitewashing Britain*, Ithaca, NY, 1997; P. Alexander and R. Halpern [eds.], *Racialising class, classifying race*, London, 2000, chs 1, 5, 6.

13 D. Powell, *Nationhood and identity: Britain since 1800*, London, 2002, chs 7, 8; M. O'Neill [ed.], *Devolution and British politics*, Harlow, 2004; V. Bogdanor, *Devolution in the United Kingdom*, Oxford, 2001; J. Mitchell, *Devolution in the United Kingdom*, Manchester, 2009; J. Davies, *History of Wales*, London, 2007, chs 11, 12; G. Jenkins, *Concise history of Wales*, Cambridge, 2007, ch. 8; T. Chapman [ed.], *The idiom of dissent*, Llandysul, 2006, chs 5–7; T. Devine, *The Scottish nation 1700-2007*, London, 2007; C. MacDonald, *Whaur extreme meet: Scotland's twentieth century*, Edinburgh, 2009; D. Denver [ed.], *Scotland decides*, London, 2000; M. Pittock, *The road to independence: Scotland since the sixties*, London, 2008; M. Gardiner, *The cultural roots of devolution*, Edinburgh, 2004; R. Ryan, *Ireland and Scotland: literature and culture, state and nation*, Oxford, 2002; S. Prince, *Northern Ireland's '68*, Dublin, 2007; H. Patterson, *Ireland since 1939*, London, 2007; J. Loughlin, *The Ulster question since 1945*, Basingstoke, 2004; T. Hennessey, *A history of Northern Ireland, 1920–96*, London, 1998; S. Bruce, *The edge of the union: the Ulster loyalist political vision*, Oxford, 1994; T. Nairn, *The breakup of Britain*, London, 1981.

14 Robin Cook, speech on immigration to the Social Market Foundation, April 2001. We might note that the dish which it allegedly replaced in that role, fish and chips, is thought by some to have partly late nineteenth-century east European Jewish immigrant origins.

15 P. Panayi, *An immigration history of Britain*, Harlow, 2010; B. Pitcher, *The politics of multiculturalism*, Basingstoke, 2009; D. McGhee [ed.], *The end of multiculturalism?* Buckingham, 2008; R. Hewitt, *White backlash*, Cambridge, 2005; P. Gilroy, *After empire: melancholia or convivial culture?*, London, 2004; B. Parekh, *Rethinking multiculturalism*, Basingstoke, 2006.

16 C. Waters, 'Dark strangers', *Journal of British Studies*, vol. 36, no. 2 (1997), pp. 207–38; D. Feldman, 'The importance of being English: Jewish immigration and the decline of liberal England', in D. Feldman and G. Stedman Jones [eds.], *Metropolis: histories and representations since 1800*, London, 1989.

17 Rich, *Race and empire in British politics*, pp. 196–200.

18 Waters, 'Dark strangers'.

19 See, for example, B. Parekh, 'British citizenship and cultural difference', in G. Andrews [ed.], *Citizenship*, London, 1991; B. Parekh, *The future of multi-ethnic Britain*, London, 2000; J. Solomos, *Race and racism in Britain*, London, 2003; A. Brah, *Cartographies of diaspora: contesting identities*, London, 1996.

20 S. Gikandi, *Maps of Englishness*, New York, 1996, pp. 69–83; S. Hall, 'New ethnicities', in D. Morley and and K. Chen [eds.], *Stuart Hall: critical dialogues*, London, 1996.

21 V. Holt, *The India fan*, London, 1988; K. Gordon's 'Peacock' series, 1978–96; E. Drummond's romances, 1979, 1983, 1990, 1991; B. and S. Keating's 'Langani trilogy', 2005–8.

22 Keating's Inspector Ghote series, 1964–2009, Michael Pearce's 'Egyptian' series, 1990–2005.

23 Vivian Stuart's 'Australian' and 'Mutiny' series, 1973–99, P. McCutchan's 'Ogilvie' series, 1969–82.

24 Important examples from a potentially very long list would include Graham Greene, Paul Scott, J.G. Farrell, William Boyd and Philip Hensher.

25 D. Cannadine, *The right kind of history*, Basingstoke, 2011; D. Cannadine, *Making history now and then*, Basingstoke, 2011; R. Samuel, *Island stories*, London, 1999; R. Samuel, *Theatres of memory*, London, 1994.

26 E. Genovese, *Roll Jordan roll: the world the slaves made*, London, 1974; E.P. Thompson, *The making of the English working class*, London, 1963; R. Hilton, *Peasants knights and heretics*, Cambridge, 1976.

27 K. Thomas, *Religion and the decline of magic*, London, 1971; D. Jones, *Chartism and the Chartists*, London, 1975; E. Royle, *Chartism*, London, 1980; G. Williams, *Artisans and sansculottes*, London, 1968; G. Rude, *The crowd in the French Revolution* Oxford, 1972; A. Forrest, *The French Revolution and the poor*, Oxford, 1981; J. Hinton, *Labour and socialism*, Brighton, 1983; S. Boston, *Women workers and the trade union movement*,

London, 1980; E. Hobsbawm, *Primitive rebels*, Manchester, 1959; E. Hobsbawm, *Bandits*, London, 1969; R.B. Dobson, *The Peasants' Revolt of 1381*, London, 1970; R. Hilton, *Bond men made free*, London, 1973.

28 M. Taylor, 'The beginnings of English social history', *History Workshop Journal*, no. 43 (1997), pp. 156–76.

29 J. Scott, 'Gender: a useful category of analysis', *American Historical Review*, vol. 91, no. 5 (1985), pp. 1053–75; R. Guha, 'Preface', in R. Guha [ed.], *Subaltern Studies*, New Delhi, 1982, vol. 1; J. de Groot '"Sex" and "race": the formation of language and image in the nineteenth century', in S. Mendus and J. Rendall [eds.], *Sexuality and subordination*, London, 1989; and J. de Groot, 'Conceptions and misconceptions: a historical discussion on women and development', in H. Afshar [ed.], *Women, survival and development in the third world*, London, 1991.

30 C. Bynum, *Holy feast and holy fast*, Berkeley, CA, 1987; C. Bynum, *Jesus as mother*, Berkeley, CA, 1982; J. Scott and L. Tilly, *Women work and family*, London, 1987; D. Gray, *Aren't I a woman: female slaves in the plantation south*, New York, 1985; L. Davidoff and C. Hall, *Family fortunes: men and women of the English middle class, 1780–1850*, London, 1987.

31 L. Hunt, *Politics, culture and class in the French Revolution*, Berkeley, CA, 1984; C. Herrup, *A house in gross disorder: sex, law and the second Earl of Castlehaven*, Oxford, 1999; M. Sinha, *Colonial masculinity*, Manchester, 1995.

32 For example the work of Foucault such as *The birth of the prison*, London 1977, *Madness and civilisation*, London 1967, *The archaeology of knowledge*, London 1972, *The order of things*, London 1974, *The history of sexuality*, 3 vols, 1978, 1985, 1988.

33 J. Cadden, *Meanings of sex difference in the middle ages: medicine, science and culture*, Cambridge, 1993; A. Bashford, *Purity and pollution: gender, embodiment and Victorian medicine*, London, 1998; C. Hall, *Civilising subjects*, Cambridge, 2002, C. Hall *et al.*, *Defining the Victorian nation*, Cambridge, 2000; A. Clark, *The struggle for the breeches*, London, 1995; S. Rose, *Limited livelihoods: gender and class in nineteenth-century England*, Berkeley, CA, 1993.

34 R. Evans, *In defence of history*, Oxford, 1997, for the former; M. Bentley, *Modernising England's past*, Cambridge, 2005 for the latter; a different view is explored in G. Eley, *A crooked line: from cultural history to the history of society*, Ann Arbor, MI, 2008.

35 Statistics taken from the government Higher Education Statistics Agency, *Students in Higher Education Institutions* annual reports 1993-2010

36 Thompson, *The making of the English working class*; Hobsbawm, *Primitive rebels*; Genovese, *Roll Jordan roll*; R. Samuel, *Village life and labour*, London, 1975; and R. Samuel, *East End underworld*, London, 1981.

37 Davidoff and Hall, *Family fortunes*; B. Taylor, *Eve and the new Jerusalem*, London, 1983; P. Fryer, *Staying power: black people in Britain*, London, 1984; J. Walvin, *Black and white: the negro in British society*, London, 1973.

38 For example A. Forrest, *French Revolution and the poor*, Oxford, 1981, D. Andress, *French society in revolution, 1789–99*, Manchester, 1999; Clark, *Struggle for the breeches*, G. Stedman Jones, *Languages of class*, Cambridge, 1983.

39 See debates as recounted in Eley, *A crooked line* and G. Eley and K. Nield [eds.], *The future of class in history*, Ann Arbor, MI, 2007.

40 Authors contributing to the 'older' *Oxford history of England*, still in use in the 1980s, included G.N. Clark (born 1890), R.G. Collingwood (born 1889), R.C. Ensor (born 1879), E.L. Woodward (born 1890), F.M. Stenton (born 1880) and F.M. Powicke (born 1879).

41 For example, the Fontana and Penguin social history series, which appeared from the 1960s.

42 Examples are V. Kiernan, *State and society in Europe*, Oxford, 1980; J. Brewer, *Sinews of power: war money and the English state state*, London, 1989; R. Swanson, *Church and society in late medieval England*, Oxford, 1993; W. Ormrod, *The reign of Edward III*, New Haven, CT, 1993.

43 For example, R. Shannon, *The age of Disraeli, 1868–1881: the rise of Tory democracy*, London, 1992; R. Harrison, *Gladstone's imperialism in Egypt: techniques of domination*, Westport, CT, 1995; M. Taylor, *The decline of British radicalism, 1847–60*, Oxford, 1995 P. Williamson, *Stanley Baldwin: conservative leadership and national values*, Cambridge, 1999; J.P. Parry, *The politics of patriotism: English liberalism, national identity and Europe, 1830–1886*, Cambridge, 2006; D. Armitage, 'Parliament and international law in the eighteenth century', and M. Taylor, 'Colonial representation at Westminster', in J. Hoppit [ed.], *Parliaments, nations, and identities in Britain and Ireland, 1660–1850*, Manchester, 2003 (which picks up these approaches more generally); C. Hall, 'Rethinking imperial histories', *New Left Review*, 1st series, no. 208 (1994), pp. 3–29; C. Hall *et al.*, *Defining the Victorian nation*, Cambridge, 2000; M. Taylor, 'Empire and parliamentary reform: 1832 revisited', in A. Burns and J. Innes [eds.], *Rethinking the age of reform*, Cambridge, 2003; M. Taylor, 'Imperium et libertas', *Journal of Imperial and Commonwealth History*, vol. 19, no. 1 (1991), pp. 1–23.

44 A.J.P. Taylor, *English History, 1914–1945*, (vol. 15 of the *Oxford history of England*) Oxford, 1965, p. v.

45 J. Pocock, 'British history: a plea for a new subject', and responses, *Journal of Modern History*, vol. 47, no. 4 (1975), pp. 601–28; J. Pocock, 'The limits and divisions of British history: a search for the unknown subject', *American Historical Review*, vol. 87, no. 2 (1982), pp. 311–36; C. Russell, 'The British problem and the English civil war', *History*, vol. 72, no. 236 (1987), pp. 395–415; and K. Robbins, 'Core and periphery

in modern British history', *Proceedings of the British Academy*, vol. 52 (1984), pp. 275–97 also opened up these issues.

46 See, for example, P. Clarke, *Hope and glory*, London, 2004, p. 2; D. Carpenter, *The struggle for mastery: Britain, 1066–1284*, London, 2004; J. Ohlmeyer, 'The baronial context of the Irish civil wars'and A. Macinnes, 'The "Scottish moment", 1638–45', in J. Adamson [ed.], *The English civil war: conflict and contexts*, Basingstoke, 2009.

47 Carpenter, *The Struggle for mastery*; C. Kinealy, *A disunited kingdom? England, Ireland, Scotland and Wales, 1800–1949*, Cambridge, 1999; M. Pittock, *Inventing and resisting Britain*, London, 1997.

48 For example, M. Hechter, *Internal colonialism: the Celtic fringe in British national development, 1536–1966*, London, 1975; H. Kearney, *The British Isles: a history of four nations*, Cambridge, 1989; N. Davies, *The isles: a history*, London, 1999; A. Grant and K. Stringer [eds.], *Uniting the kingdom?*, London, 1995; G. Burgess [ed.], *The new British history: founding a modern state*, London, 1999; B. Bradshaw and J. Morrill [eds.], *The British problem, c. 1534–1707: state formation in the Atlantic archipelago*, London, 1996; S.J. Connolly [ed.], *Kingdoms united? Great Britain and Ireland since 1500*, Dublin, 1999; S. Ellis and S. Barber [eds.], *Conquest and union: fashioning a British state, 1485–1725*, Harlow, 1995.

49 See, for example, the title of chapter 10 of P. Edwards, *The making of the modern English state, 1460–1660*, Basingstoke, 2001; J. Kenyon and J. Ohlmeyer [eds.], *The civil wars*, Oxford, 1998; C. Russell, *The fall of the British monarchies*, Oxford, 1991; J. Young [ed.], *Celtic dimensions of the British civil wars*, Edinburgh, 1997; A. Macinnes, *The British revolution, 1629–1660*, Basingstoke, 2005; A. Woolrych, *Britain in revolution, 1625–1660*, Oxford, 2002; D. Scott, *Politics and war in the three Stuart kingdoms*, Basingstoke, 2004.

50 N. Canny, *Colonial identity in the Atlantic world*, Princeton, 1993; D. Armitage, *The Ideological origins of the British empire*, Cambridge, 2000; D. Armitage, *Greater Britain, 1516–1776*, Aldershot, 2004; J. Elliott, *Empires of the Atlantic world*, New Haven, CT, 2006.

51 Hoppit, *Parliaments, nations and identities*.

52 K. Morgan [ed.], *Oxford history of England*, revised edn, Oxford, 2010, pp. x–xi, 709–10; J. Black, *A history of the British Isles*, 2nd edn, Basingstoke, 2003.

53 A sampling is J. MacKenzie and T. Devine [eds.], *Scotland and the British empire*, Oxford, 2011; T. Devine, *Scotland's empire*, London, 2004; L. Proudfoot and D. Hall, *Imperial spaces: placing Irish and Scots in colonial Australia*, Manchester, 2011; H. Bowen, *Wales and the British overseas empire*, Manchester, 2011; D. Hamilton, *Scotland, the Caribbean and the Atlantic world*, Manchester, 2005; C. Evans, *Slave Wales: the Welsh and Atlantic slavery*, Cardiff, 2010; B. Crosbie, *Irish imperial networks*,

Cambridge, 2011; M. Silvestri, *Ireland and India*, London, 2009; K. Kenny [ed.], *Ireland and the British empire*, Oxford, 2006; K. Jeffery [ed.], *An Irish empire?* Manchester, 1996.

54 S. Ellis, 'Writing Irish history: revisionism, colonialism, and the British Isles', *Irish Review*, vol. 19, no. 1 (1996), pp. 1–21; S. Howe, 'Historiography', in Kenny, *Ireland and the British empire*, this volume, published as one of the 'companions' to the *Oxford history of the British empire*, is itself an expression of the developments under discussion.

55 D. McCracken, *Forgotten protest: Ireland and the Boer War*, Belfast, 2003; D. Gleeson [ed.], *The Irish in the Atlantic world*, Columbia, SC, 2010; D. Killingray [ed.], *Policing the empire*, Manchester, 1991; P. O'Leary, *Servants of empire: the Irish in the Punjab*, Manchester, 2011; D. Tanner, *Debating nationhood and governance in Britain, 1850–1945*, Manchester, 2006.

56 A. Jones and B. Jones, 'The Welsh world and the British empire', *Journal of Imperial and Commonwealth History*, vol. 31, no. 2 (2003), pp. 57–81; A. Jones, 'Welsh missionary journalism', in J. Codell, *Imperial co-histories: national identities and the British and colonial press*, London, 2003; Bowen, *Wales and the British overseas empire*; A. MacKillop, '*More fruitful than the soil': army, empire and the Scottish Highlands*, Edinburgh, 2000; J. MacKenzie and N. Dalziel, *The Scots in South Africa*, Manchester, 2007; A. MacKillop and S. Murdoch [eds.], *Military governors and imperial frontiers: a study of Scotlnd and empires*, Leiden, 2003.

57 W.R. Louis [series ed.], *Oxford history of the British empire*, 5 vols, Oxford, 1998–99: N. Canny [ed.], *Vol. 1: origins of empire*; P. Marshall [ed.], *Vol. 2: the eighteenth century*; A. Porter [ed.], *Vol. 3: the nineteenth century*; J. Brown [ed.], *Vol. 4: the twentieth century*; R. Winks [ed.], *Vol. 5: historiography*); between 2004 and 2010 a 'Companion Series' included (in order of publication) volumes dealing with gender, the 'black experience', missions, Ireland, environment, Canada, Australia, migration, settlers and expatriates, and with Scotland in relation to empire. It can be seen that the choice of topics in that series reflected several influences, notably new historiographies of gender, race and environmental studies, and of thematic and 'four nations' analysis, as well as revived concern with the colonies of 'white settlement', redefined as the 'British world'.

58 T. Lloyd, *The British empire, 1558–1995*, Oxford, 1996; D. Judd, *Empire: the British imperial experience from 1765 to the present*, London, 1996; L. James, *The rise and fall of the British empire*, London, 1994.

59 J. Darwin, *The empire project: the rise and fall of the British world system, 1830–1970*, Cambridge, 2009.

60 N. Ferguson, *Empire: how Britain made the modern world*, London, 2003; P. Levine, *The British empire: sunrise to sunset*, Harlow, 2007.

61 K. Grant *et al.* [eds.], *Beyond sovereignty: Britain, empire, and transnationalism, 1860–1950.* Basingstoke, 2007; the latter case is made by A. Burton, 'Going beyond the global: repositioning British imperialism in world history', in C. Hall and K. McLelland [eds.], *Race, nation and empire: making histories, 1750 to the present,* Manchester, 2010; see also D. Khoury and D. Kennedy, 'Comparing empires: the Ottoman empire and the British *raj* in the long nineteenth century', *Comparative Studies of South Asia, Africa, and the Middle East,* vol. 27, no. 2 (2007), pp. 233–44; D. Ghosh and D. Kennedy [eds.], *Decentering empire: Britain, India and the trans-colonial world,* Delhi, 2006.

62 For example, P. Brendon, *The decline and fall of the British empire,* London, 2007.

63 M. Taylor, 'The beginnings of modern British social history', *History Workshop Journal,* no. 43 (1997), pp. 155–76; Bentley,*Modernising England's past,* pp. 219–32.

64 M. Berg, *The age of manufactures,* London, 1985; D. Valenze, *The first industrial woman,* Oxford, 1995; G. Gullickson, *The spinners and weavers of Auffay,* Cambridge, 1986; L. Roper, *The holy household: women and morals in Reformation Augsburg,* Oxford, 1991; A. Hughes, *Gender and the English revolution,* London, 2012; L. Hunt, *The family romance of the French Revolution,* Berkeley, CA, 1993; C. Anderson, *Subaltern lives: biographies of colonialism in the Indian Ocean world,* Cambridge, 2012.

65 J. Kelly, 'Did women have a Renaissance?', in J. Kelly, *Women, history and theory,* Chicago, 1984; R. Guha, 'On some aspects of the historiography of colonial India' in Guha, *Subaltern Studies,* vol. 1.

66 Clark, *The struggle for the breeches*; J. Cock, *Maids and madams: a study in the politics of exploitation,* Johannesburg, 1980; V. Ware, *Beyond the pale: white women, racism and history,* London, 1992; R. Lewis, *Rethinking orientalism: women, travel and the Ottoman harem,* London, 2004; L. Tuttle, *Conceiving the old regime: pronatalism and the politics of reproduction in early modern France,* Oxford, 2010: K. Cooper, *The fall of the Roman household,* Cambridge, 2011.

67 M. Rocke, *Forbidden friendships: homosexuality and male culture in Renaissance Florence,* Oxford, 1996; P. Levine, *Prostitution, race and politics: policing venereal disease in the British empire,* London, 2003; R. Phillips, *Sex, politics, and empire: a postcolonial geography,* Manchester, 2006.

68 Private information, 2002.

69 D. Harvey, *The condition of postmodernity,* Oxford, 1989; H. White, *The content of the form: narrative discourse and historical representation,* Baltimore, MD, 1987; A. Munslow, *Deconstructing history,* London, 1997; C. Steedman, *Dust,* Manchester, 2001.

70 Evans, *In defence of history,* W. Lamont [ed.], *Historical controversies and historians,* London, 1998.

71 S. Dudink *et al.* [eds.], *Masculinities in politics and war*, Manchester, 2004; J. Tosh, *A. man's place: masculinity and the middle class home in Victorian England*, New Haven, CT, 1999; I. Hull, *Sexuality, state, and civil society in Germany*, Ithaca, NY, 1996; Sinha, *Colonial masculinity*.

72 K. Clark, *Civilisation* (1969), reprint London, 2005, pp. 18–19, 27.

73 N. Ferguson, *Empire: how Britain made the modern world*, London, 2004.

74 Taylor, *English history, 1914–1945*, p. 600.

75 T.O. Lloyd, *Empire, welfare state, Europe: history of the United Kingdom, 1906–2001*, Oxford, 2002, p. 498

76 Black, *History of the British Isles*, pp. 339–40.

77 K. Morgan [ed.], *Oxford history of Britain*, Oxford, 1984, 1988, 1993, 1999, 2010, pp. 708–10; see R.H. Tawney, *The acquisitive society*, London, 1920 (last reprinted 1982).

78 A. Maddison, *Growth and interaction in the world economy: the roots of modernity*, Cambridge, MA, 2005; A. Maddison, *The west and the rest*, Cambridge, MA, 2004; K. Pomeranz, *The great divergence: China, Europe and the making of the modern world*, Princeton, 2001.

79 P. Gran, *Beyond Eurocentrism: a new view of modern world history*, Syracuse, NY, 1996 and D. Chakrabarty, *Provincialising Europe: postcolonial thought and historical difference*, Princeton, 2000, 2008; A. Dirlik *et al.* [eds.], *History after the three worlds*, Lanham, MD, 2000.

80 This term came into use in the 1880s, notably in A. Toynbee's lectures published as *The industrial revolution*, London, 1884.

81 M. Berg, 'Manufacturing the Orient: Asian commodities and European industry', *Proceedings of the Istituto Internazionale di Storia Economica*, 29 (1998), pp. 385–419.

82 R. Bartlett, *Medieval panorama*, London, 2001, pp. 258–73.

83 For example S. Marks, *Not either an experimental doll: the separate worlds of three South African women*, Bloomington, IN, 1987; Anderson, *Subaltern lives*; A. Burton, *Dwelling in the archive: women writing house, home and history in late colonial India*, Oxford, 2003.

84 L.P. Hartley, *The Go-Between*, London, 1953, p. 1.

85 J.C.D. Clark, *English society, 1688–1832: ideology, social structure and political practice during the ancient regime*, Cambridge, 1985 conducts a polemic with what is seen as the left-liberal misconceptions of a dominant historiography.

86 A. Brah, *Cartographies of diaspora: contesting identities*, London, 1996; S. Hall, *Formations of modernity*, Cambridge, 1992; Morley and Chen, *Stuart Hall: critical dialogues*; Gilroy, *There ain't no black in the Union Jack*; P. Gilroy, *The Black Atlantic: modernity and double consciousness*, Cambridge, MA, 1993; S. Gikandi, *Maps of Englishness*, New York, 1996; B. Schwarz, *The white man's world*, Oxford, 2011, B. Schwarz, *West Indian intellectuals in Britain*, Manchester, 2003.

87 K. Robbins, *Oxford history of Britain*, Oxford, 2010; Black *History of the British Isles*.

88 Kearney, *The British Isles*; J.C.D. Clark, *A world by itself: a history of the British Isles*, London, 2011

89 R. Colls, *Identity of England*, Oxford, 2002, p. 381.

90 S. Stockwell [ed.], *The British empire: themes and perspectives*, Oxford, 2008.

91 N. Canny and A. Pagden [eds.], *Colonial identity in the Atlantic world*, Cambridge, 1999; P. Geary, *The myth of nations*, Princeton, 2002; R. Chazan, [ed.] *Church, state and Jew in the middle ages*, New York, 1980; R. Moore, *The formation of a persecuting society*, Oxford, 1987; A. Lindemann [ed.], *Antisemitism: a history*, Oxford, 2010; M. Eliav-Feldon *et al.* [eds.], *The origins of racism in the West*, Cambridge, 2009; S. Mitchell and G. Greatorex [eds.], *Ethnicity and culture in late antiquity*, London, 2000; F. Millar, *The Roman Near East*, Cambridge, MA, 1993.

92 K. Kumar, *The making of English national identity*, Cambridge, 2003; R. Colls and P. Dodd [eds.], *Englishness*, London, 1986; L. Colley, *Britons*, London and New Haven, CT, 1992; R. Samuel [ed.], *Patriotisms*, 3 vols, London, 1989; S. Gikandi, *Maps of Englishness*, New York, 1996; R. Young, *The idea of English ethnicity*, Oxford, 2008; C. Kidd, *British identities before nationalism*, Cambridge, 1999; C. Kidd, *Union and unionisms*, Cambridge, 2008; R. Pope [ed.], *Religion and national identity*, Cardiff, 2001; A. Grant and K. Stringer [eds.], *Uniting the kingdom? The making of British history*, London, 1995.

93 Kumar, *Making of English national identity*; J. Campbell, 'The united kingdom of England: the Anglo-Saxon achievement', in Grant and Stringer, *Uniting the kingdom*; J. Wormald, 'The creation of Britain: multiple kingdoms or core and colonies?' *Transactions of the Royal Historical Society*, 6th series, vol. 2 (1992), pp. 175–94; J. Gillingham, *The English in the twelfth century*, Woodbridge, 2000.

94 Colls, *Identity of England*, p. 2.

95 Colls, *Identity of England*, pp. 377–81.

96 L. Colley, *Britons: the forging of a nation, 1707–1837*, New Haven, CT, 1992.

97 See Colley, *Britons*, pp. ix–x; the chosen topics are religion, economic aspects (within which empire is mentioned), 'peripheries' (with some reference to America), class, monarchy, gender and war (primarily the French Revolutionary and Napoleonic wars in Europe).

98 Colley, *Britons*, p. 8.

99 A sample of recent approaches is Levine, *The British empire*; A. Thompson, *Imperial Britain*, Harlow, 2000; A. Thompson, *The empire strikes back: the importance of empire*, Harlow, 2005; Darwin *The empire project*; B. Schwarz [ed.], *The expansion of England*, London, 1996; C. Anderson, *Subaltern lives*, Cambridge, 2012.

100 For example, Kumar, *Making of English Identity*; K. Wilson [ed.], *A new imperial history*, Cambridge, 2004; D. Hamilton, *Scotland the Caribbean and the Atlantic world*, Manchester, 2010; M. Mcclaren, *British Scotland and British India*, Akron, 2001; M. Dresser, *Slavery obscured*, Bristol, 2007; T. Barrinnger, *et.al.* [eds.], *Art and the British empire*; N. Dirks, *The scandal of empire*, Cambridge, MA, 2008; B. Schwarz, *The white man's world*, Oxford, 2011; B. Schwarz [ed.], *The expansion of England: race, ethnicity and cultural history*, London, 1996.

101 S. Hall, 'Minimal selves', in L. Appignanesi [ed.], *The real me: postmodernism and the question of identity*, London, 1987.

102 See J.C.D. Clark, *English society 1688–1832*, Cambridge, 1985; *Revolution and rebellion: state and society in England in the 17th and 18th centuries*, Cambridge, 1986; *The language of liberty 1688–1832*, Cambridge, 1993.

103 J. Clark 'Revolution and reform 1660-1832' and W. Rubinstein 'The world hegemon: the long nineteenth century', in J. Clark [ed.], *A world by itself*, London, 2010.

104 C. Holmes, *John Bull's island: immigration and British society 1871–1971*, Basingstoke, 1988, and *A tolerant society? Immigrants, refugees and minorities in Britain*, London 1991; a popular version is R. Winder, *Bloody foreigners: the story of immigration to Britain*, London, 2004; P. Panayi, *Immigration ethnicity and racism in Britain 1815–1945*, London, 1994; T. Endelman, *The Jews of Britain 1656–2000*, London, 2002; T. Kushner [ed.], *The Jewish heritage in British history*, London, 1992.

105 Black, *History of the British Isles*, p. 340; K. Morgan, *Oxford History of Britain*, pp. 708–10; Colley, *Britons*, pp. 374–5; Clark, *World by itself*, pp. 691–2.

106 J. Scott, 'Experience' in J. Butler and J. Scott [eds.], *Feminists theorize the political*, London, 1992.

CONCLUSION:
CONVERSATIONS ABOUT EMPIRE
AND HISTORY WRITING

This text has investigated possible connections between imperial involvements and history writing in the UK. This is not a matter of constructing a linear account of cause and effect, but rather of placing stories about such involvements in the same field of thought as stories about history writing. The investigation has understood those connections as one strand among the many which are woven together in the fabric of historical practice. If that practice is seen as a set of conversations between historians and material from the past and also between different historians, then we might see questions about themes of empire as one among the many topics in those conversations. Taking that metaphor a little further, we might add that this text has been concerned not only with the topics of conversation but with the vocabulary or accent in which they have been discussed. It has argued that engagement with empire affected not only the subject matter of history writing but the language and assumptions used to explore and explain the past.

Certainly, what has emerged in the course of this investigation of historical writing in the UK since 1750 is the presence of multiple voices, not all of which speak of imperial connections, and not all to the same extent or with the same clarity or the same accent. Over time the diversity of voices has increased with the enlargement of the forms and audiences for history writing. The professionalisation of historical research and writing and the growth of the study of 'history' in schools and post-school education established a demand for texts and specialists. As history texts came to be used to inform, inspire and entertain a range of publics, and to project political or commercial aims, they embedded 'history' in the worlds of entertainment, self-improvement, leisure, politics and advertising. These developments stimulated a range of separate and sometimes combined roles and expectations for history writing and possible ways of presenting information and interpretations of the past, as well as cross-overs and combinations between them.

If the period from the mid-nineteenth century to the late twentieth century saw an expansion in professional research and writing which might translate into scholarly monographs, radio or TV broadcasts, school textbooks, general surveys or popular histories, that upward curve might now be thought to be dipping down. The start of the new millennium saw declining numbers of students choosing history at school, college or university, a reduction in the time allocated for history in the school curriculum and growing criticism of 'academic' historical practice. In 2009 the Sunday broadsheet newspaper the *Observer* carried a feature entitled 'Too cool for school', which looked at members of the most recent generation of publicly successful historians, described as 'hip young historians'.[1] Their views of history writing, while not necessarily representative, and no doubt offered as a conscious provocation, provide an interesting snapshot of what a journalist thought that the broadsheet readership might want to hear about the practice and purpose of history writing. The feature highlights commercial aims ('if you look at a historian you are being offered a brand'), entertainment ('they believe that the key to revitalising history is a mixture of strong narratives, exciting personalities, and quirky facts'), modern communications ('people expect you to share your lives with Twitter updates and Facebook postings') and historical practice.

These young practitioners of history writing, while Oxbridge educated and backed by an established generation of publicly successful historians (Simon Sebag-Montefiore and David Starkey), are distant from, and critical of, academic history, which is linked to the somewhat lazy stereotype of 'tweeds' and 'ivory towers'. Storytelling and fun ('the greatest of all crimes is dullness') are at the core of their practice, which they are undertaking not necessarily in university history departments but as professional writers, sometimes combining that work with other occupations (law, acting, journalism). They distanced themselves from any concern with the conceptual or methodological underpinnings of their practice ('a thing of the past'), and saw academic history as 'facing a "what the hell are we doing" moment'. Topics are chosen because they are 'fun', and the important goal is to produce 'good narrative history which convincingly creates the world you are writing about'.

Such opinions are, of course, in the tradition of Macaulay and Trevelyan, and echo the concern of a series of politicians and commentators to reshape school history teaching to offer a clear, unambiguous (and 'British') narrative of the past which goes back to the 1980s.[2] However, the defence of this position offered by one of the 'hip six', who argues that 'writing your books with specific political aims in mind is an old-fashioned approach', differs significantly from those of their forebears. Rather than making professional or ethical objections to the presence of politics in history writing, she grounds her critique on 'fashion' and on the populist argument that if historians produce 'good narrative' and vivid recreations of the past, 'people will read it and draw their own conclusions'. Older visions of history are not just being resurrected, but refurbished for a society in which history writing is 'consumed', and in which writers have a sense of the active role of readers. However, like the writer quoted, they seem not to understand that to avoid 'politics' is itself, of course, a 'political' choice, and that authorial choices affect readers' responses. History writing is being positioned as a commodity, and as a form of accessible and entertaining communication rather than as an intellectual endeavour or a contribution to the public good. What gains and losses may follow in this shift away from approaches which have been dominant for over a century is yet to be seen.

The snapshot provided in the *Observer* should not be over interpreted, but it chimes with other political and professional critiques of academic history which have asserted the primacy of narrative and of accessibility against 'theory' and fragmentation, and returned to the question of who 'makes' history. When Cannadine wrote his biography of Trevelyan and Schama shaped his *History of Britain*, or when Raphael Samuel championed the rich diversity of ways in which people in different groups or communities might have their own engagements with the past, they too raised those issues.[3] For all of them the issues of Britain and 'Britishness' with their three centuries of imperial and global associations also looms large, but as those older associations move from public memory and knowledge into the realms of nostalgia or drama, the influence of imperial involvements may also shift. As argued in the previous chapter, circumstances since the 1970s have reinvigorated historians' self-consciousness about a 'Britain'/'England' challenged by decline, devolution, immigration and European issues, and about how colonial pasts might be recognised, avoided or analysed. Celebrations of *raj* glamour, or commemoration of the 'British' abolition of the slave trade reached out to diverse audiences, while debates over 'postcolonial' understandings of Britain and its empire continue to divide public commentators and historians.[4]

In this sense both the topic of empire and the vocabulary and ideas derived from it continue to be one of the significant elements in history writing. Among the 'six hip young historians' introduced earlier, the choice of one to write on the 'fun' topic of the history of the pineapple (apparently much less 'dull' than Roosevelt's New Deal) not only followed success by comparable works on cod, nutmeg and other products, but involved examination of global inputs to British life and taste. The interest of another in the history of Ulster unionism and the early nineteenth-century Foreign Secretary Castlereagh also has its imperial and global connections.[5] More generally, debates over universal as opposed to specific versions of 'civilisation', 'democracy', 'rights' or 'progress', and over the merits of comparative and relative analyses of these categories continue to engage historians. Controversy over the uniqueness, value and exportability of English/British/western 'achievements' and their 'difference' from those in other parts of the world is a theme which they are still addressing. Thus a historian who has traced the impact of early European expansion into the Americas on European cultures and politics recently produced a history of what is entitled *Worlds at war*, which constructs an account of a '2500 year old struggle between east and west'. It proposes a tale of continuous conflict ('battle-lines drawn twenty-three centuries ago') going from clashes between Greeks and an empire in what is now Iran in the fifth century BCE to current confrontations of Europeans and Americans with Middle Eastern states, and with migrants from that area in their own societies.[6] This reflects current western concern with real or imagined 'Muslim' threats', but also revives old western stereotypes of 'the east', visible in the text and in the use of a nineteenth-century orientalist depiction of highly sexualised 'eastern' violence on the book's cover.

As already observed, this element of historical writing was only one among many. The growth of sophisticated economic history, 'history from below', history influenced by sociological and anthropological approaches, 'third world' and global histories and histories shaped by cultural or feminist theories, has sent historical writing in many directions. This development has been reinforced by the demands from professional and market forces which encourage diversity. The range of topics, concepts, methods and audiences now available to historians exert contradictory and complex influences on their work. 'We' (the author and readers of this text) may continue to attend to the influence of imperial involvements, past or present, on the topics, ideas and vocabularies found in history writing. In order to do justice to that influence we should also attend to its associations and contests with other influences, remembering that it is one voice, albeit an important one, in the many conversations which people have about the past. These are conversations which will surely continue.

Notes

1 *Observer*, 28 June 2009: the quotations in the next three paragraphs are all from this feature.
2 Depicting and promoting 'Britishness' has been a interest for politicians as diverse as David Blunkett, Michael Gove and Gordon Brown.
3 D. Cannadine, *G.M. Trevelyan: a life in history*, London, 1992.
4 N. Ferguson, *Empire: how Britain made the modern world*, London, 2004; B. Porter, *The absent minded imperialists*, Oxford, 2004; J. Darwin, *The empire project: the rise and fall of the British world system*, Cambridge, 2009; D. Cannadine, *Ornamentalism: how the British saw their empire*, Oxford, 2001.
5 J. Bew, *Castlereagh: enlightenment, war, and tyranny*, London, 2011; F. Beauman, *The pineapple: king of fruits*, London, 2005.
6 A. Pagden, *Worlds at war: the 2500 year struggle between east and west*, Oxford, 2008.

SELECT BIBLIOGRAPHY

Major historical and related writings discussed in the text

Adair, J., *The history of the American Indians*, London, 1775.

Adams, J., *A view of universal history*, 3 vols, London, 1795.

Adolphus, J., *History of England from the accession of George III*, London, 1817.

Allen, C., *A new and improved history of England...designed for the use of schools*, London, 1793.

Anderson, C., *Subaltern lives: biographies of colonialism in the Indian Ocean world*, Cambridge, 2012.

Angus, W., *History of England*, Glasgow, 1837.

Anon., *A new history of England*, London, 1819.

Armitage, D., *Greater Britain, 1516–1776*, Aldershot, 2004.

Arnold, T., *Introductory lecture on modern history*, London, 1843.

Ashburton, C., *A new and complete history of England*, London, 1791–94.

Barlow, P., *General history of Europe*, London, 1791.

Barron, W., *History of the colonization of the free states of antiquity, applied to the present conflict between Great Britain and her American colonies*, London, 1777.

Barrow, J., *A new and impartial history of England*, 10 vols, London, 1763.

Benians, E., *et al.* [eds.], *Cambridge history of the British empire*, 8 vols, Cambridge, 1929–36.

Bentham, J., 'Essay on the influence of time and place in matters of legislation', in J. Bentham, *Collected works*, 11 vols, London 1962, vol. 1.

Berg, M., *The age of manufactures*, London, 1985.

Bicknell, A., *A history of England and the British empire designed for the instruction of youth*, London, 1791.

Birkby, T., *History of England*, London, 1870.

Black, J., *A history of the British Isles*, Basingstoke, 1996, 2003, 2012.

Blagdon, F., *A brief history of ancient and modern India*, London, 1805.

Booth, W., *In darkest England*, London, 1890.

Bowen, H., *Wales and the British overseas empire*, Manchester, 2011.

Brendon, P., *The decline and fall of the British empire*, London, 2007.

Browning, O. [ed.], *The evolutionary history of England* (a Pitmans reader), London, 1901.

Bruce, J., *Historical view of plans for the government of British India*, London, 1793.

Bryce, J., 'The relations of law and religion', in J. Bryce, *Studies in history and jurisprudence*, 2 vols, Oxford, Clarendon Press, 1901, vol. 2.

―――― *The relations of the advanced and the backward races of mankind*, Oxford, 1902.

Bryant, A., *Samuel Pepys*, 3 vols, London 1933, 1935, 1938.

―――― *The national character*, London, 1934.

―――― *The spirit of Conservatism*, London, 1939.

Bulley, E., *Great Britain for little Britons*, London, 1881.

Burke, E., *Reflections on the revolution in France*, 9th edn, London, 1791.

Burnes, A., *Travels into Bokhara*, London, 1834.

Burns, A., and Innes, J. [eds.], *Rethinking the age of reform*, Cambridge, 2003.

Calcott, M., *Little Arthur's history of England*, London, 1835.

Chapone, H., *Letters on the improvement of the mind addressed to a young lady*, 2 vols, London, 1773.

Clapham, J., *Economic history of modern Britain*, 3 vols, London, 1926–38 (reprints to 1968).

―――― *Concise economic history of Britain to 1750*, London, 1949 (reprints to 1967).

Clark, A., *The working life of women in the seventeenth century*, London, 1919.

Clark, J.C.D., *English society, 1688–1832: ideology, social structure and political practice during the ancient regime*, Cambridge, 1985.

―――― [ed.], *A world by itself: a history of the British Isles*, London, 2011.

Clarkson, T., *An essay on the slavery and commerce of the human species*, London, 1788.

―――― *The history of the rise, progress, and accomplishment of the abolition of the African slave trade*, London, 1808.

Colley, L., *Britons: the forging of a nation, 1707–1837*, New Haven, CT, 1992.

Conan, E., and Kendall, E., *A short history of England for schools*, London, 1902.

Congreve, R. [ed.], *International policy: essays on the foreign relations of England*, London, 1866.

Cooper, Rev., *A new history of England*, London, 1826.

Coupland, R., *Wilberforce*, London, 1923.

―――― *The British anti-slavery movement*, London, 1933.

―――― *The British empire*, London, 1933.

―――― *The empire in these days*, London, 1933.

―――― *Britain and India, 1600–1941*, London, 1943, 1946, 1948.

Corner, J., *History of England*, London, 1840 (many later editions).

Cowley, C., *The ladies' history of England*, London, 1780.

Craik, G., *Pictorial history of England*, 7 vols, London, 1854–58.

Creasy, E., *The spirit of historical study*, London, 1840.

—— *The rise and progress of the English constitution*, 3rd edn, London, 1856.

—— *The imperial and colonial constitutions of the Britannic empire*, London, 1872.

Davidoff, D., and Hall, C., *Family fortunes: men and women of the English middle class, 1780–1850*, London, 1987.

Davies, N., *The isles: a history*, London, 1999.

Darwin, J., *The empire project: the rise and fall of the British world system*, Cambridge, 2009.

Dawes, C.E., *King Edward's realm*, London, 1902.

Devine, T., *The Scottish nation, 1700–2007*, London, 2007.

Dickens, C., *Child's history of England* (1852) vol. 12 in *The centenary edition of the works of Charles Dickens*, London, 1910.

Dilke, C., *Greater Britain*, 2 vols, London, 1868.

Dow, A., *The history of Indostan*, London, 1768 (many later editions).

Dunbar, J., *Essays on the history of mankind in crude and cultivated ages*, London, 1781.

Edwards, J., *A concise history of England*, London, 1860.

Edwards, P., *The making of the modern English state, 1460–1660*, Basingstoke, 2001.

Ellis, C., *England and the modern world*, London, 1947.

Elphinstone, M., *Account of the kingdom of Caubul*, London, 1815 (many later editions).

Ferguson, A., *An essay on the history of civil society*, London, 1767.

Ferguson, N., *Empire: how Britain made the modern world*, London, 2003.

Freeman, E., *The Ottoman power in Europe*, London, 1877.

—— *The chief periods of European history: six lectures read in the University of Oxford*, London, 1885.

—— *The methods of historical study… with the inaugural lecture of the office of the historical professor*, London, 1886.

Feiling, K., *A history of England*, London, 1948.

Fletcher, C., *Pocket history of England*, London, 1911.

Froude, J.A., 'England's forgotten worthies', in J.A. Froude, *Short studies on great subjects*, London, 1867.

—— *The English in Ireland in the eighteenth century*, 3 vols, New York, 1872–74.

—— *Oceana, or, England and her colonies*, London, 1886.

Gardiner, S., *A student's history of England*, 3 vols, London, 1920.

George, D., *English social life in the eighteenth century*, London, 1923.

—— *London life in the eighteenth century*, London, 1930.

—— *England in transition*, London, 1931.

Gleig, G.R., *History of the British empire in India*, 4 vols., London, 1830–35.

—— *The family history of England*, London, 1836.

—— *Memoirs of the life of Warren Hastings*, London, 1841.

—— *Life of Robert, first Lord Clive*, London, 1848, 1861, 1869, 1907.

—— *History of the British colonies*, London, 1851.

Glew, D., and Plaskett, H., *History of England*, 3 vols, London, 1940.

Goldsmith, O., *The present state of the British empire in Europe, America, Asia and Africa*, London, 1768.

—— *An history of the earth and animated nature*, 8 vols, London, 1774.

Green, J.R., *Short history of the English people*, London, 1874 (I have used the Folio Society reprint, London, 1992).

Grimaldi, J., *A synopsis of English history*, London, 1825.

Guest, G., *Military and imperial history of England*, London, 1915.

Hallam, H., *View of the state of Europe during the Middle Ages*, London, 1818.

—— *Constitutional history of England*, 2 vols, London, 1827 (I have used the 1846 edn).

Harlow, V., *Origins and purpose: a handbook of the British commonwealth and empire*, London, 1944, 1949.

Henry, R., *History of Great Britain*, 6 vols, London, 1771–93.

Hickson, M., *Ireland in the seventeenth century, or, the Irish massacre of 1641–2*, 2 vols, London, 1884.

Hilton, R., *Bond men made free*, London, 1973.

Home, H., Lord Kames, *Sketches of the history of man*, London, 1774.

Hume, D., *History of England*, 8 vols, London, 1778.

Huxley, J., *et al.*, *We Europeans*, London, 1935.

Innes, A., *History of England for use in schools*, London, 1907, 1908, 1912 1926.

——, and Mee, A., *The Harmsworth history of the world*, London, 1909.

'J.S.', *Modern Europe*, London, 1757.

James, L., *The rise and fall of the British empire*, London, 1994.

Judd, D., *Empire: the British imperial experience from 1765 to the present*, London, 1996.

Kearney, H., *The British Isles: a history of four nations*, Cambridge, 1989.

Keightley, T., *The history of England*, London, 1839.

Kenny, K. [ed.], *Ireland and the British empire*, Oxford, 2006.

Kerr, P., Lord Lothian, *The growth of the British empire*, London, 1911.

King Edward history reader, London, 1901.

Kingsley, M., *Travels in West Africa*, London, 1897.

—— *West African studies*, London, 1899.

Knight, C., *The popular history of England*, 8 vols, London, 1856–62.

'A Lady', *Geography and history selected…for the use of children*, London, 1794.

Levine, P., *The British empire: sunrise to sunset*, Harlow, 2007.

—— [ed.], *Gender and empire*, Oxford, 2004.

Lloyd, T., *History of England from the peace in 1783 to the present time*, 2 vols, London, 1800.

Lloyd, T., *The British empire, 1558–1995*, Oxford, 1996.

—— *Empire, welfare state, Europe: history of the United Kingdom*, Oxford, 2002.

Louis, W.R. [series ed.], *Oxford History of the British empire*, Oxford, OUP, 1998–99 (Canny, N. [ed.], *Vol. 1: origins of empire*; Marshall, P. [ed.].

Vol. 2: the eighteenth century, Porter, A. [ed.], *Vol. 3: the nineteenth century*, Louis, W. and Brown, J. [eds.] *Vol. 4: the twentieth century*, Winks, R. [ed.], *Vol. 5: historiography*).

Macaulay, C., *History of England*, 8 vols, London, 1763–83.

Macaulay, T.B., *History of England*, 4 vols, London, 1849–55 (I have used the 6-vol. 1913 edition).

—— *Critical and historical essays*, London, 1843 (I have used the 1965 Fontana edition).

MacKenzie, J., and Devine, T. [eds.], *Scotland and the British empire*, Oxford, 2011.

Mackintosh, J., *History of England*, 3 vols, London, 1830.

MacPherson, D., *History of European commerce in India*, London, 1812.

Macpherson, J., *History and management of the East India Company since 1600*, London, 1782.

Maine, H., *Village communities east and west*, London, 1872.

—— *Lectures on the early history of institutions*, London, 1874.

Marcy, W., *Examination history of England*, London, 1925.

Markham, Mrs (Elizabeth Penrose), *History of England...for the use of young persons* (editions from 1827 to 1891; I have used the 1872 edition).

Marriott, J.A., *Commonwealth or anarchy*, London, 1937.

Martineau, H., *History of England during the thirty years peace*, London, 1849–51 (editions to 1878).

—— *British rule in India*, London, 1857.

May, T. Erskine, *Constitutional history of England*, 2 vols, Boston, MA, 1862-4.

Mill, J., *History of British India*, London, 1817 (expanded editions 1844, 1858).

Mill, J.S., *Considerations on representative government*, London, 1865.

Millar, J., *The origin of the distinction of ranks, or, an inquiry into the circumstances which give rise to influence and authority in the different members of society*, London, 1771.

Miller, E., *The beginner's history of England*, London, 1921 (I have used the 1936 edition).

Moorcroft, W., *Travels in the Himalayan provinces of Hindustan and the Panjab*, London, 1841.

Morgan, K. [ed.], *Oxford history of England*, revised edn, Oxford, 2010.

Mortimer, T., *A new history of England*, 3 vols, London, 1764–66.

Muir, R., *The expansion of Europe*, 2nd edn, London, 1917.

—— *Civilisation and liberty*, London, 1940.

Newton, A.P., *A hundred years of the British empire*, London, 1940, 1947.

O'Dogherty, W., *Epitome of the history of Europe*, London, 1788.

O'Halloran, S., *Introduction to the study of the history and antiquities of Ireland*, London, 1772.

Orme, R., *History of the military transactions of the British nation in Indostan*, London, 1763.

—— *Historical fragments of the Mogul empire...and of English concerns in Indostan*, London, 1782–83.

—— *The establishment of British trade at Surat*, London, c.1785.

Paine, T., *The rights of man*, London, 1791 (I have used the 2008 Penguin edition).

Palgrave, F., *The rise and progress of the English commonwealth*, London, 1832.

Payne, J., *An epitome of history*, London, 1794.

Philpotts, B., *Kindred and clan in the Middle Ages and after*, London, 1913.

—— *The Elder Edda and Scandinavian drama*, London, 1920.

—— *Edda and Saga*, London, 1931.

Pinchbeck, I., *Women workers and the industrial revolution*, London, 1930.

Pollard, A., *The evolution of Parliament*, London, 1920.

Prichard, J., *The eastern origins of the Celtic nations*, London, 1831.

Raymond, G., *A new and impartial history of England*, London, 1787.

Robertson, W., *History of Scotland*, 2 vols, London, 1759.

—— *History of the reign of the Emperor Charles V: with a view of the progress of society in Europe*, 2 vols, London, 1769.

—— *History of America*, 2 vols, London, 1777.

—— *An historical disquisition concerning the knowledge which the ancients had of India*, London, 1794.

Rogers, R., *A concise account of North America*, London, 1769.

Royal Institution for International Affairs, *The colonial problem*, London, 1937.

Russel, W., *New and authentic history of England*, London, 1777.

—— *The modern history of Europe*, London, 1784.

Sanderson, E., *History of the British empire*, London, 1882.

—— *The story of England: a reading book for students*, London, 1892.

Schwarz, B., *The white man's world*, Oxford, 2011.

Seeley, J., *The expansion of England*, London, 1883.

Sims, G.., *How the poor live*, London, 1883.

——*Horrible London*, London, 1889.

Smith, G., *Irish history and Irish character*, London, 1861.

—— *Three English statesmen*, London, 1867.

Smollett, T., *History of England*, 3 vols, London, 1757.

Stenton, F., *Documents on the social and economic history of the Danelaw*, London, 1920.

—— *Introduction to the survey of English place names*, London, 1924 (reprints to 1980).

—— *The Danes in England*, London, 1927 (reprints to 1957).

—— *The first century of English feudalism*, London, 1929 (reprints to 1979).

Stewart, D., 'Account of the life and writings of Adam Smith', preface to A. Smith, *Essays on philosophical subjects*, London, 1799.

Stockwell, S. [ed.], *The British empire: themes and perspectives*, Oxford, 2008.

Stuart, G., *Historical dissertation concerning the antiquity of the English constitution*, London, 1770.

Stubbs, W., *Constitutional history*, 3rd edn, Oxford, 1876.

—— *Seventeen lectures on the study of modern and medieval history*, Oxford, 1887.

Sulivan, R., *Analysis of the political history of India*, London, 1779.

Tait, C., *Analysis of English history*, London, 1878.

Tawney, R., *The agrarian problem in the sixteenth century*, London, 1912 (reprints to 1961).

—— *English economic history: select documents*, London, 1913 (reprints to 1937).

—— *The acquisitive society*, London, 1920 (editions to 1961).

—— *Tudor economic documents*, London, 1924 (reprints to 1965).

—— *Religion and the rise of capitalism*, London, 1926 (reprints to 1964).

Taylor, W. Cooke, *The history of Mohammedanism*, London, 1834, 1839, 1851.

—— *A popular history of British India*, London, 1842.

—— *Ancient and modern India*, London, 1851, 1857.

—— *The student's manual of modern history: containing the rise and progress of the principal European nations...with a history of the colonies*, 8th edn, revised and edited C. Duke Yonge, London, 1866.

Thompson, E., *History of England*, London, 1878.

Thompson, E.P. *The making of the English working class*, London, 1963.

Tout, T., *A short account of English history*, London, 1900.

Toynbee, A., *The industrial revolution*, London, 1884.

Trevelyan, G.M., *England in the nineteenth century*, London, 1922.

—— *History of England*, London, 1926.

—— *England under Queen Anne*, 3 vols, London, 1930–34.

—— *Social history of England*, London, 1941 (editions to the 1960s).

Turner, S., *History of the Anglo Saxons*, 4 vols, London, 1799–1805 (I have used the 1840 edition).

Vinogradoff, P., 'The teaching of Sir Henry Maine' (inaugural lecture 1904), in P. Vinogradoff, *Collected papers*, 2 vols, Oxford, 1928, vol. 2, pp. 173–89.

Walpole, S., *History of England from the conclusion of the great war in 1815*, 5 vols, London, 1878.

Ware, V., *Beyond the pale: white women, racism and history*, London, 1992.

White, C., *Of the regular gradation of man*, London, 1799.

Williams, G., *Artisans and sansculottes*, London, 1968.

Winterbotham, W., *Historical, geographical and philosophical view of the Chinese Empire*, 2 vols, London, 1795.

Yonge, C. Duke, *History of England*, London, 1857.

—— *Three centuries of modern history*, London, 1872.

—— *Constitutional history of England*, London, 1881.

Zimmern, A., *The third British empire*, London, 1926.

Secondary works

This is a selection of texts which readers may wish to look at in order to follow up topics further; the full range of works used to develop this text is cited in the notes.

Alford, B., *Britain in the world economy since 1880*, London, 1996.

Armitage, D., *The ideological origins of the British empire*, Cambridge, 2000.

—— and Braddick, M. [eds.], *The British Atlantic world, 1500–1800*, Basingstoke, 2002.

Barkan, E., *The retreat of scientific racism*, Cambridge, 1992.

Barkey, K., *Bandits and bureaucrats: the Ottoman route to state centralization*, Ithaca, NY, 1994.

Bartlett, R., *The making of Europe: conquest, colonization and cultural change, 950–1350*, London, 1994.

Baycroft, T., *Nationalism in Europe*, Cambridge, 1998.

Bayly, C., 'The first age of global imperialism', *Journal of Imperial and Commonwealth History*, 26:2 (1998), pp. 28–47.

Belich, J., *Replenishing the earth: the settler revolution and the rise of the Anglo world*, Oxford, 2009.

Bell, D., *The idea of Greater Britain: empire and the future of world order, 1860–1900*, Princeton, 2007.

Bentley, M., *Modernising England's past: English historiography in the age of modernism*, Cambridge, 2005.

Bitterli, U., *Cultures in conflict*, Stanford, CA, 1989.

Blyth, R., and Jeffery, K. [eds.], *The British empire and its contested pasts*, Dublin, 2009.

Bowen, H., *The business of empire: the East India Company and imperial Britain, 1756–1833*, Cambridge, 2006.

Bridge, C., and Fedorowich, K. [eds.], *The British world diaspora*, London, 2003.

Brockliss, L., and Eastwood, D. [eds.], *A union of multiple identities: the British Isles, c.1750–1850*, Manchester, 1997.

Brown, S., *Providence and empire*, Harlow, 2008.

Brundage, A., *The people's historian: John Richard Green and the writing of history in Victorian England*, Westport, CT, 1994.

Burton, A., *Empire in question*, Durham, NC, 2011.

Cain, P., and Hopkins, A., *British imperialism: decline and deconstruction*, Harlow, 1993.

—— —— *British imperialism: innovation and expansion*, Harlow, 1993.

Cannadine, D., *G.M. Trevelyan: a life in history*, London, 1992.

—— *Ornamentalism: how the British saw their empire*, Oxford, 2001.

—— *Making history now and then*, Basingstoke, 2011.

—— et al., The right kind of history: teaching the past in twentieth century England, Basingstoke, 2011.

Canny, N. [ed.], Oxford history of the British empire, vol. 1: origins of empire, Oxford, 1998.

Carey, H., God's empire: religion and colonialism in the British world, Cambridge, 2011.

Castle, K., Britannia's children: reading colonialism through children's books and magazines, Manchester, 1996.

Chancellor, V., History for their masters: opinion in the English history textbook, 1800–1914, Bath, 1970.

Chapman, S., Merchant enterprise in Britain, Cambridge, 1992.

Cirakman, A., From 'the terror of the world' to 'the sick man of Europe': European images of the Ottoman empire and society, Oxford, 2002.

Claeys, G., Imperial sceptics: British critics of empire, 1850–1920, Cambridge, 2010.

Codell, J. [ed.], Imperial co-histories: national identities and the British and colonial press, London, 2003.

Collini, S., 'Believing in England: Arthur Bryant, historian as man of letters', in S. Collini, Common reading, Oxford, 2008.

Collini, S., et al. [eds.], History, religion, and culture: British intellectual history, 1750–1950, Cambridge, 2000.

Colls, R., The identity of England, Oxford, 2002.

—— and Dodd, P. [eds.], Englishness: politics and culture, London, 1986.

Cox, J., The British missionary enterprise since 1700, London, 2008.

Daniels, C. [ed.], Negotiated empire: centres and peripheries in the Americas, London, 2007.

Darwin, J., Britain and decolonisation, Basingstoke, 1988.

—— The end of the British empire, Oxford, 1991.

—— The empire project: the rise and fall of the British world system, Cambridge, 2009.

Daunton, M., Wealth and welfare: an economic and social history of Britain, 1851–1951, Cambridge, 2007.

Dawson, G., Soldier heroes: British adventure, empire, and the imagining of masculinities, London, 1994.

Eley, G., A crooked line: from cultural history to the history of society, Ann Arbor, MI, 2008.

Eliav-Feldon, M. et al. [eds.], The origins of racism in the west, Cambridge, 2009.

Etherington, N. [ed.], Missions and empire, Oxford, 2005.

Ferguson, M., Subject to others: British women writers and colonial slavery, London, 1992.

Feske, V., From Belloc to Churchill: private scholars, public culture, and the crisis of Victorian liberalism, Chapel Hill, NC, 1996.

Finn, M., After Chartism: class and nation in English politics, Cambridge, 1993.

Garnett, J., 'Protestant histories: James Anthony Froude: partisanship and national identity', in P. Ghosh and L. Goldman [eds.], *Politics and culture in Victorian Britain*, Oxford, 2006.

Gikandi, S., *Maps of Englishness*, New York, 1996.

Gilroy, P., *There ain't no black in the Union Jack*, London, 1987.

—— *After empire: melancholia or convivial culture?*, London, 2004.

Glacken, C., *Traces on the Rhodian shore: nature and culture in western thought from ancient times to the end of the eighteenth century*, Berkeley, CA, 1973.

Goffman, D., *Britons in the Ottoman empire, 1642–60*, Seattle, WA, 1998.

—— *The Ottoman empire and early modern Europe*, Cambridge, 2002.

Goldenberg, D., *The curse of Ham*, Princeton, 2003.

Goldman, L., *Dons and workers: Oxford and adult education since 1850*, Oxford, 1995.

Gran, P., *Beyond Eurocentrism: a new view of modern world history*, Syracuse, NY, 1996.

Greer, M., *et al.* [eds.], *Re-reading the 'black legend': the discourse of race and religious difference in the Renaissance empires*, Chicago, 2007.

Gruen, E. [ed.], *Cultural identity in the ancient world*, Berkeley, CA, 2011.

Guha, R., 'On some aspects of the historiography of colonial India', in R. Guha [ed.], *Subaltern Studies*, New Delhi, 1982. vol. 1.

Gunn, S., and Vernon, J. [eds.], *The peculiarities of liberal modernity in imperial Britain*, Berkeley, CA, 2011.

Hall, C., *White, male, and middle class*, Cambridge, 1992.

—— 'Rethinking imperial histories', *New Left Review*, 208 (1994), pp. 3–29.

—— *Civilising subjects*, Cambridge, 2002.

—— *Macaulay and son: architects of imperial Britain*, New Haven, CT, 2012.

—— and McLelland, K. [eds.], *Race, nation and empire*, Manchester, 2010.

—— —— and Rendall, J., *Defining the Victorian nation*, Cambridge, 2000.

—— and Rose, S. [eds.], *At home with the empire*, Cambridge, 2006.

Hall, S., 'Minimal selves', in L. Appignanesi [ed.], *The real me: postmodernism and the question of identity*, London, 1987.

—— and Gieben, B. [eds.], *Formations of modernity*, Cambridge, 1992.

Harper, M., and Constantine, S. [eds.], *Migration and the British Empire*, Oxford, 2010.

Heathorn, S., *For home, country and race: constructing gender, class and Englishness in the elementary school, 1880–1914*, Toronto, 2000.

Hempton, D., *Religion and political culture in Britain and Ireland*, Cambridge, 1996.

Hodgen, M., *Early anthropology*, Philadelphia, 1964.

Hoppit, J. [ed.], *Parliaments, nations and identities in Britain and Ireland, 1660–1860*, Manchester, 2003.

Howe, S., *Anticolonialism in British politics*, Oxford, 1994.

Isaac, B., *The invention of racism in classical antiquity*, Princeton, 2004.

Jefferys, K. [ed.], *An Irish empire?* Manchester, 1996.

Kafadar, C., *Between two worlds: the construction of the Ottoman state*, Berkeley, CA, 1995.

Kamps, I., and Singh, J. [eds.], *Travel knowledge*, Basingstoke, 2001.

Karateke, H. [ed.], *Legitimizing the order: the Ottoman rhetoric of state power*, Leiden, 2005.

Kearney, H., *The British Isles: a history of four nations*, Cambridge, 1989.

Kelly, J., 'Did women have a Renaissance?', in J. Kelly, *Women, history and theory*, Chicago, 1984.

Kidd, C., *Subverting Scotland's past: Scottish Whig historians and the creation of an Anglo-British identity, 1689–1830*, Cambridge, 1993, 2003.

—— *British identities before nationalism*, Cambridge, 1999.

—— *The forging of races*, Cambridge, 2006.

Kinealy, C., *A disunited kingdom? England, Ireland, Scotland and Wales, 1800–1949*, Cambridge, 1999.

King, S., and Timmins, G., *Making sense of the industrial revolution*, Manchester, 2001.

Koditschek, T., *Liberalism, imperialism, and the historical imagination*, Cambridge, 2011.

Kuklick, H., *The savage within: the social history of British anthropology, 1885–1945*, Cambridge, 1991.

Kupperman, K., *America in European consciousness, 1493–1750*, Chapel Hill, NC, 1995.

—— *Indians and English*, Ithaca, NY, 2000.

Lambert, D., and Lester, A. [eds.], *Colonial lives across the British empire*, Cambridge, 2006.

Lamont, W., *Historical controversies and historians*, London, 1997.

Lester, A., *Imperial networks: creating identities in nineteenth century South Africa and Britain*, London, 2001.

Levine, P., *The amateur and the professional: antiquarians, historians and archaeologists in Victorian England, 1838–1886*, Cambridge, 1986.

Lorimer, D., *Colour, class and the Victorians*, Leicester, 1978.

McCartney, D., *W.E.H. Lecky, historian and politician*, Dublin, 1994.

MacClachlan, C., *Spain's empire in the New World*, Berkeley, CA, 1988.

MacKenzie, J., *Imperialism and popular culture*, Manchester, 1986.

McKibbin, R., *Classes and cultures, 1918–1951*, Oxford, 1998.

Mandler, P., '"Race" and "nation" in mid-Victorian thought', in S. Collini, *et al.* [eds.], *History, religion, and culture: British intellectual history, 1795–1950*, Cambridge, 2000.

—— *History and national life*, London, 2002.

—— *The English national character*, New Haven, CT, 2006.

Mantena, K., *Alibis of empire: Henry Maine and the ends of liberal imperialism*, Princeton, 2010.

Marriott, J., *The other empire*, Manchester, 2003.

Mason, P., *Infelicities: representations of the exotic*, Baltimore, MD, 1998.

Matar, N., *Turks, Moors and Englishmen in the age of discovery*, New York, 1999.

—— *Britain and Barbary*, Tampa, FL, 2005.

Meek, R., *Social science and the ignoble savage*, Cambridge, 1976.

Munslow, A., *Deconstructing history*, London, 1997.

O'Brien, K., *Narratives of enlightenment: cosmopolitan history from Voltaire to Gibbon*, Cambridge, 1997.

—— *Women and enlightenment in eighteenth-century Britain*, Cambridge, 2009.

O'Siochain, S. [ed.], *Social thought on Ireland in the nineteenth century*, Dublin, 2009.

Pagden, A., *The fall of natural man: the American Indian and the origins of comparative ethnology*, Cambridge, 1986.

—— *Lords of all the world*, New Haven, CT, 1995.

—— *Worlds at war: the 2500 year struggle between east and west*, Oxford, 2008.

Parekh, B., *Rethinking multiculturalism*, Basingstoke, 2006.

Parry, P., *The rise and fall of liberal government in Victorian Britain*, New Haven, CT, 1993.

—— *The politics of patriotism: English liberalism, national identity, and Europe, 1830–1886*, Cambridge, 2006.

Paul, K., *Whitewashing Britain*, Ithaca, NY, 1997.

Phillips, M., '"If Mrs Mure be not sorry for poor King Charles": history, the novel, and the sentimental reader', *History Workshop Journal*, 43 (1997), pp. 110–31.

Pitts, J., *A turn to empire: the rise of liberal imperialism in Britain and France*, Princeton, 2005.

Porter, B., *The absent-minded imperialists*, Oxford, 2004.

Powell, D., *Nationhood and identity: Britain since 1800*, London, 2002.

Reynolds, D., *Britannia overruled: British policy and world power in the twentieth century*, Harlow, 2000.

Rich, P., *Race and empire in British politics*, Cambridge, 1990.

Richards, J., *Film and British national identity*, Manchester, 1997.

—— [ed.], *Imperialism and juvenile literature*, Manchester, 1989.

Rose, J., *The intellectual life of the British working classes*, New Haven, CT, 2001, 2010.

Rubies, J. [ed.], *Medieval ethnographies*, Aldershot, 2009.

Samuel, R., *Theatres of memory*, London, 1994.

—— *Island stories*, London, 1999.

Schaffer, S. [ed.], *Brokered worlds: go-betweens and global intelligence, 1770–1820*, Cambridge, 2009.

Scott, J., 'Gender: a useful category of analysis', *American Historical Review*, vol. 91, no.5 (1986), pp. 1053–75.

—— 'Experience', in J. Butler and J. Scott [eds.], *Feminists theorize the political*, London, 1992.

Simmons, C., *Reversing the conquest: history and myth in nineteenth century literature*, New Brunswick, NJ, 1990.

Sinha, M., *Colonial masculinity*, Manchester, 1995.

—— 'Teaching imperialism as a social formation', *Radical History Review*, 67:1 (1997), pp. 175–86.

Smith, A., *The ethnic origins of nations*, Oxford, 1998.

—— *Myths and memories of the nation*, Oxford, 1999.

Smith, R.J., *The gothic bequest, medieval institutions in British thought*, Cambridge, 1987.

Stapleton, J., *Sir Arthur Bryant and national history in twentieth century Britain*, Lanham, MD, 2006.

Stein, B., and Stein, S., *Silver, trade, and war: Spain and America in the making of early modern Europe*, Baltimore, MD, 2000.

Streets, H., *Martial races: the military, race, and masculinity in British imperial culture*, Manchester, 2004.

Stocking, G., *Victorian anthropology*, New York, 1987.

—— *After Tylor: British social anthropology, 1885–1951*, London, 1995.

—— [ed.], *Functionalism historicized*, Madison, WI, 1984.

Sweet, R., *Antiquaries: the discovery of the past in eighteenth century Britain*, London, 2004.

Tanner, D. [ed.], *Debating nationhood and governance in Britain, 1885–1945*, Manchester, 2006.

Taylor, M., and Wolff, M. [eds.], *The Victorians since 1901*, Manchester, 2004.

Thomas, N., *Discoveries: the voyages of Captain Cook*, London, 2003.

Thompson, A., *Imperial Britain: the politics, economics, and ideology of empire*, Harlow, 2000.

—— *The empire strikes back: the impact of empire*, Harlow, 2005.

Twells, A., *Civilising missions and the English middle class*, Basingstoke, 2009.

Vernon, J., *Politics and the people: a study in English political culture, 1815–67*, Cambridge, 1993.

—— [ed.], *Re-reading the constitution: new narratives in the political history of England's long nineteenth century*, Cambridge, 1996.

Waters, H., *Racism on the Victorian stage*, Cambridge, 2009.

West, S. [ed.], *The Victorians and race*, Menston, 1996.

Wheeler, R., *The complexion of race*, Philadelphia, 2000.

Wickham, C., *The inheritance of Rome*, London, 2010.

Winks, R. [ed.], *Oxford history of the British empire, vol. V: historiography*, Oxford, 1999.

Wormell, D., *Sir John Seeley and the uses of history*, Cambridge, 1980.

Wright, A., *The Counter-Reformation: Catholic Europe and the non-Christian world*, Aldershot, 2005.

Young, R., *The idea of English ethnicity*, Oxford, 2008.

INDEX